DECADES

The Bee Gees in the 1980s

Andrew Môn Hughes & Grant Walters

SONICBOND

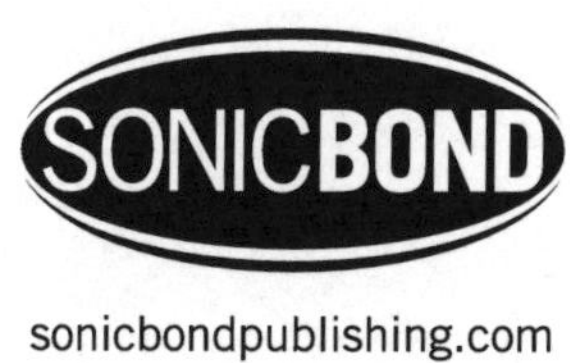

sonicbondpublishing.com

Sonicbond Publishing Limited
www.sonicbondpublishing.co.uk
Email: info@sonicbondpublishing.co.uk

First Published in the United Kingdom 2026
First Published in the United States 2026

British Library Cataloguing in Publication Data:
A Catalogue record for this book is available from the British Library

Typeset in ITC Garamond & ITC Avant Garde
Printed and bound in England
Graphic design and typesetting: Full Moon Media

DECADES

The Bee Gees

in the 1980s

Andrew Môn Hughes & Grant Walters

sonicbondpublishing.com

Dedicated to:
Enid Rees Hughes
Paula Hood
Scott Glasel
Matt Bonelli
Fred Kaarls
Dennis Bryon
Colin Petersen
Lies Spruit
Col Joye
Jon Blanchfield
Andrew Shacklock
Drew Struzan
Yuzuru Yamamae
Terry Cox

Acknowledgements

The authors would collectively like to thank the following:

Stephen Lambe and Sonicbond Publishing for giving us the opportunity to take on this project. It was good to meet you at your HQ.

Mark Crohan, our friend and colleague, to whom we owe a special – and suitably loud – thank you. The three of us began this project together, and the first two volumes were the result of that shared vision. Although Mark has now stepped back from future projects, his knowledge, enthusiasm, and generous contributions – along with the occasional wild theory – remain woven throughout this book and those to come. His fingerprints are everywhere, and, knowing him, probably on a few things he's already forgotten he contributed. We wanted to credit him as a full co-author, but in his characteristically modest way, he waved us off with, 'Just give me an acknowledgement – that's more than enough'. Mark is a remarkable bloke and a BeeGeeologist of the highest order. His expertise and good humour have been invaluable, and we will miss his presence in the day-to-day work more than he knows. Hooroo, mate.

Spencer Gibb, who has been a critical connection between the authors and his family's work and a committed, ardent supporter of this entire project from start to finish.

Albhy Galuten and Karl Richardson, for so many candid, helpful conversations in which their technical, behind-the-scenes insight has breathed so much life into many aspects of this series.

Our heartfelt thanks to Joe Mannion, the first to read the manuscript, whose insight proved an invaluable barometer of how the work would be received. His thoughtful observations – and the additional material he so generously shared – are received with genuine gratitude and appreciation.

The 'Oh No' Group – Dan Box, Mark Byfield, Mark Crohan, Judy Farrar, Michelle Gibson, Ann Grootjans, Linda Keane-Bacon, Paul Mann, Darrin Mitchell, Richard O'Donoghue, Ronnie Olsson and Sammy Jo for their friendship, banter and shared love of the Gibbs' music. This book series was written with all of you in our hearts.

Marion Adriaensen, Julio César Guzmán Arcenegui, Dick Ashby, Steve Barry, Melinda Bilyeu, Joe Brennan, Alex Brychta MBE, Dennis Bryon, Hector Cook, Tore Eriksen, Hazel Gibb, Justine Gibb, Gerard Groux, Dennis Hetzendorfer, Beth Kujala, KittLarue, Bernard Lupe, Joe Mardin, Lee Meadows, Vince Melouney, Mary Merrill, Arvid Paulsen, Erling Paulsen, Jan Paulsen, Frank & Manuela Stiller, Mike Sweeney, Faye Ward, Blue Weaver, Peta Gibb Weber, Solly Noid, Reinhard Wenesch, and Minako Yoshida, for their many heartfelt contributions and conversations along the way.

Edward Trayer, and everyone at The Wishing Shelf Book Awards – especially the reading groups – for their hard work and dedication. We are sincerely grateful to you for reading and rating *Decades: The Bee Gees In The 1960s* and *Decades: The Bee Gees In The 1970s*, and we are deeply honoured to have been finalists in the 2021 and 2023 awards.

We extend our thanks to all the websites, blogs, newspapers, magazines, radio stations, television programmes and podcasts that have reviewed our books or invited us to discuss them.

We are sincerely grateful to *Australian Herald*, *London TV*, *Tinnitist*, *The Afterword*, *RAMzine*, *Penny Black Music* and *The Light Appears*.

To the many radio hosts who welcomed us on air, including Phil Williams (BBC Radio 2), Behnaz Akhgar (BBC Radio Wales), Shan Cothi (BBC Radio Cymru), Linda McDermott (BBC Radio Merseyside), Alice Matthews (ABC Radio Canberra), Tony Jones (Môn FM) and Frank Bell (B98.7, Salt Lake City).

We are equally indebted to our colleagues in print, including Paul Donnelley at the *Daily Express* and Michael Bailey at the *Australian Financial Review*, as well as the editors and writers at *Shindig!*, *Mojo*, *The Beat*, *Eighth Day*, *Good Times*, *This Is Rock*, *North Wales Magazine*, *Shire* and *Rewind Magazine*. Special thanks to Martin Hutchinson.

Our thanks also go to *Heno* on the Welsh television channel S4C, presented by Gerallt Pennant, and to the many podcasters who generously shared their platforms with us, including David Fedor (*Bee

Gees And Me), Sarah Stacey (*Gibbology*), Walker Evans and Tim Fulton (*Confluence Cast*), Brian and Sarah Linnen (*Permanent Record Podcast*), Ben Montgomery and Jon Lamoreaux (*Records Revisited*), and Francine Brokow (*Beyond The Red Carpet*).

Very special thanks to Jayne Henry Owens of the *At A Glance ...* blog, whose generous and engaging feature introduced our work to a wider audience with real enthusiasm and care. Her thoughtful support of the *Decades* series is very much appreciated.

Thame Cricket Club, and Bragdy Cybi in Holyhead, for hosting our book talks – and all who attended – and to Thame Museum for your hospitality when we visited in 2023. To all of you: thank you for your interest, enthusiasm, and support in bringing our work to a wider audience.

Thanks also to the Independent Music Writers Alliance for its role in supporting and encouraging integrity and high standards in the field.

And last, but never least: Barry, Robin and Maurice Gibb for their unfathomable talents that gifted the world with one of the greatest musical legacies of all time. Every word written here is dedicated to you with our utmost respect and admiration.

Andrew would like to thank ... my wife Judy, whose love, patience and unfailing good sense make it possible for me to write books without accidentally derailing everyday life. She keeps things complete, calm and only occasionally asks if I'm aware that the outside world still exists.

Bella and Patch, our loyal furry sidekicks, whose mission in life is to bring joy, shed everywhere and ensure no snack is ever eaten unsupervised. And our newest recruit, Benny, who has joined the team with great enthusiasm and absolutely no respect for personal space.

My parents, Enid and Mervyn, who encouraged my love of music from the start – long before I could spell 'acknowledgements'. My mother sadly passed away during the writing of this book, but her kindness, humour, and steady encouragement remain with me.

My sons, Jonathan and Christopher, now both university
graduates and making their own way in the world. They have,
I'm pleased to say, inherited a genuine love of music. I'm
immensely proud of the men they've become. Their achievements
are entirely their own – though I remain quietly satisfied that my
influence has not been wholly detrimental.

And finally, appreciation to 'besties' Dan & Bethan Jones at Bragdy Cybi,
noble providers of beer – and cheese on Sundays – without whom our
gatherings would be noticeably more sensible – and, therefore, far less
fun. I wish you the best of luck with your new venture, Tafarn Cybi!
Keep up the good work – I'm counting on you.

Grant would like to thank … my wife Julie, for her love, humour,
encouragement, and weekly music trivia dates; Gordon and Wendy
Walters, for instilling an appreciation of music in our house from the
very beginning; Andrew and Erin Walters, for their ongoing enthusiasm
and support; Spencer Gibb of Juicy & Trouble, for his friendship, empty
envelopes, and justifiable hatred of the ghosts who live in my
hometown; Walker and Anne Evans at *Columbus Underground*, for
continuing to give me the freedom to freelance at will; Stacy Oliver-
Sikorski, for many years of general snarking; Albhy Galuten and Karl
Richardson, for their brilliance (and for their willingness to take my
phone calls); Dennis Hetzendorfer, for his kindness and storytelling; and
Joe Mardin for sharing some insight about his legendary dad, Arif.

Additional gratitude to Jacki Andre, Akio Correll, Alice Cooper, Jim
Cuddy, Lee DeWyze, Tommy Emmanuel, Cat Geletka, Michael Gerbrandt,
Scott Hall, Juliana Hatfield, Julie Malmberg, Grant Lee-Phillips, Brian
Linnen, Matt Scannell, David Wild, and many other kind friends,
colleagues, musicians and fellow Bee Gees fans who have taken a
special interest in our work.

Authors' Note
This volume represents the third entry in the *Decades* series, a
body of work dedicated to documenting the Bee Gees'
extensive and influential career.

DECADES | The Bee Gees in the 1980s

Contents

Foreword

So, here we are – the third instalment of the *Decades* series dedicated to The Bee Gees. If we were to follow the movie sequel playbook, we could assume that there's about to be more drama, more tragedy – and definitely a shitload more villains.

Well, nope. That's not what this book is about. And if you've read the first two, which I assume and hope you have since you've made it this far down the rabbit hole, you already know that. That said, outside of the recording studio and the focus of these books, it's fair to say that compared to the previous two decades, the 1980s were a much more complicated rollercoaster for the Brothers Gibb.

At the start of each of these forewords I've written, I've struggled with what to say and the direction in which I would take things. For the 1960s volume, my challenge was to write about my own family during a time in which I wasn't alive. Surely someone like Vince Melouney could do a better job? (He did, by the way.) I then had the revelation that, as a musician and performer, this period of music was pivotal for me. I had been fortunate to meet countless artists over the years and pick their brains. My mother's close working relationship with Brian Epstein and The Beatles, as well as her overall involvement with the 'London Scene', had yielded many stories. Between that and my general obsession with music history, it turns out I knew a lot about this decade. I actually knew more about what was happening overall in the 1960s British music industry than I did about what my own family was doing in it.

If only someone had written a book about that …

So, that was my key: to remove myself from them as family members entirely and just imagine what it must have been like for these three teenagers, fresh off a boat from Australia and dumped in the middle of London in 1967.

My initial battle with the foreword for the 1970s book was similar in the sense that this was a decade where monumental things – literal record-breaking events – happened for Barry, Robin and Maurice amidst circumstances of which they never could have conceived in the first chapter of their careers.

And again, I still wasn't alive for any of it. Well, kind of, anyway. Yes, I was born in the 1970s, but my memories are not entirely filled with cocaine, quaaludes, and key parties. Okay … I did see *some* cocaine on occasion.

But mine are the memories of a small child, not really understanding what was happening in the world around him. I remember living in Paris at around four years old, for example, with obviously no clue about our reason for being there: my father recording what would become one of the most musically significant (and best-selling) records of all time. By the end of the decade, I truly did *not* know that other children didn't have police escorts, security, or even access to their own plane – and I definitely had no comprehension of how my family could possibly be some of, if not the most, famous people in the world. So, lacking any legitimate and useful observational insight on that time period, I chose to give more of a historical backdrop to the 1970s in America. I particularly focused on life in major cities as a way of maybe helping readers of the book understand the political and economic climate of the times and how they dramatically shaped music, art, and popular culture. It was an almost perfect storm that allowed for The Bee Gees' meteoric success. It was important for me to set that stage – a primer, so to speak, since the series does touch upon personal events and circumstances in the lives of the brothers but doesn't provide extensive commentary, dissection, or exposition on the cultural or socioeconomic landscape.

Which gets me to this third go-round: the 1980s. I always knew this introduction would be hard to write because this time I was present – at least cognitively, anyway. I was able to observe and interact with my father and his brothers as professionals, much of it having an extremely profound impact on me. By the end of the decade, I had chosen to leave home, drop out of school, and move back to New York and pursue my own career as an artist.

I knew that writing this foreword would be personal. I went through draft after draft, sorting through poignant memories and recounting stories from that period that I thought might be relevant to this book. There was reuniting with my father after not seeing him for years, following my parents' turbulent divorce at the start of the decade. And then there was Maurice holding my feet to the fire (which he was annoyingly great at) after telling him I had been writing songs and had built my own 4-track tape recorder from parts – and him dragging me into a real recording studio to see if I was any good. There was also the mad genius of the engineer Scott Glasel. I also remember my father excitedly playing demos of songs he'd recorded just earlier that day, and me occasionally getting to write with him. There was my rapidly developing close friendship with my uncle Andy – one of the kindest, sweetest people I have ever known – and his sudden passing. I got to watch my family record music together for the first time. And then I watched them grieve. I experienced life on a huge tour and learned just how much goes into a production of that size – along with the wonderful, insightful storytelling of touring and wrangling maestro Scott Sands. As a brief side note: to any young or up-and-coming musicians out there reading this: this is absolutely *not* an experience you want to have before you've done your own touring in a shitty van, eating shitty food, and sleeping in (if you're lucky) shitty hotel rooms. That is one disappointing eye-opening reality check, let me tell you. So, when that buddy of yours is all giddy because they just landed their dream gig playing drums for Taylor Swift and they want you to come along for the summer as their roadie/assistant, say 'no'. Joking aside, it was actually insanely and unbelievably formative, and I very much appreciated the experience. It's not one that many people get to have.

Anyway, after what feels like a huge number of rewrites, I realised that I didn't want to take that approach to this foreword, either. It was starting to feel like an autobiography, and I'm fairly sure that's not what the authors had in mind when they asked me to do this…

At the start of the 1980s, the brothers began their third decade as singers, songwriters and producers – something very few of their 1960s-originated peers had accomplished. Sure, there was that brief, but not undramatic, rift between Barry and Robin going into the 1970s, but looking back, it was a mere blip considering all their subsequent achievements. This was a decade that The Bee Gees could never have anticipated, and I imagine that by the end of 1979, they probably figured they'd seen it all. And while throughout the following years they wrote and produced countless huge hits for a number of other artists, they were still 'blacklisted' by American radio as performers under their own name. Irony abounds if you consider that many of those hits sounded like them and featured their vocals – and it was by no means a secret to anyone playing or programming those records that the brothers were involved. At those same radio stations, numerous huge artists of the time, while either musically or verbally acknowledging The Bee Gees' influence on them, were *thriving*. Michael Jackson's iconic and fantastic 'Billie Jean', to name just one example, is a fairly unsubtle homage to 'Stayin' Alive', a monster hit from only five years earlier, although back then, five years in the music industry could be a very, very long time. To throw a little extra irony on top, the oft-called 'Second British Invasion' of the early 1980s was successful in part due to its often unapologetic embrace of late 1970s American music: R&B, disco and punk, which were genres that, while suddenly now taboo on US radio, had nonetheless continued to evolve in Europe. Only with the sudden rise of import records that were huge in other countries, and music publications such as *NME* from the UK being more readily available, was American radio forced to pay attention to what young people were actually listening to. Under the convenience of new labelling monikers like 'new wave' – a name detested by most of those artists, incidentally – and being able to dismissively brand these artists to the public as 'British', they were able to find some kind of radio programming loophole.

Now, in all fairness, the Brothers Gibb didn't *just* leave the spotlight due to a bizarre, hate-fuelled campaign involving burning records in a ballpark. Their music – whether under their name or that of other artists, that of their brother Andy, and even their overall sonic influence – had become heavily oversaturated at radio. It was unprecedented – and as my father once pointed out, when radio stations were advertising 'Bee Gee-free' weekends, it was probably a good time for them to take a back seat.

While withdrawing from the public eye didn't stop them from being just as prolific, and focusing on writing and producing for others might have seemed like a potential welcome break from the spotlight, deeper behind-the-scenes things were less than rosy. My dad's divorce had been unnecessarily, but not unsurprisingly, public. Maurice's alcoholism was reaching a peak. A ludicrous lawsuit was filed against them, embattling one of their greatest recordings (if not *the* greatest, in my opinion), 'How Deep Is Your Love'. Their relationship with long-time mentor and manager Robert Stigwood came to an end. They lost their younger brother. I can't imagine what it must have been like for them to make the decision to return to a more public life as performers after the blows dealt to them by the industry only a few years earlier.

That said, even in the face of that degree of humiliation and hypocrisy, it became obvious to me, for the first time personally, that these guys loved, and even savoured, a challenge. Few people, very few artists and probably even fewer family members are able to bounce back the way they did. All three brothers came together to make what I consider to be the best Bee Gees record that wasn't actually a Bee Gees record: the Robin Gibb solo album *Walls Have Eyes*. They reunited with Arif Mardin to make *E.S.P.* It was a record with undertones that varied anywhere from rock to Celtic folk to R&B, and featured the same 'throw caution to the wind' attitude that had made *Main Course* (also, probably not uncoincidentally, with Arif) as significant as it was a little over a decade earlier. And much like 'Jive Talkin'' had exploded in the US from that record, the almost impossible to categorise stylistically 'You Win Again' became a number one single – but this time, and most importantly, in the UK.

And while this was understandably a huge point of pride for the brothers as success in their homeland was always very dear to them, neither 'You Win Again' nor the follow-up single 'E.S.P.' had the American market welcoming them back with open arms. That distinction would go to their next studio effort, *One*, and its supporting world tour. Written in the wake of Andy's passing, that album boasts some of their most honest and heartfelt music – proof they were always at their best when they came together in a way that the not accidental title suggested. That last sentence, it should be noted, is how you avoid the writer's trap of falling into a potentially horrific pun. That aside, when they were unified, they were unstoppable. As a personal side note, I strongly encourage anyone reading this to *immediately* listen to the tragically under-promoted song 'Bodyguard' from that set. I believe it to be not only their best single of the decade, but one of *the* best songs of the decade. It is a nonchalant nod to their previous R&B-infused recordings and a subtle middle finger to other artists at the time experimenting with that genre. It doesn't scream from the rooftops, 'here we are – we can still do this. And we can do it better than you – don't you forget it!' But it's certainly implied.

By the end of the decade, the Brothers Gibb had experienced yet another regrouping, reinvention, and rebirth that would set them on the path to becoming living legends by the end of the next. It's a status I don't think any of them could comprehend or appreciate. In hindsight, it was their 'underdog' mentality and their mantra of 'never resting on your laurels', as my father would say, that gave them their drive and endurance.

If the 1960s were an Australian Bee Gees story, and the 1970s an American one, then the 1980s are undoubtedly a British tale. With stiff upper lips and chins up, they kept calm and carried on.

In closing, I would like to take a moment to thank those from that period that had such a strong and profound effect on me both as an artist and as a human who are sadly no longer with us today: Scott Glasel, Scott Sands, Arif Mardin, Andy Gibb, Maurice Gibb and, yep … Robin Fuckin' Gibb. I wish we'd had more time.

Spencer Gibb
November 2025, Austin, Texas, US

Prologue

As 1980 drew breath, The Bee Gees stood at a perplexing crossroads.

Exactly a year earlier, they were on the precipice of releasing *Spirits Having Flown*, their most commercially successful studio album. Their latest single, 'Too Much Heaven', was just days from becoming their fourth consecutive North American number one single. The culture-shifting tracks they contributed to the *Saturday Night Fever* film soundtrack were still in heavy rotation, while the double record set continued to cling tightly to the upper half of *Billboard*'s Top LPs & Tape chart after a staggering 72 total weeks. By that point, it had already become the biggest-selling album of all time to date.

At the close of 1979, *Spirits Having Flown* proved to be a formidable follow-up to *Saturday Night Fever*, having sold nearly 15 million copies globally – the third successive Bee Gees album to achieve platinum status. The album's extracts 'Tragedy' and 'Love You Inside Out' followed 'Too Much Heaven' to the summit of the *Billboard* Hot 100 in the US, completing a record run of six consecutive chart-toppers that duplicated what was previously believed to be an incomparable feat established by The Beatles in 1964. Moreover, the Gibbs had usurped their idols as being the sole musical act in *Billboard* singles chart history to write, perform and produce their sextet of uninterrupted number ones.

The wildly profitable, fully sold-out *Spirits Having Flown* tour took The Bee Gees to 38 North American cities, where they played 46 dates in just 100 days. As the tour wrapped, RSO Records capitalised on the turnout by issuing *Greatest*, a new double-disc retrospective that chronicled The Bee Gees' prolific output from 1975 to 1979. On 11 January 1980, it became their second number one album in the US in just ten months.

The Bee Gees had become one of the most successful musical acts in the world, fulfilling the hopes and dreams they imagined – and then some – as young boys growing up in the cold, grey suburbs of Manchester. Since Barry, Robin, and Maurice started performing and recording as The Bee Gees in 1959, they had never been more culturally relevant and commercially prosperous. At the end of the 1970s, they were seemingly everywhere. Their songs, and those they wrote, produced, and backed for other artists, permeated the airwaves. Even on recordings they had nothing to do with – from The Eagles to The Rolling Stones – their influence and ethos were plainly evident. Their faces were on almost every imaginable music and pop culture magazine, and their images adorned t-shirts, lunchboxes, cigarette lighters, and record players.

However, massive popularity always comes at a cost, and The Bee Gees' omnipresence in nearly every public outlet had pushed them beyond the brink of overexposure. In the midst of what may have been their most triumphant year, their ostensibly impenetrable cachet began to crumble. The Gibbs found themselves awash in a cultural sea change. The rise and pervasiveness of disco in the latter part of the 1970s – a grossly oversimplified corporate label for the diversity of influences and genres that propelled it – had exasperated music critics, writers, and insiders who saw it as repetitive, overproduced, and campy. More conservative corners of the industry objected to disco's amplification of marginalised artists and identities, particularly where the Black, Latine, and LGBTQ communities intersected, decrying that it had opened doors to societal depravity by glamourising sex, drugs, and irreligion.

The Bee Gees, of course, were certainly not the originators of disco, nor did their late 1970s output really fit the true sonic definition of it. But *Saturday Night Fever* became the apex of the glossy, commoditised embodiment of it. In the end, it made the Gibbs the primary and undeserving target of the eventual backlash that followed. The same media outlets that helped to bolster The Bee Gees' otherworldly halcyon started to calculatedly dismantle it in the middle of 1979 – quite literally ignited by the now-notorious 'Disco Demolition Night' baseball promotion at Comiskey Park in Chicago on 12 July. Local radio station WLUP-FM offered 98-cent tickets to a Chicago White Sox versus Detroit Tigers doubleheader in exchange for fans bringing their disco records to the stadium to be destroyed in an on-field explosion.

Meanwhile, The Bee Gees were a month into the *Spirits Having Flown* tour, blissfully playing nightly for loud capacity crowds. The signs of their falling out of favour soon became evident in the form of bomb threats and beefed-up security meeting their custom-livered Boeing 707 airliner at each subsequent stop on their itinerary.

The media and the public weren't the only ones exhausted by The Bee Gees. Barry, Robin, and Maurice struggled on various levels as they worked constantly and contended with being some of the most recognisable people on the planet. The pressure took a major toll on the brothers and their families.

This was all uncharted territory. Somewhere in those turbulent months, the Gibbs determined that, all things considered, making and releasing music as The Bee Gees – at least for the foreseeable future – wasn't feasible.

The brothers had reportedly toyed with the idea of formally bringing the group to a mutually agreeable conclusion, and said as much in a high-profile *People* magazine interview in the summer of 1979. Ultimately, they opted to take a break from being The Bee Gees to focus on writing and producing for other artists – a diversion they had winningly experimented with over the past few years. Unlike the uncharted terrain that had preceded their breakup in 1969, the Gibbs had the confidence, financial stability, family support, commercial cachet, and lived experience to weather another major career transition.

Releasing just three de facto Bee Gees studio albums in the process, the Gibbs would spend almost all of the 1980s behind the scenes, expertly crafting hit albums and singles for some of the most eminent artists of the time, intercut with a redux of their short solo careers they had left behind in 1970 – to varying degrees of success.

They would also work tirelessly to escape the shadow of their 1970s heyday, including what seemed to be a collective pact among North American radio outlets, especially, to embargo The Bee Gees' music from the airwaves regardless of its merit. By 1989, they would reclaim their rightful spot on the charts on both sides of the Atlantic.

In between, the Gibbs would also navigate some of their most difficult personal challenges to date, testing their fortitude as brothers and business partners. Their final studio effort of the 1980s, *One*, was not only The Bee Gees' most sonically cohesive work in ten years – it was a testament to their resilience and unity when it mattered most.

The latter part of The Bee Gees' career is the least-discussed stretch of their journey, something fans and enthusiasts have lamented for years. Among the myriad of Gibb-related greatest hits compilations, documentaries, interviews, and articles that have surfaced since, their 1980s output is unevenly represented at best. At worst, it's been completely overlooked.

And so, the next few hundred pages of this volume will attempt to capture the quality and prolificacy of their work across the 'Decade of Excess', with more than a few unexpected twists, turns, and detours as The Bee Gees transformed from hitmakers-du-jour into industry icons.

1980

Although the Gibbs were wrestling with the uncertainty of what their futures would hold in an industry that had become decidedly anti-Bee Gees, their commercial impact remained surprisingly powerful throughout the entirety of 1980.

The year began with the double disc retrospective *Greatest* seated at number 31 on the UK albums chart, having peaked a few weeks earlier at number 17. The Bee Gees' final single of the 1970s, 'Spirits (Having Flown)', was placed at number 61. With the benefit of radio plays, it climbed steadily, reaching its highest position at number 16 four weeks later. The bigger payoff, however, was the boost it provided to *Greatest*, which eventually landed at number six for three weeks.

On 3 January, more than a year after it had reached its number nine chart peak on the *Billboard* Hot 100, Andy Gibb's version of the Barry Gibb and Blue Weaver-penned '(Our Love) Don't Throw It All Away', the third and final single from his platinum-selling sophomore album *Shadow Dancing*, was certified gold by the Recording Industry Association of America (RIAA). It would be just a few short weeks until Andy would score yet another North American top ten hit.

In the US, *Greatest* reached the summit of the *Billboard* Top LPs & Tape chart the week of 12 January. It remained atop the tally for a single week before being replaced by Pink Floyd's *The Wall*. It would be The Bee Gees' last album to reach the top half of the survey for over 17 years. In Canada, *Greatest* would reach a peak of number four the week of 26 January, on its way to being certified double platinum.

The seventh annual American Music Awards took place on 18 January at the ABC TV Studios in Los Angeles. *Spirits Having Flown* was awarded the prize for top pop album, fending off competition from Led Zeppelin's *In Through The Out Door* and Donna Summer's *Bad Girls*. The Bee Gees were not present to accept the award, but were instead represented by brother Andy. The award was presented by Nicollette Larson (best known for her 1978 hit 'Lotta Love') and Michael Jackson. The Bee Gees were also named the top pop group for the second year in a row, beating Cheap Trick and Supertramp to the title. The award was presented by Ann and Nancy Wilson of Heart, and Andy again accepted on behalf of his elder brothers.

The first new Gibb output of the 1980s was the January release of 'Desire', the lead single from Andy's third (and ultimately final) studio album, *After Dark*, which arrived on 2 February.

After Dark – **Andy Gibb** (1980)

Personnel:
The Andy Gibb Band:
Andy Gibb: vocals
Harold Cowart: bass
Joey Murcia: guitars
George Bitzer: keyboards, synthesisers
Ron Ziegler: drums
George Terry: guitars
Guest musicians:
Joe Lala: percussion
Tom Roady: percussion (misprinted as 'Tom Roadie' in the album's liner notes)
Tim Renwick: guitar
Hugh McCracken: guitar
Albhy Galuten: keyboards
Blue Weaver: keyboards ('Desire')
Dennis Bryon: drums ('Desire')
Alan Kendall: guitar ('Desire')
Barry Gibb: vocals, guitar, synthesiser
Michael Brecker: saxophone ('After Dark')
Randy Brecker: trumpet ('After Dark')
The Boneroo Horns: Whit Sidener, Peter Graves, Neil Bonsanti, Dan Bonsanti, Kenny Faulk, Bill Purse
Vocals on 'Desire': Andy Gibb, Barry Gibb, Robin Gibb, Maurice Gibb
Vocals on 'I Can't Help It' and 'Rest Your Love On Me': Andy Gibb, Olivia Newton-John
Background vocals: Andy Gibb, Barry Gibb, Charlie Chalmers, Sandy Rhodes, Donna Rhodes
Engineers: Karl Richardson, Dennis Hetzendorfer, Mike Fuller
String arrangements: Barry Gibb, Albhy Galuten. Conductor: Albhy Galuten
Producers: Barry Gibb, Karl Richardson, Albhy Galuten
Recorded at Criteria Recording Studios, Miami, in May, October and November 1979
Release dates: UK and US: February 1980
Chart positions: Norway: 21, US: 21, Sweden: 23, Canada: 24
Gold certification: Hong Kong, US

After Dark surfaced nearly two years after the release of *Shadow Dancing*, which, at the time, was considered a significantly long gap between projects.

The cover art showed a smiling, meticulously coiffed, well-tanned, now-21-year-old Andy in a red spandex shirt channelling lightning bolts through his outstretched thumbs. It was a rather kitschy choice given that one of the objectives of the album was to help untangle Andy from his teen idolatry and demonstrate his maturity as an artist. 'I don't think there's a long life in the teen thing – three to five years and you're out', Andy told *People*'s Fred Bernstein in April 1980, claiming that *After Dark* signalled a deliberate pivot to 'more meaningful' songs because 'they're the ones who keep you going'.

Of course, the external sheen was but a façade for what had been a series of difficult recording sessions for the album that had started in the spring of 1979. Andy had been unreliable in the studio and in poor voice when he did show up because of his escalating addiction to drugs and alcohol. His meteoric rise to fame had exacerbated his chronic anxiety and self-esteem issues, and he sought respite in substances – something he admitted publicly in interviews a few years later.

Albhy Galuten recounted the situation to the authors while discussing the recording of the album in late 2024:

Andy was not really present. When we were working with other artists with Barry during that period, there was always sort of a guiding light. Every artist had a beacon to aim for. There was nothing aimed *at* Andy on this record. On the whole, for me, the recording sounds a little bland. When you have a drug problem, for the first year or two, you're still on a ride. You feel like you are sort of invincible, and you can do stuff. Then, you reach the point where you can't deal with it, which is where we were at during *After Dark*.

Andy's songwriting output, one of the important ingredients in his career thus far that had separated him from his peers in the industry, had also diminished. He penned just two known tracks during 1979 for inclusion on *After Dark*: 'Back To The Wind' and 'Warm', neither of which was used.

Despite many obstacles, the Gibb-Galuten-Richardson production team and the session players enlisted for *After Dark* managed to assemble a solid, cohesive record, and they chose good songs that made the best of Andy's vocal limitations. As a result, the entire album's aesthetic is smooth and mellow.

For all intents and purposes, *After Dark* borders on being a Barry Gibb solo album. On many of the songs, Barry double-tracks Andy's lead –

and Barry's often becomes the primary voice heard on the choruses. In some cases, the vocals that are assumed to be Andy's by the listener's ear are reportedly note-perfect impersonations by his older brother, who was forced to touch up spots where Andy's voice faltered. When Andy does actually sing, the disparity in the strength and quality of his voice between the new record and the performances he turned in on *Shadow Dancing* is startling.

By all accounts, the experience of making *After Dark* was frustrating and inconvenient, but Andy owed RSO a third album under his contract. The pressure was on everyone to follow the platinum-selling success of *Shadow Dancing*. Compared to its predecessor, it was a commercial disappointment, peaking at number 21 on the *Billboard* Top LPs & Tape chart the week of 12 April. It took just two weeks for it to tumble out of the top 40. It performed similarly in Canada, Sweden, and Norway. *After Dark* would, however, eventually receive a gold certification from the RIAA in early May.

Reviews of the album were mixed, many of which noted the change in energy from the brighter, breezier *Shadow Dancing*. *People* quipped the set had a 'clean, slick pop sound' buoyed by 'the attractive Gibb sound of melting chords and quivering sincerity. Trouble is, Andy lolls the drowsy pace that makes *After Dark* seem to be about sleeping rather than something more stirring'.

'After Dark' (Barry Gibb)

Recorded at Criteria Recording Studios, Miami, in October and November 1979

Written solely by Barry, 'After Dark' is a sultry, jazz-infused mid-tempo ballad.

One can understand why it was chosen as the album's title and opening track – if the chief purpose of *After Dark* was to showcase a grown-up Andy Gibb, it's a much more blatantly sexy song than almost anything else he'd released to date. Andy's lead vocal barely climbs above a whisper; despite it likely being a necessity given the state of his voice at the time, it does suit the playful lilt of the melody. The production team did a fine job of weaving the elements of this track together into a tasty tapestry.

Contributing to the blossoming horns ribboned around its melody were Philadelphia natives Randy and Michael Brecker, best known as the Brecker Brothers, who had cut their teeth on other high-profile projects with Todd Rundgren, Bruce Springsteen, Parliament, and Quincy Jones. Andy seemed to prefer 'After Dark' to 'Desire', performing it regularly when he made American talk show appearances in support of the album. In a July 1980 guest spot on *The John Davidson Show*, he mentioned he hoped it would be the next single. Perhaps there was some discussion at RSO about its potential, but it's likely the album's short chart life deemed it unnecessary.

'Desire' (Barry Gibb, Robin Gibb, Maurice Gibb)

Recorded at Criteria Recording Studios, Miami, in May, October and November 1979
Chart positions: US: 4, Spain: 7, Belgium: 8, Canada: 10, Netherlands: 21, West Germany: 36, New Zealand: 38, Australia: 90

'Desire' speaks volumes about the album's problematic making in that *After Dark*'s first, and presumably most confident, extract was a full-fledged Bee Gees track – an outtake from the *Spirits Having Flown* sessions that Barry, Robin and Maurice had written in 1978.

Originally titled 'Midnight', one of The Bee Gees' early demos of 'Desire' has floated around the internet for years. Barry sings the verses in his chest voice, reverting to falsetto on the choruses. Some of the finalised lyrics are recognisable at this early stage, but much of the demo track is scat-sung.

The Bee Gees finished the song after reportedly spending weeks developing it, only to drop it from the tracklist. Its similarity to 'Spirits (Having Flown)' is quite evident, which may have partially been behind the decision to shelve it for The Bee Gees' album.

For Andy's version, his lead vocal was dubbed atop his brothers' otherwise complete original recording. The Bee Gees' band (Blue Weaver, Dennis Bryon and Alan Kendall) were named in the *After Dark* album credits as 'guest musicians'.

'It was a mediocre Bee Gees record, too', Albhy Galuten said of the single in 2024. 'On most of their records, the lead singer has a personality. This lead vocal had no personality. It was milquetoast'.

'Desire's lyrics are the usual trail of abstract Gibb phrases, but the overall sentiment of the protagonist devoting themselves completely to their betrothed, despite the tension between them, punches through clearly.

The blatantly obvious Bee Gees presence on 'Desire' seemed to exemplify that the American media's rising aversion to the brothers' music was more about ostracising them in name rather than because of their actual music. The single bounded up the *Billboard* Hot 100 to reach number four in March – and number ten on Canada's *RPM* 100 singles chart in late April. Certainly, Andy's still-adoring legions of North American fans, oblivious to his mounting personal struggles at that stage, helped things along. The single failed to chart in the UK, as would anything else he would release moving forward, but it did reach the top ten in Belgium and Spain, and it became a minor hit elsewhere in Europe, Australia, and New Zealand.

'Wherever You Are' (Barry Gibb)
Recorded at Criteria Recording Studios, Miami, in October and November 1979

'Wherever You Are', another Barry composition written specifically for the album, is one of just two up-tempo songs on the entire tracklist. It may have been another song Andy especially liked among the others; he performed it along with 'After Dark' on the aforementioned appearance on *The John Davidson Show*. It would later appear on the 2018 Capitol Records compilation *The Very Best Of Andy Gibb*.

'Warm Ride' (Barry Gibb, Robin Gibb, Maurice Gibb)
Recorded at Criteria Recording Studios, Miami, in October and November 1979

'Warm Ride' follows some of the similar lyrical themes of 'Desire': passion triumphs over ambivalence. Its meaning has never been explicitly stated by the Gibbs, but one can suppose a 'warm ride' might have erotic connotations.

'Warm Ride' emerged from The Bee Gees' *Saturday Night Fever* recording sessions in early 1977. Record producer David Courtney recalled in his autobiography, *Giving It All Away*: 'The Bee Gees agreed to write a song for the Roger Daltrey album *One Of The Boys*, which I co-produced with former Shadows drummer Tony Meehan. They were recording demos at the Honky Château for a movie soundtrack at the time, which turned out to be *Saturday Night Fever*. Roger rejected the song on the basis that he felt it was not compatible with the other songs on the album'.

Despite this early rejection, 'Warm Ride' went on to enjoy a varied afterlife. In March 1978, Graham Bonnet recorded the track for his album, *No Bad Habits*, and scored a top ten single hit in Australia, where it peaked at number two, becoming one of the standout recordings of his post-Marbles solo career.

A month later, Rare Earth released their own interpretation. The Detroit-based group issued the single on the Prodigal label and promoted it with a performance on *American Bandstand* in June 1978. Their rendition was also the opening track on their album *Band Together* and circulated as an extended six-minute promotional version. The single achieved modest chart success, reaching number 33 in Canada, number 39 in the US, and number 68 in Australia.

Finally, in 1980, Andy Gibb recorded 'Warm Ride', reimagined with an acoustic guitar-driven arrangement that at times nearly washes out the softer parts of his vocal.

The unfinished Bee Gees recording from 1977 was eventually mixed and released in 2007 on a reissue of *Bee Gees Greatest*.

'Rest Your Love On Me' (Barry Gibb)

Recorded at Criteria Recording Studios, Miami, in October and November 1979

Longtime friend Olivia Newton-John was brought on board to sing two duets with Andy for the album. A new recording of 'Rest Your Love On Me' – a song Barry had written and first recorded back in 1976 during the sessions for *Children Of The World* – was a re-work of a sparser version they had performed live in early 1979 for *The Music For UNICEF Concert: A Gift Of Song* television concert broadcast and album.

The *After Dark* recording featured backing vocals from Sandy and Donna Rhoades and Charlie Chalmers of the Memphis-based singing trio Rhoades Chalmers Rhoades, who had also appeared on tracks by Al Green, Clarence Carter and Candi Staton. It was released as a single in December 1980 in select countries across Europe and South America, and also in Japan, but puzzlingly on Newton-John's EMI label instead of RSO. In Colombia, it was released as an attractive and highly desirable transparent purple vinyl 12" single. It failed to chart anywhere.

'I Can't Help It' (Barry Gibb)

Recorded at Criteria Recording Studios, Miami, in October and November 1979

Chart positions: US: 12, Spain: 23, Belgium: 27, Canada: 32, Australia: 62

The other Andy-Olivia duet on the album was a new Barry-written song, 'I Can't Help It', the album's second and final wide-release single.

Karl Richardson recalled recording the track in a conversation with the authors in December 2024:

Olivia was great. She had a lot of patience. In the studio, the two of them were singing while looking at each other, although the microphones weren't 180 degrees apart, so that we didn't have a lot of spill from the other. But they could read each other's faces and voices, and they had their music stand so they could read the lyrics and react to the other person singing at the same time. So, the emotional ad libs you hear in the song are all real – they were really going for it. We tried to capture as much of that live as possible.

'I Can't Help It' reached number 12 on the *Billboard* Hot 100 the week of 24 May, staying at its peak for two weeks. Coincidentally, Olivia's 'Magic', the lead single released from the *Xanadu* film soundtrack, also made its chart debut the same week on its way to number one.

Andy and Olivia's pairing during the *Music For UNICEF* project and on *After Dark* fuelled rumours that the two were romantically involved. Both denied it, although Andy's coy media commentary on the topic alluded to the fact that he might have had an interest. However, nobody seemed too eager to quell the illusion of them being linked if it helped to sell records. *People* magazine even dedicated their 21 April issue's front cover story to it with the tagline 'Andy & Olivia – the youngest Gibb talks frankly about drugs, his Bee Gee brothers and the Newton-John rumours'.

'One Love' (Barry Gibb, Andy Gibb)
Recorded at Criteria Recording Studios, Miami, in October and November 1979

'One Love' is one of two Andy-Barry co-writes on the album, although the moody melody and rhythmic pacing suggest it was mostly guided by the eldest brother's hand. It has a similar tempo to The Bee Gees' 'Stop (Think Again)' from *Spirits Having Flown*, but without the falsetto histrionics; Andy's vocal is mostly kept to a whisper. A thick layer of Barry harmonies lifts the choruses.

'Someone I Ain't' (Barry Gibb, Andy Gibb)
Recorded at Criteria Recording Studios, Miami, in October and November 1979

Given the smoke and mirrors propping up *After Dark*, Andy singing a track called 'Someone I Ain't' is an interesting choice. Still, it's a pretty ballad. The choruses have enough folksiness to sound like something

Andy would have previously written for himself, but the wordy phrasing and big flourishes of falsetto harmonies on the choruses are certainly Barry's compositional trademarks.

'Someone I Ain't' is also the only track from *After Dark* to appear as a B-side to a single; it backed 'I Can't Help It' in all markets.

'Falling In Love With You' (Barry Gibb, Albhy Galuten)
Recorded at Criteria Recording Studios, Miami, in October and November 1979

'Falling In Love With You' is a song Barry and Albhy Galuten had written in 1977, copyrighted at the same time as Barry's compositions 'An Everlasting Love' – which became Andy's second single from *Shadow Dancing* – and 'Ain't Nothing Gonna Keep Me From You' that was given to singer Teri DeSario. It's unknown if Barry had either of those projects in mind when it was conceived.

It's a tender ballad that has some of 'After Dark's sensuality (and more nighttime imagery). Brushed drums, electric piano, and smooth guitar sweetening keep things light. The vocals are essentially an Andy and Barry duet most of the way through, and it suits both their breathy voices well.

Andy performed the song along with 'Desire' on American singer and actress Dinah Shore's daytime talk variety show, *Dinah!,* on 22 February, and did so again with the addition of 'After Dark' while serving as guest host on the 14 March episode of *The Midnight Special*.

'Dreamin' On' (Barry Gibb)
Recorded at Criteria Recording Studios, Miami, in October and November 1979

The album's final track, 'Dreamin' On', written by Barry alone, is reminiscent of 'Dance To The Light Of The Morning' from *Flowing Rivers* with its easy, country-hued melody. It has Barry's classically meandering verses. Like most of the other tracks on the album, Barry's vocal supports Andy's almost word-for-word on the chorus.

In February, Andy made a two-week trip to Europe to promote *After Dark*, visiting London, Munich, Paris, and Amsterdam for radio and television appearances and press interviews. During his visit to London, he attended the British Rock and Pop Awards at the Café Royal on 26 February. The ceremony was introduced by BBC presenters Sue Lawley and Dave Lee Travis, and Andy presented the award for the best group to The Police. The event was shown in its entirety on BBC television the following evening and simulcast on BBC Radio 1 with commentary by Mike Read.

While in Munich, Andy visited British rock band Queen, who were in the middle of recording their forthcoming studio album, The Game, at Musicland Studios. Freddie Mercury invited Andy to join the session and contribute vocals to a few takes of the song 'Play The Game'.

Andy's personal assistant, Scott Sands, later recalled, 'We were in Munich, Germany and we met Freddie Mercury. We were in the studio one night and Freddie Mercury couldn't hit a high note. And, he told Andy 'Get out there. That's your famil[y]'s forte – the high notes'. So, Andy went and sang with Queen backtracks and it just sounded so incredible'.

The track would eventually serve as the album's third single in May 1980, although Andy's vocals were not used in the released recording. The existence of those outtakes has been confirmed by producer Reinhold Mack. At the time, the Queen Fan Club reported that the finished version of the song featured Andy singing the first verse.

The tapes of Andy's vocals were later found in a search of Queen's archives in 1990 when the band was considering bonus material for a CD reissue of *The Game* on Hollywood Records, but they were ultimately not included. It is not known if the tapes have survived over subsequent years.

Also in February, Robin and Blue Weaver's work with American soul singer Jimmy Ruffin began to see the light of day as the single 'Hold On (To My Love)' hit radio and retail. It debuted on the *Billboard* Hot 100 chart at number 63 on the week of 1 March. Four days later, the single debuted on the UK singles chart at number 36.

Barry, Albhy Galuten, and Karl Richardson were focused squarely on Barbra Streisand's forthcoming album. After demos for the tracks had been completed in October 1979, work began on proper recordings for the project in February at Criteria. Karl Richardson told *Albumism* in 2020:

We cut the first versions of the tracks at Criteria to take them to Los Angeles so we could capture Barbra singing there. She was filming a movie at the time. Recording was sort of like a hobby for her at that moment, and we could only get her for so many hours of so many days, originally. So, the decision was to cut the music in Miami, then produce her vocals, then come back to Miami to do the mix.

With the basic instrumentals in place, the sessions moved to Sound Labs Studios in Hollywood, California, in March to record Streisand's vocals. Post-production continued through the summer.

The problems of music piracy under the guise of bootlegging and counterfeiting were compounded when a major controversy erupted in Denmark in March. This resulted from a massive promotional campaign for BASF blank tapes, who used the names of superstar acts to promote their products. Posters featuring ABBA, The Bee Gees, Bryan Ferry, and Wings were mailed to those who responded to press advertisements, which were aimed at the teenage market, saying: 'You can hear the sounds of these artists by recording them on BASF tapes'. Danish music industry executives saw this as a direct encouragement of BASF's customers to copy major artists' product onto blank tape.

Back in The Bee Gees arena, a *Billboard* article on 22 March broke news that Ronald H. Selle, a Chicago-based musician and antiques dealer, had filed a lawsuit against The Bee Gees, alleging that their 1977 hit song, 'How Deep Is Your Love', was 'copied largely' from his own 1975 composition, 'Let It End'. The lawsuit was filed in the US District Court for the Northern District of Illinois and named Barry, Robin, and Maurice Gibb as defendants, along with their record label distributor Polygram and Paramount Pictures. The lawsuit also included RSO Records, Stigwood Music, Unichappell Music, and Warner Bros. Music.

Selle's legal team approached The Bee Gees in early 1980. According to the group's personal manager, Dick Ashby, their lawyers advised them to settle the case to avoid costly litigation. 'We were told to offer something like $25,000 just to sort of make him go away', Ashby revealed. Road manager Tom Kennedy echoed the sentiment, explaining, 'Everyone was fair game. Rather than spend millions of dollars defending it, most people would just give them a few thousand to go away'. However, Selle was determined to see the case through. 'He said he wanted six figures', Ashby recounted. 'That was when we said, 'See you in court'. But, of course, we were pretty new to this whole thing'.

The case gained significant media attention as it pitted an independent musician against one of the biggest music acts in history. The central question in court would be whether the similarities between the two songs were coincidental or if The Bee Gees had, in some way, had an opportunity to hear and copy Selle's work.

The lawsuit would highlight the challenges independent musicians face when battling major industry players over intellectual property rights. It also underscored the complexities of proving musical plagiarism, a debate that continues to this day in the music industry.

The Fairlight CMI (short for Computer Musical Instrument), a digital synthesiser, music sampler, and digital audio workstation, was introduced in 1979 by Fairlight, a Sydney, Australia-based firm. Priced at $36,000 at the time, it was one of the earliest electronic music workstations with an embedded sampler and is credited with coining the term 'sampling' in music. It rose to prominence in the early 1980s and competed with the Synclavier from New England Digital.

The 10 May 1980 edition of *Billboard* magazine reported that only four Fairlight CMIs were in use in the US and were owned by Lindsey Buckingham of Fleetwood Mac, Stevie Wonder, Geordie Hormel of the Village Recorder studio in Los Angeles, Ri and Barry Gibb. Fairlight's first customer in the UK was John Paul Jones of Led Zeppelin.

While Barry evidently wanted to be at the cutting edge of digital technology in music production, and the Fairlight CMI was likened to a much more reliable and versatile digital version of the Mellotron, musicians slowly began to realise that the CMI could not match the expressiveness and control that could be achieved using acoustic instruments, and that sampling was better applied as imaginative sound than pure reproduction.

Albhy Galuten told the authors in December 2024:

The Fairlight was not as useful to us as the Synclavier. It became very popular. Yes' 'Owner Of A Lonely Heart' used the Fairlight. It led to some incredibly creative stuff, but it used a different kind of approach than the Synclavier, which had a higher sampling quality. Fairlights were more user-friendly, but I didn't really care about that kind of stuff because I knew how to navigate around things technically. But for people who used Fairlight, it was easier to create things because of how the experience was set up. A lot of great artists did great things with it.

Sunrise – Jimmy Ruffin (1980)

Personnel:

Jimmy Ruffin: vocals

Marcy Levy: vocals ('Where Do I Go')

Blue Weaver: keyboards

Alan Kendall: guitar

Bobby Cadway: guitar
Pete Carr: guitar
George Terry: guitar
George Perry: bass
Chuck Kirkpatrick: bass
Dennis Bryon: drums
Joe Lala: percussion
The Boneroo Horns ('Jealousy'): Whit Sidener, Kenny Faulk, Jeff Kievett, Don Bonsanti, Jamis Marshall
Backing vocals: Yonne Lewis, Krystal Davis, Janet Wright, Robin Gibb, Dennis Bryon, Jimmy Ruffin, Marcy Levy, Charlie Chalmers, Sandy Rhodes, Donna Rhodes, Barry Gibb, George Perry
Engineers: Greg Kolotkin (Kingdom Studios), Dennis Hetzendorfer (Criteria Recording Studios)
String arrangements: Blue Weaver, Mike Lewis
Conductor: Mike Lewis
Producers: Robin Gibb, Blue Weaver
Recorded at Kingdom Sound Studios, Syosett, Long Island, NY, in November 1979 and Criteria Recording Studios, Miami, in January 1980
Chart position: US: 152

In May, Jimmy Ruffin's seventh and final studio album, *Sunrise*, was released. Robin explained, 'I've known Jimmy for years, and one day he simply phoned me up and asked if I would like to produce some tracks for him. I said yes, and it all evolved from there'. In fact, their friendship went back to about 1974, and Ruffin recalled, 'We talked about working together and then the band had a hit with 'Jive Talkin'' and it just became impossible. Eventually, Robin was able to find time to work with me in the studio, and the result is the new album'.

Ruffin, a Mississippi native, was born into a musical family who were a travelling gospel act called The Dixie Nightingales. His younger brother, David, became one of the lead singers of the pivotal Motown R&B/soul outfit The Temptations, and provided the guiding vocal for many of the group's classics like 'My Girl' and 'Ain't Too Proud To Beg'. Jimmy joined the Tamla-Motown ranks as a session vocalist in 1961 and began releasing material as a solo artist for the stable in 1966.

Robin's involvement resulted in Ruffin enjoying a new chapter of recording success with his RSO label debut. He had first scored with the now classic 'What Becomes Of The Brokenhearted', which rose to the top ten on the US singles and R&B charts in late 1966. In the UK, it reached the top ten twice; first in 1966 and again in 1974 after it was reissued. A string of other hits followed in the UK after his American success began to dry up, including 'I've Passed This Way Before' and 'Farewell Is A Lonely Sound', but after a change of record label, Ruffin went through a fallow commercial period. However, he was still playing the UK's Northern clubs with tremendous success.

Ruffin lived in London for four years until 1976, when he decided to return to Detroit. He recalled: 'The problem was that I found the London promoters would not take me seriously. I was playing dates in the South of England, the Midlands and the North, and there were full houses everywhere, but it was different in the capital. When they heard me, they'd just say: 'Well, he's fine for the Northern clubs but not down here'. Eventually, a friend of mine told me to get out of the country and return to the US if I wanted to keep my prestige, and that's exactly what I did'.

And so it was in November 1979, Robin and Blue Weaver decided to begin their downtime from The Bee Gees by writing and producing for Ruffin. The earliest songs featured on the album, which would eventually be titled *Sunrise*, were recorded at Kingdom Sound Studios in Syosset, Long Island, New York, close to Robin's house in Lloyd Neck. Later tracks were laid down at the more familiar surroundings of Criteria Recording Studios in Miami. The album cover photographs were also taken in Miami, with the front featuring a silhouetted profile of Ruffin overlooking Biscayne Bay.

Sunrise featured a mix of musical styles. The first single and the opening track, 'Hold On (To My Love)' (sometimes formatted without parentheses), was a Transatlantic hit, but its up-tempo R&B pulse was not particularly representative of the rest of the album. There are, however, several other noteworthy and captivating cuts. Sadly, this wasn't enough to stimulate sales sufficiently for the album to achieve notable chart success anywhere. On the *Billboard* Top LPs & Tape chart, it only mustered a peak of number 152 the week of 14 June.

'Hold On (To My Love)' (Robin Gibb, Blue Weaver)
Recorded at Kingdom Sound Studios, Syosett, Long Island, NY, in November 1979
Chart positions: UK: 7, Ireland: 8, US: 10
'Hold On (To My Love)' is a strong track with good commercial hooks – not melodically dissimilar to the aforementioned Teri DeSario's 'Ain't Nothing Gonna Keep Me From You'. *Billboard* magazine raved about it,

saying it was 'a sprightly, finger-popping tune which mixes infectious Gibb-style hooks with Ruffin's soulful vocal inflections. It contains outstanding ingredients of performance, arrangement and production to ensure it is a favourite for both DJs and radio play. Ruffin's voice captures the earthy feeling of Al Green and the rich and moving quality of Joe Simon's 'I Need You, You Need Me".

During a promotional trip to London to support the single, Ruffin appeared on *Top Of The Pops* on 1 May. It climbed quickly to its peak position of number seven and spent a total of seven weeks in the top 40. It also fared well in the US, reaching number ten on the *Billboard* Hot 100 on the week of 3 May, amassing a total of 14 weeks on the chart overall.

An instrumental version appeared on the B-side of the single, and the song's enduring popularity was cemented when Robbie Leslie reworked it for the US-based Disconet remix service, which was issued on the label's August 1981 *Volume 4, Program 4* 12" single. It subsequently appeared on a further Disconet 12", *Volume 7, Program 1*, in August 1984. It became available commercially as a bonus track on the 12" version of 'Young Heart (Hang On)' in March 1985. Stephen L. Freeman also remixed the track for Hot Tracks in 1991 when it appeared on the *Hot Classics #9* CD.

Ruffin re-recorded the song in 2005 along with several of his other best-known songs on an album titled *Hold On To My Love*. Only the revamped version is currently available on streaming services.

A version of the track featuring Robin on lead vocals was also recorded, although it is often mistaken for a demo. In reality, no demos were created specifically for this album. It was recorded after Ruffin's take was completed, following a suggestion from Blue Weaver, who believed the song suited Robin's voice perfectly. Robin delivers a stunning vocal performance, elevating the song's conclusion into an impressive falsetto range. His rendition has been available on his official YouTube channel since the summer of 2020.

'Forever' (Barry Gibb, Robin Gibb, Maurice Gibb)
Recorded at Criteria Recording Studios, Miami, in mid 1978 and January 1980
The mid-tempo 'Forever' was one of the first songs laid down for the album. Its composition is credited to Barry, Robin and Maurice as its origin lies in the sessions for *Spirits Having Flown*, although in its original form it was titled 'Nobody'. With lyrical adjustments by Robin, the song later evolved into 'Forever Forever', a title most likely designed to prevent

copyright confusion with another song titled 'Forever' that the brothers had written in 1966. On the album, however, it does appear as 'Forever'.

Blue Weaver remembers 'that was a Bee Gees backing track and we used it'. Robin rewrote the lyrics. It's a strong track instrumentally, with nice lead guitar licks and lush string arrangements in the introduction and instrumental break, and vocally with Ruffin digging deep into his range for the first line of the chorus and pushing the upper limits for the finale. It would have made a solid second single.

'Night Of Love' (Robin Gibb, Blue Weaver)
Recorded at Kingdom Sound Studios, Syosett, Long Island, NY, in November 1979

'Night Of Love' was chosen as the album's second single, released in June 1980 in the UK with 'Songbird' on the B-side. It appeared in July in the US.

It's quite similar in style to 'Hold On (To My Love)' but lacks the memorable melody of its predecessor. Perhaps it's the chorus; Ruffin should have been able to own it with a powerful vocal, but he ends up lost in the mix behind the backing vocalists. There are sections on the bridge in which he ventures into falsetto range and a tight-throated high register highly reminiscent of Robin's singing style. It failed to make a dent on any chart.

'Searchin'' (Robin Gibb, Blue Weaver)
Recorded at Kingdom Sound Studios, Syosett, Long Island, NY, in November 1979

The short ballad 'Searchin'' features a pretty piano melody typical of Blue Weaver's writing style, but it's overpowered by loud synthesised strings that at times sound unpleasantly discordant alongside the vocals and other instruments. The song was released as the B-side to 'Night Of Love' in all markets.

'Changin' Me' (Robin Gibb, Blue Weaver)
Recorded at Criteria Recording Studios, Miami, in January 1980

The most overtly 'disco' track on the album, 'Changin' Me' has composer credits for Robin and Blue on the album itself, but Broadcast Music Incorporated (BMI), a performance rights organisation in the US, also lists Jimmie Lee Ruffin [*sic*] as a co-writer.

The track sounds rather dated even for 1980 and has a feel akin to a 1970s television show theme with its scratchy guitars and sweeping strings.

'Where Do I Go' (Barry Gibb, Robin Gibb, Maurice Gibb, Andy Gibb)
Recorded at Criteria Recording Studios, Miami, in January 1980
'Where Do I Go' is noteworthy as a composition being credited not only to Barry, Robin and Maurice, but also Andy Gibb.

The idea of all four brothers recording together had been brought up in 1978; 'Where Do I Go' seems to have been originally conceived with that intent. After the four-piece Gibb project didn't materialise, the track was resurrected here as a duet with Marcy Levy – who was at that time best known as a backup singer for Eric Clapton and the co-writer of his 1978 hit single, 'Lay Down Sally'.

The original country-flavoured demo features Barry singing alone and strumming an acoustic guitar. The finished recording adds some nice lead guitar licks and even some slide guitar. Making the song into a duet was a nice idea, although the contrast between Ruffin's deep, rich voice and Levy's more high-pitched nasal tone makes the interplay of their vocals less interesting.

'Two People' (Robin Gibb, Blue Weaver)
Recorded at Kingdom Sound Studios, Syosett, Long Island, NY, in November 1979
'Two People' is another reflective ballad, albeit less interesting than the others on the album. At points, it's apparent the song's melody and key might be just slightly outside Ruffin's vocal range, and a few of the higher notes he hits sound rather strained.

'Jealousy' (Robin Gibb, Blue Weaver)
Recorded at Criteria Recording Studios, Miami, in January 1980
The hard-edged rouser, 'Jealousy', is a good commercial pop song that might have been a better choice for a single than 'Night Of Love'. Finally, we can hear Ruffin's tenor soar to full capacity on the choruses.

'Songbird' (Barry Gibb, Robin Gibb, Maurice Gibb, Blue Weaver)
Recorded at Criteria Recording Studios, Miami, in January 1980
'Songbird' is historically significant among The Bee Gees' compositions as the first writing collaboration the three Gibb brothers collectively undertook outside the family. Previously, Barry had co-written with Johnny Devlin, Robin with Vic Lewis, and Maurice with Nat Kipner and

Billy Lawrie, but this song, which was written in early 1975 and appeared on the *Main Course* album, became Blue Weaver's first songwriting credit as a member of The Bee Gees' band.

This is Ruffin's most soulful vocal performance on the album, but it falls considerably short of the benchmark set by The Bee Gees' beautiful original version.

All told, *Sunrise* is a solid effort, although a couple of low points drag it down, and it's not a comfortable experience to listen to in one sitting. The production feels somewhat stale, despite Robin and Blue's respective talents and instincts. Ruffin's classic Motown vocal prowess should have given the writing and production team a lot to work with, but on many songs, it sounds like he's struggling to fit his voice into the track as opposed to it serving as a good vehicle for his capabilities.

Sunrise has never been released on CD, nor has it been reissued in any format. It also remains unavailable on any current streaming platform.

The BMI Awards, held at the Plaza Hotel in New York City on 10 June, proved fruitful for The Bee Gees, who scooped up three awards. The most performed BMI song of 1979 was 'Too Much Heaven', which received further accolades for its proceeds helping underprivileged children through UNICEF. Robin was there to represent The Bee Gees and was presented with special glass plaques by the children of two BMI executives: Claudia Granville, aged six, daughter of Elizabeth Granville, assistant vice president of publisher relations; and Ernest Clayton, also aged six, son of Linda Booker of the writer relations section. James Grant, under-secretary of the United Nations and executive director of UNICEF, noted that $3.5 million had been donated to UNICEF so far as a result of the total income derived from 'Too Much Heaven'.

With Maurice by her side, Yvonne Gibb gave birth to a second child – a daughter, Samantha Amanda – on 2 July in Miami.

The Bee Gees' massive appeal, coupled with their newfound post-1970s disparagement, left them wide open for parody. British comedian Kenny Everett, renowned for his outlandish humour and musical parodies, had delivered a classic spoof of the Gibbs with his 'Do It Yourself Bee Gees Kit' sketch on *The Kenny Everett Video Show* on 19 March 1979. The segment hilariously deconstructed the formula for becoming a Bee Gee, complete with a series of transformation pills. Everett began with Bottle 'A', containing the 'world-famous Bee Gee teeth' pill, followed by Bottle 'B', which provided the 'shirt open to the navel exposing hairy chest and revealing large golden medallion' pill. Bottle 'C' contained the 'world famous Bee Gee hair' pill. Initially, only one Bee Gee, modelled after Barry, appeared, but Bottle 'D' miraculously split him into three, completing the trio with Robin and Maurice. The final touch was Bottle 'E', containing the most important part of a Bee Gee: the world-famous vibrato. Once the transformation was complete, the newly cloned Bee Gees launched into the opening of the song 'Children Of The World'. Everett's affectionate lampooning remains a fan favourite; Maurice was later quoted in an interview saying his send-up was 'the best'.

Another memorable Bee Gees caricature came from comedians Angus Deayton, Michael Fenton Stevens, and Philip Pope of the UK radio series *Radio Active*. In 1980, they formed The Hee Bee Gee Bees, a fictitious singing group that created original music that poked fun at not only the Gibbs but many other big names in the industry. Their album, *439 Golden Greats – Never Mind The Originals Here's The Hee Bee Gee Bees*, included the band's irreverent send-ups of Michael Jackson (as Jack Michaelson), The Beatles (as The Beagles), David Bowie (as David Bowwwow), Kenny Rogers (as Kenny Rogered), Status Quo (as Status Quid), The Police (as The PeeCees), Neil Young (as Neil Dung), Bob Dylan (as Bob Vylan), The Band (as The Bland), Frank Sinatra (as Frank Sumatra), Dean Martin (as Dean Martian), Leonard Cohen (as Leonard Crowing) and George Harrison (as George Harassing). Deayton, Stevens, and Pope each assumed a persona corresponding to the three Gibb brothers: Garry Cribb, Norris Cribb, and Dobbin Cribb, respectively.

Signed to Original Records, The Hee Bee Gee Bees released their first single, 'Meaningless Songs (In Very High Voices)' (clearly poking fun at often-parenthetical Gibb song titles), in the summer of 1980. Sounding an awful lot like 'Too Much Heaven', the group have to be commended for their rather solid falsetto mimicry. A picture sleeve for the single featured the Brothers Cribb copying the pose and wardrobe from The Bee Gees' *Children Of The World* cover art – with the humorous addition of them each holding a hair dryer. The back of the sleeve, with the title of the single's B-side, 'Posing In The Moonlight', shows the Cribbs in a pastiche of the now infamous folded-arms-in-white-suits photograph of The Bee Gees on the *Saturday Night Fever* soundtrack album. 'Meaningless Songs ... ' would eventually reach number 79 on the Australian singles charts in the spring of 1981.

The UK trade publication *Music Week* featured two half-page adverts for the single in its 16 and 30 August issues, the first of which boasted an offer of a 'special colour bag on first 10,000,000 only!' The second featured reviews from *Sounds* and *Record Mirror*, with the former saying the single 'captured The Bee Gees' sound so convincingly that I doubt you'd realise what was going on if it was on in the background while you were painting the missus or ironing the dog, or whatever'. The latter recognised the comedians' 'truly inspired and grotesquely vicious dissection of the techniques and devices of the Brothers Gibb'.

The 1980 Edinburgh Fringe Festival, which took place between 17 August and 8 September, featured The Hee Bee Gee Bees as part of *Radio Active*'s showcase – one of over 400 acts to appear. No doubt it was one of the reasons 'Meaningless Songs … ' was propelled to number 21 on the UK Independent Singles Chart on the week of 20 September, spending six weeks in total on the tally.

Meanwhile, the actual Gibbs were keeping busy with other projects. Robin surfaced next with a contribution to the *Times Square* motion picture soundtrack. *Times Square*, another Robert Stigwood production, was a dramatic vehicle starring American actors Trini Alvarado and Robin Johnson, along with British actor Tim Curry. Canadian director Allan Moyle was at the helm, who eventually became better known for his work on the films *Pump Up The Volume* and *Empire Records* in the 1990s. Alvarado and Johnson play teenagers Pamela Pearl and Nicky Marotta from disparate backgrounds who meet and befriend one another while in treatment at a neurological hospital. After they run away and escape to the streets of New York City, the film follows their trials and tribulations. Curry, playing radio DJ Johnny LaGuardia, becomes involved as the pair are reported missing, and eventually helps them discover their musical talents and form a punk duo, The Sleez Sisters.

The film continued Stigwood's apparent love affair with gritty portrayals of life in New York, which recurred in his subsequent productions, *The Fan* and *Staying Alive*. If *Times Square* feels like it follows a similar blueprint as *Saturday Night Fever*, it's no accident. Robin Johnson's casting was reportedly part of a longer-term vision to market her as the female counterpart to John Travolta, and she was signed to a three-year exclusive film deal with RSO. With Stigwood's production company and record label both on a gradual downward slide, none of those projects were made before RSO folded in 1983.

Like *Saturday Night Fever*, the film's plot was driven by a double-disc soundtrack of industry heavyweights, consisting mostly of already released punk and new wave songs by acts like Talking Heads, Joe Jackson, Suzi Quatro, Lou Reed, and Joey Ramone.

'Help Me' (Robin Gibb, Blue Weaver)

Recorded at Criteria Recording Studios, Miami, in mid-1980
Chart position: US: 50

Robin's contribution to the soundtrack, which bucked the harder-edged tone of the remainder of the set, is the mid-tempo pop song 'Help Me', a duet with Marcy Levy that had materialised after she had participated on Jimmy Ruffin's *Sunrise* as a guest vocalist earlier in the year.

The single was Levy's first as a headlining artist. She had been signed to RSO since the mid-1970s, and at the time had reportedly been in the process of recording her debut solo album with then-fledgling producer David Foster, but the project was shelved. Instead, she served as Eric Clapton's primary backing vocalist and occasional co-writer between 1974 and 1979.

Melodically, 'Help Me' is a good showcase for both vocalists, but it sticks out like a sore thumb among its contemporaries on the soundtrack album. In the film, the song plays over the closing credits.

The Cars' song 'Dangerous Type' – in the film but not on the soundtrack – would have been a more appropriate choice for a lead single, but given the solid track record Stigwood had amassed by featuring Gibb songs in his films, he seemed compelled to put RSO-signed Robin out in front.

'Help Me' peaked at a disappointing number 50 on the *Billboard* Hot 100. On the flip side was an instrumental version of the track. Two different versions of the B-side exist; US issues of the single featured Gary Brown playing saxophone – he had previously contributed to *Spirits Having Flown* and played on the instrumental take that backed Frankie Valli's 'Grease' single.

RSO seemed to have a decent amount of confidence in the film and album, taking out a full-page ad in the 13 September issue of *Billboard* and committing $1.5 million to promote the project via radio adverts. *Times Square* didn't come close to matching the box office mojo of *Fever* or *Grease*, only taking $1.4 million in ticket sales against its $5 million production budget. Critical praise for the film was also sparse, but some detractors saw the film as a good idea in concept that became a missed opportunity in execution.

Despite its star power, the soundtrack album only managed to reach number 37 in the US and fizzled out at number 56 in Australia. It did not chart in other markets.

With Andy's future prospects as a recording artist dimming quickly, RSO seemed eager to have him fulfil his final contractual obligation to the label in order to capitalise on whatever popular momentum remained among his fans. Another motivation was most certainly to recoup the million-dollar loan Robert Stigwood had allegedly fronted Andy to cover his growing tax obligations, which he'd accrued while overspending on lavish purchases, drugs, and alcohol. It was a shocking scenario to imagine, given the magnitude of Andy's recent success.

Knowing Andy was likely in no position to tackle another full album project, RSO made the decision to repackage all of his singles, some of which were only seven months old at the time, along with the title track to *After Dark* that Andy seemed to favour, plus three new recordings. *Andy Gibb's Greatest Hits* was released in September.

If RSO had wished to provide a thoughtful review of Andy's career to date, they might have included the version of 'Words And Music' used on the Australian single issued by ATA Records before he arrived in the United States, or a couple of his own good compositions like 'Flowing Rivers' or 'I Go For You'.

What materialised instead was 'Time Is Time', a new song and lead single co-penned by Andy and Barry, which Andy claimed was his creation with only a minor change suggested by his older brother. The song veers more into rock territory than pop, with an oddly compressed guitar solo that sounds almost like a synthesiser, plus a good drum line furnished by accomplished session player Steve Gadd. Barry is audible in a layered set of backing vocals that seems to mimic a gospel choir, and it's done rather effectively.

'Time Is Time' was puzzlingly pushed out almost two months after the release of the *Greatest Hits* album, eventually reaching number 15 on the *Billboard* Hot 100 the week of 24 January 1981. While respectable, it broke Andy's *Billboard* top ten singles streak that had begun more than four years earlier when 'I Just Want To Be Your Everything' jumped to a new number seven peak on the week of 7 July 1977 on its way to the pole position.

A full-page advert appeared in *Billboard*'s 15 November issue to promote the single and album together, and Andy made appearances on

Solid Gold and *The Mike Douglas Show* in the US to perform the song.

Internationally, 'Time Is Time' only surfaced on the Austrian and German pop singles charts, summiting at number 17 and 44, respectively.

In a surprising change of approach by RSO, the set's second single, 'Me (Without You)', is a ballad written by Andy only. He delivers a strong, impassioned vocal against a backdrop of a pipe organ-like electric piano and dramatic strings. It was probably the kind of exposure Andy had hoped for all along for his individual writing, although it was a little late at this point. Released in February 1981, it peaked at number 40 on the *Billboard* Hot 100 the week of 11 April. It was his very last appearance in the top half of any chart.

Andy performed the song on 2 February on *The John Davidson Show*. During an interview segment with the host, Andy was surprised by an appearance by *Dallas* actress and future significant other, Victoria Principal, to whom he'd written a fan letter. It was reportedly the first time the two had met face-to-face.

The third new track recorded for *Andy Gibb's Greatest Hits* was a cover of 'Will You Love Me Tomorrow', the classic Gerry Goffin-Carole King composition originally released by The Shirelles in 1960. Singer P.P. Arnold (appearing as Pat Arnold in the album credits) was recruited to sing the song as a duet with Andy.

Arnold was a known quantity to the Gibbs, having previously worked with Barry in the late 1960s. In 1978, Arnold was unexpectedly contacted by Dick Ashby, The Bee Gees' personal manager. Although she had long been out of Hollywood circles, Ashby reached out with an invitation to meet Barry after the Hollywood premiere of *Sgt. Pepper's Lonely Hearts Club Band*. After the event, Arnold was whisked to the Beverly Hills Hotel for a reunion with Barry and Linda Gibb, whom she hadn't seen since 1970. 'They seemed genuinely pleased to see me after all those years', she recalled. Over the course of their conversation, Barry reportedly appeared ready to rekindle their professional relationship. 'Barry told me that if I ever came to Miami, we could finish the recordings we'd started all those years ago. He didn't say when, but it didn't matter. What he gave me that night was hope, and hope was in short supply in my life'.

Arnold eventually did come to Miami, and Dick Ashby arranged for another meeting with Barry shortly after she arrived. While a full album project she had discussed with him wasn't on the cards due to his busy schedule, he offered an alternative:

He asked me if I would like to do a duet with Andy on the Carole King classic, 'Will You Love Me Tomorrow'. I love this song, and I felt it would be an honour to sing with him. The last time I'd seen him, he'd been maybe 12 years old. This was a golden opportunity for me, and it wasn't hard to say yes.

'Will You Love Me Tomorrow' was a long-standing favourite of the Gibbs; The Bee Gees would eventually record a version themselves for a Carole King tribute project, *Tapestry Revisited*, in 1995. The Arnold-Gibb take for this project was a jazzier, R&B interpretation, rife with Rhodes piano and a saxophone solo. While it was an inoffensive addition to the package of songs on the album, there were more than enough good Andy-only recordings that could have taken its place to highlight his own artistry.

Andy Gibb's Greatest Hits would eventually peak at number 46 on the *Billboard* Top LPs and Tape chart the week of 31 January 1981, spending a total of 12 weeks on the survey.

Guilty – Barbra Streisand (1980)

Personnel:

Barbra Streisand: vocals

Barry Gibb: vocals ('Guilty', 'What Kind Of Fool'), backing vocals, acoustic guitar

Richard Tee: electric piano, elephant grand piano, clavinet

George Bitzer: electric piano, elephant grand piano, synthesiser

Albhy Galuten: synthesiser

George Terry: guitar, gut string guitar, slide guitar

Cornell Dupree: guitar

Pete Carr: guitar, acoustic guitar

Lee Ritenour: guitar

Harold Cowart: bass

David Hungate: bass

Steve Gadd: drums

Dennis Bryon: drums

'Bernard Lupe': drums

Joe Lala: percussion

Jerry Peel: French horn

Peter Graves: trombone, half-speed bass trombone

Russ Freeland: trombone

Mike Katz: trombone

Ken Faulk: trumpet
Brett Murphey: trumpet
Bud Burridge: trumpet
Neil Bonsanti: tenor saxophone
Dan Bonsanti: tenor saxophone
Whit Sidener: baritone saxophone
Backing vocals: Denise Maynelli, Myrna Mathews, Marti McCall
String arrangements: Albhy Galuten, Barry Gibb
Horn arrangements: Albhy Galuten, Barry Gibb, Peter Graves
Engineers: Karl Richardson, Don Gehman, Sam Taylor, Dennis Hetzendorfer, Michael Guerra, Dale Peterson, Patrick Von Weigandt, Carl Beatty, Robert Shames
Producers: Barry Gibb, Albhy Galuten, Karl Richardson
Recorded at Middle Ear, Miami Beach, in February 1980; Criteria Recording Studios, Miami, in February 1980; Sound Labs Studio, Hollywood, in March 1980; Media Sound, New York, in June 1980
Release dates: UK: 27 October 1980, US: 23 September 1980
Chart positions: Australia: 1, Austria: 1, Finland: 1, France: 1, Italy: 1, Netherlands: 1, New Zealand: 1, Norway: 1, Spain: 1, Sweden: 1, UK: 1, US: 1, Canada: 3, West Germany: 4, Japan: 9
Silver certification: Portugal
Gold certification: Sweden
Platinum certification: Australia (6×), Belgium (2×), Canada (5×), Finland, France (2×), Hong Kong, Italy, Netherlands, New Zealand, UK, US (5×), West Germany

The full year of studio work that Barry, Albhy Galuten, and Karl Richardson had invested in the Barbra Streisand album was finally ready for public consumption. *Guilty* arrived on 23 September.

Streisand had been making music for as long as the Gibbs; her first appearance on a record was on the Broadway cast recording of the musical *I Can Get It For You Wholesale* on Columbia Records in April 1962 at the age of 19. Her proper debut, *The Barbra Streisand Album*, followed in February 1963, immediately landing her in the top ten of the *Billboard* Top LPs chart. Her earlier studio efforts were a multifarious blend of standards, show tunes, and a handful of original songs with classic undertones, but she had more recently become a major force in contemporary pop. *Guilty*'s predecessor, 1979's *Wet*, had produced the rhythmic smash 'No More Tears (Enough Is Enough)', a duet with Donna Summer that reached number one on the *Billboard* Hot 100.

In her 2023 autobiography, *My Name Is Barbra*, Streisand recalled *Gulity*'s origin story:

In 1979, there was one project constantly on my mind ... *Yentl* ... and this was the year when I promised myself that I was going to do whatever it took to get it made. So, when [CBS Records head of A&R] Charles [Koppelman] started talking about yet another album even before *Wet* was finished, my reaction was, 'I don't have time'. I didn't want to look for songs. I didn't even want to hear them. But Charles, who had his eye on the market, wanted to take advantage of discomania while it lasted. It had worked for [previous singles] 'The Main Event/Fight' and then 'No More Tears (Enough Is Enough)', so he thought, 'Why not keep the party going and try for a third?'

I don't know whose idea it was to put me together with The Bee Gees – Charles and [Streisand's then-producing partner and significant other] Jon [Peters] had become friends, and both claimed credit. But it couldn't have been too hard a sell because I loved their music for *Saturday Night Fever*. So, I said yes when Charles invited Jon, me and the kids to a Bee Gees concert at Dodger Stadium. We sat in the midst of 56,000 screaming fans, the show was very exciting, and afterward, Charles made his pitch. He told me that Barry Gibb, one of the three brothers who made up the group, had written and produced five of the current top ten *Billboard* singles – an unprecedented feat – and was looking to branch out and produce albums for other artists.

Without a doubt, *Guilty* was the highest profile project Barry and the production team had worked on outside of The Bee Gees, and expectations were high. For all Barry's musical expertise and success, the prospect of producing someone who was essentially an American institution was slightly nerve-wracking. He told *Billboard* in early 1981:

I wasn't going to do the album at one point. Barbra is rumoured to be a tough lady. I'd heard about the time 'Evergreen' was written and how Paul Williams was sent backwards and forwards to write lyrics – and I was afraid that was going to happen to me, but the wonderful thing is it never did. Apart from the fact that Barbra's a total professional, she's a very nice lady. You can't go wrong with an artist like that. I'd have to say at least 80% of the success of the record belongs to her.

In *My Name Is Barbra*, Streisand recalls the first conversation she had with Barry about the project:

> He was very sweet. He told me he had been a big fan ever since he heard 'People' in Australia, where he was living when it came out. I told him that I was a big fan of his music, and then asked if he would be interested in making an album with me. There was silence on the line for a moment. And then Barry said, 'I'm bowled over. Could you give me 24 hours to get up off the floor before I give you an answer?'
>
> It wasn't until years later that I found out he had actually been nervous and intimidated about taking the job. So, he called Neil Diamond and asked what I was like to work with. 'Just relax', Neil said. 'She's fantastic to work with. Go for it'. And Barry's wife told him she'd divorce him if he turned me down.

The album's cover art took the excitement of a Barbra-Barry collaboration a step further. Using a similar motif as her 1977 album *Superman*, a playful photo of Streisand appeared on a stark background under a simple banner of her last name and the album's title – with one minor modification: she was in a flirtatious embrace with her producer. It was a bold choice given that Barry is not actually credited on the cover and his image was associated with a musical act that was actively being rejected by the media. But poking at that might have been at least part of the goal.

Streisand commented on the design choices in *My Name Is Barbra*:

> The art director from Columbia had an idea ... he wanted to photograph me with an angel on one shoulder and a devil on the other. That made no sense to me. Instead, I asked him to hire Mario Casilli, the photographer who had done such a good job on my *Playboy* cover and the *Wet* album. Mario came over to the recording studio where Barry and I were working to do some publicity stills before we had a concept for the cover. I happened to be wearing a white blouse and white pants that day, and when I looked at the shots, I said, 'That's it. We should both be wearing white, and let's shoot it against a simple white backdrop'. I thought Barry was very handsome,

and if we were both in white, against white, that would distil the photo to its simplest form. It would also create a monochromatic frame, the kind I always like.

An assistant ran out for a huge roll of white paper, another went to Barry's hotel to pick up his white shirt and pants, and we shot the cover then and there, with no drama and no fuss. I'm looking at it again ... all that white had such purity and yet the album was called *Guilty*. That's an interesting dichotomy, but I wasn't thinking of that then.

Despite all the positive vibes in front of the camera, the cover art stoked a controversy that delayed the album's release. Barry allegedly requested additional payment from CBS for the use of his image. Robert Stigwood and RSO also lodged a complaint centred on Barry's royalties arising from his participation in the album. Since Barry had been approached by Streisand and her representatives at The Entertainment Co. to write for, produce, and perform *Guilty*, he reportedly considered himself an independent solo artist, likely freezing RSO and the other Bee Gees from any royalties. CBS president Walter Yetnikoff managed to negotiate the issue out of court. RSO apparently received no compensation, but it's unknown if Barry did. As a point of interest, Barry was the only member of The Bee Gees at the time who was not signed to an individually exclusive recording contract with RSO.

As with *Spirits Having Flown*, the production team had a vision for *Guilty*. 'I knew what she'd done, but what we had in mind was bringing her more into the mainstream', Barry told *Billboard*. 'She certainly has the voice. She's easily the finest female vocalist in the world'.

Albhy Galuten said that Barry writing songs for Streisand's voice and point of view needed a paradigm shift from what had been written for The Bee Gees. 'It's interesting how the lyrics are Barbra-relevant rather than Bee Gees-relevant', he told *Albumism* in 2020. "I've got nothing to be guilty of' is sort of the whole Jewish guilt thing. It's the same thing with 'I am a woman in love'. It's uncompromising. It's not 'I love you, please come back to me', it's 'I love you and I'm strong about it'. It's Barbra's image and the things that were relevant to her, and Barry was writing about them with her in mind'.

Barry and Robin wrote an initial batch of songs following the completion of The Bee Gees' *Spirits Having Flown* tour: 'Woman In Love', 'Run Wild', 'Promises' and 'Life Story', which were committed to demos with the production team's support in October 1979. 'We went into Studio A and we [put them down]', Albhy Galuten explained to *Albumism* in 2020. 'I think we had maybe the LinnDrum machine, and I played piano and Barry played acoustic [guitar] on … some of the songs. On some, he didn't play because they were musically different than what he'd usually play on a guitar'. Barry's demos were sung almost completely in falsetto to precisely match the key and tone of Streisand's voice.

A second set of songs, likely written after Robin had departed Miami to begin work on the Jimmy Ruffin album, was completed by Barry and Albhy Galuten: 'What Kind Of Fool', 'Never Give Up', and 'Make It Like A Memory'. They were perhaps more rhythmically and melodically adventurous than the Barry and Robin compositions, but the sum of all parts was a bold and beautiful set of tracks for a distinctive voice.

Streisand soon visited Miami to hear what the team had been working on. She recounts in *My Name Is Barbra:*

I sat in the studio and listened to demo tapes Barry had made of the new songs, with him singing my part in his unique falsetto. I instantly responded to the melodies and the feel of the songs, but I was less certain about the lyrics. They were kind of abstract, with lots of intriguing, impressionistic images that were open to interpretation (in other words, I didn't know what they meant). It was clear that my usual method of analysing lyrics just as I would analyse a script, looking for subtext and nuances of meaning, was not going to work here. I was used to approaching each word literally, whereas Barry was writing figuratively. And his writing was nonlinear. There was no conventional narrative with a beginning, middle and end, so there wasn't the kind of storyline I was used to.

But I listened again and talked to Barry and made a decision. I decided to trust him, to just put myself in his hands and go with the flow. Barry recorded all the tracks in Miami and then came out to Los Angeles to record my vocals. The whole process was incredibly streamlined. Barry just asked me to sing each song ten times, and then he would take care of the rest. Really? It seemed so simple.

Capturing Streisand's performances was one of the easier parts of making *Guilty,* taking just two weeks in total. But the brevity of that process didn't diminish the production team's awe of her vocal singularity. 'When she opened her mouth,' Albhy Galuten remembers with astonishment, 'and we were on the other side of the glass, we were, like, 'what ... the ... *fuck*?!'"

With the extended period the three producers had spent engineering every note of *Spirits Having Flown* as the precedent, the bar for technical precision was set high. Barry, Albhy, and Karl were in the studio non-stop for three additional months working on the album's post-production, syncing the pitch and timing of Streisand's vocal takes to the instrumentals. Karl Richardson told *Albumism* in 2020:

It took us two weeks just to combine the vocal – I spent days in the studio with an oscilloscope and looking at her and the rhythm of the song and moving things in milliseconds because, again, these are rhythmic songs, [*sings, emphasising the beats*] 'and we got nothing to be *guil*-ty of…' and all that stuff. You've got to have that nailed. She wasn't exactly there all the time.

Albhy Galuten explained:

Barry's feeling and his vision are that the meter is pretty much on time. There's a beat and it goes *right there*. And the same thing with the pitch. You don't really scoop into pitches; you're supposed to hit the pitch and nail it. So, in order to adjust Barbra's vocal so that it met with Barry's sensibility, we were moving the time. And this was before the days of sampling and being able to move vocals around with these little tiny offsets and fractions and punch-ins and delays. And doing the same thing with harmonisers to do three or four passes at the beginning of a vocal word, so it would hit it right on and not slide up the way Barbra liked to do.

Karl Richardson elaborated:

I had two machines locking up and punching a cross-fading machine into the recording machine was a several-week process to do for the entire album. I had a book of lyric sheets … I think I used a loose-leaf binder that was about six inches thick by the time we got done with the album with all my notes. Every little nuance with ad-libs or breaths because you have to cross them before breaths, and things like that. From a technological perspective, when you listen to *Guilty*, you don't realise that behind the scenes, a lot of editing was going on.

There was much public and industry anticipation for the well-publicised Streisand-Gibb collaboration, so no detail was too small to ensure the album showcased everyone's best work. Karl: 'We wouldn't release a record unless we knew it was our best foot forward. We just couldn't let it out of the studio unless we'd done everything we knew was humanly possible, because once you release a record, you've released a record. You can't go back in the studio when it's in the shrink wrap'.

'The definition of 'best', though, is an interesting concept', Albhy interjects. 'Lots of people have an opinion about what they think is best. What happened during this phase of my and Karl's relationship with Barry was that there was a synchrony, and there was an understanding of the goal of everything; what this project is and was, and how it would be executed. In this case, 'best' was when everything we knew intuitively was accomplished the way it was supposed to be. There was this clear vision about the way Barbra's vocal would sound and how it would work'.

'Guilty' (Barry Gibb, Robin Gibb, Maurice Gibb)

Recorded at Middle Ear, Miami Beach, in February 1980; Criteria Recording Studios, Miami, in February 1980; Sound Labs Studio, Hollywood, in March 1980; Media Sound, New York, in June 1980
Chart positions: US: 3, Norway: 4, Belgium: 9, Spain: 11, New Zealand: 12, Canada: 13, Netherlands: 15, West Germany: 15, Ireland: 21, UK: 34, Australia: 37
Silver certification: UK

The album's opener and second single, 'Guilty', was one of two duets Barbra would record with Barry. Streisand says in *My Name Is Barbra*:

When we were finished with the album, it dawned on me that we were missing a certain kind of song – something very up-tempo, maybe a bossa nova. Barry understood exactly what I meant, and he went off and came back with 'Guilty', the only cut on the album written by all three Bee Gees. I really loved that one and said, 'I think it should be the first song on the record and the title of the album. 'Guilty' is such a powerful word. It has all sorts of psychological implications, and people will respond to it". Besides, I knew a lot about guilt … I am Jewish!

Barry had discovered the agility that capable session players could offer while producing projects for Andy, Samantha Sang, Teri DeSario, and

Frankie Valli, and he became enamoured with the idea of hiring the right people at the right time to give him exactly the sound he was looking for. Drummer Steve Gadd, guitarists Pete Carr and Cornell Dupree, bassist David Hungate, and pianist Richard Tee were among the experienced hands hired for *Guilty*.

Albhy Galuten, talking to *Albumism* in 2020, recalled a particularly memorable moment while recording the song's instrumental tracks:

Steve Gadd is one of the finest drummers that ever lived, and right now he's straight and he's still fantastic. But, at the time, he was pretty loaded. When we cut the track, his timing was great, but he was so loaded he could barely stand up. And I realised after the first run-through what it should be. We used to do these chord charts, and they were just, you know, bar lines with chord names on top of them.

Steve came into the control room; Steve and [Richard] Tee and whoever else. And while we played back the first take, I was scribbling and hen-scratching the bass drum patterns on this chord chart while Barry was singing him drum turns that he wanted. And when the playback was done, Steve went back out and sat at the drums, and we played back the tape – and it was the take. He had remembered every bass drum pattern I'd written, and every drum turn Barry had sung to him, and just nailed it. He and Tee were so incredible.

Perfecting the now storied Barbra-Barry duet also required some creativity in meshing their voices. Albhy remembers:

When we recorded 'Guilty', we'd already cut the track. Originally, Barry was not going to do any duets. They talked him into it. So, for his verses, we had to change the key and had worked out modulations to go from one key to another, from verse to chorus, and then overdub the instruments, fit them in, and fly that stuff around to literally create the verses for Barry that were in another key. Wherever Barry sang verses, those were never recorded in that key; they were originally recorded in different keys in different parts with everything but the drums.

'Guilty' made its debut on the *Billboard* Hot 100 chart at number 68 the week of 1 November. It would eventually peak at number three the week of 10 January 1981, spending a total of 22 weeks on the chart. In the UK, the reception was surprisingly lukewarm given the strong performance of the album and its first single. It entered the singles chart at number 70 the week of 30 November, climbing slowly to its highest position of 34 the week of 17 January 1981. It achieved top 20 status in Canada, Belgium, the Netherlands, New Zealand, Norway, Spain, and West Germany. In Mexico, it was issued as a red vinyl 12" single.

Barry and Barbra performed the song live for the very first time for Streisand's *One Voice* concert broadcast and album on 6 September 1986. The Bee Gees would eventually include a shortened version of 'Guilty' in the medley section of their concert sets beginning in the late 1990s. It was captured for the first time on their 1997 live album, *One Night Only*. Barry additionally sang the song as a duet with Olivia Newton-John during the Sound Relief charity concert in Sydney, Australia, on 14 March 2009, which benefited locals affected by the Victorian bushfires that had scorched the state in February.

'Guilty' was covered by Australian pop vocal group Human Nature with the variant title 'Guilty (One In A Million)', releasing it as a single from their fourth studio album *Walk The Tightrope* in August 2004. It peaked at number 33 on the country's singles chart.

More recently, the track played during the opening sequence of the 2021 American comedy film *Barb And Star Go To Vista Del Mar,* starring Kristen Wiig, Annie Mumolo, Jamie Dornan, and Damon Wayans, Jr.

'Woman In Love' (Barry Gibb, Robin Gibb)

Recorded at Middle Ear, Miami Beach, in February 1980; Criteria Recording Studios, Miami, in February 1980; Sound Labs Studio, Hollywood, in March 1980; Media Sound, New York, in June 1980

Chart positions: Australia: 1, Austria: 1, Belgium: 1, Canada: 1, Finland: 1, France: 1, Iceland: 1, Ireland: 1, Italy: 1, Netherlands: 1, Norway: 1, South Africa: 1, Spain: 1, Sweden: 1, Switzerland: 1, UK: 1, US: 1, West Germany: 1, Zimbabwe: 1, Argentina: 2, New Zealand: 2, Japan: 42

Gold certification: Australia, Italy, UK, West Germany

Platinum certification: France, US

'Woman In Love' was the song selected as the album's first single. The ethereal, haunting ballad sounds a world away from anything on *Spirits Having Flown*, and the (likely intentional) absence of any detectable Gibb vocals gave Streisand's voice complete ownership of the song. The track does, however, have a visceral connection to *Saturday Night Fever* that was likely overlooked by most listeners. Albhy Galuten: "Woman In

Love' used the same drum loop we used for 'Stayin' Alive', just slowed way down and EQ'd radically. The loop is credited to 'Bernard Lupe' in the album's liner notes'.

While the brass at CBS had full confidence in 'Woman In Love', Streisand had some reservations, which she explained in *My Name Is Barbra*:

It was not the melody, which I liked – it even sounded vaguely Hebraic, with its progression of minor chords – it was the lyric. And I started questioning it, forgetting my resolve to just go with the flow. It begins like this: 'Life is a moment in space, when the dream is gone it's a lonelier place' ... Okay, so does that mean this couple broke up? It continues: 'I kiss the morning goodbye, but down inside you know we never know why ... ' Is she questioning why they're breaking up? 'The road is narrow and long, when eyes meet eyes, and the feeling is strong. I turn away from the wall, I stumble and fall, but I give you it all ... ' Is she talking about meeting eyes with a new person, or is she remembering her past with this person? And what kind of wall? Is it figurative or emotional?'

And then there's the chorus. 'I am a woman in love, and I'd do anything to get you into my world and hold you within…' Anything? This is the part I found really hard to sing. I suppose there are women who will 'do anything' to get a man, but I just couldn't relate to that. And please don't misunderstand. I don't mean to put down anyone. But this made the woman sound like some sort of clever manipulator. Maybe I'm a little bit envious of that kind of woman, but it sure as hell isn't me. I wouldn't even know how to manipulate a man. Usually, I just build up my nerve and ask bluntly for what I want – although my husband says I do have my ways.

Back to the lyric – I also questioned the next line: 'It's a right I defend, over and over again ...' What right? The right to use any means to get her man? And who is she defending against? Society? It's interesting ... if you're just listening to Barry's music and not paying particular attention to the words, the song sounds like an anthem of women's empowerment ... it just wasn't the kind of empowerment I was working toward. So, I was having a hard time identifying with this character. And then I realised I was being too literal again. Everyone at Columbia was thrilled with the song. So, I thought, 'Fuck it. Forget the words. Just do it'.

Streisand's decision to abandon her objections led to her scoring her most successful international single ever. Released on 16 August in the US (it was delayed until 2 September in the UK), 'Woman In Love' made an impressive entrance on the *Billboard* Hot 100, debuting at number 49. On 25 October, just seven weeks after its debut, it began a three-week run at the top of the charts. It was her fifth number one single on the survey overall. In the UK, it ascended the singles chart even more quickly after debuting at number 48 on 4 October. It took just three weeks to rise to the summit, spending ten weeks in the top 40, and 16 weeks in the top 100. It would be her sole UK chart topper. It also reached the pole position in Canada, Australia, New Zealand, Ireland, West Germany, Spain, South Africa, Norway, Sweden, Switzerland, and France. Two interesting variants of the single appeared in 12" formats: in Colombia, it was released on transparent yellow vinyl, while in Mexico, it was issued on transparent green vinyl.

By 1981, the single had sold over two and a half million copies globally.

The Bee Gees performed a brief and comedic excerpt of the song with Barry taking the lead vocal during their special episode of the *Live By Request* television series for the A&E network, airing in April 2001.

Despite its global acclaim, Streisand didn't perform the song on stage until 2013, when it was added to the European setlist of her *Barbra Live* tour. It was also in regular rotation on her 2016 outing, *Barbra: The Music, The Mem'ries, The Magic*.

'Woman In Love' has been covered by several artists, most notably released as a standalone single by Atomic Kitten's Liz McClarnon in 2006, which was produced by Robin. It peaked at number five in the UK and became a moderate hit in several European countries. McClarnon had opened for Robin during the tour to support his solo album *Magnet*. Israeli singer and Eurovision winner Dana International's version of the track was featured on the 1998 Bee Gees tribute album *Gotta Get A Message To You*, which was released to benefit Live Challenge '99 – a charitable effort to combat poverty and homelessness in the North West of England. American rapper and Wu-Tang Clan frontman RZA sampled it extensively on his 2008 song 'Put Your Guns Down'.

'Run Wild' (Barry Gibb, Robin Gibb)

Recorded at Middle Ear, Miami Beach, in February 1980; Criteria Recording Studios, Miami, in February 1980; Sound Labs Studio, Hollywood, in March 1980; Media Sound, New York, in June 1980

While *Guilty*'s singles are outstanding highlights, the entire album is strong from start to finish. 'Run Wild', which served as the B-side to 'Woman In Love' in all markets, is a lush, rich ballad, and its spacious soundscape provides Streisand plenty of room to ebb and flow vocally.

British actress and singer Kate Robbins recorded a version of 'Run Wild' for her 1981 eponymous debut album for RCA Records. She had achieved a number two UK hit with the set's first single, 'More Than In Love'. 'Run Wild' was released as the follow-up, but it failed to chart. It was produced by Barry Leng and Simon May, who had previously been at the helm of American singer Amii Stewart's 1979 international hit 'Knock On Wood'. May would eventually compose the theme song for the long-running British television series *EastEnders*.

'Promises' (Barry Gibb, Robin Gibb)

Recorded at Middle Ear, Miami Beach, in February 1980; Criteria Recording Studios, Miami, in February 1980; Sound Labs Studio, Hollywood, in March 1980; Media Sound, New York, in June 1980
Chart position: US: 48

'Promises' notches up the album's tempo and uses Barry's background vocals effectively to propel Streisand's lead and add rhythmic interest.

It was released as *Guilty*'s fourth and final single in May 1981, but missed the top 40 in the US, peaking at number 48 on the *Billboard* Hot 100 the week of 20 June. It did fare significantly better on the American and Canadian adult contemporary charts, where it landed at number eight and number five, respectively.

'The Love Inside' (Barry Gibb)

Recorded at Middle Ear, Miami Beach, in February 1980; Criteria Recording Studios, Miami, in February 1980; Sound Labs Studio, Hollywood, in March 1980; Media Sound, New York, in June 1980

The gorgeous 'The Love Inside' closes out *Guilty*'s first side. Streisand sings softly with her head voice for the majority of the song, achieving full throttle only for the last verse and refrain. It's an incredible showcase for her full range.

'The Love Inside' was released as a single in the UK only on 13 November 1981, but missed the singles chart. In the US, it was used as the B-side for 'What Kind Of Fool'.

The copyright registration for the song, filed in 1978, was credited to Barry, Robin, Maurice, and Andy Gibb as its writers, which has caused speculation that it may have initially been intended for the aforementioned four-piece Brothers Gibb project – or perhaps for Andy's forthcoming third studio album. Barry's demo recording is sung with an exceptionally light touch that seems to mimic what Andy would sound like in his breathy voice. *Guilty*'s liner notes, however, credit Barry as the sole writer.

'The Love Inside' was later covered by American folk singer Joan Baez on her *Live Europe '83* album.

'What Kind Of Fool' (Barry Gibb, Albhy Galuten)

Recorded at Middle Ear, Miami Beach, in February 1980; Criteria Recording Studios, Miami, in February 1980; Sound Labs Studio, Hollywood, in March 1980; Media Sound, New York, in June 1980

Chart position: US: 10

Guilty's third single, 'What Kind Of Fool', which hit radio and retail in the US and UK in January 1981, is certainly one of the most beautiful compositions in the Gibbs' songwriting catalogue.

Dennis Hetzendorfer, one of the album's assistant engineers working at Criteria Recording Studios, recalled to the authors in September 2025 the evening he heard Barry playing the song for the very first time for him and others in the production booth during the 1979 sessions for *Spirits Having Flown*:

We'd be working all day in Studio D, and around midnight or one o'clock in the morning, we would start winding down and sit around and talk. It was just Barry, Karl, Albhy, and me in the control room. I remember after one particularly productive day, I turned to Barry during a pause in the conversation and said, 'Hey, Barry – play me a song I haven't heard'. And he knew that meant 'play me something you've been working on'. And he'd go, 'okay'. There was always an acoustic guitar in the control room, and he picked it up and played 'What Kind Of Fool'. He had some of the lyrics – 'there was a time when we were down and out' – but not much else. He didn't have the bridge or anything like that, and he had only maybe 30% of the verse vocal and a bit of the chorus. Those were the kinds of things you experienced while working with them that you thought, 'Oh, wow – that's *really* pretty special'.

Albhy remembers it being one of the earliest compositions written for *Guilty,* and he and Barry finished the song together during an evening session at his house around a piano.

The track begins with a mellifluous Rhodes piano line, furnished by Richard Tee, and both Barry and Barbra vocalising with tender restraint; two voices that are completely disparate in tone, but complement one another superbly. That blend is especially impressive given their vocals were recorded separately.

The song escalates in intensity throughout, peaking during a dramatic bridge that alternates the time signature between 4/4 and 3/4. It's a heartbreaking, emotional piece that's beautifully produced and sung.

Once again, the production team employed 'Bernard Lupe' to drive the rhythm section, which is modified to sound like brushed snares. Drummer Steve Gadd provides the appropriate fills.

'What Kind Of Fool' entered the *Billboard* Hot 100 at number 72 the week of 31 January 1981, peaking at number ten the week of 21 March. It fared even better on *Billboard*'s Adult Contemporary chart, spending four weeks at number one beginning the week of 14 March. It also rose to and spent three weeks at number 17 on the Canadian *RPM* singles chart starting the week of 4 April. The single surprisingly didn't chart in the UK.

Barbra and Barry performed the song live (albeit in a different key) along with 'Guilty' on Streisand's *One Voice* concert special and album. The original track from *Guilty* appeared on numerous Streisand compilation albums, but on *Partners* (2014), Barbra revamped 'What Kind Of Fool' with R&B artist John Legend. It's a beautiful version but has a decidedly more classical feel than the original.

American actor and singer Darren Criss, who starred in the popular US musical dramedy series *Glee*, covered the song in 2011 for one of the show's soundtrack albums, *Glee: The Music Presents The Warblers*. The song appeared only on the album and did not surface in an episode of the show. The a cappella arrangement, interestingly, mirrors Barry's original demo rather than the released version.

'Life Story' (Barry Gibb, Robin Gibb)

Recorded at Middle Ear, Miami Beach, in February 1980; Criteria Recording Studios, Miami, in February 1980; Sound Labs Studio, Hollywood, in March 1980; Media Sound, New York, in June 1980

'Life Story', another powerful Barry and Robin composition, is urgent and tense, using celestial keys, punchy brass, and stuttered acoustic guitar as its fuel (frequent Bee Gees percussionist Joe Lala even got to use a whip as part of the rhythm section). It backed the 'Guilty' single in most markets.

Once again, the 'Stayin' Alive' drum loop makes an appearance with an altered tempo and an echo effect.

'Never Give Up' (Barry Gibb, Albhy Galuten)

Recorded at Middle Ear, Miami Beach: February 1980; Criteria Recording Studios, Miami: February 1980; Sound Labs Studio, Hollywood: March 1980; Media Sound, New York: June 1980

'Never Give Up' chugs along with a catchy, Nanigo-esque rhythm, showcasing veteran Harold Cowart's expert bass playing and a pleasantly acidic synth solo by pianist George Bitzer. The dissonant double tracking of Streisand's voice on the bridge is a great effect, and the multiple key changes give it good momentum.

It served as the flip side of the 'Promises' single in the UK.

'Make It Like A Memory' (Barry Gibb, Albhy Galuten)

Recorded at Middle Ear, Miami Beach, in February 1980; Criteria Recording Studios, Miami, in February 1980; Sound Labs Studio, Hollywood, in March 1980; Media Sound, New York, in June 1980

The album's closer, 'Make It Like A Memory', is a sweeping seven-and-a-half-minute opus that merges multiple musical styles and varying tempos. The track is sectioned into movements, swaying between pop, classical, rock, and jazz influences, reaching its first peak with a wailing guitar solo by Pete Carr and cascading piano runs by Richard Tee. The second begins after a false ending where Streisand's vocal finishes, followed by an orchestral blitz that ramps up for the final two minutes of the song.

Albhy Galuten believed Streisand's classical acumen allowed her to navigate the tricky timing of 'Make It Like A Memory', which put the R&B sensibilities of Barry and the production team to the test. He told *Albumism* in 2020:

When we were recording, there was a long pause when she sang 'make it like a … memory'. The downbeat is supposed to be on 'memory'. I remember doing the demo; it took Barry, like, ten times to get the vocal to come in on time with the downbeat because there was no time through there. There was no beat going on. For Barbra, it's not her natural thing to sing like Michael [Jackson] or Barry rhythmically. In fact, we ended up having to do a lot of fine-tuning and adjustment to get her meter to line up in a way that was, you know, sufficiently rhythmic for Barry. But on 'Make It Like A Memory', she did five takes, and on every single one she nailed the downbeat. So, even though Barry has incredible, detailed meter and absolute accuracy, Barbra has this intuitive sense of long-time [classical sustained phrasing] that she knows when to come in based on some aesthetic that is not countable by the rest of us R&B musicians.

The months of hard work Barry and his associates invested in *Guilty* paid off in dividends. However, there was a feeling midstream that it had the potential to be something special. 'We could tell about halfway through that we had something very different from what she'd been doing and that it could be an extremely big album', Barry told *Billboard* in February 1981. 'I'm pretty sure we could follow it with an even better album because we know each other better'.

The week of 11 October, just 12 days after its release, *Guilty* entered the *Billboard* Top LPs and Tape chart at number 15 and rose to the top two weeks later, where it spent three further weeks at the summit. In total, it spent 49 weeks on the survey.

In the UK, Streisand became the first female artist to have simultaneous number one entries on the album and singles charts (with 'Woman In Love'). Its initial chart run lasted 81 weeks, from 11 October 1980 through 24 April 1982. However, the album appeared on the chart three additional times over the next 33 years: number 97 the week of 15 May 1982; number 93 the week of 10 September 2005, coinciding with the release of *Guilty*'s sequel, *Guilty Too* (*Guilty Pleasures* was the alternate title for the project outside the UK and Ireland); and number 64 the week of 27 August 2015. *Guilty* also topped album charts in Australia, Austria, the Netherlands, Finland, France, Italy, New Zealand, Norway, Spain and Sweden.

CBS was so confident in *Guilty*'s sales power that it simultaneously released a limited half-speed master issue of the album on its CBS Mastersound subsidiary with the regular retail version – the first time in its history. The audiophile pressing retailed for approximately $12 USD at the time – about double what a traditional pressing cost.

Critics were broadly positive about the Barbra-Barry collaboration. *Rolling Stone*'s Stephen Holden, who was often dour about the Gibbs' work, wrote:

One reason that the Streisand-Gibb team proves to be the most sensational artist-producer duo since Michael Jackson and Quincy Jones created *Off The Wall* is that both principals are basically traditional pop sentimentalists who complement each other in convenient ways. Barbra Streisand's steel-belted soprano gives more dramatic authority to Gibb's chromatic mini-arias than practically any other voice could.

Streisand herself gave her experience of making the album a glowing review in *My Name Is Barbra*. 'I've always looked back on the *Guilty* album as the easiest, most pleasant recording experience I've ever had. Barry just made the whole process a delight. He knew exactly how to showcase me as an artist because he's a wonderful artist himself'.

To celebrate its 25th anniversary in 2005, *Guilty* received a DualDisc CD reissue, remastered and accompanied by bonus interview footage, an extended digital album of Mario Casilli's photo shoot for the album, and the live performances of Barry and Barbra singing 'Guilty' and 'What Kind Of Fool' during the *One Voice* concert special.

While the revamp didn't feature any bonus material, Barry released *The Guilty Demos* exclusively as a digital-only album on Apple's iTunes platform on 10 October 2006. All of *Guilty*'s songs are accounted for, with the exception of 'Never Give Up'. However, demos for two tracks intended for *Guilty* that were shelved during the recording process are present: 'Secrets', which was given to British singer Elaine Paige, and 'Carried Away', which would surface on Olivia Newton-John's landmark album, *Physical*, the following year.

The arrival of *The Guilty Demos* came as somewhat of a surprise to fans. Although many of the prototype tracks had been circulating on bootleg recordings for years, an official packaging of them was a detour from the Gibbs' usual aversion to making their unfinished works publicly available.

The friction between Barry, RSO, and CBS resulting from his work on *Guilty* was a foreshadowing of something much more ominous that would not only significantly alter The Bee Gees' future but also expose surprisingly deep fractures in their seemingly idyllic relationship with Robert Stigwood.

The Bee Gees had become wary of Stigwood sometime in 1979 after an audit ordered by one of their lawyers had reportedly uncovered millions of dollars in royalties unpaid to the Gibbs. Their legal team planned to file a lawsuit in late October 1980, but events escalated when a furious Maurice, upon learning the full extent of the alleged discrepancies, drove from his country home near London and stormed into Stigwood's London office to confront him.

Relations between Stigwood and The Bee Gees had been notably strained in recent months. Tensions had apparently flared further when filmmaker George Lucas directly approached The Bee Gees with a project proposal. The brothers were reportedly warned that any deal would need to go through the Stigwood Group, with legal action threatened otherwise.

The Bee Gees' most recent contract with Stigwood, negotiated in August 1975, was set to last five years or cover eight albums, whichever was longer. On 2 October, The Bee Gees stunned the music world by filing an unprecedented lawsuit against their long-time manager and record label head. The lawsuit was a culmination of years of tension, alleging fraud, misrepresentation and financial mismanagement. They accused Stigwood of maintaining an excessive degree of control over The Bee Gees' professional lives, stemming from a management agreement signed when the brothers were, in the words of their lawyer, John Eastman, 'inexperienced in business affairs'. Eastman, the brother-in-law of Paul McCartney, was a high-profile lawyer known for helping The Beatles extricate themselves from their contract with former manager Allen Klein in 1977.

The Gibb brothers claimed that Stigwood's management was rife with conflicts of interest and contractual breaches, and that he had taken advantage of their naivety to negotiate contracts that heavily favoured him.

The Bee Gees' lawsuit alleged that Stigwood appropriated copyrights and master recordings owned by the group, surreptitiously diverted millions of dollars through self-serving corporate entities and resisted and discouraged their efforts to work with companies outside the RSO fold. The suit also claimed that Stigwood International, a Bermuda-based corporation, was created as 'a conduit … to remove funds from the Stigwood Group in New York and elsewhere for personal use and benefit'. Additionally, it accused the PolyGram Group, the worldwide distributor for and partial owner of RSO, of collaborating with Stigwood through these corporate 'alter egos' to defraud The Bee Gees of royalties and other owed payments.

The suit asserted that the Gibb brothers were lacking business experience when they signed their first contract with Stigwood in 1967, agreeing to give him a 25% manager's fee on their recording earnings while receiving only an 'unreasonably small percentage' of the retail price of their records and the net profit from their songwriting.

The lawsuit further alleged that during contract renegotiations in 1975, Stigwood 'concealed from the Gibbs the fact that the Stigwood Group owed the Gibbs millions of dollars and instead falsely represented that the Gibbs personally owed substantial sums of money to the Stigwood Group'. This alleged deception led The Bee Gees to believe they had a minimal bargaining position and could not terminate their relationship with Stigwood. The suit also claimed that Stigwood, with the assistance and in part through the instrumentality of the PolyGram Group, created unnecessary corporate structures to retain and delay millions of dollars in royalties and to facilitate override payments and fees. These mechanisms, the lawsuit contended, were designed to skim income from the plaintiffs and delay payments, enabling the defendants to earn millions of dollars of interest on such sums. Further accusations included Stigwood striking deals with BMI to secure large advances on The Bee Gees' songs without sharing those funds with the group.

The lawsuit sought a staggering $75 million from Stigwood (equivalent to nearly $270 million in 2026 terms), $75 million from the PolyGram Group (which owned half of the Stigwood Group Companies), $50 million in punitive damages and millions more in interest and back royalties. It also demanded the return of all The Bee Gees' master recordings, the reassignment of song copyrights, the termination of all their many contracts with Stigwood and his companies, and repayment of all management fees under their most recent contract from 1977 to date.

The central issue in the Bee Gees-Stigwood conflict was the 1975 agreement, which required the group to deliver eight albums and bound them to an exclusive relationship with Stigwood for at least five years. Stigwood's executives argued that the group still owed the company five albums. However, The Bee Gees countered that *Main Course* should count toward the contract, despite their claim that the 1975 release was unfairly subjected to the lower royalty rates established in their 1967 agreement.

The lawsuit sent shockwaves through the music industry. Stigwood, who had managed The Bee Gees since 1967, vehemently denied the allegations, issuing a statement from his Bermuda home:

I am angry, dismayed, revolted. I will fight this attack on my integrity. These ridiculous allegations are false, baseless and without foundation. I have instructed counsel to see that the truth is told and that those responsible for this travesty are made to account for their misconduct.

Stigwood's business allies rallied to his defence. Fredric 'Freddie' Gershon, president of the Stigwood Group, accused The Bee Gees of attempting to renegotiate their contracts through the press. He claimed Barry had admitted to using high initial demands to bargain for a better deal, stating, 'We have to start with a high number, Freddie, so we can re-negotiate down to a new deal'. Gershon further alleged that Robin and Maurice had denied knowledge of the lawsuit's contents. He dismissed the accusations as 'revolting' and pointed out that Stigwood had never discouraged outside collaborations, even playing a key role in securing Barry's work with Barbra Streisand.

RSO Records president Al Coury also defended Stigwood, describing the lawsuit as a betrayal, saying:

I have worked in this industry for over 20 years, and to the best of my knowledge, The Bee Gees have received the highest royalty rate ever given to any artist, and that includes 17 years at Capitol, where I worked with such major talents as The Beatles, Bob Seger, Steve Miller and Paul McCartney. It appears that The Bee Gees are not happy with the extraordinary money they have already earned, and they seem to be unaware, or insensitive to the fact, that a record company working for them requires money for the highest quality manpower. The Bee Gees have made significantly more money than RSO Records has in the past five years. If RSO had given them more, the record company simply could not have stayed in business. In all my years in the business, I have never seen so much lavished on any one group.

Recalling negotiations over the songs featured in *Saturday Night Fever*, Coury shared:

They were asking for so much money for four songs on the *Saturday Night Fever* album that I threatened to resign from my position as president. If Robert Stigwood and The Bee Gees had forced me to accept their deal, the record company would have lost approximately 15 cents per album. The Bee Gees still wound up with an excessively high royalty, and I believe that Robert Stigwood even gave them a percentage of the film.

In their lawsuit, The Bee Gees alleged that independent accountants identified over $16 million in unpaid royalties owed to them by Stigwood. Responding to this claim, Coury remarked:

It seems they have forgotten the costs involved in selling records and are asking for even more than what has already been given. It is impossible for us to be more generous without putting ourselves out of business. The Bee Gees' relationship with Robert Stigwood is far more than that of manager. He has known them and cared for them, both personally and professionally, for about 20 years, and this action is a shocking, incomprehensible and disgraceful betrayal on their part.

The lawsuit left The Bee Gees navigating a delicate balancing act. Despite the publicised animosity, Robin and Maurice maintained cordial relationships with RSO's London executives, even dining with them shortly after filing the suit. Meanwhile, Barry remained in the US, focusing on personal projects.

RSO's swift and outspoken defence was highly unusual, as it allowed corporate executives to speak so openly about an ongoing legal case. Jeanne Theis, RSO's director of promotion and publicity, explained the company's approach: 'When the allegations are as ridiculous as they are, and as outrageous as they are, we have no problem responding to them publicly'. Publicity, however, seemed to be at the core of the controversy, prompting speculation among members of the press that the lawsuit may be part of a larger strategy. Some suggested it might be aimed at re-negotiating The Bee Gees' five-year/eight-album deal with RSO Records. Freddie Gershon hinted at such motives, stating, 'This is some sort of a means to an end'. Theis was even more direct, asserting, 'It's an obvious stunt'.

If the battle between the Gibbs and Stigwood was indeed a ruse, *Village Voice* reporter and veteran music writer Maureen Orth may have been the first to be fooled by it. Orth worked from the 42-page complaint filed on behalf of The Bee Gees to write her story, meeting her Tuesday night deadline. However, the document was not officially filed in New York's Supreme Court until Friday.

On Wednesday, the day Orth's story hit the newsstands, reporters rushed to the downtown courthouse seeking details but found no records. A phone call to The Bee Gees' attorney John Eastman's Manhattan office eventually led to the complaint being distributed to newsrooms across the city.

Speculation was rife that this was a calculated move to manipulate the press. Orth disagreed, stating, 'I wrote my story from a complaint by a group, The Bee Gees, that has no other publicity people or managers other than Stigwood himself. It is a fairly serious length to go to for a publicity stunt, and it is an awful lot of time and trouble and money to go to in hiring the lawyers to do it'.

While Stigwood and his associates painted The Bee Gees as ungrateful, the brothers maintained that they were simply seeking justice and the right to control their artistic and financial destiny. Their lawsuit detailed years of alleged financial mismanagement, delayed royalty payments, and restrictive contracts that they claimed had stifled their creativity. The Gibbs insisted their grievances were not about greed but about reclaiming what was rightfully theirs.

Robert Stigwood responded swiftly and aggressively, escalating the legal battle by filing a $310 million countersuit in New York's Supreme Court on 27 October. He accused The Bee Gees of libel, extortion, corporate defamation, and breach of contract. Stigwood's filing portrayed himself as the architect of The Bee Gees' success, claiming he had transformed them 'from penniless youths into multi-millionaires', and that the lawsuit was a calculated attempt to tarnish his reputation and force him into concessions. Stigwood also sought an injunction to prevent The Bee Gees from pursuing new management and requested that the case be tried under English law.

The countersuit alleged that The Bee Gees' legal action was not a legitimate attempt to resolve contractual disputes, but a strategic ploy designed by their lawyer to bludgeon Stigwood 'into more extra-contractual concessions by disseminating false accusations to the worldwide press'. The claim stated: 'Plaintiffs' publication of the false allegations in the unverified complaint is a flagrant abuse of the judicial process. It is a shameful effort at blackmail by legal pleading and constitutes actionable misconduct under the laws of the State of New York and elsewhere'. Stigwood's brief also alleged that at least two of the Gibb brothers admitted this tactic during conversations with him.

The suit alleged that The Bee Gees authorised their attorney to commence this action after having been advised that they could not win a litigation seeking to terminate or rescind their contracts with Robert Stigwood, and implied that the real reason was to put pressure on Stigwood through the widespread media coverage the group knew the suit would engender.

The counterclaim included an affidavit from Freddie Gershon, himself an attorney, which characterised The Bee Gees' lawsuit as a 'bargaining chip in the latest round of contractual sparring between the Gibbs and certain of the defendants'. Stigwood asked the court to dismiss the case, arguing that English courts are the appropriate venue for resolving the dispute as the contracts in question were negotiated in England and stipulate English jurisdiction.

Stigwood's countersuit referenced six contractual agreements between The Bee Gees and his companies, asserting these agreements were periodically updated not to confuse royalty payments, as alleged by The Bee Gees, but to help the group avoid English taxes. The filing stated that The Bee Gees were represented by their own lawyers and tax advisors during each renegotiation, countering the group's claim that they were inexperienced in business affairs when they first signed a major contract with Stigwood in 1967.

The countersuit also rebutted claims that Stigwood failed to fulfil his contractual duties, detailing his involvement with the group since their 1967 debut. Stigwood credited himself with mediating disputes among the Gibb brothers, helping Barry after his solo career faltered, and overseeing their major successes – including their contributions to the *Saturday Night Fever* and *Grease* soundtracks. The suit highlighted Barry's receipt of a $3 million payment for composing the *Grease* title track as evidence of Stigwood's role in securing substantial financial opportunities for the group.

The countersuit further alleged that The Bee Gees, either directly or through their representatives, falsely represented that they were no longer under contract to Stigwood to various individuals and organisations, including Jerry Weintraub of Concerts West; CBS Records president Walter Yetnikoff; founder of Casablanca Records Neil Bogart; Charles Koppelman of The Entertainment Company; BMI; and Charles Webber, president of Lucasfilms, the company that produced the *Star Wars* sagas. The suit also charged that Barry Gibb's deal with CBS, vis-à-vis Barbra Streisand's *Guilty* album, violated existing contracts with Stigwood, and that the group entered into merchandising deals in violation of existing agreements with Stigwood. It was alleged that The Bee Gees sidestepped existing agreements in arranging with Concerts West to manage their 1979 US tour, leaving one of the Stigwood companies liable for expenses incurred on the tour.

Regarding the films *Grease* and *Saturday Night Fever*, Stigwood charged that the group wrote and produced music for those films at his behest and received compensation far in excess of the norm.

As for The Bee Gees' contributions to the UNICEF benefit, Stigwood's countersuit accused the group of threatening to withdraw from the television special and to renege on their promise to donate the rights to 'Too Much Heaven' to UNICEF. Stigwood claimed these threats forced him to concede to the group's late 1970s financial demands, which he estimated cost his companies $20 million over recent years. These actions formed the basis of Stigwood's extortion charges.

While the countersuit suggested that Stigwood sought to reclaim copyrights to The Bee Gees' songs, a lawyer from Paul, Weiss, Rifkind, Wharton & Garrison, which represented Stigwood, denied this intention.

The Bee Gees' lawsuit against Robert Stigwood highlighted the challenges faced by artists navigating the complexities of the music industry. The case exposed the potential for exploitation in management relationships and raised questions about the balance of power between artists and record labels. It also underscored the importance of financial literacy for artists entering into long-term contracts.

As the legal battle unfolded, one thing became clear: the ties that had once bound The Bee Gees and Robert Stigwood were irrevocably severed, leaving a legacy of both artistic triumph and bitter contention. Whether the courts would side with the brothers or Stigwood remained uncertain, but the case would forever alter the trajectory of one of music's most iconic partnerships.

The lawsuit posed immediate financial and operational repercussions for RSO Records. In November, the label dismissed 19 staff, including vice-president Bob Ursury, in a major cost-cutting move. With no new Bee Gees material expected in the near future due to the legal standoff, RSO's revenue stream was likely to suffer. The situation was exacerbated by strained relations with PolyGram, RSO's parent company, which was reconsidering its partnership with the label.

In the thick of this intense legal crisis, The Bee Gees completed the construction of their own recording facility, Middle Ear, located at 1801 Bay Road in Miami Beach. The studio was housed in a former warehouse, a windowless and unassuming structure that offered a high level of anonymity. The decision to build their own studio was influenced by the rising costs of recording, with sessions at Criteria Recording Studios at the time estimated to cost around $250,000 per album.

Middle Ear was designed by Seth Snyder, a renowned studio designer, engineer, and professional audio equipment dealer who had previously worked with Fort Lauderdale-based professional audio equipment manufacturer MCI (Music Center Incorporated). Snyder's expertise extended to designing Sunshine Studios for K.C. & The Sunshine Band and Bob Marley's Tuff Gong Studio in Kingston, Jamaica.

Middle Ear was initially kitted out with MCI equipment: a JH-556-LM automated console, two JH-24 multitrack recorders with a JH-45 auto-lock synchroniser, and JH-110B stereo recorders. Later, The Bee Gees adopted a more cautious approach to emerging technology, opting to rent digital equipment as needed while waiting for industry standards to solidify.

Despite the Gibbs having a space where they were in complete control and could perform their work with the most advanced equipment, some felt the move might have done more to hinder their creativity than help it. Albhy Galuten told the authors in late 2024:

Leaving Criteria was a mistake. We tend to fall into the trap of thinking that things are about resources and quality. But it's really more about social stimulus. The thing about Criteria was that there were always other bands in the next studio; you know, the Jackie Gleason Orchestra, The Eagles, Black Sabbath, Donny Hathaway. There were just so many people around. That's how we got Don Felder and Joe Walsh on Andy's records because there was all this cross-pollination and this buzz of people listening to each other's stuff.

When we were at Middle Ear, we were just sort of stuck in this cave by ourselves. We'd bring in some musicians, but it wasn't the same thing. There was no serendipity. Everything was planned and organised. Building and moving to Middle Ear allowed them to have control and state-of-the-art stuff. They wanted to be in the driver's seat. But I think the main reason was to be near home. It was more like a place the family could hang out. And, by the way, I never blame anybody for placing their family high in their hierarchy of values. Family and friends are, in most ways, more important than your work. If you can't pay your bills, obviously, your family suffers. But they didn't have to worry about paying their bills.

Despite the negative American sentiment toward most things disco, the *Saturday Night Fever* film made its primetime television debut on 16 November 1980 on the ABC network. More intriguingly, the PG-rated version aired that evening contained scenes that had been previously unseen in any of the theatrical releases, cobbled together as the network edited the film to fit the scheduled time block and to satisfy strict television censorship laws and guidelines.

RSO, certainly eager to generate a profit in any form, given their precarious financial status, capitalised on the event by reissuing 'Night Fever' and 'More Than A Woman' as a double-sided single. The effort didn't return either of the songs to the charts, but it did offer Bee Gees completists three distinctly labelled versions of the single: one on the newly-adopted RSO sliver label motif; a second on RSO's special 'Top Line' branding that had been unveiled as part of a reissue program for some of its catalogue's biggest hit singles since 1977; and a third issued by Polydor instead of RSO, using an orange-and-gold label branding tagged as its 'Band of Gold Series'.

Amidst many controversies and transitions, the brothers, their band and their producers gathered in the new studio in late October to begin mapping out the next Bee Gees album.

Blue Weaver, Dennis Bryon, and Alan Kendall had become so much more than the Gibbs' backup musicians – they were stakeholders in The Bee Gees as a creative and commercial enterprise. They had contributed substantively to the recordings that defined their 1975-1979 halcyon, and, in Blue's case, had written significant components of songs like 'How Deep Is Your Love' and 'Night Fever' – and even shared writing credits with the brothers on *Main Course*'s 'Songbird' and *Children Of The World*'s 'The Way It Was'. Unlike other bands, the three were not just paid for their services; they were provided a cut of the proceeds received from the recordings.

There was an emotional connection, as well – the band's spouses and families had become close with the brothers and theirs. They spent time at each other's homes, vacationed together, and supported one another through challenging circumstances.

Setting up shop at Middle Ear was reportedly part of a greater master plan the collective had discussed to form a production company and record label for which they could all work freely with other artists and produce their own projects. But according to Dennis Bryon in his book, *You Should Be Dancing: My Life With The Bee Gees*, that 'had been forgotten' when they began work on the new Bee Gees album.

But operating as a real band required a high level of investment in all its members. Barry, Albhy, and Karl had become a results-oriented production powerhouse, accustomed to summoning whatever expert musician they desired to fit their needs, giving them specific directions, cutting them a paycheque and sending them on their way so the team could focus on perfecting the recordings for release. Barry was unquestionably the creative compass for The Bee Gees now, and it didn't appear that was going to change anytime soon. Having to balance eight stakeholders' needs and interests equitably throughout the making of a record probably felt stifling.

It had also been two full years since everyone had been together, finishing up *Spirits Having Flown*. A lot had changed since then, and the separate professional projects and personal affairs everyone had been attending to outside the group's bubble had likely given each of them varying ideas of how they wanted to move forward.

And then there was the small matter of The Bee Gees' fall from public and media favour. They had gone from hedging bets on how many weeks their new record would spend at number one to wondering if anyone would even listen now. Dennis remembers that the weight of it all caused the sessions for the new album to deteriorate rather quickly:

From day one, the vibe in the studio was terrible. I was sitting next to Karl in front of the mixing console when Maurice came in and told me to get out of his chair. I couldn't believe it, I thought he was joking, but he was serious. Blue and Albhy were at each other's throats all the time, disagreeing over everything. There was no flow or excitement about the music. Everybody just sat around reading magazines and comic books or played pool. Nothing was getting done. It was sad.

The fledgling album had, ironically, been given a working title of *Sanctuary*. The atmosphere was anything but, as Dennis recalled:

Besides a LinnDrum machine, Albhy had a Fairlight CMI set up in the control room. We were working on a song called 'Cornerstone'. Albhy had programmed a bassline that he wanted me to play drums to. The bassline had a super-fast techno feel that was impossible for me to play along with. I remember trying to record it 70, 80 times. I'd never been through anything like this before. I played it so many times that a huge blister emerged on my finger. Soon, that blister burst, and a second blister appeared. When the second one burst, the wound started to bleed everywhere. When I saw blood on my dreams, I went home.

Work on the album came to a screeching halt. If The Bee Gees had any hope of returning to form with new music and regaining the popular traction they'd lost in the last year, some major internal changes would be needed.

1981

A new year brought a new addition to Barry and Linda's family. On 10 January, their third son, Travis Ryan Crompton Gibb, came into the world nearly two months early. Weighing just four pounds and five ounces, Travis spent the first seven weeks of his life in an incubator as his parents anxiously watched and waited for him to grow strong enough to come home.

When the day finally came, their joy was short-lived. Within days, Travis developed pneumonia and was rushed back to Variety Children's Hospital in South Miami. 'Our ordeal started all over again', Barry recalled. 'Pneumonia is serious for anyone, but for a premature baby, it's usually fatal. It was an experience Linda and I never want to go through again – but it hasn't discouraged us from having more children'.

While Barry was focusing on a particularly tough situation at home, Dick Ashby, The Bee Gees' personal manager, was tasked with a rather unpleasant chore on the business front. The decision had been made by the Gibbs to part ways with Blue Weaver, Dennis Bryon, and Alan Kendall after more than half a decade of making not only the biggest hits of The Bee Gees' career, but also some of the most successful music in history.

In his autobiography, *You Should Be Dancing: My Life With The Bee Gees*, Dennis Bryon remembered clearly the day that changed absolutely everything:

It was the second weekend in January of 1981. Linda was in the hospital giving birth to their third child. I was working in my house with two carpenters; we were building a new self-contained apartment over the garage. The phone rang. 'Hi, Denny, it's Dick. I'm afraid I have some bad news ... the boys want to use another band'. I just stood there in shock as the carpenters hammered away. 'Oh', I said. Then there was silence. 'Sorry, Denny. I guess we'll be talking over the next couple of days ... I knew things hadn't been going well in the studio,' he continued, 'but I had never expected this'.

Another, and even more perplexing, phone call followed, this time from Dennis' former Amen Corner bandmate, Clive Taylor, who had reportedly heard the news before Dennis: 'L.A.'s buzzing with the news. Jeff Porcaro [the drummer and co-founder of the American rock band Toto] has been asked to be in the new band'.

Tensions between the band and production team had apparently run high for some time, particularly with co-producer Albhy Galuten; Dennis believed he, Blue Weaver, and Alan Kendall were 'never good enough for him'. Upon learning of Jeff Porcaro's supposed hiring, Dennis firmly believed his and the rest of the band's ouster was Albhy's decision. Albhy refuted this in a late 2024 conversation with the authors, in which he explained why The Bee Gees made the radical departure:

I certainly don't take responsibility for letting the band go. I *am* responsible for introducing Barry to all these other musicians because we used them on other records, and we were in love with them. And he thought, 'Okay, well, you have Steve Gadd and Jeff Porcaro, who every drummer in the world will tell you they look up to and bow down to them'. And Dennis was a lovely man, but not the same calibre of drummer.

Albhy added a reflective caveat:

I was not as aware at the time because I was so focused on getting parts right, of how important the chemistry was. Not the quality of the drumming, but the quality of the personality. And that's what we lost with Dennis and Blue. They were in the studio all the time expressing their opinions and doing stuff. I was young, and I didn't realise how important that was.

When Dennis finally came face-to-face with Barry the day after his firing, Barry revealed the brothers had made the call with their co-producers' cooperation, but he had been 'too embarrassed' to deliver the news himself. Allegedly, Dennis, Blue, and Alan were provided a $150,000 severance payment (which translates to just over a half-million dollars in 2026 terms). According to Dennis, the sum was 'a non-refundable but recoupable advance on future earnings. My next royalty cheque would come 18 years later in the fall of 1999'.

With the departure of their band mates, The Bee Gees would soon return to Middle Ear, armed with an arsenal of top session players, to resume work on their next studio album. Recording and production would last until June.

In January, Walter Yetnikoff, president of the CBS Records Group, presented Barry with a special plaque in honour of his work as the co-producer of Barbra Streisand's *Guilty*. The album had sold seven-and-a-half million copies, and its singles had sold six million units worldwide to date. CBS anticipated sales would eventually reach 20 million – a rather accurate prediction as of 2026.

On 25 February, the 23rd Grammy Awards ceremony took place at Radio City Music Hall in New York City, celebrating the year's most outstanding musical achievements. Barry and Barbra Streisand were among the evening's highlights, earning multiple nominations and a significant win.

The song 'Woman In Love' received three nominations: Record of the Year, Song of the Year, and Best Pop Vocal Performance, Female. Additionally, the album *Guilty* was nominated for Album of the Year. However, the duo's crowning achievement of the night came when their duet on the song 'Guilty' won the Grammy for Best Pop Vocal Performance by a Duo or Group with Vocal, earning Barry his seventh statue.

The buzz surrounding Streisand was palpable that evening. At the previous year's ceremony, she and Neil Diamond had delivered a show-stopping performance of their hit duet 'You Don't Bring Me Flowers'. Barry and Barbra appeared during the televised portion of the ceremony to announce the award for Best Rock Vocal Performance, Male, which was won by Billy Joel for his 1980 album *Glass Houses*. When Paul Simon introduced Barbra and Barry to the stage, the audience erupted into applause, giving the duo a standing ovation. Diana Ross was even caught on camera clapping enthusiastically and exclaiming 'Wow!' as the pair, dressed in matching white outfits, made their way to the podium. Streisand recounted the evening in *My Name Is Barbra:*

Barry and I won a Grammy that night for Best Pop Performance by a Duo or Group. I had asked him to wear white, and so did I, to continue the concept from the cover. And I had written a few lines for us to say when we both walked out onstage.

Barbra: Barry, do you feel guilty?
Barry: No.
Barbra: I do.
Barry: Why? Why would you feel like that?
Barbra: I don't know. I feel like I'm cheating on Neil Diamond.

That got a big laugh, and Barry gave me a big kiss.

On 21 February, American country singer-songwriter Conway Twitty released Barry's now omnipresent composition 'Rest Your Love On Me' as a single. It climbed the *Billboard* Hot Country Singles chart slowly to become his 25th solo number one hit on 2 May, summitting for one week. It was also used as the title of Twitty's 42nd studio album, which peaked at number 12 on the *Billboard* Top Country Albums survey – one of two he would release in the same calendar year.

Twitty had been actively recording music since 1955 and was best known for his country standards 'It's Only Make Believe', 'Hello Darlin'' and 'You've Never Been This Far Before'. Twitty had recently visited The Bee Gees at their newly constructed Middle Ear Studios and a photo was published in *Billboard* with the caption suggesting he was trying to convince the brothers to record a country album.

In March, California-based Nautilus Recordings used the licence it had received from RSO late in 1980 to issue *Spirits Having Flown* as an audiophile LP. The multi-platinum disc was half-speed mastered at the JVC Cutting Center in Los Angeles and pressed on imported virgin Teldec vinyl at KM Records in Burbank.

Spirits Having Flown's reputation as a production masterpiece and showcase for the Gibbs' complex vocals no doubt caught Nautilus' attention. Their mastering process was specifically geared to emphasise an album's middle and upper frequencies, and the bright, detailed sound of the original masters was a great foundation.

The album's opening track, 'Tragedy', instantly demonstrated the benefits of half-speed mastering; the vocals have a crisper and more defined quality, allowing listeners to appreciate their intricacies. However, this intensified upper-end energy sometimes proves challenging for the vinyl format. In 'Tragedy', the synthesiser part exhibits noticeable distortion, hinting at the limits of the mastering technique.

Despite these occasional distortions, the overall clarity and sharpness in the rest of the album are commendable. The impeccable production quality comes through beautifully in tracks like 'Too Much Heaven' and 'Love You Inside Out', where the vocals and instrumental arrangements are presented with remarkable precision.

In March 1981, it was announced that Barry would star in a remake of *A Face In The Crowd*, a film about a pop singer who rises to fame but succumbs to greed and corruption. Production was slated to begin in July. The project, however, was ultimately never made.

The remake was to be based on the original 1957 movie of the same name, with Barry reprising American actor Andy Griffith's role as Larry 'Lonesome' Rhodes, a drifter whose charm and talent are discovered by radio producer Marcia Jeffries, played by stage and screen star Patricia Neal. Marcia helps transform Rhodes into a media sensation, but his success exposes his manipulative, egotistical nature. Rhodes gains immense influence, swaying public opinion and even reshaping a presidential candidate's image. However, his offscreen persona destroys his relationships, including with Marcia. Rhodes's downfall begins when Marcia secretly broadcasts his derisive comments about his audience and allies. The public backlash ruins his career, leaving him isolated and powerless.

On 27 March, further cutbacks at RSO Records saw its once bustling Los Angeles office reduced to a skeleton staff with the termination of 55 employees. This marked a dramatic reversal for the label, which only a few years ago had dominated the US record industry. RSO moved forward with a drastically thinned-out team, including President Al Coury, Senior Vice President Bob Edson, with marketing, sales, and promotion handled by parent company PolyGram.

The downsizing followed the label's financial struggles tied to disappointing returns on releases like *Sgt. Pepper's Lonely Hearts Club Band* and *Times Square*, as well as ongoing issues with counterfeit products and a strained relationship with PolyGram. These challenges were compounded by the legal dispute with The Bee Gees, who were still RSO's most prominent and profitable asset, which halted new material and left the label's revenue in decline.

Robert Stigwood remained optimistic, stating at the time his intent was to focus on soundtracks and A&R activities in major cities to develop new talent. Despite the turmoil, Al Coury insisted that RSO would remain viable, albeit as a smaller operation.

In early 1981, reports emerged in a Norwegian newspaper detailing a transformative period for singer Demis Roussos. The Greek star and former member of progressive rock outfit Aphrodite's Child had embarked on a successful solo career with hits including 'Goodbye, My Love, Goodbye', 'From Souvenirs To Souvenirs', and 'Forever And Ever', which became a number one single in the UK in 1976. The article revealed that he was preparing to collaborate with Barry. Roussos hoped that Barry's Midas touch would elevate his career to new heights. Despite the excitement generated by these revelations, the collaboration never came to fruition. Like many prematurely announced projects involving the Gibbs, the pairing faded into obscurity.

In early 1981, Maurice quietly pursued a solo project, composing five instrumental pieces. He produced the recordings himself, playing keyboards and synthesisers throughout. The collection, which was never released, included 'Image Of Samantha', 'Follow My Love', 'In The Beginning', 'Strings And Things', and 'Hello, My Love'. All were registered for copyright in April 1981, indicating they were intended as a complete set for an instrumental album titled *Strings And Things*. The first piece was almost certainly inspired by his daughter Samantha, born in July 1980.

While the copyright filings list 1981 as the date of creation, it is possible that some of the music was begun in mid-1980. Maurice may not have been working on this material concurrently with the Bee Gees' *Living Eyes*, but it may have occupied him in January or February before work on the group's album resumed.

One of the instrumentals, thought to originate from this batch, later circulated within the fan community. Built on a firm drum track with a flowing synthesiser melody, it stands as a strong composition. The piece shows striking similarities to 'In And Out of Love', a song co-written by Maurice and Robin which would appear on Robin's *How Old Are You?* album in 1983. If the attribution is accurate, the recording shows Maurice at a point of renewed inspiration, signalling a short but significant burst of creative energy.

After months of legal conflict, all disputes between The Bee Gees, Robert Stigwood, the Stigwood Group of Companies, and PolyGram had been settled. According to an official joint statement issued on 8 May by RSO Records, 'The Bee Gees deeply regret the distress caused by allegations made ostensibly in their name, and they continue to have the utmost regard for Robert Stigwood'. As part of the resolution, all allegations on both sides had been 'unreservedly withdrawn'. The Bee Gees were to continue their longstanding association with RSO, with a new album slated for worldwide release later in the year.

Starting 1 July, the Gibb brothers would also manage an independent music publishing venture, marking a fresh chapter in their career alongside the renewal of ties with Stigwood. A spokesman for The Bee Gees told the press, 'Things will open up down the line, but for now, the press release is all we have to say'.

The ongoing legal battle became increasingly public as both sides revisited the terms of the settlement. Initially bound by confidentiality, the dispute re-emerged in the spotlight, fuelled by a series of contentious statements.

The conflict gained renewed attention following comments by RSO Records President Freddie Gershon in a *Rolling Stone* interview, published on 25 June. Gershon stated: 'If you've been in the business long enough, you know that all artists go through periods of temporary insanity. The Bee Gees started investigating the facts, and I think they realised it wasn't worth it to go through several years of litigation, only to have a judge or jury tell them the same thing they found out for themselves, that Robert Stigwood has always treated them fairly and correctly. I believe they were embarrassed to find that out, and they dropped the suit and went away with their tails between their legs'.

Rather than easing tensions, Gershon's pointed remarks further strained relations between the two parties. His statements provoked an emphatic response from The Bee Gees, who published a detailed rebuttal as a full-page advertisement in both *Rolling Stone* and *Variety*. In their statement, they denied ever apologising to Stigwood, insisting they would never do so, and they clarified key terms of the agreement. They owed two more albums to RSO under their 1975 contract. The advances for these albums had been significantly increased, with foreign royalty rates substantially improved.

The Bee Gees also emphasised their newfound independence with the termination of Robert Stigwood's longstanding role as their manager. They claimed the freedom to pursue outside projects without RSO's approval. Royalties allegedly owed by RSO had been settled, with some claims paid in full, others compromised, and some conceded by the group.

In the realm of music publishing, the group announced the creation of a new entity to oversee their entire song catalogue, including works dating back to 1967. While RSO would retain a modest financial interest in their catalogue and upcoming releases until 31 December 1989, this interest would gradually diminish and ultimately cease altogether.

The statement was signed by Barry, Robin and Maurice, and counter-signed by their lawyer, Michael Eaton.

Stigwood quickly countered that The Bee Gees' statement misrepresented the settlement. He asserted that the group's statement contradicted the agreed-upon terms and the press release issued at the time of the settlement. Stigwood claimed the resolution was contingent on a worldwide apology from The Bee Gees – something they categorically denied. He also insisted that despite the termination of direct management agreements, RSO would continue to receive managerial commissions under the settlement terms. Regarding royalties, Stigwood contended that payments withheld during negotiations were made with the group's full knowledge.

The ongoing dispute highlighted the acrimony between the two parties, despite the formal resolution. While the specifics of the settlement remained disputed, the fallout highlighted a fractious relationship that marked the end of a significant chapter in The Bee Gees' career.

The Gibbs appeared eager to distance themselves from Stigwood and RSO, focusing on greater control over their future projects and legacy. Meanwhile, Stigwood remained steadfast in defending his reputation and the fairness of his business practices.

Robin later explained the ordeal:

It was a total misunderstanding, and we patched it up. We made friends with each other. At that time, RSO was folding up anyway as a record company, and everybody was parting ways. It was just that time when everybody was moving on, and I think it was the right thing to do. Robert didn't really feel like he wanted to keep managing artists all the time. With Polydor and RSO splitting, and Robert wanting to do personal things with his life, and we were coming off the back of all this huge chaos, we needed to clean our heads out; we needed a break. We just wanted to concentrate on writing and producing for other people, which we did.

Adding to the list of complicated relationship issues in The Bee Gees camp, Molly Gibb publicly announced the dissolution of her marriage to Robin on 22 May:

I have hardly seen Robin for the past three years, and I have sadly come to the conclusion that our marriage is over. There is no one else involved, but there comes a point when a woman has to say she has had enough. I have filed for divorce and the papers are due to be served tomorrow. The more successful the group became, the less I saw of Robin. It's really due to the pressures of the pop business and the length of time Robin is now away. When we married, Robin was not such a big star and life was easier to manage. I do not want to air private grievances in public, and I hope everyone will respect our wish for privacy through this difficult time.

Unfortunately, Molly's wish to keep the particulars of their divorce under wraps would unravel spectacularly over the next year and would impact them and their children significantly.

The 11 July 1981 issue of *Billboard* mentioned Andy Gibb was working with American producer and engineer Michael Barbiero on a cover of The Everly Brothers' 1958 classic 'All I Have To Do Is Dream' as a duet with his significant other, Victoria Principal. The track was a lifelong favourite of his older brothers, so Andy's desire to record it with his new love wasn't surprising – but the fact that Barry had absolutely nothing to do with the track was. It was the first time Andy released material without any sibling support since 1975. It is also Andy's only known co-producing credit.

To date, Barbiero had served as a staff producer for Paramount Records, helming and earning a Grammy nomination for the soundtrack to the 1973 film *Serpico*, starring actor Al Pacino. Later, he would be attached to projects by major industry names like Guns N' Roses, Counting Crows, Ziggy Marley, and Maroon 5.

The track was recorded at Media Sound in New York City and arranged by American session musician Leon Pendarvis, best known as the musical director and house band keyboardist for *Saturday Night Live*. It's possible that Pendarvis played keyboards and guitar on the song, but the remaining personnel are unknown. The instrumentals don't seem to have the same trademarks of Andy's usual studio players, like Tubby Ziegler or Harold Cowart.

RSO put out the single in August (it was delayed until October in the UK). It was backed with the *Shadow Dancing* album cut 'Good Feeling', which meant that every track from Andy's sophomore album had now been issued as a single A- or B-side between the US and UK markets.

Robert Stigwood was on the verge of dropping Andy from the label due to his mounting personal issues and declining commercial success, but he must have thought Andy's well-publicised romance with Principal would at least rekindle some of the media buzz that buoyed his duets with Olivia Newton-John the year before – and some revenue for his now-financially strapped label.

In the end, it did neither – the single rose to just number 51 on the *Billboard* Hot 100 the week of 12 September. Andy and Victoria's performances of the song on *Donahue* and *The John Davidson Show* seemed to have little impact. It did slightly better in Canada, peaking at number 29 on the national singles chart and at number eight on the adult contemporary tally.

While there really isn't anything particularly wrong with Andy and Victoria's interpretation of the song, it's completely unremarkable musically and pales in quality to all his previous singles. For that reason, and quite possibly due to the fact that their relationship was so scrutinised by the public and the media, 'All I Have To Do Is Dream' never resurfaced on any widely-issued future retrospective of his work. It did appear on a Brazilian compilation titled *All About Andy Gibb* on the Elenco label in 1983, and again on the 1995 various artists package *You & I* on the Som Livre imprint, also released in Brazil. The latter is the only known occasion the song has been available on CD.

'All I Have To Do Is Dream' was Andy's last RSO output – and, very sadly, the final recorded material he would release for the rest of his life.

On 29 July 1981, the world turned its eyes to London as Prince Charles, heir to the British throne, married Lady Diana Spencer in a spectacular ceremony at St. Paul's Cathedral in London. The event drew widespread media attention, with the wedding broadcast live to a global audience of an estimated 750 million viewers.

That same evening, ITV broadcast the full-length version of *Saturday Night Fever* for the first time on UK television. Seizing the moment, RSO Records issued a promotional single featuring two of the film's most famous tracks: 'Night Fever' and 'Stayin' Alive'. Released under the catalogue number SNF 1, the promo's sleeve notes directly tied the re-release to the royal wedding broadcast, stating the expected surge in audience figures:

At 7:30 pm on Wednesday 29 July, the day of the royal wedding, ITV will be showing the full-length version of *Saturday Night Fever*. This will attract one of the highest audience viewing figures this year – an estimate of no less than 20 million people has been forecast. Included on this promotional single are two tracks from the soundtrack album, *Saturday Night Fever*, which were hit singles in their own right.

Following the television broadcast, the *Saturday Night Fever* soundtrack briefly re-entered the UK album charts, landing at number 91 for the week of 15 August.

In the summer, the brothers upgraded their Middle Ear recording facility with the acquisition of a cutting-edge Sony PCM 1610 digital audio processor. By integrating this state-of-the-art digital processor into their studio setup, The Bee Gees were poised to create recordings with unparalleled clarity and precision. Among its many features, Sony touted its 90-decibel dynamic range, which eclipsed that of most high-end analogue processors that maxed out at 30 decibels. It also gave users the ability to use master recordings over and over again without any loss of quality.

On 12 September, Andy began a stint co-hosting the syndicated American music television series *Solid Gold* with American singer, actress, and presenter Marilyn McCoo, best known as one of the lead vocalists for the vocal group The 5th Dimension. The show, which had made its debut in September 1980 and was hosted by Dionne Warwick in its first season, was taped at the Golden West Broadcasters studio facility in Los Angeles. Usually airing on Saturday evenings, *Solid Gold* was one of several shows – not dissimilar to *American Bandstand* – that focused on the popular music of any given week and featured many of the artists lip-synching their hit songs. The show also included a dance troupe that performed routines choreographed to the week's featured songs. Andy would frequently perform solo or in duets with the guests. On this, the first show of the second season, he was joined by Olivia Newton-John to perform their single, 'Rest Your Love On Me'.

In October, *Billboard* reported the music industry had raised over $4.2 million to support the world's needy children through the Music For UNICEF project. Founded in 1978 by The Bee Gees, Robert Stigwood, and British television presenter and journalist David Frost, the organisation was launched in January 1979 with *The Music For UNICEF: A Gift Of Song* television special.

An accompanying LP, released globally by Polydor, generated $3 million in revenue, while music publishing royalties, administered by Chappell Music, contributed an additional $1 million. The concert itself raised $200,000, bringing the total to over $4.2 million for UNICEF's efforts. The Bee Gees donated the full proceeds of their number one single, 'Too Much Heaven', to the cause.

The two songs left over from the *Guilty* project also surfaced in October on projects by two other artists: 'Secrets' and 'Carried Away'. Albhy Galuten noted: 'When we wrote those songs, it was not Streisand's style – it was Barry being stimulated by what he thought would be interesting and fun to do with her'.

The Barry and Robin composition 'Secrets' was recorded by British singer Elaine Paige, best known for her portrayal of the character of Grizabella in the original West End cast of Andrew Lloyd Webber's stage musical *Cats*. 'Secrets' appeared on Paige's second album, simply titled *Elaine Paige*, which was produced by Lloyd-Webber's frequent co-writer Tim Rice. Rice was a fervent Bee Gees fan, having written the sleeve notes for the 1973 *Best Of Bee Gees Vol. 2* compilation.

Rice collaborated with several other songwriters for the album, including Francis Lai, Florrie Palmer, Paul McCartney, and Mike Batt. It is possible that 'Last Affair Of The Heart', a song that he co-wrote in 1980 with Maurice, might have been considered for inclusion. In 2005, Rice thought the song had not been recorded at all; however, the March 1981 US copyright registration for the track was submitted as a cassette recording, although none of the contributors are named.

Olivia Newton-John's 'Carried Away' was included on her 11th, and what would become her most successful, studio album, *Physical*. A gentle mid-tempo song, it is filled with tight background vocal harmonies seemingly designed to offer the illusion the Gibb brothers themselves are singing alongside her. Newton-John's longtime collaborator and producer, John Farrar, took on the Gibb-like singing duties, aided by a vocoder to enhance the effect.

Farrar recalls how Olivia came to record the song, saying, 'She got a hold of it somehow. I think maybe Barry gave it to her. He's always been a hero of mine from way back when The Bee Gees first started, and I was in Australia. I met him a few times over the years, and he's just the sweetest guy'. Olivia's connection to The Bee Gees stretched back years, having previously recorded their song 'Come On Over', which became a top-five country hit in the US in 1976. Her version of 'Carried Away' remained faithful to Barry's original demo. Albhy Galuten, who co-wrote the song with Barry, describes the recording as a tribute, remarking:

I think John's a brilliant producer. I have a tremendous amount of respect for him. The thing with 'Carried Away' is that it seems so straightforward. It's not your average time signature, but it doesn't seem so unusual because the melody leads you there. It's not like you have to count. It seems totally natural.

Every song on the *Physical* album had its own music video filmed for the *Physical* video album, which was directed by British filmmaker Brian

Grant (who would work with The Bee Gees in 1983). In 2021, the deluxe CD reissue of the album included an alternate mix of 'Carried Away', plus its accompanying music video, on DVD.

English lyricist Don Black, whose work spans musicals, film, television themes, and chart hits, wrote two songs with Maurice in 1981. Black's collaborations include a broad range of composers and performers, including John Barry, Andrew Lloyd Webber, Quincy Jones, Henry Mancini and Robbie Williams. He is perhaps best known for co-writing the James Bond themes 'Thunderball', 'Diamonds Are Forever', and 'The Man With The Golden Gun'.

He recalls co-writing two songs at Maurice's house in the UK – 'He Made Me Laugh' and 'While I'm Here' – over several days, with stage actress Marti Webb providing lead vocals on demo recordings. Although neither track was ever officially released on record or CD, Webb later performed 'He Made Me Laugh' on the BBC television programme *The Two Ronnies* on 19 December 1981, a performance subsequently made available on *The Two Ronnies – Series Nine* DVD in 2011.

As promised in the wave of back-and-forth statements exchanged between the Gibbs, RSO Records, and Robert Stigwood earlier in the year, The Bee Gees finally delivered their 16th studio album, *Living Eyes*, in October.

Living Eyes (1981)

Personnel:
Barry Gibb: vocals, acoustic guitar
Robin Gibb: vocals
Maurice Gibb: vocals, acoustic guitar
Don Felder: guitar
George Terry: guitar
Chuck Kirkpatrick: guitar, slide guitar, sitar
Harold Cowart: bass
Bob Glaub: bass
Jeff Porcaro: drums
Steve Gadd: drums
Russ Kunkel: drums
'Solly Noid': Drums
Ralph McDonald: percussion
Joe Galdo: military snare drum

Richard Tee: piano, Rhodes piano
George Bitzer: piano, Rhodes piano, synthesiser
David Wolinski: Rhodes piano
Albhy Galuten: synthesiser
'Sidney': bass, synthesiser
The Boneroo Horns: Peter Graves, Ken Faulk, Brett Murphey, Neil Bonsanti, Don Bonsanti, Whit Sidener
Brass Sextet: Peter Graves, Ken Faulk, Brett Murphey, Jerry Peel, Greg Lonnman, Ken Waldenpfuhl
String arrangements: Barry Gibb, Albhy Galuten, Maurice Gibb
String conductor: Albhy Galuten, Gene Orloff
Horn arrangements: Barry Gibb, Albhy Galuten, Maurice Gibb
Engineers: Karl Richardson, Don Gehman
Assistant engineers: Dale Peterson, Samii Taylor, Lincoln Clapp, Don Brewer, Nick Kalliongis, Jim Pace, Dennis Hetzendorfer, Alex Clarke
Producers: Barry Gibb, Robin Gibb, Maurice Gibb, Karl Richardson, Albhy Galuten
Recorded at Middle Ear, Miami Beach, horns recorded at Criteria Studios, Miami, and strings recorded at Media Sound, New York, between February and June 1981
Release dates: UK: October 1981, US: October 1981
Chart positions: Spain: 4, Norway: 6, Netherlands: 7, Italy: 8, New Zealand: 13, Sweden: 18, Japan: 26, Australia: 30, Canada: 32, West Germany: 37, US: 41, UK: 73
Gold certification: Spain
Platinum certification: Canada

Sonically, *Living Eyes* felt more like a follow-up to *Guilty* than *Spirits Having Flown*, and it seems there was at least an attempt to recapture some of the magic Barry and the production team had created with Barbra Streisand by employing many of the same session hands they had used during those sessions. In theory, their expert abilities supporting the Gibbs' stellar songwriting and vocals should have been a faultless combination. But in practice, almost everything fell short.

While the musicians-for-hire did their jobs, the soulful sympatico of The Bee Gees' dedicated band was clearly missing. Dissolving it was intended to eliminate the challenging dynamics that had evolved in the studio and stoke more musical creativity and range, but the opposite seemed to transpire. Karl Richardson told the authors in late 2024 that 'there was a certain amount of tension at that time, and we said, 'Well, let's try something different'. So, we collected some L.A. hot-shot musicians to do *Living Eyes*. And the result was pretty much chaos'.

Among the expert hands recruited for the album were Richard Tee, Harold Cowart, and George Terry, all of whom had appeared on *Guilty*. Eagles guitarist Don Felder appeared throughout the album, almost as if he was replacing the role of Alan Kendall. Drumming duties were largely handled by Steve Gadd, with Russ Kunkel (who previously worked with Jackson Browne, James Taylor, and Bob Dylan) appearing on a trio of tracks. The industry whispers from early in the year were at least partially fulfilled when Jeff Porcaro was brought on board to play on three of the album's songs. Percussionist Ralph McDonald, who had his own song, 'Calypso Breakdown', on the *Saturday Night Fever* soundtrack, is featured on four of the ten tracks.

The brothers themselves seem to have gotten lost in the shuffle. Streisand's vocal was the undisputed star of *Guilty*. On *Living Eyes*, the Gibbs' usually pristine performances lack the clarity and warmth they achieved on their latter-1970s recordings, and they sometimes struggle to find space in the arrangements. Instrumentally, Maurice was constrained to playing just his acoustic guitar while a revolving door of bassists and guitarists filled in parts he'd normally contribute.

Fresh from the work they had completed on their own side projects, Maurice and Robin didn't appear to be interested in taking a backseat as they had on *Spirits* ... while Barry, Albhy, and Karl did much of the creative work. As a result, the sessions were rife with tensions and disagreements regarding the album's direction, and if one takes a critical listen, the push-and-pull is palpable.

While the Gibbs' music is often inherently melancholic, the audible 'top-of-the-world' vivacity that propelled *Spirits Having Flown* is absent from *Living Eyes*. Some of the tracks are outwardly sad and introspective – understandably so, given the personal and professional issues the brothers had been contending with over the past year-and-some. But the post-halcyon backlash they were experiencing also seemed to zap their confidence and their focus.

Albhy Galuten told the authors in late 2024 that the album struggled to find an audience: 'So much about making a good record is about having a vision and going somewhere and trying to accomplish something and making a statement and connecting with a group of people. Taylor Swift is so popular because she gives voice to young women who have no one speaking for them. The Beatles gave voice to adolescents. And *Saturday Night Fever* gave voice to working-class Americans who just wanted to go out on the weekend and let go. It's not clear that *Living Eyes* was giving a voice to anything'.

He points out that the album was also stymied by the Gibbs' family issues that bubbled underneath the recording process. 'The brothers were never very good at candour', he explains. 'They don't tell you what's really going on. Whenever there were internal things going on, you just didn't talk about anything. We never even talked about Maurice's drinking, but everybody knew that he had vodka in his Perrier bottle. When you're in a family dynamic like that, life can't be a meritocracy. As I said before, I don't blame anyone for putting family ahead of their careers, but in this case, the music suffered'.

For everyone involved, *Living Eyes* seemed to be an uninspiring venture. While The Bee Gees owed RSO an album, one questions whether or not they were ready to make one.

Despite the challenges that accompanied the making of the album, those working with the Gibbs at the time still remember being inspired by the experience. Criteria engineer Dennis Hetzendorfer shared an anecdote with the authors in September 2025 about a fascinating critical technical detail that, unbeknownst to their listeners, helped to shape The Bee Gees' vocal soundscape in the studio:

So, one interesting thing Karl [Richardson] said to me was, 'You know what gives [the brothers] their sound?' I said, 'What?' He said, 'It's not just the three of them singing'. First of all, in their headphones, they liked the playback nice and loud, with a nice stereo mix. Usually, as an engineer, you have to tailor the headphone mix to what the singer needs – what helps them sing their best. Some singers like a lot of keyboard because they get their pitch from that. Olivia Newton-John told me she got her pitch from the bass, interestingly. Others want rhythm, so they can lock into the beat.

The Bee Gees wanted to hear the *whole* thing. They wanted reverb on their voices, the right amount of reverb in the mix. They wanted to hear the whole record in their headphones. But here's the twist: when they sang around one microphone, Barry would lift his headphones off his ears a little bit – both sides – so he could hear his brothers acoustically in the room. Maurice would see Barry do it and copy him, lifting his headphones off just a bit. Robin, meanwhile, kept his headphones hanging around his neck. He was listening acoustically in the room, with the headphone sound just bleeding out.

So, think about it: you've got three sets of headphones open, loud, off their ears or around their necks. From a technical standpoint, no, you wouldn't want that – you'd get a lot of headphone bleed into the vocal mic. But that's the way the Bee Gees sang. That was their reality. If you soloed one of their vocal tracks, you'd hear a lot of headphone spill. But what could you do? Nothing. It became part of their sound.

When you'd listen to a Bee Gees harmony – doubled or tripled, which was common – you'd have all these tracks of singing, plus all this headphone bleed. And you just dealt with it, because it was part of the sound.

That's one of the reasons the Bee Gees sounded the way they did. Of course, the main reason is that they knew exactly what they were doing, and their singing was among the best of our lifetime. But wrapped up in that was this little engineering quirk – the headphone bleed – that became part of the magic.

The Gibbs' own feelings about *Living Eyes* appeared to ebb and flow. When it was released, Barry declared, 'It's our finest album in terms of depth, performance and quality of the production. It's been about 11 months working on this album, and we do tend to work an awful long time on our albums because we want to be sure'.

But three years later, his views had changed considerably. 'Obviously, we had a scare with *Living Eyes*. It wasn't the kind of album we should have brought out at that point. It was a little too downbeat, as opposed to having energy. But we were trying to go for a change, to draw ourselves away from the falsetto vocals and do something that might be a little different. We knew the risks when we did that'. Robin also offered that '*Living Eyes* was a turkey, I think, for a good reason. I don't think that last album does any harm, but I'm really glad it was a turkey'.

Affirming the brothers' mixed sentiments toward the album, the material from *Living Eyes* was largely omitted from the many future Bee Gees greatest hits compilations, save for the 1990 box set *Tales From The Brothers Gibb: A History In Song 1967-1990*, on which only the first single, 'He's A Liar', appeared.

The brothers wrote six additional songs during the *Living Eyes* sessions, almost all of which have floated around the internet for years as bootlegged demos – 'The Promise You Made', 'City Of Angels', and

'Mind Over Matter'. A mid-tempo ballad, 'Heat Of The Night', was reportedly on an earlier running setlist for the album but was later shelved in favour of 'Nothing Could Be Good'. Another song, 'Loving You Is Killing Me', was also never used. One of the outtakes, 'Heart (Stop Beating In Time)', was eventually given to British singer Leo Sayer for his 1982 studio album *World Radio*.

Another product of the sessions was the ballad 'Hold Her In Your Hand', penned by Barry and Maurice. It would be re-recorded and released as a solo single by Maurice in 1984 in association with the soundtrack for the film *A Breed Apart*.

The declining record market had also forced RSO to make cuts to its marketing staff and budgets, which certainly didn't help, but given its legal entanglements with the Gibbs, there may not have been much motivation to tout a new Bee Gees record. And with the European synth-pop explosion dominating radio and retail, *Living Eyes* also just didn't sound contemporary and lacked good public appeal. Even serious Bee Gees fans are divided in their opinions on it several decades on. Perhaps that also points to the issue of whether or not The Bee Gees had a solid 'will buy anything' fanbase when you compare the difference between sales of *Spirits Having Flown* and *Living Eyes*.

In the end, the public appeared to be as conflicted about the album as its creators. *Living Eyes* debuted at number 65 on the *Billboard* Top LPs & Tape chart the week of 21 November; a far cry from the number four entry *Spirits Having Flown* made on the same tally in February 1979. Just four weeks later, the album stalled at a disappointing peak of number 41 and slid quickly south. In the UK, the album didn't climb past number 73. There was some small consolation that it landed in the top ten in Spain, Norway, the Netherlands, and Italy.

Given the mounting Gibb-averse sentiments of the mainstream media at the time, *Living Eyes* was, quite surprisingly, reasonably well received by many critics who sympathised with the brothers' daunting task of escaping the weight of their own massive commercial success. Many acquiesced to admitting The Bee Gees' vocal work remained top-notch, even if the arrangements lacked the adrenaline of their previous few efforts.

Demos for *Living Eyes* were created in early 1981, but much like the blueprints the collective made for *Spirits Having Flown*, they're just early, unfinished versions of the fully produced tracks without strings and a few other live instrument dubs. In some cases, the demos sound a bit cleaner and punchier than the mixes included on the released album.

The album's artwork appears to be a conscious effort to banish the often mocked 'white suits' imagery of *Saturday Night Fever*, which, if only the Gibbs knew it at the time, they would never shake. The front and inner photos were taken by Japanese photographer Minsei Tominaga as part of a shoot commissioned by TDK. The front cover shows the brothers in smart black evening wear. It appears the stylist couldn't quite convince Barry and Maurice to eschew their open shirts and glowing medallion and crucifix, respectively, but Robin's white silk scarf balances out the equation. Maurice is also seen wearing a fedora-adjacent hat in all the album's photos – a precursor to the look that would become his signature in a few years' time.

The front cover photo was taken at sunset on a terrace of what is believed to be Turtle Bay Towers, located at 310 East 46th Street on the east side of the New York City borough of Manhattan. The Towers are a pre-war structure originally built in 1920 as a printing factory. In 1979, they were converted to luxury residential units. Behind the brothers, looking slightly to the southwest, are the silhouettes of the Wells Fargo, Chrysler, and MetLife Buildings. The Turtle Bay neighbourhood in which the building is situated borders the East River and is also home to the world headquarters complex of the United Nations.

The inner gatefold photograph was taken on the grand Art Deco lobby staircase at Radio City Music Hall in midtown Manhattan. Again, the outfits are more sober, this time showing the brothers in woolly sweaters and tweed jackets.

The Gibbs are in the same attire on the back cover photograph, taken by The Bee Gees' personal photographer, Bob Sherman, posing next to a beautiful 1937 Packard Super Eight convertible sedan. The backdrop is still in New York, but much less urban, featuring the front of the historic Dairy Barn Complex at Caumsett State Historic Park Preserve on Lloyd Neck, Long Island, near one of Robin's homes.

The album was released at an interesting time for the music industry. A new format, the digital compact disc, was about to be launched – and it would soon revolutionise the music listener experience globally. *Living Eyes* was chosen to be the first album to be manufactured on CD for demonstration purposes, and this was seen on the BBC's science and technology programme *Tomorrow's World*. A photograph of The Bee Gees was also featured on the front cover of the inaugural issue of the

Compact Disc trade magazine, with Maurice holding a disc and a CD player, Barry a *Living Eyes* CD sleeve, and Robin the album's LP sleeve for size comparison.

In Japan, a special promotional record from the album was issued to DJs and record dealers. It featured six songs from the album, three on each side, and as a novelty, it played from the centre outwards.

'Living Eyes' (Barry Gibb, Robin Gibb, Maurice Gibb)

Recorded at Middle Ear, Miami Beach, between February and June 1981
Chart positions: Austria: 7, Belgium: 37, US: 45, West Germany: 58
The album's title track was released as the second single from the album on 30 October in the UK (it was held back until November in the US), backed with 'I Still Love You'.

It's an outstanding tune, melodically strong throughout with a killer bridge section – and it has no less than five key changes. Its lyrics, however, are as inscrutable as 'Holiday' or 'I Started A Joke', but references like 'my destiny that would arrive the moment you're born', 'I leave you heaven and the earth, I leave you never', and 'the soul and the magic of you' would suggest it might be a heart note to the Gibbs' children – quite possibly Travis Gibb, specifically, who had overcome many complications upon his arrival earlier in the year.

Considering his talent, Jeff Porcaro's drumming is inexplicably soft and tentative throughout the track, although it's possible he was instructed to play on top of the drum machine that was used in the song's demo. Some extra punch in the rhythm section certainly would have been welcome. Albhy Galuten plays the synthesiser, double-tracking Barry's vocal on the intro.

The promotional video, directed by Martin Pitts, was quite a departure from the cinematic motif he'd employed for the single's predecessor, 'He's A Liar': the Gibbs are dressed casually, playing and singing seated on stage in front of a group of children at Barry's son Stephen's school in Miami. There is a brief moment of levity near the end of the clip as the brothers and their young audience are showered with balloons and confetti, and the camera focuses on Maurice, who grins as he spits out bits of paper as they fall onto his face while trying to sing. The video debuted on the 4 December broadcast of *Solid Gold* in the US, with an introduction by Andy.

The single charted, but it performed slightly less well than 'He's A Liar'. It did the best in Austria, the only territory where it made the top ten, peaking at number seven. In other important countries that had previously given their material the warmest reception in recent years, it fared poorly. The US would become the most unforgiving market for them post-1979; 'Living Eyes' became the first Bee Gees single since 1974 to miss the top 40. Even more alarming was West Germany's showing – a country that had championed them so much in the past – where the single peaked at just number 58. In their native Britain, despite high-profile television exposure on the *Parkinson* chat show, it completely failed to chart.

'He's A Liar' (Barry Gibb, Robin Gibb, Maurice Gibb)

Recorded at Middle Ear, Miami Beach, horns recorded at Criteria Studios, Miami, between February and June 1981
Chart positions: Greece: 1, Italy: 5, Spain: 6, Belgium: 10, Netherlands: 12, France: 19, Austria: 30, US: 30, Canada: 33, Australia: 38, West Germany: 68, UK: 82

'He's A Liar' was chosen as the lead single from *Living Eyes* with an instrumental version as the B-side – a curious choice by RSO given the fact that The Bee Gees' ace was always their vocals and there were a number of options on the album that were good enough to be a flipside. The 12" single featured a slightly extended version of the A-side, which was later issued on a Japanese-only LP and CD called *Rare Collection*. As a curio for collectors, the Austrian edition of the single is the only record ever released credited to the 'Gibb Brothers' on the label.

'He's A Liar' is often discussed among fans and experts as a dreadful attempt to reintroduce The Bee Gees to radio and the record-buying public after a long hiatus – and as such a stark departure from the explosive singles that preceded it. Barry voiced a similar sentiment in a post-release interview with *Billboard*, claiming it was 'simply the wrong choice'. 'We originally felt the single should have been 'Living Eyes', but I don't want to put the blame on anyone's shoulders', he continued. "He's a Liar' was the choice of everyone involved'.

Instrumentally, the song has strength with Don Felder of The Eagles taking on the lead guitar line. Years later, Felder recalled that it was one of the most challenging session gigs he'd ever played, noting that Barry made him record at least ten separate takes of his part – undoubtedly so the production team could choose portions of each and edit them together to their liking. Steve Gadd turns in one of the better drumming performances on the album.

The track's lyrics offer a lot of powerful imagery, and Barry's lead vocal in his natural voice is a good reminder that it, too, was a robust instrument for those who were accustomed to hearing just his higher register by now. Barry's low growling of the title phrase on the chorus, which is resolved by a shrill '*ahh!*', detracts from the well-sung verses by adding an almost melodramatic musical theatre quality rather than making it sound like a serious contemporary rock song.

With The Bee Gees' recent legal tussle with Robert Stigwood and RSO barely in the rearview mirror, releasing a lead single titled 'He's A Liar' was provocative, to say the least. 'A few people thought it had something to do with Stigwood', Barry later said. 'It was wrongly timed. At another time, it could have been the right single. It doesn't reflect the rest of the album'.

An early demo of the song has Barry scat-singing most of the song to a synthesised rhythm track and piano, with only the title and the lyric 'and I should know' vocalised, demonstrating the brothers' frequent songwriting process of starting with a title and melody before other lyrics are wrapped around them.

The promotional video, also directed by Martin Pitts, illustrated the story in the lyrics with Maurice taking the lead role on camera. The parts where the brothers harmonise show them in profile, consciously dressed in black against a dark background to purposely exorcise the mythically white-suited icons of the *Fever* era. There are humorous elements to the video that hark back to their home movie-making days in Australia.

In terms of chart performance in the three most important world markets, the single did not fare well. In the US, it peaked at number 30 on the *Billboard* Hot 100 the week of 24 October, breaking their sterling streak of number one singles. In West Germany, it petered out at just number 68, and in the UK, it was a flop, not even making the all-important published top 75. The brothers must have been deeply disappointed.

Retrospectively asked about 'He's A Liar' for the liner notes of the *Tales From The Brothers Gibb: A History In Song* box set in 1990, Barry commented, 'This piece of work raises more questions than answers … '.

'Paradise' (Barry Gibb, Robin Gibb, Maurice Gibb)
Recorded at Middle Ear, Miami Beach, between February and June 1981
'Paradise' is a lush, three-verse song, and an excellent bridge provides a good mid-track lift. It was issued as a third single from the album but

received only a limited release in the Netherlands and Japan. The flipside was 'Nothing Could Be Good'. No money was invested in the promotion of the single, and no video was made to accompany the release. Bearing in mind that this was the new age of MTV, a single now had a much more difficult time gaining wide exposure without visual promotion. Needless to say, it failed – a great pity as it deserved to be heard by a wider audience.

'Don't Fall In Love With Me' (Barry Gibb, Robin Gibb, Maurice Gibb)
Recorded at Middle Ear, Miami Beach, horns recorded at Criteria Studios, Miami, between February and June 1981

A dramatic symphonic introduction, not dissimilar to the outro of Barbra Streisand's 'Make It Like A Memory', leads into a beautiful piano-led, Robin-fronted ballad, although it never achieves the heights expected. It follows a song form that's atypical for the Gibbs, front-loading the chorus with the verses following. The second pass of the chorus changes a few lyrics before a short bridge and then a repeat of the verse and chorus. Given Robin's state of affairs at the time, 'Don't Fall In Love With Me's sombre lyrics are almost certainly tied to his divorce from Molly.

Robin's son Spencer covered the song with a full orchestra for a 2017 tribute album, *The Gibb Collective – Please Don't Turn Out The Lights*, which included a series of covers of the brothers' songs by many of their children.

'Soldiers' (Barry Gibb, Robin Gibb, Maurice Gibb)
Recorded at Middle Ear, Miami Beach, between February and June 1981

"Soldiers' *killed* me', Albhy Galuten told the authors in late 2024. 'It was really, *really* good. I loved Jeff Porcaro's drumming on it. The feel is just incredible with these 7/8 bars – it's like it goes through glass'. It's the only time on *Living Eyes* that Barry uses his falsetto lead full throttle, and it may have been a good choice for a lead single as a transitional piece, employing his familiar high-register voice against a decidedly more rock-oriented background than their most recent hits.

Like other tracks on *Living Eyes*, 'Soldiers' has a stunningly good bridge section. Lyrically, and in classic Gibb fashion, there are a few interesting grammatical liberties taken – especially on lines like 'shower your love to me there' and 'for what are we living for?' But in contrast with the absolute power of Barry's vocal, those indiscretions fade to the background.

'I Still Love You' (Barry Gibb, Robin Gibb, Maurice Gibb)
Recorded at Middle Ear, Miami Beach, between February and June 1981
Another Robin-led ballad kicks off the second side of the album, which feels like a bit of a letdown after the peak energy of 'Soldiers'. While parts of the melody are somewhat reminiscent of 'Country Lanes' from *Main Course*, the chorus isn't nearly as memorable – and it repeats for almost a full two minutes of the track's four-and-a-half-minute length. Like 'Don't Fall In Love With Me', it's quite easy to make lyrical connections to Robin's divorce.

Session musician Chuck Kirkpatrick plays a sitar on the chorus. Kirkpatrick was a co-engineer on the album *Layla And Other Assorted Love Songs* for Eric Clapton's early 1970s band Derek and the Dominos, along with Karl Richardson and Criteria Recording Studios founder Mac Emerman. Its inclusion was perhaps a little nod to George Harrison, although the sound on this track is almost indiscernible from an electric guitar riff.

'Wildflower' (Barry Gibb, Robin Gibb, Maurice Gibb)
Recorded at Middle Ear, Miami Beach, between February and June 1981
The lovely Maurice-sung ballad 'Wildflower' is his first lead vocal on a Bee Gees record in almost a decade; he last turned in 'You Know It's For You' on *To Whom It May Concern*, although one could pedantically argue it had only been three years since he sang the opening line on 'Being For The Benefit Of Mr. Kite' on the *Sgt. Pepper's Lonely Hearts Club Band* soundtrack.

Maurice explained: 'When we first started writing it, each one of us was singing the lead, we were all singing together, and it just came out that this would be a nicer song for me'. However, he had plenty of support; Barry and Robin are in full-throated harmony on the bridges, and Barry's falsetto backing is heard throughout.

One could argue that Maurice would have been a better lead voice to feature more frequently on the album, as it had a more modern, neutral sound to fit a 1980s aesthetic, but that may not have landed well with his older brothers, who desired to be out in front.

Barry and Maurice's acoustic guitars provide a warm, comfortable backdrop, and they contrast well with Don Felder's restrained electric.

'Nothing Could Be Good' (Barry Gibb, Robin Gibb, Maurice Gibb, Albhy Galuten)
Recorded at Middle Ear, Miami Beach, between February and June 1981
'Nothing Could Be Good', written by the brothers and co-producer Albhy Galuten, was a late addition to the album. It's a piano-forward ballad with jazz overtones, and features Barry singing in a somewhat mannered natural voice.

Albhy told the authors in 2025: 'We wrote it together. As usual, Barry was mostly responsible for the lyrics and melody, and I for the chords, feel and structure, though we both had input in each other's domain – Barry more so than me'.

'Cryin' Every Day' (Barry Gibb, Robin Gibb, Maurice Gibb)
Recorded at Middle Ear, Miami Beach, between February and June 1981
Another obvious choice for a single passed over was this first glimpse of Robin's voice against synthesiser-driven Euro-pop. It would have been a refreshing change from the Barry-centric falsetto leads of the previous years, and it would have given a wider audience an opportunity to hear a Robin-led single that wasn't a ballad.

The arrangement boasts a Giorgio Moroder-style pulsating synthesiser and synth bass, and drums – plenty of them, with *three* drummers credited. One, however, wasn't an actual human; former Criteria Recording Studios engineer Seth Snyder had built a machine that played real drums triggered by an electric pulse, cleverly named Solly Noid (read: *solenoid*). Russ Kunkel and Jeff Porcaro provide support, supplying the cymbals and fills.

The bass and synthesiser on the track are curiously credited to 'Albhy Galuten and Sidney'. According to Albhy, 'Sidney' was the nickname the team gave to the new Synclavier that had been purchased for Middle Ear, a nod to the co-founder of New England Digital and co-inventor of the technology, Sydney Alonso.

The song was much more in tune with what was happening in popular music at the time than most of the rest of *Living Eyes*, but still with The Bee Gees' trademarks. Barry singing rhythmically with the cymbal fills on the bridges is a notable moment on the album, as is the gorgeous pseudo-church choir that the brothers emulate in the background. That could simply be replicated by a synthesiser these days, but this is undoubtedly multi-tracked Gibbs simply doing what they do best.

Upon further reflection, one wonders if 'Cryin' Every Day' is an evolution of the fast-paced synthesised track 'Cornerstone' that Dennis Bryon mentioned he'd struggled to play with during the final Bee Gees band sessions from late 1980.

'Be Who You Are' (Barry Gibb)

Recorded at Middle Ear, Miami Beach, horns recorded at Criteria Studios, Miami, and strings recorded at Media Sound, New York, between February and June 1981

'Be Who You Are' is the first song to appear on a Bee Gees album with writing credited solely to Barry since the four tracks he composed on his own for the 1973 album *Life In A Tin Can*.

The orchestral overture at the start of the track borrows pieces of melodies from other songs on the album (lines from 'Paradise', 'Wildflower', and 'Soldiers' are easily identifiable) before the song begins in earnest with Don Felder's capable electric guitar. It's an outstanding track; a song of encouragement and strength with a fine melody line and a showcase for Barry's vocal talents, his lead switching seamlessly between his full-blown, powerful chest voice, breathy tones, and falsetto.

Barry explained that it 'started out as a simple song' but they 'decided to write a reprise of the rest of the album, in other words, to incorporate some of the little melodies, like 'Living Eyes' within that reprise, done by a 40-piece orchestra, which has turned out real nice'.

October 1981 saw the beginning of promotional activity for the album, including a BBC interview with Paul Gambaccini. The recording was subsequently repurposed by RSO Records for a US promotional interview LP intended for syndication across radio stations.

The 31 October edition of *Record Mirror* featured an article penned by British journalist Chas De Whalley. The piece was supposed to include a full interview with Barry, until it was cut prematurely short:

Barry Gibb of The Bee Gees has just thrown an almighty wobbler and hung up on me. It may be 85 degrees out there on the street in Florida, but the mercury is rising fast under the collar of the elder Bee Gee. And it would seem to be all my fault. In an effort, you see, to get the properly balanced story you expect in your *Record Mirror*, I hazarded the guess that despite – or maybe even because of – The Bee Gees' worldwide success, some people in Britain didn't take New Zealand's favourite sons too seriously. And then I ventured the opinion of one notable *Record Mirror* scriber, namely that The Bee Gees' music was meaningless pap.

And did Mr. Gibb senior go through the roof? You're telling me, he did.

'That's bullshit!' he blustered. 'And you can quote me on that! Our songs mean a lot more than your avant-garde or new wave things. You've just got to listen to them properly. You've been listening to those 'Meaningless Songs' guys, haven't you?'

You mean The Hee Bee Gee Bees, I suggested. But Barry Gibb wasn't hanging around. We were talking on the telephone, and it would have taken two seconds for my words to reach his ears via the satellite. But he wasn't waiting for them. 'If you think we mind being copied, then you're wrong, too. Imitation is the best form of flattery, and I think Kenny Everett did the best spoof of us ever. But when it gets offensive, that's when you can throw it out of the window. If you think our songs are meaningless pap, then so are Paul McCartney's. I don't want to talk to a magazine that thinks The Bee Gees are meaningless pap'.

Yeah, but wait, what I was trying to say was…

Too late. Thousands of miles away in a dreamhouse in Biscayne Bay, Miami, Florida, a busy man who has barely been up an hour and has the dubious prospect of an afternoon of business meetings before him just slammed the phone down. Probably because he reckons he doesn't need the brain damage he believes a conversation with me offers. And all I can think is I'm glad I wasn't interviewing him face-to-face because he might easily have taken a swing at me. And all because I did a rather silly thing and voiced somebody else's opinion before voicing my own. I shall not do that again.

With Barry's abrupt departure from the conversation – a preview of what would be an even more infamous walkout by the eldest Gibb some 16 years later whilst the brothers were guests on *Clive Anderson All Talk* – one could possibly accuse him of taking himself a little too seriously, although De Whalley did offer a mea culpa mid-piece that he'd apparently not had enough time to intently listen to *Living Eyes* to ask him better questions about the songs and potentially avoid the blowup. However, at the end of the article, De Whalley clapped back:

> I'm dazed and confused. What do you think? Is Barry Gibb simply an over-successful, egotistic and ageing symbol of everything that's bad about AOR rock? Or beneath those smooth features that stare suavely from the album covers do you reckon there beats the brain of a true artist who resents doubts cast on his integrity?

Still, De Whalley interjects several compliments about the quality of *Living Eyes*, and penned an entirely separate review of the album in the same issue (entitled 'Prime Beef Gees') in which he calls the record 'a winner' that boasts 'a bunch of exquisite melodies with so much colour and harmony to them'.

On 2 November, the brothers appeared on the American talk show *Donahue*, presented by veteran media personality Phil Donahue and recorded at the studios of WGN-TV in Chicago. In addition to an interview with Donahue himself, the format allowed for questions from audience members, interspersed with acoustic performances of 'Bye Bye Blackbird', 'Lollipop', 'New York Mining Disaster 1941', 'How Can You Mend A Broken Heart', 'Lonely Days', and 'Stayin' Alive'.

On 26 November, The Bee Gees returned to their childhood home in the Manchester suburb of Chorlton-cum-Hardy. For Barry, Robin, and Maurice, it was a loving trip down memory lane. Their first stop was 51 Keppel Road, the best known of their many childhood homes. The house was owned at the time by 74-year-old Peter Bartosiewicz, a Polish immigrant who came to Britain with the Free Polish forces. He welcomed the brothers inside, although he admitted he had never heard of The Bee Gees.

The visit stirred up many memories. The parlour, once their parents' bedroom, remained much the same. The passage alcove that had once been their kitchen was still there, and their old bedroom at the back of the house had now become home to Mr. Bartosiewicz's pet pigeon. Barry reflected, 'We all slept in here. Things were hard in those days, so the three of us shared a double bed while our sister Lesley had her own single bed'.

As they strolled through the back alleys and cobbled streets, they encountered many changes. The old fish and chip shop had become a Chinese takeaway, and the hut they accidentally set on fire as children had been replaced by a modern factory. The Gaumont Cinema, where they had made their first public performance, had been converted into a funeral parlour. Maurice, with his trademark sense of humour, quipped, 'I wonder if that's significant!?'.

The visit continued at Oswald Road School, where they reminisced about their youthful mischief; stolen kisses behind the sheds, learning 'nothing in the art class', and the 'messing about on the way home'. Maurice, looking at the children playing, mused, 'I can see myself in some of these kids'.

Despite their fame, The Bee Gees' bond with their childhood home remained strong. 'It was here that we decided what we wanted to do', Barry said. 'We knew we wanted to sing. We even ran off to the BBC studios in Manchester as kids and asked the doorman for an audition'.

Their visit concluded with a heartwarming moment when Maureen Nicholls, a former neighbour, recognised them. Seeing them for the first time in 23 years, she cheerfully asked, 'It's been a long time! How are things going with you?' Robin, with a shy smile, responded, 'Well, we're millionaires now'.

While in Manchester, the brothers also reunited with two old school friends, Kenny Horrocks and Paul Frost. In late 1957, they had formed The Rattlesnakes, a skiffle group that marked The Bee Gees' first step into performing. Barry played guitar and sang, Robin and Maurice provided backing vocals, while Paul played drums and Kenny took up the tea-chest bass. One story, often retold with varying details, recalls how they were due to mime to a record at the local Gaumont cinema. On the way to the theatre, the fragile shellac 78rpm disc they intended to use was accidentally dropped and broke. With no backing left, the boys had no choice but to sing for real, and in doing so revealed the harmonies that would become their trademark.

Their schedule in Manchester also included an official industry record launch at the Piccadilly Hotel and an appearance on the *Mike Sweeney Show* on Piccadilly Radio, where they spoke about their memories of the city and their new album. He remembered the encounter vividly: 'I hadn't even been told the band were coming in. The studio door just opened and in walked The Bee Gees – and I only realised when they sat down in front of me. At that exact moment I'd been on air, in the middle of this daft debate about my mam making me cold toast for school, wrapped in greaseproof paper – whether you buttered it hot and let it go cold, or wait and butter it after'.

'Robin Gibb looked at me and said, 'Was that live?", Sweeney continues. 'I said, 'Yeah, of course'. And he just smiled and said, 'Our mam used to do that for us'. It was my first ever interview – completely unannounced – and there I was, talking about cold toast to what turned out to be an audience of about a million listeners. One of those surreal moments you never forget'.

In the 28 November issue of Billboard, Barry appeared eager to explain why Living Eyes had not achieved the commercial success everyone had hoped for, suggesting the significant time gap between Spirits Having Flown and the new album was at least partly responsible for the flub. 'I hoped that the Streisand album would be treated as our last album because to us it was our last project. We figured that would take care of the time in between. But to the rest of the industry, maybe it wasn't'.

Barry also spoke to the pressure he and his brothers had been under to recapture their stratospheric *Saturday Night Fever* heights, which had certainly set an impossibly high bar for a transitional album like *Living Eyes*. 'As good as you are and as hard as you work, you can't always pull it off'.

While the making of *Living Eyes* was turbulent for the brothers and their co-producers, Barry seemed confident the group would push forward together, citing the possibility of their next studio album and final contractual obligation to RSO arriving in 1983 with a world tour to support it. 'The element of The Bee Gees' success is to never give up. That's the element that destroys groups. Ten years ago, we stopped working and didn't have hits. We sat on our laurels. What happened then was a great education for us. Our enthusiasm and drive are still there. We feel the same way about a hit today as we did 12 years ago. We are avid fans of music and charts'.

Of course, there would be no de facto Bee Gees album released for years; however, the article did make mention of planned solo projects for each of the brothers, the potential of them contributing music to another soundtrack, as well as Barry possibly producing an album for singer Dionne Warwick – all of which would happen over the next three years.

Following the success of *Saturday Night Fever* and *Grease*, Robert Stigwood was increasingly involved in film projects, and in 1981, he acquired the rights through Paramount Pictures to develop a cinematic version of Andrew Lloyd Webber and Tim Rice's musical *Evita*. Director Ken Russell was initially attached, and by November 1981, screen tests were reportedly being held at Elstree Studios for the role of Eva Perón. Amid the flurry of casting speculation, Barry's name surfaced as a possible candidate for the role of Che Guevara, alongside other pop stars such as Peter Gabriel, Adam Ant, and Elton John. On 17 November, *The Sun* reported that Barry was 'just days away from signing the contract which will have him making his big screen debut'. No official announcement, contract, or credited screen test ever confirmed his involvement, yet the rumour persisted, largely due to Stigwood's habit of casting musicians in cinematic roles. The project stalled by 1982, and Russell's version of the film never moved into production.

Commenting on his being perennially considered for major motion picture roles at a fan gathering in Miami in November 1988, Barry said: 'Of the film offers that I've had – I've had dozens – and I've never done one of them. That should tell you what state the film business is. In fact, I was supposed to do *Miami Vice* three times. What people do is they offer you something and then they never follow through'.

The Evita film would eventually be made in 1996, directed by Alan Parker, starring Madonna as Eva Perón and Antonio Banderas as Che Guevara. At the time, however, Barry firmly denied press reports linking him to the project, insisting during an interview with Roger Scott, that: 'There's no truth in that. The newspaper that printed it didn't even speak to me - they don't know anything about it - it's mere presumption on their part. There have been discussions and approaches made, but I've never even discussed the project with anyone'.

The interview was again part of the promotional push for the new album and took place at Capital Radio. The one-hour live broadcast segment featured a wide-ranging set of live studio performances that showcased both their own catalogue and a couple of their key influences. They sang 'Massachusetts', 'Words', 'I've Gotta Get A Message To You', 'Jive Talkin'', 'How Can You Mend A Broken Heart', 'New York Mining Disaster 1941', and 'The Three Kisses Of Love', alongside covers of 'Bye Bye Love' (the first hit for the Everly Brothers in 1957) and 'Save Your Heart For Me' (a US top ten hit for Gary Lewis & The Playboys in 1965), as well as 'Paradise' and 'Stayin' Alive'.

On 4 December, BBC Radio 1 listeners were treated to a special edition of *Round Table* with host Richard Skinner. The programme, known for featuring guest artists reviewing the latest record releases, welcomed The Bee Gees to share their insights and opinions on a selection of contemporary tracks.

They brought their seasoned ears and distinct musical sensibilities to the discussion, weighing in on a diverse lineup of songs from various genres and artists. The eclectic playlist included emerging new wave sounds, classic rock, R&B-infused tracks, and festive holiday tunes: Altered Images' 'I Could Be Happy'; Rush's 'Closer To The Heart'; Davis Gamson's 'Sugar Sugar'; Bruce Springsteen's 'Santa Claus Is Coming To Town'; Chic's 'Burn Hard'; Maria La Palma's 'Jerolas'; The Gibson Brothers' 'Quartier Latin'; Nona Hendryx's 'It's A Holiday'; B. E. F. featuring Tina Turner's 'Ball Of Confusion'; Tenpole Tudor's 'Wunderbar'; The Jacksons' 'Things I Do For You'; and Nils Lofgren's 'I Go To Pieces'.

Richard Skinner wisely saved Status Quid's 'Boring Song' for last. The track, released as a single, was actually The Hee Bee Gee Bees under another pseudonym. Addressing the parody, Skinner prompted discussion on whether The Bee Gees found it amusing: 'You know that these fellers did the famous Hee Bee Gee Bees send up? So, let's talk about that. Did you find that amusing?' Barry responded:

I think it's important that you have a sense of humour. I think it's great to have someone send you up and all that business – I think that's very flattering. When I said earlier, 'Oh, great', I thought you were going to introduce Status Quo's new single ['Rock 'N' Roll'], which I love. This, however – we're not talking about a legit group. But let's at least say that when a group like The Hee Bee Gee Bees go out of their way to send somebody up, I think they ought to send people up and be glad of doing that, instead of saying things like 'Boring Song'. All I can say is that Status Quo would not be flattered – that is almost an attack, and it makes you feel very upset because it's your life, and when somebody says boring songs as a send up, well, you think, 'My God, is that the general opinion?' – because that's what they're doing – everything they consider to be the general opinion. And when they put ours out, it was called 'Meaningless Songs' – two points for originality, boys! What I'm saying is that when they say things like meaningless songs or boring songs, that upsets the artist. And I think if it's their aim – it upset me – I don't know if it upset the group, and it upset me because my life is writing songs, and I don't care to have them call them a meaningless song. And I don't think Status Quo feel too good about it, either. The sense of humour is great, but I don't think you ought to attack the group.

After seemingly friendly and polite thanks and farewells, Skinner wrapped up the show with an introduction to *The Andy Peebles Show*, which followed. Peebles adopted a northern accent and introduced The Bee Gees performing a live, acoustic performance of 'Massachusetts'.

The Bee Gees closed out the year with a series of UK radio and television appearances, including a prime-time spot on *Nationwide*, the BBC's flagship current affairs television programme, broadcast in the early evening following the news, where they were interviewed by Fran Morrison.

Of greatest note, however, was the 19 December airing of *Parkinson* on BBC1, guesting with Elaine Paige, who had recorded the Gibbs' song 'Secrets' the year before. The brothers sat with Michael Parkinson for a 25-minute interview segment, with banter interspersed by an a cappella performance of 'Lollipop', which they had sung regularly as young performers. Thrillingly, they also sang short, but excellent, acoustic versions of their early Australian singles 'The Three Kisses Of Love' and 'Wine And Women', followed by 'New York Mining Disaster 1941' and 'Massachusetts'. With the Christmas season imminent, the show wrapped with The Bee Gees singing a rendition of 'Silent Night' over the closing credits.

On 29 December, Barry was seen on BBC1's *Pop Quiz*, hosted by presenter Mike Read. The two-team panel consisted of singer David Grant of Linx, Status Quo's Rick Parfitt, and singer Cliff Richard serving as captain, versus Barry, presenter and writer Paula Yates, and captain and Ultravox lead singer Midge Ure. Singer-songwriter and Electric Light Orchestra co-founder Roy Wood joined the episode as a special guest.

1982

'The 32nd annual Sanremo Music Festival was held between 28 and 30 January and was transmitted through the Eurovision network by RAIUNO, the Italian state-owned television company. Apart from the Italian artists competing in the song contest, a number of international acts also performed, including Donovan, America, Gloria Gaynor, Van Halen, Daryl Hall and John Oates, Stray Cats, Marianne Faithfull, and the Village People. Rockers Kiss appeared via a satellite link-up with New York, and Maurice did likewise from Las Vegas.

The Bee Gees were scheduled to perform 'He's A Liar' and accept awards as a group, but according to Italian newspaper reports, Barry went home to Miami with a bad back, and Robin went back to his house in New York because of an accident. Maurice explained: 'I'm alone because my two brothers aren't feeling too well – they're in Miami, and New York, so I'm in Las Vegas on holiday, so I wouldn't have missed this for the world – I'm glad I'm here'.

Rather than being formally presented with the awards, the presenter casually handed him the *Telgatto Di TV Sorrisi E Canzoni* award to The Bee Gees as the most popular group of the decade and did similarly with a gold record award for *Living Eyes* from PolyGram. As he didn't have his brothers to perform with him, Maurice took the opportunity to deliver a solo rendition of 'Wildflower' with a backing track.

In early 1982, a Norwegian newspaper reported that Agnetha Fältskog of ABBA was on the verge of a collaboration with Barry. Inspired by Barry's production of Barbra Streisand's *Guilty*, Agnetha saw the opportunity to further her solo ambitions. Stig Anderson, ABBA's manager, explained, 'The girls in ABBA have a greater need than the boys to present themselves on a solo album. Remember, both girls started out as solo artists, and their new solo albums help to further develop their talent'. However, Anderson also emphasised the importance of keeping the solo projects distinct from ABBA's signature sound. 'In order to present music that is not ABBA in miniature, we deliberately choose to avoid Björn Ulvaeus and Benny Andersson as producers'.

The planned collaboration between Agnetha and Barry was a bold step in this direction, with Anderson himself encouraging the endeavour. 'Both Barry and Agnetha hope this will work out', he shared, noting that only Barry's potential film commitments posed a risk to the partnership. However, as the discussions progressed, logistical challenges emerged. Barry, accustomed to working in his own Miami studio, was insistent on recording there. Agnetha, deeply rooted in Sweden, was reluctant to leave her home country for an extended period. The impasse proved insurmountable, and the collaboration ultimately, and sadly, fell through.

A *Billboard* article from 20 March revealed The Bee Gees were among the first musicians to own the Synclavier II, a groundbreaking digital music system created by New England Digital. With a price tag of $13,750 (close to $50,000 adjusted for inflation in 2026 terms), the Synclavier II combined a real-time synthesiser with a 16-track digital recorder. It allowed musicians to sample, modify, and store audio digitally, create new sounds, mimic traditional instruments and even print musical scores. These capabilities offered a level of creative control that was revolutionary for its time. Other notable early purchasers included Oscar Peterson, Leon Huff, Pat Metheny, and Neil Young.

In March, Barry was announced as the choice for the role of Lord Byron in a forthcoming film about the English Romantic poet and revolutionary. His casting came as a surprise to fans and the entertainment world alike. However, the film's producers, Mikola and Elizabeth Shevchek, believed they had found something unique in him – a connection and a kindred spirit they felt mirrored Byron's own.

'Barry's own life kind of parallels Byron's', noted Tom Rosa, the film's screenwriter. 'Byron was followed in his escapades, his adventures in the Italian and Greek revolutions and in his writing by his contemporaries. Keats and the others were groupies, in a sense. Barry and Byron were contemporary heroes in their different time periods'. Barry, who had never before acted in a dramatic role, was intrigued by the challenge. This wouldn't be his first time on a movie set – he had appeared with his brothers in *Sgt. Pepper's Lonely Hearts Club Band*, a film in which The Bee Gees sang Beatles songs. But *Lord Byron* was to be his first foray into a serious, historical portrayal.

To the Shevcheks, Barry was more than just an actor for the part – he was the very essence of Byron they hoped to capture. The filmmakers designed the project around Barry himself, even granting him script approval – a rare move that underscored their faith in him. It was an opportunity that demonstrated the producers' commitment to the project and their willingness to trust Barry's creative vision, despite his lack of prior acting experience. Speaking to *The Daily Star*, Barry said:

Now that I have landed my first big straight acting role in a film, I want to make sure I can act. So, I am going to learn the business from scratch. I don't have any illusions about it. I know I have the potential, but it is up to me to prove I can do it by the time the cameras start rolling.

Mikola Shevchek, who helmed the project alongside his wife, had made a name for himself in film, having graduated from UCLA Film School and the American Film Institute. He built his career through work in both the American and Japanese film industries, producing and directing films and documentaries. Shevchek's experience working with The Bee Gees previously, particularly on the commercial side with TDK tapes during the recording of *Living Eyes*, gave him insight into Barry's character and potential for the role of Byron.

But the story of Barry Gibb as Lord Byron would end as a fascinating 'what if' rather than a finished film. By August 1982, production on the film was postponed until 1983 – a delay that clashed with Barry's full schedule, ultimately forcing him to pull out. But, also, as Barry explained: 'The Lord Byron film was on the cards for a solid year. There was $200,000 in advance that went into my account to do the part. Everything was there, and then in the last three months, the whole deal fell apart. The producers ran out of money. All these different games went on'.

It was disappointing for both Barry and the Shevcheks, who had high hopes for the project. Barry's music commitments took priority, and the opportunity to portray the fiery Romantic hero slipped away.

A small group of songs from early 1982 points to a parallel strand of writing activity by the Gibb brothers, separate from their work for Dionne Warwick and likely intended for an as-yet unidentified project. 'My World (In The Palm Of Your Hands)' and 'Human Being' both date from March 1982, according to their US copyright registrations, placing them in the same creative period as the songs written for Dionne Warwick, though evidently intended for a different project. The former is a Robin and Maurice composition, while the latter brings Barry into the fold – albeit with his name listed last on the registration, which hints that this may have begun as a primarily Robin and Maurice undertaking with Barry contributing more marginally rather than acting as a principal collaborator.

There has been speculation that these songs were recorded with another Jimmy Ruffin project in mind, though 'Human Being', in particular, feels ill-suited to his style. Instead, it points toward an early Europop sound – the synthesiser-led successor to disco – which aligns far more naturally with Robin's cooler vocal approach and Maurice's keyboard-driven arrangements. It's a direction they would soon pursue more fully on Robin's 1983 solo album. A third song, 'Love Is Just A Calling Card', also written by Robin and Maurice, has no confirmed creation date, but is stylistically close to 'Human Being' and would have sat comfortably alongside that later material.

On the morning of 6 April, New Yorkers awoke to an unseasonal blizzard that blanketed the city in snow. Streets were nearly impassable, and even seasoned New Yorkers were taken aback by the intensity of this late-season winter onslaught. Central Park recorded a remarkable 9.6 inches (24.4 cm) of snow, and temperatures in the city plunged to 21°F (-6°C), a truly rare phenomenon for the month of budding blooms.

In the midst of this unexpected wintry scene, a visitor from much warmer climes was trying to adjust to the icy surprise. Maurice, having just arrived in New York City from the warmth of Florida, stepped into the storm with his wife, Yvonne. According to the *New York Daily News*, Maurice looked up at the snow swirling around them, shook his head and turned to Yvonne with a laugh, 'I told you we should have brought along some warm clothing!'

Maurice had come to New York to make a guest appearance on the long-running CBS soap opera *The Guiding Light*. Yet even his anticipation of the new role did not fully prepare him for the cold. 'I left 85 degrees for this?' he joked. 'All I have is a light suit jacket. I guess we may have to go over to Macy's to get some warm outfits or something'. His stint on *The Guiding Light* was broadcast on 7 May. He made a brief but memorable 15-minute cameo where he appeared as himself, alongside regular cast members Gregory Beecroft as Tony Reardon, Tom Nielsen as Floyd Parker, Carol Ann Clark as Lesley Ann Monroe, and Robert Newman as Josh Lewis. Reflecting on his experience, Maurice shared his excitement, saying, 'I loved it. I'd never done anything like this before, and it's a lot of fun'.

For Maurice, the snowy backdrop of New York offered an ironic yet timely inspiration for his work. While his brief foray into drama unfolded amid wintry conditions, his musical endeavours remained active. He revealed that he and his brothers were collaborating on nine new songs for Dionne Warwick's upcoming album, with Barry leading the production. Maurice's creativity didn't stop there; he shared with the

Daily News that he was also working on the score for a unique television adaptation of *A Christmas Carol*, which he initially understood to involve puppets – a detail that piqued his interest. However, he later discovered the project was actually planned as a traditionally animated, or 'cel animation', film, produced by Burbank Films Australia.

Thinking about a Christmas project in April might seem unusual to most, but Maurice's boundless creativity kept him constantly open to inspiration, and with the city streets blanketed in snow, he had all the reminders he needed of winter's grip. From copyright registrations, however, it would appear that Maurice only completed one piece of music for the film, an instrumental titled 'Spirit Of The Snow', and so, *A Christmas Carol* would ultimately take a different musical direction.

The film was designed to reach a wide television audience in Australia and brought a new interpretation of Dickens' 1843 classic tale of redemption. It premiered on 22 December on the Australian Nine Network. For the music, the producers ultimately turned to composer Neil Thurgate, who crafted the score, which was conducted by Billy Burton.

The track 'Heart (Stop Beating In Time)' was written by Barry, Robin, and Maurice during the sessions for *Living Eyes*. Although The Bee Gees themselves never released the track, they did record it in demo form with Barry singing the lead vocal in falsetto. It's a complex ballad with a tricky time signature and multiple key changes that does bear some melodic similarity to 'Living Eyes'.

It found a new life when British artist Leo Sayer included it as the opening track on his album *World Radio*, which was produced by Arif Mardin. It was released on 14 May and reached number 30 on the UK album charts. Sayer later released 'Heart (Stop Beating In Time)' as the second single from the album, with UK listeners getting the single on 28 May via Chrysalis Records. Notably, it was also issued as a special 7" picture disc in the UK, offering fans a collectible format. To promote 'Heart (Stop Beating In Time)', Leo Sayer made several television appearances that brought the song wider recognition. He performed on *The Cannon & Ball Show* on 12 June and delivered a live vocal performance on *Top Of The Pops* on BBC1 on 24 June, which was repeated on 15 July. The single reached number 22 on the UK charts and achieved moderate international success, peaking at 71 in Australia and its best placing of number 17 in Ireland. Leo had been told the song was written specifically for him, but when Canadian singer Véronique Béliveau recorded it in 1984 with French lyrics as 'Please (Dis-Moi C'que

Tu As)' on her album *Transit*, she was informed it had originally been intended for Andy Gibb. Sayer's voice, however, is a perfect fit, and he handles the challenging melody with gusto.

'Heart (Stop Beating In Time)' has also been covered by a number of other artists. Marilyn McCoo released it as a single in November 1983 and included it on her unsurprisingly titled album *Solid Gold*. American R&B singer Stevie Woods released his version as the opening track on his album *Attitude* in November 1983, and also as a single in April 1984. Also in 1984, Bruce Murray, brother of Canadian songstress Anne Murray, recorded a version for his album *Two Hearts*. Dutch singer Josephine Hoenjet from Voerendaal in the Netherlands, who performed under her first name only, released her version as a single in 1985.

Bee Gees Greatest Volume 1 – 1967-1974 (1982)

Side One: 1. 'New York Mining Disaster 1941' 2. 'To Love Somebody' 3. 'Massachusetts' 4. 'World' 5. 'Words' 6. 'I've Gotta Get A Message To You' 7. 'Idea'
Side Two: 1. 'I Started A Joke' 2. 'Melody Fair' 3. 'First Of May' 4. 'Saved By The Bell' 5. 'Sun In My Morning' 6. 'The Lord' 7. 'I.O.I.O.'
Side Three: 1. 'In The Morning' 2. 'Lonely Days' 3. 'Lay It On Me' 4. 'How Can You Mend A Broken Heart' 5. 'Israel' 6. 'My World' 7. 'Sea Of Smiling Faces'
Side Four: 1. 'Saw A New Morning' 2. 'Wouldn't I Be Someone' 3. 'King And Country' 4. 'Give A Hand, Take A Hand 5. 'It Doesn't Matter Much To Me' 6. 'Throw A Penny'

Bee Gees' Greatest Volume 1 – 1967-1974, a double album released exclusively in the former Republic of West Germany in June 1982, presents a mix of the group's early hits, some deep cuts, and a few lesser-known B-sides showcasing the Gibbs' musical evolution from 1967 to 1974. While it falls short of a conventional greatest hits compilation, this collection, curated by Norbert Lippe, offers a distinctive look at The Bee Gees' diverse output, capturing both their chart-topping singles and a few hidden gems from this period.

The album opens on side one with early classics like 'New York Mining Disaster 1941' and 'To Love Somebody', both of which established The Bee Gees as songwriters capable of tackling both storytelling and emotive ballads. Tracks like 'Massachusetts' and 'Words' add to the nostalgic appeal, and the inclusion of 'I've Gotta Get A

Message To You' emphasises the band's early lyrical themes of longing and heartbreak.

As the album progresses, we encounter 'Melody Fair', 'Saved By The Bell' and the lesser-known 'Sun In My Morning' on side two. Deep cuts like 'Lay It On Me', 'Israel', and 'Sea Of Smiling Faces' feature on side three, while 'King And Country' (from their unreleased 1973 studio album *A Kick In The Head Is Worth Eight In The Pants*), 'Wouldn't I Be Someone', and 'Throw A Penny' on side four add depth. Notably, some of these tracks were originally single A- or B-sides in other territories. A hype flash on the cover promises 'never released on an album' – a somewhat sweeping claim which is not entirely true, unless it comes with the caveat that this applies only to West Germany.

The album cover was an inverse of 1979's *Bee Gees Greatest* artwork, with a purple background and the roundel logo design with a white background. Inside the gatefold, black-and-white photos from the band's early years through to 1974 capture the visual history of The Bee Gees, while Norbert Lippe's sleeve notes provide context.

During the Cold War, music behind the Iron Curtain was tightly controlled by state-run record labels. These labels were more than just commercial enterprises – they were tools of cultural policy. At the heart of this network was the Soviet Union's Melodiya, founded in 1964 as the state-owned monopoly for music production and distribution. It became the primary source of recorded music for millions across the USSR.

Melodiya's catalogue spanned classical music, folk and Soviet pop, but also included select Western artists carefully curated to align with ideological guidelines. When Eric Clapton's *Slowhand* album was released, for example, the song 'Cocaine' was omitted to align with state censorship policies.

Among the rare Western acts granted this semi-official exposure were The Bee Gees. Although the group's global popularity surged in the 1970s, Soviet music fans had limited access to their music. July 1982 marked a milestone when *Spirits Having Flown* was released in the Soviet Union – only the second Bee Gees album to appear there (following *Main Course* in 1977), although it was officially untitled.

Before full albums were available in the USSR, Bee Gees songs were only accessible on more modest and ephemeral formats. In 1975, an EP featuring 'To Love Somebody', 'New York Mining Disaster 1941', 'Holiday' and 'I Can't See Nobody' was released with several label colour variations, which often came from the pressing plants: Aprelevka, Leningrad, Riga, Tashkent, and Tbilisi, which used different inks and papers. Aprelevka typically pressed pink or cream labels, while Leningrad and Riga sometimes used blue, green, or red. By the mid-1970s, with Melodiya pushing mass production, such inconsistencies became normal. The EP was repressed in 1980 and 1982, even appearing as a special red vinyl variant.

The same four tracks were circulated on a flexi-disc through *Krugozor*, a hugely popular literary and musical magazine that focused on documentaries, history, classical, and contemporary art, literature and music (including that from Western countries). It was in immense demand by young Soviet consumers, who would form long waiting lines in stores and kiosks during release days. Each magazine contained up to six blue 33 RPM double-sided flexi-discs.

Beyond the USSR, other Eastern Bloc countries maintained similar models. East Germany's Amiga label, Poland's Tonpress, Czechoslovakia's Supraphon, Hungary's Hungaroton, and Bulgaria's Balkanton all released records by The Bee Gees and played pivotal roles in shaping their nations' soundscapes. These labels, despite operating under censorship, became unlikely preservers of both national culture and a filtered window into Western artistry.

Meanwhile, the brothers continued to write and produce for other artists outside of The Bee Gees, and their next project would generate another round of international hits.

Heartbreaker – Dionne Warwick (1982)

Personnel:
Dionne Warwick: vocal
Barry Gibb: vocal, acoustic guitar
Steve Gadd: drums
Richard Tee: piano
George Bitzer: piano, synthesiser
Albhy Galuten: piano, synthesiser
Tim Renwick: guitar
George Terry: guitar
George Perry: bass
Joe Lala: percussion
Dennis Bryon: percussion
Daniel Ben Zebulon: percussion

Anita Lopez: percussion
Gary Brown: saxophone
The Boneroo Horns: Peter Graves, Brett Murphey, Whit Sidener, Dan
Bonsanti, Neal Bonsanti, Ken Faulk
String arrangements: Barry Gibb, Albhy Galuten
String conductor: Albhy Galuten
Horns arranged by Barry Gibb, Albhy Galuten
Engineers: Karl Richardson, Dale Peterson, Neal Kent, Sam Taylor-Porter,
Andy Hoffman, Nicky Kalliongis, Mike Fuller
Producers: Barry Gibb, Albhy Galuten, Karl Richardson
Recorded at Middle Ear, Miami Beach, and Mediasound Studios, New York,
about April and May 1982
Release dates: UK: October 1982, US: 28 September 1982
Chart positions: Norway: 1, Sweden: 2, UK: 3, Netherlands: 5, Finland: 9,
Austria: 13, Australia: 14, West Germany: 18, US: 25, New Zealand: 32
Gold certification: Netherlands, US
Platinum certification: UK

The Gibb-Galuten-Richardson production team followed the massive
success of their Barbra Streisand collaboration by producing an album
for Dionne Warwick, a singer already renowned for her earlier hits
written by Hal David and Burt Bacharach.

Like The Bee Gees, Warwick began her singing career at a young
age, and by 1982, her remarkable journey had already spanned two
decades. She initially performed with her family's vocal gospel group,
The Drinkard Singers, and then with sister Dee Dee in The
Gospelaires. She later pursued music studies at The Hartt College of
Music, funding her education through regular session work. In 1960,
while recording for American soul outfit The Drifters, she caught the
attention of Brill Building composer and producer Burt Bacharach,
who asked her to sing demos for songs he was writing with his
partner Hal David. This marked the beginning of a long-lasting
professional relationship. Bacharach and David later presented one of
her demos to Scepter Records, whose president, Florence Greenberg,
turned down the song but signed Warwick, kickstarting her 12-year
tenure with the label.

For *Heartbreaker*, Warwick's 23rd studio effort, the production team
employed a similar approach to their previous work with Streisand.
Songwriting was a mix of contributions from the three Gibb brothers

and collaborations between Barry and Albhy Galuten. Once again, Barry played rhythm guitar and provided backing vocals alongside an impressive list of hired session hands.

The original plan for the album didn't solely involve Dionne Warwick. Instead, the production team had envisaged a collaborative album featuring three prominent female singers: Gladys Knight, Dionne Warwick, and Jessica Cleaves, known for her work with Earth, Wind & Fire. The concept was to bring together artists with distinct vocal ranges – low (Knight), medium (Warwick) and high (Cleaves) – creating opportunities for duets and trio performances that would provide a fresh, creative challenge for the songwriters.

However, after Barry had a discussion with the founder and president of Arista Records, Clive Davis, the project shifted direction. Barry recalled in a BBC Radio 2 interview with Gary Barlow in 2020:

[Clive] came to see me in Miami. I'd never been to see him. I knew of him – of course, the whole business knew of him – but I'd never met him. He came to see me in Miami, and it was after the *Guilty* album, and he said, 'Would you do an album for someone with us?', and I said, 'Well, have you got a list of the artists?' That's how that came about. So, he gave me a list of all the artists, and I went down the list. Linda and I always loved the *Freewheelin'* album, and *Valley Of The Dolls*, and all those incredible songs. And I said, 'Dionne Warwick – Dionne Warwick, no question'.

Presenter Barlow knew Davis of old and related further on the story: 'Clive said, 'I'll send her down to Miami'. And you said, 'No, no, no, no, she's the lady – I'm going to Vegas to record her'. And he said, 'And that's the kind of man Barry Gibb is". Caught a little off guard by the compliment, Barry stumbled a little before confirming:

Well, that's correct. I mean, I didn't think that she should come and function in that way. I thought it was our job to go see her because we're making the record – we're the producers – and we had to show her that respect. And that was a pleasure. She was performing in Vegas, and we didn't want to interrupt that schedule or her life, so we said we'll go there and make it work. We're writing songs in the MGM ballroom when there are no seats, so there's this giant sort of room with a piano.

Barry, Robin, and Maurice wrote seven songs for the project, but two of them, 'Broken Bottles' and 'Oceans And Rivers', were rejected. Warwick would, however, revisit 'Broken Bottles', produced by Barry Manilow, during sessions for her album *Finder Of Lost Loves* (released in non-US territories as *Without Your Love*), but the track remained on the shelf until the expanded edition was released in 2014. Danish singer Gitte Hænning was rumoured to have recorded 'Oceans And Rivers', but it has never surfaced.

To complete the album, Barry teamed up with Albhy Galuten to write four more songs. Albhy noted that the songwriting process was specific to the project, with Barry's ideas evolving based on the needs of the album. 'If they had been for the other project, he would have written some different songs', Albhy said. Dionne Warwick's album was an example of Barry and Albhy's specific sympatico. They went into the studio and, within two days, had created demos of the album in the correct keys for Dionne's voice. These demos circulated within Bee Gees fandom for many years on cassettes and were bootlegged on CD numerous times from the early 1990s. They received a legal release via the iTunes platform in 2006, but stopped short of a tangible product.

Barry's falsetto was an essential tool for both composing and performing these demos. Albhy explained, 'Barry could sing in falsetto for any key, which made it easy to create songs for different vocalists. We would do basic arrangements, and then just bring in musicians to play'. Barry's falsetto provided him with a greater vocal range and flexibility than his natural voice, which had more limitations. Albhy noted that while Barry had good vocal range and control in his natural voice, his falsetto was where he truly excelled. 'He could do almost anything in falsetto', Albhy explained. This flexibility made falsetto a powerful writing tool for Barry, especially when working with female vocalists, as he could easily match their range. When writing for male vocalists, however, Barry had to rely on his natural voice, which was more limiting for him. Creating songs for female singers like Dionne Warwick, Barbra Streisand, or Samantha Sang allowed Barry to fully explore his creativity without those constraints'.

Recording for the album began with the instrumental tracks, using the original demos as rough guides but not simply dubbing over them. Drummer Steve Gadd and bassist George Perry laid down the rhythmic foundations, after which layers of keyboards and guitars were added. Albhy Galuten, George Bitzer, and Richard Tee shared the piano and synthesiser duties, bringing depth and texture to the songs. Apart from George Terry, who played on the title track only, the only guitarist employed for the album beyond Barry's own rhythm work was Tim Renwick, a familiar collaborator from the Andy Gibb albums. Later, strings were added as a final touch at Mediasound Studios in New York, adding a smooth polish to the arrangements. Dennis Bryon's percussion credit certainly refers to the use of his famous drum loop, previously nicknamed 'Bernard Lupe', on several tracks.

As the wheels of promotion began to turn, Arista called *Heartbreaker* 'Dionne's landmark album' and there was no doubt that it was certainly an ambitious and expensive project. An advertising campaign in *Billboard* magazine featured three different full-page advertisements in the 30 October, 20 and 27 November editions. Meanwhile, the UK was graced by Dionne's presence for a number of television appearances. She appeared on BBC1's lunchtime magazine programme, *Pebble Mill,* on 8 October. When asked by presenter Donnie MacLeod about the album, Dionne replied:

> Barry Gibb and his brothers wrote about three tracks together, and there's another songwriter that Barry writes with frequently, Albhy Galuten, who wrote the majority of the other tracks with him. But by and large, it was a whole conglomeration of people who contributed to the album, and I think it just turned out beautifully. I'm thrilled with the album.

As if to prove the point, she performed four songs on the show, three of which were from the album: 'Heartbreaker', 'Yours', and 'Take The Short Way Home'.

Later in the month, she appeared on BBC1's *Saturday Superstore* and the prime-time evening programme *The Late Late Breakfast Show* on 23 October, followed by *Top Of The Pops* on 28 October. This appearance featured a re-recorded backing track for 'Heartbreaker' and Dionne performed a live vocal.

'Heartbreaker' (Barry Gibb, Robin Gibb, Maurice Gibb)
Recorded at Middle Ear, Miami Beach, and Mediasound Studios, New York, about April and May 1982
Chart positions: Portugal: 1, Sweden: 1, Australia: 2, Denmark: 2, Ireland: 2, Norway: 2, UK: 2, Belgium: 3, Finland: 3, Spain: 3, Zimbabwe: 3, New

Zealand: 4, South Africa: 4, Switzerland: 4, Netherlands: 5, Austria: 10, US: 10, West Germany: 10, Canada: 15, France: 17, Italy: 24

The lead single was the title track, 'Heartbreaker' – a good choice to pre-empt the album release, as it was without doubt the strongest song that had been assembled for it. Written by all three brothers, it was a simple verse-chorus ballad with a typically irresistible hook and a melody and rhythm that keep moving the song forward. It had 'hit single' written all over it and became a global smash, reaching the top ten in most countries, but notably reaching the top slot in Portugal, Sweden, and most significantly on the *Billboard* Adult Contemporary chart. Meanwhile, on the *Billboard* Hot 100, it reached number ten and just missed out on the top placement in the UK, peaking at number two.

For Maurice, the title of the song felt especially meaningful. 'I cried my eyes out after we wrote it', he remembered. 'I drove home and thought, 'We should be doing this one', and when she did it, it was brilliant. We sang on it, and it became like a duet between The Bee Gees and Dionne Warwick'.

In a conversation with Tom Cridland on the *Greatest Music Of All Time* podcast in December 2024, Warwick opened up about her initial hesitation to work with Barry. While she admired his talent, the thought of recording 'Heartbreaker' initially didn't resonate with her, much like her reluctance to record 'Do You Know The Way To San Jose' years before. Reflecting on the experience, she explained:

I did not want to record 'San Jose' – I *really* didn't want to record 'Heartbreaker'. Just like with 'San Jose', it didn't feel like me, and between him and his brothers and Clive Davis saying, 'You *will* record the song', I said, 'Oh, I will ... okay'. I know it's the same thing that happened with 'San Jose'. 'You *are* going to record this one'. I said, 'okay', because of the insistence of not only Barry but Maurice and Clive Davis in my ear – 'You will, you will, you will, you will'. Maybe they know more than I do, and by and large, anybody knows more than I do. Don't ever ask me what's going to be a hit. I have no criteria when it comes to that. But they knew something I didn't know.

Reflecting on the success of the collaboration, Maurice noted that 'it became her biggest single since 'Do You Know The Way To San Jose', which, when we were kids, we *adored*'. The song not only marked a significant achievement for Warwick but also demonstrated The Bee Gees' enduring talent for crafting hits that resonated deeply with listeners. So much so, 'Heartbreaker' became the 50th British chart hit written by some combination of Gibb brothers. The only songwriting teams to top that total at this point in time were Lennon & McCartney, Bacharach & David, Goffin & King, and Holland-Dozier-Holland.

A handful of notable cover versions materialised after Warwick's original, courtesy of Australian singer Diana Trask in 1985; British singer Katie Melua in 2016; and British singer-songwriter Nick Lowe (for his *Tokyo Bay/Crying Inside* EP with Los Straitjackets) in 2018.

When The Bee Gees returned to touring in 1989, 'Heartbreaker' was incorporated into the acoustic medley portion of the concert – and it remained intact in most of their future major live performances. They recorded their own studio version in 1994, intended for a proposed compilation, *Love Songs*, that was shelved, but it eventually saw release on the 2001 hits collection, *The Record*.

'It Makes No Difference' (Barry Gibb, Albhy Galuten)
Recorded at Middle Ear, Miami Beach, and Mediasound Studios, New York, about April and May 1982

The soulful and atmospheric ballad 'It Makes No Difference' is the first songwriting collaboration between Barry and Albhy Galuten on the album's tracklist. Released as the B-side to 'All The Love In The World' in most territories – the exceptions being the US and Argentina – the track takes a slower, more dramatic tone, giving Dionne a deeply emotive song to bring to life.

Rich in mood and melodrama, the song unfolds in two parts. Dionne's warm, expressive vocals take the lead in the verses, while the chorus sees a multi-tracked Barry joining her – their voices intertwine effortlessly to create a gorgeous blend of harmonies. It's probably the closest they would get to a duet on this album.

'Yours' (Barry Gibb, Robin Gibb, Maurice Gibb)
Recorded at Middle Ear, Miami Beach, and Mediasound Studios, New York, about April and May 1982
Chart position: UK: 66

Released as the third single from the album in the UK in February 1983, 'Yours' is a sweeping, theatrical ballad that showcases Dionne's ability to turn a simple love-lost theme into something deeply moving – evoking shades of her 1979 hit, 'I'll Never Love This Way Again'. It was reportedly one of Warwick's favourites on the album. Although it didn't achieve major chart success – peaking at number 66 – it remains a standout performance. It was included on several of Warwick's future hits compilations.

The song is beautifully structured, opening with a unique passage that never repeats, setting the stage for the story. The arrangement slowly intensifies, with Warwick's soaring vocals guiding the listener through waves of swelling emotion. Just when it feels like the song is reaching its conclusion, an instrumental break sweeps in, only for Dionne to return for a powerful, final chorus. Barry's layered 'Bee Gee chorus' vocals lilt in the background.

'Take The Short Way Home' (Barry Gibb, Albhy Galuten)
Recorded at Middle Ear, Miami Beach, and Mediasound Studios, New York, about April and May 1982
Chart position: US: 41

'Take The Short Way Home' is an infectious, upbeat track that evolves into a similar horn-driven energy to The Bee Gees' 'Search, Find' from *Spirits Having Flown*. The second Barry and Albhy composition on the album's tracklist was released as *Heartbreaker*'s third single in the US and Canada, and in some European countries, in February 1983. In the UK, it was relegated to the B-side of 'Yours'. In the US, it peaked at number 41 on the *Billboard* Hot 100, enjoying a 13-week chart run from late February to May 1983. It also reached number five on the magazine's Adult Contemporary survey and number 43 on the Hot Black Singles chart.

From the moment the beat kicks in, the track exudes momentum and spirit, driven by a funky R&B groove that makes it irresistibly catchy. Warwick's vocals shine with a playful, effortless charm, and when Barry's signature falsetto background harmonies come into play, the track fully leans into that unmistakable Bee Gees sound.

'Misunderstood' (Barry Gibb, Robin Gibb, Maurice Gibb)
Recorded at Middle Ear, Miami Beach, and Mediasound Studios, New York, about April and May 1982

Closing out side one, 'Misunderstood' is a smooth, mid-tempo track that effortlessly blends warm piano and shimmering guitars into a laid-back, almost breezy groove. A true throwback to Dionne Warwick's iconic 1960s sound, this song feels like a respectful nod to the classic Bacharach and David era.

Dionne's vocal delivery is, as always, flawless, her effortless phrasing and warmth bringing a timeless quality to the track. The third, fourth and final choruses – the last of which fades out – feature a clever staggered vocal interplay between Barry (in his now infamous breathy timbre) and Warwick, adding an extra layer of richness to the melody.

'All The Love In The World' (Barry Gibb, Robin Gibb, Maurice Gibb)

Recorded at Middle Ear, Miami Beach, and Mediasound Studios, New York, about April and May 1982

Chart positions: Netherlands: 3, Belgium: 7, UK: 10, Ireland: 19, New Zealand: 23, West Germany: 50, Australia: 53, US: 101

'All The Love In The World' was the second single extracted from the album and was released in November 1982. It was an obvious choice, with a hook that grabs the listener on first hearing and some discernible similarities melodically and rhythmically to the album's title track. However, it didn't perform as well on charts, with its best showings being a respectable number three in the Netherlands and number seven in Belgium. Peaking at number ten in the UK was a good result, no doubt helped by the promotional video being shown on *Top Of The Pops*. In the US, the single narrowly missed the *Billboard* Hot 100, peaking at number 101 on the magazine's Bubbling Under Hot 100 survey, but it did reach number 16 on the Adult Contemporary chart.

'I Can't See Anything (But You)' (Barry Gibb, Albhy Galuten, Maurice Gibb)

Recorded at Middle Ear, Miami Beach, and Mediasound Studios, New York, about April and May 1982

'I Can't See Anything (But You)' was the B-side to the 'Heartbreaker' single. It's the third Barry and Albhy collaboration on the album, although for this song only, they are joined by Maurice. After its dramatic minor key opening chords, the song settles into a pleasant if unspectacular ballad before returning to a high drama bridge and a key change prior to the fade. Barry's presence as a backing singer is clearly evident as he subtly adds depth as the song slowly builds to a powerful climax.

'Just One More Night' (Barry Gibb, Albhy Galuten)

Recorded at Middle Ear, Miami Beach, and Mediasound Studios, New York, about April and May 1982

Dionne delivers a masterclass in understated emotion with 'Just One More Night', a beautifully crafted piano ballad that stands as one of the most underrated tracks on the album. Written by Barry and Albhy, the song thrives on its dreamy production, allowing Warwick's soulful vocals to take centre stage.

The verses build theatrically, creating a sense of longing before melting into an intimate, delicate chorus. The sparse arrangement enhances the vulnerability in Warwick's plea for love to linger just a little longer. As the song progresses, Barry's harmonies gracefully weave into the mix, adding warmth and depth. Then comes a standout moment – the instrumental break – where Gary Brown's saxophone injects a touch of sensuality, heightening the romanticism.

With its sweet yet melancholic tone, 'Just One More Night' is an elegant slow burn, proving that, sometimes, the most understated tracks carry the deepest emotional weight.

'You Are My Love' (Barry Gibb, Robin Gibb, Maurice Gibb)
Recorded at Middle Ear, Miami Beach, and Mediasound Studios, New York, about April and May 1982
As the penultimate track on the album, 'You Are My Love' arrives with a burst of synthesised energy, giving the record a shift in tone as it moves into its final stretch. Written by Barry, Robin, and Maurice, the song carries many of the familiar hallmarks of the Bee Gees – polished pop structure, layered melodies, and a sense of optimism that runs through large swaths of their work.

From its opening moments, the track leans into a clear commercial sensibility, built around a melody that settles in quickly. Dionne moves through the verses with warmth and control before the chorus expands, with Barry's backing harmonies woven in behind her vocal.

The production remains clean and measured, matching the song's tone while giving the album one of its more distinctive late-sequence moments.

'Our Day Will Come' (Bob Hilliard, Mort Garson)
Recorded at Middle Ear, Miami Beach, and Mediasound Studios, New York, about April and May 1982
Bringing the album to a close, 'Our Day Will Come' stands apart as the only track without songwriting input from any of the Gibb brothers. Instead, the song was written by Mort Garson with lyrics by Bob Hilliard, first becoming a hit for Ruby & The Romantics in 1963. For Dionne, the song carried personal significance – she recorded the

publisher's demo in 1962 and had long hoped to release her own version. That wish is finally realised here in a rendition that feels graceful and unforced.

Warwick's interpretation is measured and understated, unfolding over a laid-back, jazz-tinged arrangement. It begins with soft Rhodes piano, light percussion, and a rounded bassline that establishes a mellow foundation. Strings drift in gradually, adding texture, while Warwick's voice remains at the centre – controlled, intimate, and precise as she moves through the melody.

Barry's backing harmonies subtly colour the track, appearing and receding without ever distracting from the lead vocal. At the midpoint, a saxophone solo introduces a warm instrumental passage before easing into the final stretch, where the arrangement broadens slightly without losing the song's restraint.

As the album's closing moment, 'Our Day Will Come' works as a reflective farewell – a nod to Warwick's earlier years as much as a reminder of how well her voice still inhabits material built on nuance rather than force. It is a carefully judged cover that ends the record on a quiet, fitting note.

'Let It Be Me' (Gilbert Bécaud, Pierre Delanoë, Manny Curtis)
Recorded at Middle Ear, Miami Beach, and Mediasound Studios, New York, about April and May 1982

A bonus track from the album sessions appeared in 2020 on *Déjà Vu – The Arista Recordings*. 'Let It Be Me' was a demo of a duet by Dionne and Barry and was probably never seriously considered for inclusion on the album. The song was composed by French singer Gilbert Bécaud with lyrics by Pierre Delanoë in 1955 as 'Je T'appartiens'.

It was adapted into English by Manny Curtis under the title 'Let It Be Me', and it became an international standard thanks to the Everly Brothers' version in 1960. Later versions by Elvis Presley, Bob Dylan, and Nina Simone helped popularise the song.

Dionne had previously recorded 'Let It Be Me' for her 1970 album, *Very Dionne*, but it wasn't released at the time and only appeared as a bonus track when the album was reissued in 2004. She did, however, perform the song live at the 1971 Grammy Awards ceremony.

The demo features a basic arrangement dominated by a Rhodes piano, and while it could have been developed further, it really would not have fit well with the other songs in the set, which are far more melodic.

Barry's vocal is strong and forceful at times, but never overbearing, complementing Dionne's part well. The two-part harmony section is particularly pleasing.

In an interview with Dionne, which aired on 23 March 1985 on the UK's Channel 4 music and chat show *The Other Side Of The Tracks*, host Paul Gambaccini noted that *Heartbreaker* was her biggest record ever in Britain. 'That's right,' she replied, 'and the whole continent as well, all of Europe. I've never had a record as big, and it was fun'. When Gambaccini asked, 'Was it a different kind of studio experience?', she replied:

> You know, by and large, no. They are very, very professional. And they're also perfectionists. I mean, they don't want to hear one note different, really, but I did have a little bit of swing with Burt. But it got to the point where they kind of relied upon me to do what I do best, as I relied upon them to do what they do best. And we finally got into the groove, and it worked.

Barry was also very pleased with the album's performance: 'What we're most proud of is that just about every record we made with all those people set some sort of record for that artist', he marvelled. 'It's amazing. I think Dionne Warwick had the biggest album of her career in Europe with that album'.

Looking back on her experience, Dionne told the *Greatest Music Of All Time* podcast:

> I had a wonderful time recording with them. And what interests me more, after the album was finished, was that they did not try to make me a Bee Gee; they respected that I was Dionne Warwick, and there was nothing they wanted to do to interfere with my sound. You know, they just enhanced it by surrounding me with music that was appealing – and still is appealing.

Many may see *Heartbreaker* as just one of several successful albums from Dionne Warwick's 1980s comeback, which ultimately led to her 1985 US number one hit, 'That's What Friends Are For'. However, *Heartbreaker* arguably represents the creative high point of this chapter in her career. With its stunning production, exceptional songwriting, and the kind of vocal performances that define Warwick as a legend, the album stands as one of her most remarkable works.

The song 'Rest Your Love On Me', written by Barry, received a BMI Country Citation of Achievement in 1982. This award is presented by Broadcast Music, Inc. (BMI) to recognise songs that have achieved significant performance milestones in the country music genre. 'Rest Your Love On Me' stands as a unique entry in The Bee Gees' catalogue, being a country ballad that achieved crossover success. Originally released as the B-side to their 1978 hit 'Too Much Heaven', it marked The Bee Gees' only appearance in the *Billboard* Country Top 40 as artists when it peaked at number 39 on 13 January 1979. It was, however, performances of Conway Twitty's version that topped the *Billboard* Hot Country Singles chart in May 1981 that gave the song the boost required to earn the citation.

Barry was a passionate tennis fan. His love for the sport extended beyond just playing – he actively participated in charity tournaments, using his influence to support meaningful causes. On 13 December, he took part in Linda Evans' International Tennis Tournament, an event dedicated to raising funds for Spina Bifida research. Just a week later, on 20 December, he joined another tournament, this time hosted by tennis star Ilie Năstase. This event aimed to benefit the American Cancer Society, further highlighting Barry's commitment to philanthropic efforts through the sport he loved.

These professional and celebrity charity events deeply inspired Barry. Witnessing firsthand the impact that sports and philanthropy could have, he decided to establish his own charitable initiative. A few years later, he launched the Barry Gibb Love & Hope Tennis Festival, combining his passion for tennis with his dedication to helping others.

1983

The Bee Gees began 1983 with a new worldwide publishing agreement with Chappell Music, reuniting with the company that had previously managed their copyrights through Robert Stigwood's RSO Music. The deal was officially announced by Heinz T. Voigt, president of PolyGram's publishing division, alongside Irwin Robinson, president of Chappell/ Intersong. This renewed partnership marked a more direct and collaborative relationship between The Bee Gees and Chappell, following the group's retrieval of their RSO material through a legal settlement with Stigwood. Under this new arrangement, Chappell Music would handle the administration of both past and future works by Barry, Robin, and Maurice. The agreement covered the extensive catalogue of Gibb Brothers Music, which held copyrights from their first major hit, 'New York Mining Disaster 1941', to more recent successes like Dionne Warwick's 'Heartbreaker'.

The Gibbs started writing and recording new Bee Gees material for the soundtrack of *Staying Alive*, the long-discussed sequel to *Saturday Night Fever*. Directed by Sylvester Stallone, who also co-produced the film alongside Robert Stigwood for Paramount, *Staying Alive* once again featured John Travolta in the lead role. Although no official soundtrack deal had been announced yet, there was significant excitement given The Bee Gees' proven ability to create hit songs for major film projects.

On 21 January, Robin and his partner, Dwina Murphy, whom he had met almost three years earlier, welcomed a son, Robin John. Initially, they chose to keep the happy news within their inner circle, sharing it only with family and close friends.

On 20 February, a federal court in Chicago became the setting for a dramatic trial involving The Bee Gees and Ronald H. Selle, an amateur musician and antique dealer. The lawsuit centred around Selle's claim that The Bee Gees had plagiarised his song 'Let It End' to create their 1977 hit 'How Deep Is Your Love' – a cornerstone of the massively successful *Saturday Night Fever* soundtrack.

The case was heard by the Honourable George N. Leighton, United States District Judge for the Northern District of Illinois. The atmosphere in the courtroom was tense as both parties prepared to present their cases in what would become a landmark trial. The Bee Gees, with two decades of experience as successful and published songwriters, were confident in their defence. They firmly believed that the allegations against them were unfounded.

Their confidence was bolstered by the presence of trusted colleagues – Dick Ashby, Blue Weaver, and Albhy Galuten – who were prepared to testify about the authentic creative process behind 'How Deep Is Your Love'. These collaborators had been integral to the band's development and their creative journey. They understood the nuanced and organic way The Bee Gees crafted their music, often building songs through a mix of spontaneous inspiration and collaborative effort. The defence had also lined up expert witnesses to reinforce their argument, hopeful that reason and evidence would prevail. As Barry stated:

I have no malice towards this man. I believe that he acted in good intentions on his behalf, that certain notes in these songs resemble each other enough for him to believe that we took his song. I only hope that at the end of the day, no matter how this goes down, he just takes into consideration that he could be wrong.

Selle was born on 7 August 1946 and lived in Hazel Crest, Illinois. He earned a master's degree in music education from the University of Illinois and was a skilled musician. At the time he wrote 'Let It End', he was supporting his wife Joanne and their three children by working as a clothing salesman for the Carson, Pirie & Scott department store in Chicago. In addition, he also led a three-piece band, performing at local engagements around the Chicago area, worked as a church choir director, and occasionally wrote both religious and secular music.

According to Selle, the melody for 'Let It End' came to him spontaneously one morning in the fall of 1975 while shaving. 'I wrote it down and developed it further while at work', he recounted, explaining how he later refined the composition on his piano that same evening.

Selle registered 'Let It End' with the US Copyright Office on 17 November 1975; the fee for doing so was, at that time, $6. He performed the song with his band two or three times in the Chicago area, and they recorded the song in a studio setting, where Selle himself provided the lead vocals. Eager to secure a publishing deal, he sent out 11 copies of his demo tape along with lead sheets to various music publishers. However, eight of them returned the materials without interest, while three never responded. Importantly, there was no record of the song being sent directly to The Bee Gees or their associated publishing companies. This was the extent of the public dissemination of Selle's song.

In May 1978, Selle was outside working in his yard when he overheard his teenage neighbour playing 'How Deep Is Your Love' on a cassette player. The song, featured on the soundtrack of *Saturday Night Fever*, was a massive hit at the time. 'I recognised the melody immediately, but with different lyrics', Selle later recalled. Curious, he examined the cassette jacket and discovered that the songwriting credit belonged to Barry, Robin, and Maurice Gibb. Still uncertain, he later attended a screening of *Saturday Night Fever*, where he heard the song again and confirmed his suspicions that it resembled his own composition.

However, proving or disproving plagiarism is complex, largely reliant on circumstantial evidence. Typically, a plaintiff must demonstrate that the defendant had access to the work in question. Selle's attorneys did not present evidence to show how The Bee Gees might have accessed his song 'Let It End'. Instead, they relied heavily on the testimony of Arrand Parsons, a professor of music at Northwestern University and an expert in classical music. Despite his lack of experience in analysing popular music, Parsons' testimony was technical and comprehensive. Through a series of graphs and charts, he demonstrated a bar-by-bar comparison of the two songs.

According to his analysis, the first eight bars – referred to as Theme A – of each song contained 24 identical notes. Out of the 34 notes in 'Let It End' and 40 in 'How Deep Is Your Love', these overlapping 24 notes appeared in symmetrical positions. Parsons noted further that of the 35 rhythmic impulses in Selle's composition and the 40 in The Bee Gees' song, 30 were the same. The final four bars of the songs, known as Theme B, had 14 identical notes, and of the 14 rhythmic impulses, 11 matched precisely. Moreover, both themes appeared in analogous positions within their respective songs. Based on this structural comparison, Parsons concluded, 'the two songs have such striking similarities that they could not have been written independently of one another'.

Selle's lawyer, Allen Engerman, argued that such striking similarities effectively established inferred access. Engerman's approach shifted the focus from proving direct access to asserting that the similarities were too profound to be coincidental. Under cross-examination by The Bee Gees' attorney, Robert Osterberg, Parsons appeared less certain of his absolute conclusions. When asked directly if the only way Theme B of 'How Deep Is Your Love' could have been composed was through copying, Parsons stumbled. He initially asserted the improbability of independent composition but quickly reconsidered, clarifying, 'I believe that elements which are in common between the songs in question are of such striking similarity that the second song could not have come into being without the first'.

Osterberg sought to dismantle Parsons' testimony by emphasising that similarity alone does not equate to copying. Given the finite number of notes and rhythmic variations available, some overlap between songs is almost inevitable. To reinforce this, Osterberg highlighted apparent similarities between 'Let It End' and The Beatles' 'From Me To You', attempting to illustrate that melodic resemblance does not automatically imply theft.

A pivotal moment in the trial occurred when Maurice took the stand as a witness for the plaintiffs. In a moment that the plaintiffs deemed critical, Maurice was played a section of Selle's song. Upon hearing a piano section from 'Let It End', Maurice responded, 'I believe that's 'How Deep Is Your Love'. Yes, I'm sure it's 'How Deep Is Your Love''. This misidentification was presented as near-irrefutable evidence that the melodies were indistinguishable to the very creators of the disputed song. Selle's team capitalised on this moment, confident that it demonstrated a subconscious familiarity at the very least. This misidentification, combined with Parsons' testimony, appeared to solidify the jury's perception of infringement.

For the defence, Blue Weaver, who had been instrumental in the song's creation, presented a working tape of the 'How Deep Is Your Love' writing sessions to demonstrate the creative process: Barry described how the song originated: 'The idea was to get Blue to play the chords that I could hear in my head and turn that into a song'. Robin and Maurice contributed to the lyrics and harmonies, weaving their collaborative talents into the composition. The defence aimed to emphasise the organic nature of their songwriting, suggesting that any similarities were purely coincidental.

However, the integrity of the working tape was called into question due to a 12-minute blank section. The plaintiffs implied that the tape had been altered, potentially to obscure evidence of copying. Weaver refuted this assertion, insisting, 'If you listen to that tape, there's no way that you could contrive anything like that. Really – if you were contriving it, it would sound differently – you would do it so people could understand what was going on … you wouldn't have the repetition, the trying to home in'.

As the trial wore on, frustrations mounted. During a routine scheduling meeting, Judge Leighton voiced his impatience, urging the attorneys to expedite the proceedings. He suggested that had he been deciding the case without a jury, he could have reached a verdict based on the evidence already presented. Interpreting these remarks as a sign that the case could be dismissed without further defence, The Bee Gees' legal team chose to rest without calling their planned experts. Barry recalled, 'The judge gave us indications at least two times during the trial that we should rest our case. If it was obvious to us that the court didn't think we were guilty, why not rest our case?'

This decision would prove costly. After five hours of deliberation, the jury ruled in favour of Selle. Jury foreman, Earl Wilke, cited the unchallenged testimony of Parsons as a crucial factor, stating, 'There was nothing to contradict the plaintiff's witness. There was no expert for the defence. Dr. Parsons talked of the improbability of independent composition, and nobody disputed that'.

The verdict in the case marked a dramatic turning point for both parties involved and left a lasting impression on the music industry. For Ronald Selle, it was a 'victory for the little guy', a validation of his claims that his work had been unfairly taken by one of the world's most successful pop groups. Selle's lawyer, Allen Engerman, expressed optimism about the financial gains from the ruling, hinting at the significant damages that could be awarded due to the massive success of the *Saturday Night Fever* soundtrack.

In stark contrast, The Bee Gees reacted to the decision with a mix of shock, disbelief, and defiance. Barry described the experience as feeling like he had 'stepped into *The Twilight Zone*', a surreal nightmare that called into question their integrity as songwriters. Robin's reaction was more direct and vehement, dismissing the verdict as 'a lie – a lie – a lie'. The group, steadfast in their conviction of innocence, immediately filed a motion to overturn the decision and vowed to appeal if necessary. As Barry declared, 'We intend to fight this to the end'.

Beyond the immediate fallout for The Bee Gees and Selle, the ruling raised significant concerns within the broader music community. Steve Massarsky, an entertainment law expert, predicted a ripple effect that could embolden others to pursue similar claims. 'This case will create a whole batch of litigants who will say, 'This guy beat The Bee Gees; so-and-so has my song", he cautioned. The verdict signalled a potential surge in copyright disputes, where the boundaries between inspiration and infringement would be increasingly scrutinised.

For The Bee Gees, the financial implications of the ruling were considerable, given the monumental success of 'How Deep Is Your Love' as part of the multi-platinum *Saturday Night Fever* album. However, the financial stakes paled in comparison to the threat posed to their reputations. Barry articulated the emotional toll, stating, 'I guess you have to be accused of something you didn't do to really feel how we feel. We're outraged; it's very difficult to describe'.

Despite Selle's victory in front of a jury, The Bee Gees' legal team took a decisive step on 22 April by submitting a motion for *judgment notwithstanding the verdict* (JNOV), a rarely granted yet powerful legal mechanism aimed at overturning the jury's decision. This move marked a critical moment in the ongoing legal battle. A JNOV, which stands for the Latin legal terminology 'judgment non obstante veredicto', allows a judge to override a jury's verdict if it is determined that no reasonable jury could have reached the same conclusion based on the evidence presented. Typically filed after a jury's decision but before the judge issues a final judgment, a JNOV challenges the validity of the verdict by asserting that it contradicts the weight of the evidence or misinterprets the law.

In response to The Bee Gees' motion, Judge Leighton carefully reviewed the evidence and arguments presented during the trial. It would be a further 15 weeks before he issued his final judgement.

How Old Are You? – Robin Gibb (1983)

Personnel:
Robin Gibb: vocals
Maurice Gibb: backing vocals, bass guitar, piano, synthesiser, acoustic guitar, electric guitar
Alan Kendall: acoustic guitar, electric guitar
Dennis Bryon: drums, percussion, backing vocals
George Bitzer: piano, synthesiser
Engineers: Samii Taylor, Dale Peterson, Larry Janus, Mike Fuller
Producers: Maurice Gibb, Robin Gibb
Co-producer: Dennis Bryon
Recorded at Middle Ear, Miami Beach, between October and November 1982
Release dates: UK: May 1983, US: 11 October 1983
Chart positions: West Germany: 6, Netherlands: 26, Switzerland: 26

In late 1982, Robin began working on new material for what would become his second studio album, 12 years after his debut, *Robin's Reign*. He had initially hoped that Arif Mardin would produce the album, but was disappointed when prior commitments prevented Mardin from taking on the project.

Shortly before the album's release, Robin was interviewed for Italian radio station Radio Studio 105 by presenter Federico L'Olandese Volante, which ultimately wasn't broadcast, during which he revealed a significant amount of detail about its making:

> I'm doing work with Maurice and Dennis Bryon, The Bee Gees' drummer, who helps with production. Maurice was co-producer, and he played a lot of the instruments and some harmony. We even agreed with each other not to do too many harmonies together because we wanted a different harmony sound from Bee Gees records.

Maurice also contributed significantly as a songwriter and arranger for the project. Though officially labelled as a Robin Gibb album, it was, in essence, a collaboration between Robin and Maurice. Maurice's efforts were so extensive that he deserved a co-credit, although he modestly and characteristically kept himself in the background.

Robin, Maurice, and Dennis recruited former Bee Gees band member Alan Kendall to play guitar – perhaps an attempt on Robin and Maurice's part to extend an olive branch to their old friends after they had been unceremoniously relieved of their duties two years earlier. Frequent Gibb collaborator George Bitzer would contribute piano and synthesiser.

The instrumental arrangements heavily feature electronic elements but are carefully crafted to avoid sounding overproduced. Maurice, as co-producer, emphasised clarity and separation in the mix, resulting in a tight, balanced aesthetic. Reflecting Robin's earlier solo work on *Robin's Reign*, electronic drums were integral to the recording process. Technology had, however, come leaps and bounds over the intervening years, and the device of choice was the programmable LinnDrum, which was gaining popularity within the industry at that time. Robin spoke specifically about the machine in his conversation with Radio Studio 105:

> We used the Linn before anyone else. We used the Linn on *Spirits Having Flown*. We used the Linn on the Dionne Warwick album. It's a very advanced piece of equipment, but at the same time, you've got to

remember that these machines are not just machines that you can just press a button and get what you want – you have to be a musician to use these machines. You have to actually know music, and you have to know, especially with a Linn machine, how to play the drums to use it as well. I have to have a drummer use it. So, you're not really getting away with anything. It is difficult to use these things. They're a damn sight more difficult to use than having the drummers and real guitarists and musicians in there.

The programmed drums were then paired with basslines played by Maurice on either a bass guitar or synthesiser. Maurice and Alan Kendall further built on these foundational elements with guitar and electric piano alongside George Bitzer's significant work on the keys.

The result was a clean, lean sound that complemented Robin's high-range vocals. Some critics noted the consistency of Robin's voice gave the album a cohesive feel, but the lack of vocal variety made listening to the entire record somewhat monotonous.

Dennis was a latecomer to sessions, becoming involved when Maurice called him out of the blue. Dennis recalled the excitement of getting back into the studio in his autobiography, *You Should Be Dancing: My Life With The Bee Gees*: 'This was just what I needed; I was excited, and I felt like I had a purpose in life again'. Determined to be fully prepared, he headed to the music store. 'I bought some new sticks and fresh drumheads. When I got home, I unpacked my drums, gave them the once-over, and tuned them up'.

The following week, he arrived at Middle Ear eager to begin. 'I drove to the studio and set up. The engineers on the project were a former Criteria employee named Samii Taylor and one of the Middle Ear engineers, Dale Peterson.' It took some time to get the drums sounding right, but soon the rest of the musicians arrived. 'Alan walked in with his guitar and amplifier, setting up behind a baffle.' Finally, Maurice and Robin entered, and the energy in the room shifted. 'Everybody was so happy to be together again; it was almost a reunion. There was a warm atmosphere in the room.' The session took on a collaborative feel as the group settled into working together.

Maurice played a demo he had recorded at home, a song called 'Kathy's Gone'. After making some notes, it was time to record. 'Samii got a headphone mix to everybody's liking, and we were off. It felt right to be playing with the band again, and to have Maurice on bass'. The session went smoothly. 'Everything sounded wonderful. Samii was a really good engineer; she made my drums sound huge'. After adding more keyboards, guitars, and cymbal swells, they called it a day.

The next morning, the work continued with Maurice playing the demo for 'In And Out Of Love'. Once they nailed the track, Robin recorded a guide vocal, and more instrumentation was added.

By Monday, the momentum hadn't slowed. 'At 11 o'clock, we started recording again', Dennis continues. 'We cut two more tracks that day: 'How Old Are You?' and 'Another Lonely Night In New York''. As the session wrapped, Alan and Blue packed up their instruments, but Maurice had one more request. 'I was about to pack up my drums when Maurice asked me if I would play some drum fills and cymbals on some of the other tracks. Of course, I agreed'.

Dennis found himself taking on an even bigger role in the project than he had expected. 'The next day, I came in as usual at 11 in the morning to do some drum parts, but instead, Maurice asked me if I would help him record Robin's vocal track'. Robin arrived and spent about an hour in the booth, recording multiple takes before heading home. 'Then Maurice and I started going through the different performances, choosing what we thought were the best parts'.

At the end of the session, Maurice turned to him with another request. 'He asked if I would come in the next day to help him again. This happened every day, until it reached the stage where, at the end of the day, Maurice would just say, 'See you tomorrow, Den Den''.

Weeks passed, and Dennis continued coming in every day, but something gnawed at him. 'Nobody had mentioned anything about me getting paid for the work I was doing. I didn't even know whether I was officially part of the project or just 'hanging out' at the studio'. One day, when Barry visited Dennis' house, he brought it up. 'He told me I should discuss it with Maurice. He said that for the amount of time I was putting in, he thought I should at least be co-producer'. So, Dennis finally spoke to Maurice – 'I talked to him, and he agreed'. As a result, Dennis was credited under Alternate Productions, while Maurice continued using Moby Productions, the company he had originally founded in 1970 with his then brother-in-law, Billy Lawrie.

Robin was deeply committed to maintaining an open and collaborative approach during the production process. 'Even though I know I'm producing with my brother, or whatever, I see it as a team', he explained in an interview with *Billboard*. 'I don't think you can get things done if you see yourself as a leader. You've got to be able to take feedback and input. Maurice is very good at that. If either one of us had an idea the other didn't like, we'd talk about it. We could discuss it. When you're in the studio a while, it becomes very relaxed'.

In the 9 April 1983 edition, *Billboard* reported: 'Also wrapped is Robin Gibb's 'Heart From The Fire' Polydor album'. This was the first mention of the album's possible title – which wasn't entirely correct; it was actually 'Hearts On Fire'. However, that would soon change.

How Old Are You? marked a distinct shift in Robin's musical direction. For Robin, it was vital that the record stood apart from The Bee Gees' sound. 'My album has to have a separate identity', he explained. 'It was important that it didn't sound like The Bee Gees. It was important that people wouldn't say, 'Oh, this is a Bee Gees album in disguise'. It was again the music that I liked to do'. He further emphasised the need for artistic growth, adding, 'What's important for a producer and songwriter is that you shouldn't always sound the same. You have to explore different avenues of music. You have to work in a large field'.

Yet, Robin acknowledged that some similarities with The Bee Gees' music were inevitable, given their shared songwriting style. 'You have to be born a writer, certainly a writer with a style', he said. 'I think that's why a lot of Bee Gees songs are easily identifiable; they have that stamp on them that you can always say, 'Well, that sounds like a Bee Gees song'. And even I have been unable to escape that, even on my solo album. Although I've escaped the sound identity, I think I've kept the signature of The Bee Gees' songs'.

This maturity in Robin's musical style reflected his evolution as an artist. Comparing the new album to his first solo effort, *Robin's Reign*, he observed: 'I was still in my teens, and I was doing stuff that was just off the wall. I wasn't following any set musical direction at all. But I've matured musically, and I'm developing in a certain direction. I could never have done this kind of stuff then'.

Despite its unique identity, *How Old Are You?* retained Robin's natural commercial instincts. When asked about the album's accessible sound, Robin remarked to *Face Rocks*, 'I didn't purposely try to make the album commercial – it's just me. It's not an image or anything like that – it's just the music I write. I get up in the morning, put on my jeans and T-shirt, and go to work. By being yourself, you're not selling anything except yourself. It's genuine, and you've got to believe in yourself if you want other people to believe in you'.

The album's lead single, 'Juliet', became a significant hit in Europe, particularly in West Germany, but Robin expressed doubts about releasing the album in the US. 'I was in the middle of changing labels, and I didn't want PolyGram to release it because I was not able to support it', he told *Billboard*. 'I didn't want it to come out and die without my support. I didn't feel they had its best interests at heart'. Despite these concerns, *Billboard* reported that Polydor had set 11 October as the release date for the album in the US. About 40,000 copies of the album were sold after being imported from West Germany.

Robin was quick to emphasise that *How Old Are You?* was not an attempt to establish himself as an independent solo artist outside The Bee Gees. 'I don't really look for a steady solo career as an artist', he told *Face Rocks*. 'It's really a project with Maurice outside The Bee Gees, but I'm not looking to be separate from The Bee Gees. My priority is still The Bee Gees'.

How Old Are You? may not have revolutionised Robin's career, but it demonstrated his ability to create music that was both personal and commercially viable.

The album cover design was attributed to The Cream Group with photography by Jimmy Wormser, a distinguished photographer renowned for his contributions to British advertising. His most iconic work includes the surreal 1977 Benson & Hedges campaigns, featuring a gold cigarette packet amidst Egyptian pyramids, and also as a giant sardine can floating in a pool. His portfolio encompassed collaborations with brands like British Airways, Martini, Volkswagen, Nike, Guinness and Rolex, and extended to the performing arts, notably the Royal Ballet.

The front cover photograph was captured outside the Electric Cinema at 191 Portobello Road in the Notting Hill district of London. Opened in 1910, it is one of the oldest working film theatres in Britain. It was one of the first buildings in Britain to be designed specifically for showing motion pictures, and one of the first in the area to be supplied with electricity – hence the name. Vintage movie posters for James Dean's *Rebel Without A Cause* and Vincent Price's *Masque Of The Red Death* decorate the lobby entrance. Robin, dressed in a brown leather bomber jacket, a red-and-black plaid shirt, jeans, and white tennis shoes, leans casually against a wall with one foot propped up. The main poster featuring the album title incorporates an image of Clark Gable and Ava Gardner taken from the 1953 movie poster for *Mogambo*. This may have been more than a decorative choice: at the time of the film's release,

Gable was 52 and Gardner 30 – a noticeable age gap that subtly echoes the question posed by the album's title. Whether intentional or coincidental, the pairing hints at themes of age and attraction.

Robin offered further insight into the album's artwork during his Radio Studio 105 interview:

> Funnily enough, that was all done when the album was going to be called *Hearts On Fire*. It was only more recently that I changed it to *How Old Are You?* because I wanted a little bit more, I don't know, a little bit more tongue in cheek, street level sort of humour on the title, rather than *Hearts On Fire* – something like *How Old Are You?* can actually raise a question. It gets people thinking about the title. And I wanted to do that, you know. So, it gets you thinking – it gets people thinking automatically. It doesn't have to mean anything, but it doesn't hurt to have something that makes you think.

The album's back cover photograph, taken inside the same cinema, depicts a courting couple sharing a kiss. Robin, seated a few rows in front of them, glances back over his shoulder, catching sight of the scene. 'That was my idea as well', Robin explained to Studio Radio 105. 'I did two pictures of that, actually – there's a couple kissing, and then there was me at the front. I was looking right at the camera. So, I said, later, 'No, I don't think I should be looking right at a camera' – apart from them, I'm the only one in the theatre – it looks more cheeky, not looking at the movie and looking at them instead. I liked the idea of having an empty cinema with two people and they're kissing'.

Artwork for all the album's singles consisted of cropped sections from the front cover photograph.

'Juliet' (Robin Gibb, Maurice Gibb)
Recorded at Middle Ear, Miami Beach, between October and November 1982
Chart positions: Italy: 1, Switzerland: 1, West Germany: 1, Austria: 2, Belgium: 7, Netherlands: 11, Australia: 70, UK: 94
Gold certification: West Germany
The opening track on the album, 'Juliet', stands as a quintessential example of early 1980s synth-pop. Released as a single in Europe in May and the US in June, the song combines a classic verse-chorus structure with layers of inventive production designed for maximum impact. The

track opens with a dramatic, atmospheric introduction, leading into an infectious electronic beat and Robin's soaring vocal delivery. Avoiding falsetto, he reaches for the highest parts of his regular register. The stuttered refrain 'J-J-J-Juliet' adds an irresistible hook.

Lyrically, the song is about the transformative power of love. The protagonist begins as a carefree and somewhat reckless individual, but finds true meaning through Juliet. Her love teaches him how to truly connect, breaking down his emotional walls and allowing him to grow. The reference to being a 'Romeo' alludes to Shakespeare's famous lover and aligns with classic themes of passionate devotion to his Juliet.

The song's standout bridge section showcases the Gibb brothers' mastery of melody and arrangement. Maurice's gentle interlude – 'Close your eyes, Juliet, don't let go' – transitions into Robin's intense, impassioned vocal, culminating in a triumphant return to the chorus. These dynamic shifts, coupled with a wordless vocal outro, make 'Juliet' a rich listening experience.

A high-budget promotional video, directed by Brian Grant and filmed at Wykehurst Place in West Sussex, further elevated the single's appeal. The historic mansion, known for its appearances in films like *The Legend Of Hell House* and *The Eagle Has Landed*, provided a visually striking backdrop.

Robin told Studio Radio 105 that the video is 'a fantasy. The guy finds this old house in the country. He's a writer. He's in the country, and he stumbles across this deserted old house, goes in, and sees a typewriter – of course, he's a writer – so he starts typing and puts himself in the story that he's thinking about. That film we did that day goes on for about ten minutes, but we had to get it down to under three minutes'.

Critically, 'Juliet' drew praise for its infectious hooks and polished production. *Billboard* described it as 'a hooky piece of synth-pop which recalls some of ELO's craftier singles'. While it only reached number 94 in the UK, the single was a major success in Europe, topping the Italian, Swiss, and West German charts and performing well across the continent where Euro-pop was emerging from disco's remnants. The single achieved gold record certification in West Germany with sales in excess of 250,000 copies.

Televised performances across Europe played a crucial role in cementing the song's success and establishing 'Juliet' as Robin's signature solo hit of the 1980s. His promotional appearances began on 21 April with a performance on *Musikladen* in West Germany. This was followed by an appearance on Italy's *Superflash* on 12 May and a performance on the Dutch *Voetballer Van Het Jaar* (Footballer Of The Year) programme on 27 May.

On 10 September, Robin took the stage at the 20th *Festivalbar* held at the Arena di Verona, performing both 'Juliet' and 'How Old Are You?'. The event was broadcast a few days later on 15 September in Italy. On 16 December, he returned to German screens on *Thommy's Pop Show Extra*, again performing the same two songs.

'Juliet' was incorporated into the setlist of The Bee Gees' 1989 *One For All* tour, performed in a lower key with all three brothers joining in on the chorus in full harmony. The live version from their Melbourne, Australia tour stop was first heard widely on the box set compilation *Tales Of The Brothers Gibb: A History In Song 1967-1990*. The *One For All Tour Live!* VHS and Laserdisc releases served as its debut on video in 1990. Later, Robin would include the song in several live solo performances in the mid-to-late 2000s.

'How Old Are You?' (Robin Gibb, Maurice Gibb)

Recorded at Middle Ear, Miami Beach, between October and November 1982

Chart positions: West Germany: 37, UK: 93

The album's title track was released as the second single in October 1983. Musically, it carries the signature elements of the era. Maurice's backing vocals punctuate the track, with the refrain 'How old are you?' adding an intriguing hook. While Barry's productions often leaned toward polished sophistication, this song stood out for its raw, pop-rooted energy.

The promotional video for 'How Old Are You?' cleverly embraces a *St. Trinian's*-inspired theme. In the clip, Robin takes on multiple roles, including a schoolteacher, an elderly taxi driver and a spiv – soundly based on George Cole's character Flash Harry from the *St. Trinian's* films. Robin claimed that his then-girlfriend and future wife, Dwina, appeared as one of the schoolgirls in the video, although she is not readily identifiable upon close scrutiny – if she is actually in the video at all. A photograph of the two of them in character on the set does exist, however.

Filmed at Bearwood, a grand Victorian country house in Sindlesham, Berkshire, the location originally belonged to John Walter, the owner of *The Times*. The house has since served as a filming location for various television productions, including *Lord Mountbatten: The Last Viceroy, Restless, Midsomer Murders, Endeavour, The Crown*, and *Soldier Soldier*.

In the video, the school is humorously renamed 'St. Bumblesbury Academy for Young Ladies'. The narrative follows a light-hearted, exaggerated take on the protagonist's predicament, satirising his melodramatic turmoil over an underage girl. 'It's cheeky – it's not a fantasy', Robin once commented. 'I think it's a lot of fun. I just liked the *St. Trinian's* idea of the English school'. Despite its engaging concept, the song only charted modestly, reaching number 37 in West Germany and a disappointing number 93 in the UK.

Beneath its upbeat exterior, however, 'How Old Are You?' presents a morally complex narrative. The lyrics delve into a man's conflicted feelings about an underage girl, centring on his uncertainty about her age and his awareness of the inappropriateness of his attraction. While the protagonist expresses fear and guilt, he ultimately succumbs to temptation, creating an unsettling tension between self-awareness and a lack of accountability. The recurring line, 'You said you were 17, but you are somewhere in between', underscores the blurred moral boundaries, while the song's emphasis on the girl's 'women's charms' shifts responsibility away from the narrator, raising ethical concerns. Robin said it was 'probably the most controversial song' on the album.

Compared to Gary Puckett's 'Young Girl', which explicitly calls for separation due to the age difference, 'How Old Are You?' offers no clear moral resolution. Instead, it lingers in the man's internal struggle, offering no perspective on the girl's experience or the broader implications of his actions. While the protagonist's vulnerability may evoke some degree of empathy, the song's indulgence in his conflict risks glamorising or excusing predatory behaviour. Unlike similar works such as The Police's 'Don't Stand So Close to Me', which critiques power imbalances, 'How Old Are You?' lacks a critical perspective, raising questions about its treatment of consent and responsibility.

'In And Out Of Love' (Robin Gibb, Maurice Gibb)

Recorded at Middle Ear, Miami Beach, between October and November 1982

'In And Out Of Love' reflects on love, loss, and emotional renewal. The lyrics depict a journey of searching for something real while navigating the pain of past heartbreaks. The opening lines – 'Out in the world, lost in the night, broken inside, the dream's out of sight' – set a wistful tone, conveying feelings of loneliness and disillusionment. The last line of the chorus – 'I've been crazy falling in and out of love so long' –

highlights the weariness of past romantic disappointments. The imagery of 'a storm within an ocean of heartache and wonderland' perfectly captures the emotional turbulence of love – both its pain and its magic. Robin's lyrics beautifully convey these emotions, making the song deeply relatable.

One of the song's greatest strengths is its vocal harmonies, which evoke the classic Bee Gees sound. Dennis Bryon, who also plays drums on this track, was asked by Robin to join him and Maurice to add a third harmony part. He remembered, 'Robin told me to stand between him and Maurice. [Engineer] Dale [Peterson] came out and plugged in a third set of headphones. I knew the melody to the song quite well by now, and the lower third harmony came naturally to me'. As they rehearsed, reality hit him. 'I suddenly realised where I was. I was standing between Robin and Maurice Gibb, singing harmony on a Bee Gees song'.

'Kathy's Gone' (Robin Gibb, Maurice Gibb)

Recorded at Middle Ear, Miami Beach, between October and November 1982

'Kathy's Gone' was issued as the B-side to the 'How Old Are You?' single in Italy only. Robin, who claimed it was one of his favourite songs on the album, had apparently designated it as his first choice for the lead single in the US.

The track tells the story of a woman who leaves behind a mundane suburban life in pursuit of fame and excitement as a movie star. Robin's storytelling ability shines through on this track, as he paints a vivid picture of Kathy's ambitions and the emotional wreckage in the wake of her departure. His distinctive voice enhances the song's intensity. Expressing both sorrow and desperation, the listener feels the weight of his heartbreak. It's a beautifully crafted song about love, loss and the pursuit of dreams at the cost of personal relationships.

Billboard noted in their review of the album that the song had 'the warm, poignant sound of pre-disco Bee Gees'.

'Don't Stop The Night' (Robin Gibb, Maurice Gibb)

Recorded at Middle Ear, Miami Beach, between October and November 1982

'Don't Stop The Night' is Robin at his paradoxical best. It's an upbeat, dancefloor-ready pop track laced with heartbreak, jealousy, and emotional uncertainty. The protagonist is left in emotional limbo – watching the girl he loves pass him by with someone else, clinging to hope, and refusing to let go. A textbook example of his knack for pairing melancholic lyrics with buoyant production – a formula he turned into an art form.

The song opens with a simple synthesiser riff set against a chugging drum machine rhythm, giving the song its danceable quality. Robin's vocals mirror the synth melody on the first four lines of each verse, creating a tight melodic cohesion that anchors the track. The final line of each verse sees him shifting into a higher pitch, which acts as a natural bridge into the more climactic chorus. It's a clever technique, and one that helps maintain the song's forward momentum.

Robin's vocal delivery has a pained quality – especially evident in the chorus. There's a noticeable strain as he reaches for the high notes – perhaps too ambitious at times – but it's that very struggle that underscores the vulnerability of the song's primary subject.

'Another Lonely Night In New York' (Robin Gibb, Maurice Gibb)

Recorded at Middle Ear, Miami Beach, between October and November 1982

Chart positions: West Germany: 16, Switzerland: 19, Belgium: 36, UK: 71

Released as the third single from *How Old Are You?* on 27 January 1984 in the UK, 'Another Lonely Night In New York' peaked at number 71, but it was a moderate success in other parts of Europe.

It's yet another song about heartbreak and solitude, themes that were prevalent in the Robin-led songs on *Living Eyes*, with his primary writing inspiration being the dissolution of his marriage to Molly. Bearing in mind that at this time Robin did also have an apartment in Manhattan, the song could be perceived as autobiographical, although Robin would defiantly claim that *How Old Are You?* overall had 'no message in the album. You know, I'm not trying to get a message across about my personal life or situation. I didn't want to get too personal'.

Lines like 'The city of dreams just keeps on getting me down' and 'If my heart and my soul had their way, you would still be here' highlight the narrator's deep sense of longing and regret, while New York serves as both a romanticised backdrop and a symbol of isolation.

The song opens with an ethereal, dreamy cloud of keys that release into a soft, atmospheric arrangement with lush synths and gentle percussion, characteristic of early 1980s soft rock. Robin's delicate, emotive vocals bring depth to the lyrics, making the listener feel the weight of his reflections. It's not only a standout track on the album – it's one of the strongest tracks in Robin's entire solo discography.

In the UK, the single was released with 'I Believe In Miracles' as the B-side. A limited-edition double pack in a gatefold sleeve was also issued. The bonus disc was the original 'Juliet'/'Hearts On Fire' single – probably in an effort to shift stock of the single, which, upon its original release, sold poorly. It did little to stimulate sales the second time around.

Robin revamped the song in 2003 for his solo album *Magnet* (altering its title slightly to 'Lonely Night In New York'), giving it a refreshed sound and faster tempo for the 21st century. The keyboard and percussion tracks are newly recorded, but his original vocal was kept intact.

The promotional video for 'Another Lonely Night In New York' lacked the flair and creativity seen in the big-budget clips for 'Juliet' and 'How Old Are You?'. Featuring Robin performing alone on a circular stage illuminated by footlights, the video was intercut with split-screen stock footage of New York landmarks and skylines. While visually serviceable, it didn't capture the emotional depth or cinematic ambition of his earlier videos.

Despite this, the single received strong promotional support on television, particularly in West Germany and the Netherlands, where Robin appeared on prominent music shows such as *Musikladen* and *TopPop*.

In the UK, a series of performances helped maintain visibility, including a notable appearance on *The Cannon & Ball Show*, where, in addition to performing the single, he took part in a light-hearted sketch that included a rendition of 'Three Bells' – a song which had previously charted in the US and UK for The Browns in 1959, and later in the UK for Brian Poole & The Tremeloes in 1965.

This was followed by a guest spot on the debut episode of *Leo*, singer Leo Sayer's BBC2 series, which featured both a performance of the track and scenes of Leo and Robin visiting iconic Bristol landmarks: the S.S. Great Britain and the Clifton Suspension Bridge. His final UK television appearance for the single came on *Rod Hull And Emu*, filmed at the Sun Centre in Rhyl, notable for featuring a unique alternate backing track not used elsewhere. These varied appearances helped to ensure the song reached audiences across Europe, even if commercial success in the UK proved elusive.

'Danger' (Robin Gibb, Maurice Gibb)
Recorded at Middle Ear, Miami Beach, between October and November 1982

'Danger' is a beautifully constructed song with mainstream sensibilities, enriched by strong vocal performances and thoughtful production. The chorus is especially radio-friendly, built with an ear for accessibility and melodic memorability – it's reminiscent of Smokey Robinson and the Miracles' 1967 track 'More Love' (a hit in 1980 for American singer Kim Carnes).

Vocally, Robin demonstrates real range and control here – most notably in the verses, where he moves fluidly into a higher register on key lines. These shifts not only inject emotional contrast but also serve a structural purpose, giving the chorus a satisfying lift when it arrives. The production supports these transitions, with the arrangement swelling just enough to carry him there without overpowering his voice.

Lyrically, 'Danger' leans into Robin's signature themes of longing, transformation and the almost cosmic pull of love. The lines about being 'rescued' and 'paralysed' by affection are classic Robin – poetic, romantic and tinged with just enough existential angst to keep things interesting.

On 19 December, during a promotional visit to Italy, Robin performed 'Danger' on *Ric E Gian Folies*, broadcast on the Italia 1 television channel. Although the song was never released as a single, its inclusion was a surprising yet welcome choice, highlighting its strength as an album track.

'He Can't Love You' (Robin Gibb, Maurice Gibb)
Recorded at Middle Ear, Miami Beach, between October and November 1982

With 'He Can't Love You', Robin revisits the storytelling tradition that defined much of his earlier solo work and Bee Gees balladry, but with a more polished 1980s sensibility. From the outset, the song dives into a familiar narrative setup – the love triangle. Robin's protagonist watches the woman he loves swept up in a glamorous but ultimately hollow affair. The verses paint vivid, cinematic scenes – weekends in Paris, champagne in Monte Carlo, model-esque beauty on the Champs-Élysées – all of it delivered with a sense of detached observation. It's a classic Robin Gibb lyrical device – glamorous surface, emotional void underneath.

One of the most striking aspects of the song is its chorus, arguably one of the best on the album. Leading into it, the pre-chorus takes on a surprising twist – Robin's vocals shift into a more guttural, almost pleading tone before soaring into the melodic high of the chorus. It's that contrast – the twist and lift – that gives the song its emotional payoff.

The vocal blend between Robin and Maurice is particularly effective here. Maurice's harmonies sit just behind Robin's lead, never intruding but always enriching, creating a blend that's sonically satisfying. It's one of those understated production choices that elevates the track.

'He Can't Love You' might be rooted in familiar themes, but it doesn't feel recycled. It's more refined, more mature – reflecting the changes in both Robin's artistic voice and the production values of the 1980s.

'Hearts On Fire' (Robin Gibb, Maurice Gibb)
Recorded at Middle Ear, Miami Beach, between October and November 1982

'Hearts On Fire', the B-side to Robin's hit single 'Juliet', stands as a moody, atmospheric track that leans heavily into its nocturnal themes. Beginning with a slow drum track and sparse instrumental backing, the song immediately sets a dark, shadowed tone that mirrors the urban nightscape painted in the lyrics. The instrumental restraint early on gives the piece a certain cinematic ambiance, with tones and textures that align with the imagery of twilight and city lights.

Robin's performance in the verses is fragile and emotional. However, this haunting elegance begins to fray as the song moves into the chorus. His vocals strain as he attempts to rise above the increasingly intense backing. The emotional intensity is clear, but it comes at the cost of clarity and control; the high notes feel forced, and the lyrics in the chorus become almost unintelligible amidst the swelling instrumentation.

By the time the second chorus fades, the track introduces a guitar solo from Alan Kendall, which adds a slight lift in energy, but it feels somewhat disconnected from the earlier sombre mood and lacks the cohesion needed to bring the song full circle.

'Hearts On Fire' is arguably the darkest track on the album, and as a single B-side, it may have deterred casual listeners from engaging with the full LP. Its ambition is notable, but the execution falters, particularly in the chorus, where it loses both vocal and lyrical clarity. Ultimately, it's probably the weakest track on the album – more of an experimental mood piece than a fully realised song.

'I Believe In Miracles' (Robin Gibb, Maurice Gibb)
Recorded at Middle Ear, Miami Beach, between October and November 1982

'I Believe In Miracles' is not only the closing track on the album, but it also served as the B-side to *two* singles: 'How Old Are You?' and 'Another Lonely Night In New York'. It's a strange decision by the record company to reuse the same track as the B-side for both releases, especially considering the wealth of material that could have showcased different aspects of Robin's solo work. While the song does carry thematic weight, it doesn't quite have the standalone strength one might expect from a track used so prominently in the single campaigns.

As an album closer, the song aims for a message of resilience and romantic faith, ending the record on a positive emotional note. Robin's vocal delivery here is oddly restrained and lacks the dynamic range he was capable of. The production, built around sparse 1980s synthesisers and a drum machine, feels a little thin, and by this point in the album, that minimalist aesthetic begins to wear out its welcome.

That said, the chorus redeems much of what comes before. With a burst of brightness, Robin lifts the mood and the addition of a catchy synth run injects much-needed energy. It's easy to see why the song was chosen to finish the album, even if it is somewhat of a letdown in the build-up.

Despite its flaws, 'I Believe In Miracles' does have its moments – particularly in the chorus. But its dual use as a B-side only highlights how uneven it is as a recording. In the context of the full album, though, it serves its purpose: a final note of optimism in a project that otherwise does a great job capturing the sound and spirit of the early 1980s. It also reinforces the adventurous spirit of Robin and Maurice stepping out from Barry's shadow, proving they could modernise without losing their melodic soul.

In December 1982, Maurice flew to Los Angeles to meet with arranger Jimmie Haskell to discuss a new movie score that he was composing. *Misunderstood* was an American drama film directed by Jerry Schatzberg and produced by Accent Films Ltd. Based on Florence Montgomery's 1869 novel of the same name, the movie tells a poignant story of loss, family and resilience, and had been previously adapted into the 1966 Italian film *Incompreso*, starring Anthony Quayle.

The cast of *Misunderstood* included Gene Hackman as Ned Rawley, a busy and often absent father who must care for his two sons following the death of his wife, Lilly. Henry Thomas, widely recognised for his lead role as Elliott in *E.T. The Extra-Terrestrial*, portrayed the elder son, Andrew, while Huckleberry Fox played the younger son, Miles. The family's story unfolds in Tunisia, where they reside due to Ned's job. The narrative delves into the emotional challenges of their loss, with Andrew coping better than his younger brother.

Principal photography for the film took place in Tunisia between October and December 1982, so by the time Maurice had registered the music that he had written for copyright in June 1983, the film was almost nine months into production.

Maurice composed a series of instrumental themes: 'Misunderstood', 'Andrew Alone', 'Andrew's Theme', 'Welcomed Friend', and 'Lilly'. These tracks reflected the film's emotional tone, with 'Lilly' accompanying scenes featuring the late mother, played by Susan Anspach, in flashback scenes. Maurice's compositions were first recorded as demos using synthesisers to represent orchestral parts, followed by full orchestral arrangements conducted by Hollywood veteran Jimmie Haskell at Criteria Studios with recording engineer Mark Draeb.

Maurice offered candid insights into the challenges faced by musicians working in the film industry during a couple of notable interviews. He shared his experiences navigating the complex dynamics between filmmakers and composers. During an appearance on *The Don Lane Show* on Channel 9 in Australia, Maurice was asked about his involvement in creating the score. He responded cautiously, revealing the delicate nature of the ongoing negotiations. 'Well, it's like this – it's in the middle of negotiations at the moment. I have been working on the score, but at the moment, I'm dealing with a very difficult director', he remarked.

This sentiment of creative friction was further elaborated on in a July interview with David Hartman on *Good Morning America*. When asked about the often-strained relationship between directors and composers, Maurice acknowledged the tendency for music to be undervalued in the filmmaking process. He explained:

It seems that in most cases, not so much in ours, but in some cases, it's usually the last say by the director, and the music is usually the last thing that's thought of. Sometimes they may say it doesn't fit. You may have worked hard on it, and it doesn't get used in the end. But there are a lot of decisions that have to be made. I think the producers and the directors now have to realise how important music is for film.

Maurice's comments highlighted a broader issue within the industry: the perception of music as an afterthought rather than a core element of storytelling.

> The director, basically, as I say, has the final say on where the music goes in the film. So, if it suits his film and the way it has to be, then he obviously knows what he's doing. But it would be nice to contribute to some of the actual editing of your songs, and so forth, things like that – a place in the picture.

Despite his best efforts, Maurice's score was ultimately not used in the film. According to Haskell, producers often commission multiple scores and select the one that best fits their vision. In this case, Maurice's compositions were deemed unsuitable. The final score was composed by British composer Michael Hoppé, with additional music by Argentinian composer Carlos Franzetti.

However, the Gibbs didn't have to wait long for their music to make it to the silver screen again. In the summer of 1983, five new Bee Gees songs would appear on the soundtrack of the *Saturday Night Fever* film sequel, *Staying Alive*.

Staying Alive (1983)

Personnel:
Barry Gibb: vocals, guitar
Robin Gibb: vocals
Maurice Gibb: vocals
George Terry: guitar (lead guitar on 'Someone Belonging To Someone')
Tim Renwick: guitar
David Sanborn: saxophone
Engineers: Karl Richardson, Steve Klein
Producers: Barry Gibb, Robin Gibb, Maurice Gibb, Karl Richardson, Albhy Galuten
Recorded at Middle Ear, Miami Beach, between October and December 1982, and between February and March 1983
Release dates: UK: July 1983, US: June 1983
Chart positions: Switzerland: 1, Italy: 2, Japan: 2, US: 6, UK: 14, Australia: 28

Saturday Night Fever's monumental success in late 1977 and early 1978 quickly catalysed talks of a follow-up film. *Fever* screenwriter Norman

Wexler had reportedly written a screenplay, but any forward momentum was stymied by John Travolta's refusal to agree to reprise his leading role as Tony Manero because he didn't like how his character was portrayed in the script. Robert Stigwood intervened and solicited Travolta's feedback, finally getting him on board after they made compromises on the storyline. Travolta also apparently inspired Stigwood's decision to bring in Sylvester Stallone as director after he had raved about the intensity of *Rocky III* after seeing it in the theatre.

And so, *Staying Alive* was born, revisiting the life of the agile but dim Manero, who had been struggling since his Brooklyn nightclubbing days to carve out a career as a professional dancer. It ended up being reviled by critics for being contrived, insipid and lacking the raw guts of its predecessor. Despite its reputation (Maurice later mockingly referred to the film as 'Rocky in Legwarmers'), it still managed a reasonably strong draw at the box office, grossing $165 million worldwide.

Saturday Night Fever had incited a cultural revolution by exposing and capitalising on a phenomenon that had mostly existed underground. *Staying Alive*, however, was chasing a well-established dance film trend that had already been propelled by arguably better films like *Flashdance* and *Fame* – the latter of which also happened to involve RSO in releasing its soundtrack.

As he did for *Saturday Night Fever*, Stigwood commissioned The Bee Gees to write and record some new songs that would feature prominently on the album's first side. But instead of filling the rest of the album with licensed material from well-known artists, the label ultimately leaned on three virtual unknowns to supply the balance of the tunes: Frank Stallone – the then-unknown brother of the film's director; Tommy Faragher – who had had minor success in the 1970s with his family act The Faragher Brothers; and Cynthia Rhodes, a dancer, actress, and eventual lead singer of the American pop group Animotion, who co-starred in the film with Travolta as Tony Manero's love interest, Jackie.

Interestingly, The Bee Gees hadn't initially intended to be involved at all. Speaking to Robyn Carter of *Channel Four News*, Barry explained that they had actually hoped to step away from the project: 'We thought, 'It's been done, and let's leave our music out of it this time, and you get somebody else to do it', and we felt a lot safer'. Robin echoed that sentiment, saying, 'I think because the first one was such a phenomenon, that it would be right for someone else to do it. People would automatically compare our new music with the old music, and it would be wrong'.

Ultimately, though, their contractual obligation to furnish one more album project to Stigwood and RSO pushed them to participate. Barry later admitted in the same interview that they had their doubts: 'We still don't know if it's a wise career move – but what we do know is that we believe in the music we presented, and with or without the movie, we believe the music will be successful'.

He also hoped fans would hear a different kind of growth in the new material, saying, 'Hopefully, I think you're going to hear a bit more maturity in the music – and that's the best word I can think of to use. I just think that we've grown up a little more, that the music has grown a little more with us, and you're going to hear things that we didn't do before'.

In 1983, The Bee Gees were in a completely different place collectively and individually than they were in the spring of 1977 when they were asked to contribute songs to *Saturday Night Fever*. In addition to their legal woes and the commercial disappointment they had experienced with *Living Eyes*, they were also still in the thick of a pervasive radio embargo in North America that was a painful remnant of the last time they had contributed their music to a film. It was not exactly the best timing for a reconstitution of The Bee Gees. However, *Staying Alive* would complete their contract with RSO and would free them to pursue other avenues in the near future.

It would appear the songs for *Staying Alive* were likely created as an extension of the sessions that the Gibb-Galuten-Richardson production team had been involved in for singer Kenny Rogers' forthcoming album *Eyes That See In The Dark*, rather than a true return to form for The Bee Gees. Robin and Maurice's presence on the finished recordings seems minimal – some fans have jested over the years that *Staying Alive* qualifies more as half a Barry Gibb solo record than as a true Bee Gees effort.

Details like firm recording dates, a comprehensive list of session players, and production notes for the *Staying Alive* songs don't really exist, nor are they discussed to any great extent in press clippings or interviews. Albhy Galuten recalled in 2024 that the musicians used for *Eyes That See In The Dark* were likely the same ones employed for the project. Guitarists Tim Renwick and George Terry, who had played on a number of other Gibb projects, have reportedly claimed they participated in the sessions. Besides the Gibbs, famed American saxophonist David Sanborn is the only other musician formally credited on any of the tracks – his name appears in print on the label for 'I Love You Too Much', the B-side of the 7" 'Someone Belonging To Someone' single. It's fair to presume he played the other tracks' saxophone parts, as well.

In an interview with David Hartman on *Good Morning America* in July 1983, Barry admitted the challenge of living up to the unprecedented success of *Saturday Night Fever*:

Well, that's really difficult. There is an enormous pressure. And I don't really know how you follow it. You have to treat it as a different project, rather than treat it psychologically as a follow-up. You know, it just takes a little bit of the pressure off. But you're right. It's a tough thing to follow up, and we just enjoy making the music and hope for the best.

Still, the production team worked on the music earnestly, although they had little input as to how it was used in the film itself – a distinction they made clear in multiple interviews.

On the *Don Lane Show* on Channel 9 in Australia, when asked whether they were unhappy with how the music had been handled, Barry replied diplomatically:

We don't really want to judge or say anything at this point, but the best way we can answer is that you really have to get Sylvester Stallone on your satellite and ask him what he thinks of the music in the film and where he put it. Our opinion is that if Sylvester Stallone wanted something as he has, he got what he wanted. And I think that you have to ask him any other points. I think that's the only way for us to answer it.

Robin added:

Sylvester Stallone directed the movie. He has complete control of all the music – it's not ours. We write the music. He asked us to write the songs. He phoned us a few times to say what he wanted here and there for different parts of the music, and we gave him the music. That's where our job ends. We can't go into the scenes and [can't] do the coordination? Our job ends with the director and Sylvester Stallone.

Robin reiterated this division of responsibilities when speaking to David Hartman on *Good Morning America*, stating:

He came down to the studio while we were writing the songs for *Staying Alive*, and heard quite a few of them. He was in touch, by and large, with the process of the writing right up to the end of the film. Of course, it is his decision how the music is worked into the film, along with the other people's music. Our job is to write the songs and go into the studio and produce them, and then it's up to the director, who, of course, in this case, is Sylvester Stallone, on how that music is worked into the movie.

When asked by Hartman if they were pleased with how their songs had been used, Barry deferred:

Well, it's very difficult for us to be the judges of it at this point in time. It's really the eve of release, and I think we have to be patient, rather than judge it right now, and see what the public think. You really have to ask Sylvester if he's pleased because it really is down to what he wanted. And as far as we're concerned, he got what he wanted.

An article in the 13 August edition of *Billboard* observed:

It's generally accepted that the *Saturday Night Fever* soundtrack went to number one on the strength of The Bee Gees' cuts, and that the other acts were largely along for the ride. Here, the situation seems to be reversed: it's the other music that's selling the album, and The Bee Gees, for once, are coat-tailing into the top ten. The John Travolta association is also no doubt triggering a lot of album sales. This is the fourth soundtrack from a Travolta picture to crack the top ten, following the blockbusters *Saturday Night Fever*, *Grease* and *Urban Cowboy*.

In the end, The Bee Gees' music was not utilised in the film with the same prominence or impact as it had been in *Saturday Night Fever*, which might have dulled the chart performance of their singles from the soundtrack.

The Bee Gees had written and recorded a sixth track for the film, 'River Of Souls', that was an explosive seven-minute-long epic slated for use in the film's final dance number, but it was never used. Instead, American singer-songwriter Joe Esposito's (better known for his song

'The Best' from the 1984 film *The Karate Kid*) 'The Winning End' was chosen for the scene. That song was inexplicably omitted from the soundtrack album, but Esposito co-wrote several of the tracks that did appear on the second side of the LP.

The album itself was a hit, peaking at number six on the *Billboard* Top LPs & Tape chart the week of 27 August. It reached number 10 in Canada, number 14 in the UK, and number 28 in Australia. It performed the best in Switzerland, where it topped the album charts, and it placed at number two in both Italy and Japan. Still, it was a far cry from the record-shattering run of *Saturday Night Fever*.

The soundtrack's biggest hit was Frank Stallone's 'Far From Over', an energetic dance song. It reached number ten on the *Billboard* Hot 100 the week of 1 October. It fared poorly in the UK, peaking at number 68.

Staying Alive was the last original album issued by RSO Records, which was defunct and then absorbed by its distribution company, PolyGram, by the end of 1983. 'I'm Never Gonna Give You Up', a duet between Frank Stallone and Cynthia Rhodes that featured on side two of the soundtrack LP, was RSO's final single release.

Industry veterans Mo Ström and Bill Levy were responsible for the soundtrack album's design and art direction. The cover's focal point is an intense image of a weathered, perspiring John Travolta captured from the film's finale. The title logo typeface consists of illuminated points with an ombre effect, emulating the banks of stage lighting behind Travolta in the photograph.

The inner of the gatefold sleeve features a number of production stills from the movie, with another scene from the finale as the centrepiece.

The back cover features a backlit photograph of The Bee Gees, a clear attempt at modernising their infamous, white-suited pose on the rear of the *Saturday Night Fever* soundtrack album. Barry and Robin's sleeveless T-shirts and Maurice's leather bomber jacket do the trick. American photographer Mario Casilli, known for his long-term work for *Playboy* magazine, snapped the image of the Gibbs. He was also responsible for the playful photos of Barry and Barbra Streisand that were used for *Guilty*. Unlike *Saturday Night Fever*, however, no photos of the other contributing artists are shown.

The album received a nomination for Best Album of Original Score Written for a Motion Picture or Television Special at the 26th Grammy Awards. The other nominees were *Star Wars: Return Of The Jedi*, *Tootsie*, and the eventual winner, *Flashdance*.

'The Woman In You' (Barry Gibb, Robin Gibb, Maurice Gibb)

Recorded at Middle Ear, Miami Beach, around March 1983
Chart positions: Spain: 2, Belgium: 16, Netherlands: 21, France: 23, West Germany: 23, US: 24, Australia: 73, UK: 81

'The Woman In You' was the final track recorded for the soundtrack but was the first single to be released – barely two months separated each of those events.

It wasn't a typical Bee Gees song, lacking the usual melodic structures expected. The main hook is the keyboard-guitar riff that kicks the track off, but it's held together with a funky groove and has a catchy chorus sung by all three brothers.

In all markets, the 7" single was backed with the full-length original version of 'Stayin' Alive'. The 12" single release included an extended version with a longer introduction and fade out. The flip side featured a megamix of sorts called 'Saturday Night Mix', which segued 'More Than A Woman', 'Stayin' Alive', 'Night Fever', 'Jive Talkin'', and 'You Should Be Dancing'. These tracks only made it to album format on the Japanese *Staying Alive Dance Mix Album*. he Woman In You' fared slightly better commercially than the singles from *Living Eyes* that preceded it. It landed at number 24 on the *Billboard* Hot 100. Its best showing was on the Canadian *RPM* Contemporary Adult chart, where it went to the top for the week of 23 June, dislodging former RSO stablemate Irene Cara's 'Flashdance ... What A Feeling' from the pole position.

The promotional video was conceptualised by Keith Williams and directed by Brian Grant. It features each brother working in a mundane day job: Maurice as a taxi driver, Robin as a server in a diner, and Barry working in a print shop. They are, however, all uncontrollably distracted by a beautiful woman who walks by as they are working. This was actually Cynthia Rhodes, who played the part of Jackie in the film. The video closes out on an elaborate set with Rhodes and a host of female dancers performing a routine while the brothers sing and strike macho poses atop a stylised representation of the Statue of Liberty's crown in the midst of the neon-lit set. A still photograph from this part of the video was used for the sleeve photo of the Japanese single release of 'Life Goes On'.

'The Woman In You' was nominated in the movie category of the 5th annual US National Publishers' Association Song Awards in 1984.

'I Love You Too Much' (Barry Gibb, Robin Gibb, Maurice Gibb)

Recorded at Middle Ear, Miami Beach, around November/December 1982

A strong mid-paced track with Barry, who is in fine vocal form using his versatile natural voice – varying from a sonorous full belt to softer, breathier tones. Maurice and Robin aren't audible on this particular song, and the meandering melody and long verses signal Barry may have written much of it on his own.

The lyrics of 'I Love You Too Much' show maturity in writing and are on the knife-edge of being sensual and risqué – a line like 'under me is where you should be' doesn't leave much to the imagination.

An instrumental version of the song with a saxophone solo by David Sanborn appeared as the B-side of the 'Someone Belonging To Someone' 7" single, and also on the Japanese *Staying Alive Dance Mix Album*.

'Breakout' (Barry Gibb, Robin Gibb, Maurice Gibb)

Recorded at Middle Ear, Miami Beach, around February 1983

A brilliant, rhythmic dance track with layered percussion and synth bass creates a firm foundation for Barry to throw himself headlong into this. He uses three different voices: full force, natural, and breathy – he ad-libs over the drum outro with some light falsetto sweetening but stops short of employing his famed high-register yelp.

It certainly had potential to be a single, but the closest it got was as the B-side to a Japanese-only 7" release of 'Life Goes On'. However, it was performed on the Italian television show *Fantastico* in preference to the two singles released from the album.

'Someone Belonging To Someone' (Barry Gibb, Robin Gibb, Maurice Gibb)

Recorded at Middle Ear, Miami Beach, around November/December 1982

Chart positions: Belgium: 23, Netherlands: 30, UK: 49, US: 49, West Germany: 55

The second Bee Gees single to be released from the soundtrack was 'Someone Belonging To Someone', a slow, romantic song with long melodic verses sung by Barry. Robin and Maurice are seemingly not present on either this track or 'Breakout', but they presumably added some harmony vocals mixed into Barry's.

In 1990, Barry accurately described it as a 'fair ballad from a silly film'. Released in July 1983, it became a minor hit in the US and UK, peaking at number 49 in both markets. It should have fared better given its quality, but also the phrase 'someone belonging to someone' is up there among the Gibbs' more confounding lyrical choices. RSO may have been aiming to balance the up-tempo 'The Woman In You' with a modern answer to 'How Deep Is Your Love'. A more adventurous choice might have improved their chance at a hit. The B-side of the 7" single featured an instrumental version of 'I Love You Too Much' while the 12" featured 'Saturday Night Mix'.

The promotional video was directed by Charlie Allen for Cinema East and features a staged performance in a dark setting with coloured lights filmed using star filters. There are unidentified musicians in the background, although the lead guitarist's beautiful mother-of-pearl-inlaid guitar does feature in a number of close-ups. Barry is shown playing a highly uncharacteristic guitar for him, a Gibson Les Paul, while Maurice plays a Fender Precision bass. Poor Robin looks rather uncomfortable miming on a Moog Liberation, one of the first commercially produced 'keytar' synthesisers. The video is padded out with the obligatory scenes cross-promoting the movie.

'Life Goes On' (Barry Gibb, Robin Gibb, Maurice Gibb)
Recorded at Middle Ear, Miami Beach, around October 1982
One of the first songs written especially for the movie soundtrack was 'Life Goes On', and it was recorded towards the tail end of 1982, shortly after RSO had formally announced the film.

It's a pleasant and bouncy mainstream pop song and has a good hook line in the chorus. Of all the new tracks the Gibbs wrote for *Staying Alive*, it's perhaps the most stereotypically Bee Gees-esque; the changing keys and dense harmonies are somewhat reminiscent of 'Living Eyes'. It was released as a single, but only in Japan. It should, perhaps, have been considered as a single in other territories.

'Stayin' Alive' (Edited Version) (Barry Gibb, Robin Gibb, Maurice Gibb)
The Bee Gees' contributions to the album were sealed with a pointlessly edited 'Stayin' Alive' appended to the end of the LP's first side–at just over a minute and a half, it was over before it began. As the title of the movie was inspired by the song, it should have been given more

prominence and recognition; even a remix would have been more interesting.

In a late 2025 conversation with the authors about his involvement in various Gibb-related projects during the 1980s, former Criteria Studios engineer Dennis Hetzendorfer offered an intriguing anecdote about the track's 1977 recording that had not been previously revealed:

Recording 'Stayin' Alive' was one of my first involvements with the Bee Gees. We were mixing it in Studio B on a 500-series MCI console – it had early automation, which felt pretty advanced at the time. One of the last things recorded was Barry's vocal in the middle section: 'life going nowhere, somebody help me'. To get that thin, bite-y sound, we did something a little unconventional. The track had been recorded at 30 inches per second with Dolby A noise reduction. Normally, you encode the signal going to tape and decode it on playback – but for that section, we took the Dolby out. That was Karl [Richardson]'s idea. What you're hearing there is the encoded signal without decoding, which gives it that thin, almost 'stretched' quality. The tricky part was that there was no way to automate it. The vocal was spread across a few tracks – probably tripled – so when we rolled the two-track mix, I had to manually flip three switches right on cue every time that line came in, then flip them back so the rest of the song sounded normal. All in real time.

On 8 July, Ronald H. Selle's lawsuit against The Bee Gees took another dramatic turn. Judge George N. Leighton of the US District Court for the Northern District of Illinois overturned the 23 February jury verdict against the Gibbs. The reversal marked a significant victory, as the brothers had vehemently denied the allegations throughout the trial.

Judge Leighton issued a 28-page decision nullifying the jury's verdict, which had initially sided with Selle. Although no evidence was ever presented to demonstrate that The Bee Gees had access to Selle's song, his legal team had argued that the similarity between the two tracks implied unauthorised borrowing.

In New York, attorney Jerry Gold confirmed that an appeal was being considered, maintaining confidence in the jury's original decision.

Appearing on CNN's *Freeman Report*, Barry expressed relief at the ruling, emphasising that without proof of access or copying, there had never been a legitimate case:

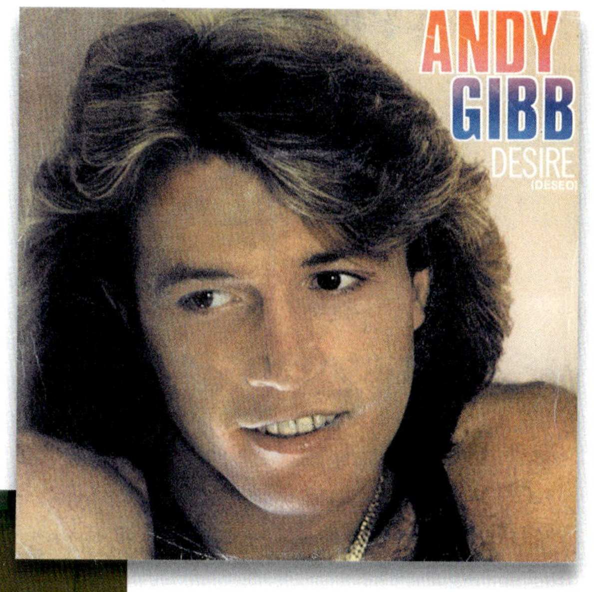

Right: Spanish picture sleeve for Andy Gibb's single 'Desire' – the first of only two songs on which all four Gibb brothers sang. (*RSO*)

Left: Robin with Jimmy Ruffin during the recording of the *Sunrise* album.

Right: Robin and Marcy Levy recording their contribution to the *Times Square* movie soundtrack, 'Help Me'.

Left: Karl Richardson, Albhy Galuten and Barry at work with Barbra Streisand, overseen by her manager Charles Koppelman. (*Mario Casilli*)

Right: The Bee Gees behind the mixing desk at their Middle Ear Studio in 1981.

Left: The label of the Austrian edition of 'He's A Liar' – the only record ever released credited to the Gibb Brothers. (*RSO*)

Right: A Japanese promo LP featuring six tracks from *Living Eyes*, notable for its reverse groove (playing from the inside out). (*RSO*)

Left: Although not the first commercially available CD, *Living Eyes* was famously used as the demonstration model for the new format. (*Compact Disc*)

Right: The Bee Gees at Piccadilly Radio in Manchester with presenter, Mike Sweeney.

Left: The Bee Gees with presenter Roger Scott at Capital Radio, where they performed a live acoustic set on air.

Right: Bee Gees *Greatest* 1967-1974. *(RSO)*

Left: Maurice at his home studio, Panther House, in early 1982.

Right: Barry with Dionne Warwick.

Left: Robin in character as a schoolteacher in the 'How Old Are You?' promotional video. His then-girlfriend, Dwina Murphy, is dressed as a schoolgirl but does not actually appear in the clip.

Right: Sylvester Stallone and John Travolta with the brothers at Middle Ear Studio during the recording of the *Staying Alive* soundtrack.

Left: Barry with Alex Brychta, the illustrator of *The Legend*. (*Jody and Tracy/Namara Features Ltd.*)

Right: *The Legend* – the illustrated story of the Bee Gees, written by David English and illustrated by Alex Brychta. (*Quartet Books*)

Left: Kenny Rogers, Dolly Parton and Barry Gibb. (*RCA*)

Right: Maurice Gibb – 'Hold Her In Your Hand' UK 7″ single in gatefold sleeve. Theme to the film *A Breed Apart*. (Audiotrax)

Below: Robin Gibb in discussion with producer Mark Liggett at Criteria Studios during the making of the *Secret Agent* album.

Left: An enamel badge given to all involved in the making of the *Now Voyager* video.

Right: Barry in early make-up for the 'I Am Your Driver' segment of his long-form video, *Now Voyager*. Among the other characters is his ten-year-old son Stevie, standing to his left. (*Andy Hosie*)

Left: A rare first edition of Surfside's 'Rockin' Reggae Jam' on the Surf label (1984). It was produced by Maurice together with Bee Gees physician Dr Ron Stander, and was later reissued on the Soaring label in 1985. (*Surf Records*)

Right: A Swiss fan club, BG News, interview record from 1984, limited to just 200 copies, featuring short interviews with Barry, Robin and Maurice conducted by Andreas Anderegg. (*BG News Switzerland*)

Left: Maurice in character as a Union soldier in the film *The Supernaturals*. He composed a soundtrack, but it was not used in the theatrical release. (*Embassy Pictures*)

Right: Barry in the studio with Michael Jackson and Diana Ross, recording 'Eaten Alive', for which Jackson wrote an additional section. (*Capitol Records*)

Left: The intended front-cover image for Barry's unreleased 1986 album *Moonlight Madness*. (*Rick Garcia*)

Right: Robin from the photo shoot for his *Walls Have Eyes* album.

Left: 'We're The Bunburys' UK single in booklet sleeve. (*Island Records*)

Right: Barry and Barbra Streisand at rehearsals for her September 1986 fundraising concert at her Malibu ranch.

Left: Maurice and Swedish pop star Carola Häggkvist in Miami during the recording of her album *Runaway*, which Maurice produced.

Right: The Bee Gees at Middle Ear, adding harmonies to their *E.S.P.* album. (*Bravo*)

Left: 'You Win Again' – the UK chart-topping single, with sales boosted by the release of a 12″ picture disc. (*Warner Bros*)

Right: A rare UK special-edition 12″ single of 'E.S.P.' featuring Arthur Baker remixes. (*Warner Bros.*)

Above: On 7 October 1987, Andy Gibb earned his private pilot's licence at CAV-AIR Flight School in Fort Lauderdale with instructor Ken Winters. (*Bee Gees Quarterly*)

Right: The programme for Barry Gibb's fourth Love & Hope Tennis Festival, at which Barry and Andy performed at the gala dinner.

Left: The Bee Gees performing at the Atlantic Records 40th Anniversary concert at Madison Square Garden on 14 May 1988 – their first concert-stage appearance since the 1979 *Spirits Having Flown* tour.

Right: The Prince's Trust Rock Gala at the Royal Albert Hall – The Bee Gees' first concert performance in Britain since 1974.

Left: The Bee Gees meeting Diana, Princess of Wales, after The Prince's Trust Rock Gala concert.

Right: The Bee Gees appeared before an audience of over 72,000 people at the Nelson Mandela 70th Birthday Tribute at Wembley Stadium.

Left: Barry with Timothy Dalton and Anthony Edwards, stars of the movie *Hawks*. (*Georges De Keerle*)

Top right: The promotional badge given to attendees of the gala world premiere of the film.

Right: The Argentine edition of the soundtrack album. (*Polydor*)

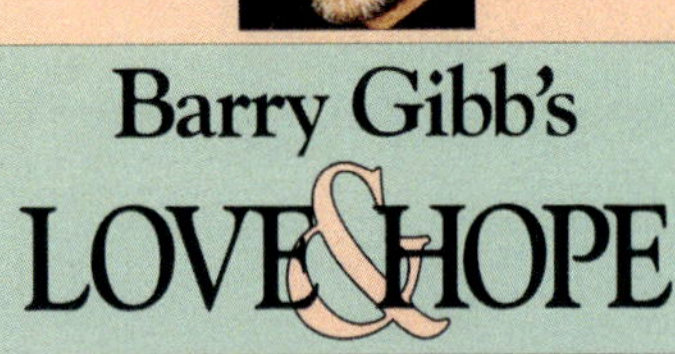

Left: The programme for Barry Gibb's fifth Love & Hope Tennis Festival, marking the first appearance by all three Bee Gees at the event since its launch in 1984.

Right: The Bunburys' second UK single in a booklet sleeve. (*Island Records*)

Left: Sitting on the dock at Barry's house on Biscayne Bay, Miami Beach. (*Hello*)

Right: Awards for the *E.S.P.* album from *Hollywood* magazine in Germany in 1989. (*PPW/Kohr*)

Left: The European edition of the *One For All* tour programme.

Left: A *One For All* tour backstage pass.

Right: Performing the ever-popular medley segment at the Waldbühne in Berlin. (*Andrew Môn Hughes*)

Left: Reunited with former bandmates, drummer Colin Petersen and guitarist Vince Melouney, at the Sydney concert on the Australian leg of the *One For All* tour. (*Kay Barclay*)

You cannot prove what didn't happen, and the truth of the matter is the song was never heard by any of us … There has to be at least some sort of proof of access, some reasonable evidence that we would have heard his song, and that is simply not the case. So, the judge had to give us our honour back, which was taken away and should not have been.

He also reflected on the implausibility of the accusation, framing it in more personal terms:

In my mind and in my heart, the question is, why would we do this? Why would three people who have been writing all their lives, who have had considerable success with many songs, stoop to stealing an unknown writer's song? It's quite possible that Ronald Selle believed that we took his song – but he was wrong. He was wrong then, and he's wrong now.

The publicity surrounding the lawsuit appeared to prompt further claims. Robin revealed that the band were already facing another case: 'We're being sued again now for 'Woman In Love', just for the title... The record sounds about as much like our 'Woman In Love' as 'Chattanooga Choo-Choo".

Reflecting on the experience, Barry acknowledged the longer-term impact of the case, admitting it had altered how the band viewed their position within the industry:

I guess now we'll have to live with the feeling that somewhere, somehow, somebody's going to take action against us again... We've written a lot of songs and had a lot of successes, so we're a good target. But hopefully, this case, and the way it's gone down, is going to stop people from wanting to hit established songwriters quite so easily.

Despite their eventual vindication, Barry remained frustrated that the outcome received far less attention than the accusation itself: 'What was heartbreaking was the six months waiting to be vindicated by the judge – and when we were found innocent, nobody publicised it, so that was even more devastating'. He noted that their decision to fight rather than settle had resonated with other artists who had faced similar accusations.

In a subsequent appearance on *The Don Lane Show* in Australia, Robin clarified that the ruling had not come through appeal but through the judge's direct intervention, with the original jury decision simply set aside.

Barry, however, remained cautious about what might follow: 'It would be nice for us to go home and think it's all over, but we don't think it is… We get the feeling that the plaintiff will indeed go for an appeal, and it's very possible that the judgment could be overturned again'.

Reflecting more broadly on the case, Barry later pointed to a fundamental disconnect between the legal system and the realities of songwriting:

From the justice point of view, it seemed like their opinion of writing a song was totally different … The general opinion is that a song is written with a pen and not in the mind – that you have to sit at a piano and write notes. And that is simply not the case… people have been writing songs in their heads for years.

Maurice echoed that frustration, suggesting that the jury's limited understanding of the music industry had complicated the trial:

To go through all that pressure and be judged by people who don't know anything about the music industry, don't know how people write songs… it was very hard. It was held in his hometown in Chicago, so people were very supportive of the so-called underdog. We became a target in this particular episode.

In August, an unconventional Bee Gees biography was published. Its origins, however, date back to 1979. At that time, The Bee Gees created a unique and humorous illustrated biography titled *The Legend*, a book that captured the band's history in an imaginative way. Written by their close friend and the first president of RSO Records, David English, and illustrated by Alex Brychta, the book depicted Barry, Robin and Maurice as animals, presenting their journey in a light-hearted and entertaining manner.

The idea for *The Legend* originated during a holiday on Robert Stigwood's yacht, *Sarina*, in Corfu. David English recalled a moment of chaos aboard the yacht:

We had a minor shipwreck, and while various stars were leaping around in panic, they suddenly looked like animals to me. I went down to my cabin and wrote a story called *Animals In Wonderland*. Everyone loved it. And when The Bee Gees heard about it, they wanted me to do a follow-up based on the band's history.

Explaining how he became involved in the project, Alex Brychta told the authors in September 2025:

David English met my late father, Jan, when they were both working on a BBC children's programme, when David did a short stint as presenter. My dad, also an illustrator like me, as well as a painter, was producing some drawings for the programme – I think it was *Play School*.

The two became friends, and later, when David wrote the *Sarina* cruise saga, he asked my father to illustrate it. When my dad found out that the job wasn't paid and was just a personal gift for Robert Stigwood, whom he didn't know, he politely declined. At that time, I wasn't long out of art college, but had already published a couple of books, so David asked me instead. As I had time on my hands, I agreed. Since this was a one-off book, the text also had to be written by hand, and my mum, a professional calligrapher, was persuaded to help me out.

The finished product was a great hit with Robert, and when The Bee Gees saw it, they wanted a book about their lives illustrated the same way.

The first edition of *The Legend* was published in 1979, but only a few thousand hardcover copies were printed as a vanity project. The Bee Gees personally financed the project, spending approximately £30,000 to produce a red-covered hardback edition embossed with the classic Ernie Cefalu-designed Bee Gees logo. These copies were sent to close friends, family, and select fans.

A limited commercial release followed in the US through The Official Bee Gees Fan Club. This version featured a cover illustration of the animal representations of Barry, Robin and Maurice bursting out of a bass drum.

In August 1983, an updated version of *The Legend* received a full commercial release, concluding with the Ron Selle court case, Kenny Rogers' album, and the *Staying Alive* film. This edition introduced a new front cover, depicting the characters on top of the Pan Am Building in New York.

Reflecting on the time spent with the band while working on the books, Alex Brychta recalled:

Both editions of the book took a combined total of maybe a year to produce, and during that time, my mum and I spent a lot of time with the brothers since they enjoyed checking the progress on a regular basis. We met up with the brothers regularly in London, Miami and L.A., where we attended their, at the time, biggest concert at the Dodger Stadium. They invited us onto the stage at one point during the concert, and to this day, I blame that experience for my tinnitus. Mum and I were positioned next to one of the building-sized banks of speakers at the side of the stage.

The book's promotional campaign included a book signing at Liberty in Regent Street on 27 August, and appearances on *Good Morning Britain* and *The Late, Late Breakfast Show* with Noel Edmonds.

The humour and creativity behind *The Legend* made it an endearing project for the band. In an interview with Sharon Feinstein for *Woman*, Robin shared: 'You can find an animal in most people, and I think the book is a terrific idea'. He explained his own portrayal: 'I have been portrayed as a red setter because I own one called Penny, and because I used to have red hair. Also, I am very alert, just like a hunting dog'. Maurice was depicted as an eager beaver, while Barry was illustrated as a lion. 'My wife, Linda, always said I seemed to resemble a lion because of my long mane of hair', Barry said.

The book also included playful representations of other key figures in The Bee Gees' journey. 'Everyone gets sent up in the story', Barry noted. 'For instance, Robert Stigwood, producer of the *Saturday Night Fever* and the *Grease* movies, is always portrayed hanging upside down because his life is so topsy-turvy'.

Discussing the creative freedom he had, Alex Brychta reflected:

In one way, it was the best job I ever had because I was allowed to go mad and draw things that couldn't be published today. The only restrictions concerned areas where the brothers thought they might get sued. One such episode was an illustration of The Osmonds. 'How will you draw them, since they have big teeth and you already draw us with big teeth', Barry asked. 'I can just draw them as big teeth on legs', I said. The brothers roared with laughter and told me to go for it. 'Hang on, are they going to sue us?' one of them asked. 'Not if you don't name them', I said – and so it was passed.

The book's appeal extended beyond the band's inner circle. Robin said in the *Woman* interview:

People found the book incredibly addictive. Neil Sedaka, John Travolta and Barbra Streisand all told me they were taking it to bed with them every night – and loving it. People find it much more absorbing to read a funny biography with lots of pictures than a thick volume of print. There is no real dirt in this book, no heavy sexuality or unnecessary violence, so I know it is going to appeal to a lot of different people. My kids actually prefer it to their *Tintin* books.

Earlier plans to adapt *The Legend* into a full-length animated film stalled amid creative disagreements over how the project should be approached. At one stage, a proposal to turn it into a horror movie was put forward but ultimately rejected. This was followed by the idea of reimagining it as a *Monty Python*-style comedy starring the brothers themselves, with a team of writers developing the concept – but none of these ideas ever came to fruition.

On 10 August, MCA held a press conference at New York's Carlyle Hotel to announce a major signing to the label. Invitations mailed out the week before the event said only that the guest of honour was 'responsible for sales of more than 100 million records', but label officials confirmed that it was going to be Barry Gibb.

In December, he signed with Polydor International as a solo artist for the world outside the US and Canada. The Bee Gees as a group would remain signed to RSO – for now.

Eyes That See In The Dark – **Kenny Rogers** (1983)

Personnel:
Kenny Rogers: vocals
Barry Gibb: vocals, guitar
Maurice Gibb: guitar, bass, synthesiser, vocals
Tim Renwick: guitar
George Terry: guitar
George Bitzer: piano, synthesiser
Albhy Galuten: synthesiser, piano

Ron Ziegler: drums
Joe Lala: percussion
The Boneroo Horns: Peter Graves, Whit Sidener, Ken Faulk, Neal Bonsanti
('You And I', 'Islands In The Stream')
Dolly Parton: vocals ('Islands In The Stream')
Denise DeCaro: vocals ('I Will Always Love You')
Myrna Mathews: vocals ('I Will Always Love You')
Marti McCall: vocals ('I Will Always Love You')
The Gatlin Brothers (Larry Gatlin, Steve Gatlin, Rudy Gatlin): vocals ('Buried
Treasure', 'Evening Star')
The Bee Gees (Barry Gibb, Robin Gibb, Maurice Gibb): vocals ('Living With
You')
Fred Tackett: guitar ('Evening Star')
Mitch Holder: guitar ('Evening Star')
John Hobbs: piano ('Evening Star')
Paul Leim: drums ('Evening Star')
Engineers: Karl Richardson, Steve Klein
Producers: Barry Gibb, Karl Richardson, Albhy Galuten
Recorded at Middle Ear, Miami Beach; Lion Share Recording Studios, Los
Angeles, about May 1983
Strings recorded at Ocean Way Recording, Los Angeles, about May 1983
Release dates: UK: October 1983, US: August 1983
Chart positions: New Zealand: 2, Norway: 2, Sweden: 4, Canada: 5,
Australia: 6, US: 6, Austria: 9, Netherlands: 13, Switzerland: 14, UK: 53
Platinum certification: Australia, Canada (4x), New Zealand, US (2x)

In the final weeks of 1982, country music icon Kenny Rogers, seeking to
expand his musical horizons, decided to approach Barry, hoping to
discuss a new musical project. Barry's reputation as a songwriter and
producer was unmatched, with a track record of crafting iconic hits.
Rogers, keenly aware of his success producing albums for Barbra
Streisand and Dionne Warwick, sought a similar transformative
collaboration. To initiate the project, Rogers demonstrated his
commitment by sending his private jet, a luxurious BAC One-Eleven with
20 seats upholstered in white kid leather, to fetch Barry and his wife,
Linda, for a discussion at his home. The purpose was clear: Rogers
wanted Barry to produce his next album.

Barry's initial response encapsulated his enthusiasm and commitment:
'Someone might say, 'Would you do a couple of tracks?' If I really loved

that artist, I'd say, 'Well, I'd actually love to do a whole project". The notion of a single song quickly grew into a full-album endeavour, a concept that excited Barry. 'I think an album has an identity', he explained. 'You work for the whole identity, and you do it as a project. Then your heart's in it, and it's better than doing just two songs. I don't think it works otherwise'.

It wasn't just Kenny's fame that drew Barry to the project – it was the challenge. Barry admitted:

My first thought was, 'How wonderful!', because of the challenge. He's the thoroughbred country singer and the major male artist in this country. I was very flattered because people like that don't often approach someone like me. This was unique, and I was very pleased. I looked forward to this project from the beginning – as opposed to Barbra Streisand, whom I was terrified to produce until I started working with her – and I thoroughly enjoyed it.

For longtime Bee Gees fans, the pairing with Rogers made more sense than Streisand or Warwick, as Barry's affinity for country music was well-documented, even earning him a BMI Country Citation of Achievement for 'Rest Your Love On Me'. Barry admired Kenny's unique connection with the public, explaining in a 1983 *Billboard* interview:

Kenny isn't going to appreciate this, but I think he has sort of a father image. It's a very solid, warm feeling you get when you look at the guy or hear him sing. It's terrific. When he's on television, he comes across as a very warm person, which is what he really is. There's a very big space in this business for someone like that, and Kenny has captured it.

What didn't surprise me, I suppose, is that he is the talent he's made out to be, that he hasn't just been sold. Everyone in our business is the victim of high-publicity hype. No one is ever quite as good as they're made out to be. This is a larger-than-life business, but Kenny stands up. That didn't surprise me because that's the reason I wanted to work with him.

Kenny also saw the collaboration as an opportunity to expand his image, remarking, 'You have to stick your neck out and hope that your audience will stretch out their musical tastes with you. Just the thought of me working with The Bee Gees has to make people a little curious about these two different musical styles'.

Albhy Galuten noted Barry's enthusiasm: 'Barry wanted to work with Kenny. The basic rule of thumb was that if there was anybody who was inspirational for Barry to work with, then it would be great to work with them. Everything was tied to Barry writing great songs. If Barry was inspired, that was all that was needed. If he wasn't, you were wasting your time'.

Barry took a meticulous approach to creating Kenny Rogers' album, recording rough versions of every track before reworking them with session musicians and Rogers himself. He adapted his vocal delivery for the demos to suit Kenny's range, departing from his usual falsetto. The process began in mid-1982 when Barry and Maurice recorded the first demo, which would become the title track 'Eyes That See In The Dark'. At this stage, Barry had not yet met with Kenny.

Albhy Galuten described this initial phase as 'the two-day demos', explaining the swift and focused process: 'I put down a drum machine track, Barry played acoustic to it, I added bass, and then other elements'. These rough demos, crafted in their studio using guitars, drum machines, and layered vocals, became the foundation for the album. Barry's dedication was evident, with Albhy recalling that 'Barry would sing all the vocals in two days', ensuring the songs were ready for the next stage of development.

Late in 1982, after meeting Kenny and agreeing to write an entire album for him, the brothers created a batch of songs and demoed them in January 1983. These included 'You And I', written by Barry, Robin and Maurice; 'This Woman', a collaboration between Barry and Albhy Galuten; and 'Midsummer Nights', another Barry and Albhy composition.

The next set of songs, written by all three brothers, included some of the album's standout moments. 'Hold Me' emerged as a gentle, quiet ballad accompanied on the demo by synth strings played by Albhy. 'Living With You' featured harmonies that included all three brothers; a feature retained in the final recording. In 'Buried Treasure', Maurice provided the harmonies later recreated by the Gatlin Brothers for the released version. Notably, the brothers initially conceived 'Islands In The Stream' as an R&B ballad in the style of Smokey Robinson. However, it evolved into a country song, and at the demo stage, it was not yet planned as a duet, remaining in the same key throughout. This early version featured backup vocals from Robin and Maurice.

For the final batch of songs, Barry and Maurice worked as a pair, crafting three additional country tracks. 'Saying Goodbye', a poignant and beautifully crafted song, didn't make it beyond the demo stage. 'Evening Star' was a lively, harmony-rich track later enhanced by the Gatlin Brothers for its release, while a somewhat clichéd instrumental break was removed. The dramatic ballad 'I Will Always Love You' completed this group.

These demos, created as a foundation for Rogers' recordings, were never meant for public release. However, in November 2006, they were officially issued as *The Eyes That See In The Dark Demos* on iTunes, offering fans a behind-the-scenes glimpse into the creative process behind the album. Fans have frequently lamented Barry not releasing the tracks himself as a solo effort – and they have a point as his vocals on the demos are outstanding. However, Barry was more driven to give Kenny the strongest possible set of tracks to fit his aesthetic. Mission accomplished.

The recording sessions proper commenced in May 1983 at Middle Ear in Miami. Instrumental tracks were laid down by a top-tier studio band featuring Maurice on guitar, bass, and synthesiser, alongside seasoned session musicians that included Tim Renwick and George Terry on guitar, Ron Ziegler on drums, Joe Lala on percussion, and George Bitzer on synthesiser.

Once the instrumental tracks were completed, Rogers' vocal recordings took place at Lion Share Studios in Los Angeles, a facility he had personally upgraded from its previous incarnation as ABC Recording Studios. Additional string arrangements were recorded at Ocean Way Recording, also in Los Angeles.

Many instrumental elements from the original demo recordings were preserved in the final mix, showcasing Barry and his team's forward-thinking techniques.

The Bee Gees relished the challenge of working for someone else. Barry explained the creative freedom that came with writing for other artists: 'It's great input for us because it gives us another dimension to our songwriting. Writing for other people is like stretching – suddenly you can stretch the songs; you can make them do other things'. Discussing his approach as a producer, he recalled: 'Once the songs were selected, Kenny didn't have much to do with cutting the tracks, which were done in Florida. But during the time in L.A., cutting his vocals, there was a lot of intense to-ing and fro-ing about exactly how they should be. There was possibly a little more anguish on Kenny's part than he might have experienced on the last few albums. He would get unhappy about things. In other words, the full spectrum of emotions came out of the guy; I expect a little more than on previous albums'.

What began with enthusiasm soon gave way to unexpected challenges as the recording process unfolded. Kenny, although a seasoned performer, struggled to adapt to the Gibbs' polished demos, and his laid-back approach to the lyrics frustrated the team. 'We sent all the songs,' Maurice explained, 'and when he came to start singing, he didn't know the words'. Barry echoed this sentiment, lamenting: 'The fact that they have to have a piece of paper in front of them, and they've been working on this album with you for three months, and they haven't actually learned the songs – it's frustrating', Barry admitted. 'If I were the artist, I'd be at home memorising these words. It's a different thing when you read and sing'. Despite these frustrations, the team pressed on, determined to shape the album into something extraordinary.

Rogers also struggled to infuse his distinctive style into the songs. Instead, he safely mimicked Barry's demo vocals, which ended up creating tension between him and the production team. Albhy Galuten recalled the situation in conversation with the authors in late 2024:

Kenny was singing *awfully*. I mean, he really was. He was trying to do an imitation of Barry Gibb's little boy voice, and it just wasn't Kenny Rogers at all. I kept telling him, 'Please, just be yourself. Don't try to sing like Barry Gibb'. Then his manager, Ken Kragen, came to me and said, 'Kenny would prefer if you weren't in the studio during his vocals'. So, I wasn't there when he recorded them. At the time, I was renting a house in Malibu and was going windsurfing every day, so I didn't really care. My thought was, 'Fine – I'm still the producer, I wrote the songs, I did the arrangements, I'll take care of the strings, horns, mixing ... everything. But I just won't be there when Kenny sings'.

Karl Richardson told the authors in December 2024 that 'Barry and I didn't mind finishing the record because we knew the band. And Albhy was always there anyway – it wasn't like he really left the sessions. He was conscious of all the music being made. The basic tracks were probably already cut by then, so it was mostly vocals'.

Karl adds that Dolly Parton's arrival in the studio to record what was to become the historic duet 'Islands In The Stream' was a significant turning point in resolving Rogers' vocal issues:

I was there to rehearse Dolly and Kenny for the first time, while Barry was out doing an interview for TV or radio. Thank *God* I had the demo tapes from Miami, where Barry had laid down the pilot vocals. He actually sang Dolly's part and Kenny's part, so I could tell each of them in their headphones, 'this is your part, Kenny' and 'this is your high part, Miss Dolly'. Dolly was wonderful – she'd lilt and flirt with the tracks, change lyrics, scat sing. Meanwhile, poor Kenny was trying to figure out what day it was [*laughs*]. She got on him, too. She said, 'How come you make more money than I do? Because you're stupider than I am!' It was this constant tension because she already knew she could figure this out in her sleep.

Some of the harmony parts were tricky for Kenny. I'd play them over and over, and Dolly would say, 'Come on, *Kenny*! You got that, right? Let's *go*! [*singing*] Islands *in* the stream!' She was over there wailing, and Kenny was like, [*bellowing in monotone*] islands in the stream…' I'd have to say, 'No, no! *Phrasing*!'

All in all, Barry believed the creative push-and-pull that occurred was all in a day's work whilst collaborating with an accomplished artist:

It's a little easier when you think that they're all record producers themselves to begin with. Kenny makes records himself. It's not like we have to push too hard. They come prepared to be pushed. There's no point in using a producer unless you're prepared to be pushed a little bit. You've got to get a camaraderie going, and both the artist and the producer work for that. We meet in the middle, and it works.

'Islands In The Stream' emerged as a serendipitous triumph. Originally written with Diana Ross in mind as an R&B song, it evolved into something completely unexpected. Barry reflected on the track's transformation: 'That was the cream of the cake for me. Dolly is my favourite female singer at the moment'.

Eyes That See In The Dark was released on 22 August 1983 in the US and about two months later in the UK. While its reception varied across markets, the project exceeded commercial expectations. The album achieved considerable success in the US, reaching number six on the *Billboard* Top LPs & Tape survey. On the magazine's Top Country LPs chart, however, it was an absolute blockbuster, spending four months in the pole position.

The album's reception in Britain was lukewarm. The cross-ocean disparity was especially highlighted by the performance of the singles. 'Islands In The Stream' became a global sensation, topping pop, country and adult contemporary charts in multiple countries. It was even declared the RCA label's best-selling single of all time – a remarkable feat for an imprint synonymous with Elvis Presley's output.

However, the British arm of RCA initially overlooked the track, opting instead to release the album's title song as the first single. It only reached number 61, prompting a rushed release of 'Islands In The Stream', which then peaked at number seven. Remarkably, the album charted for just one week in the UK, peaking at number 53.

'This Woman', 'Buried Treasure', 'Eyes that See In The Dark', and 'Evening Star' also became hits in the US, solidifying the album's success in multiple formats.

Despite the challenges, *Eyes That See In The Dark* remains a landmark collaboration. It bridged the worlds of country and pop at a time when crossover between the two genres was still developing, showcasing the Gibbs' versatility as songwriters and producers. As Barry reflected, 'If you write a song, it never really floats away. It's still yours. You do go through that and sometimes find yourself thinking, 'God, I wish I hadn't given that one away'. But you can't be like that. You have to be objective and just keep on writing. We have enough faith in our writing that everyone gets the strongest songs we can give them. You can't hold songs back'.

For Kenny Rogers, the album marked a high point in his career, achieving double platinum status in the US and triple platinum in Canada. 'I think the tracks Barry did on that album are spectacular', Kenny said in a 1984 interview. 'After it was all over, I wished I had gotten more involved. It wouldn't have been any better, but it would have been a little more 'me".

Decades later, 'Islands In The Stream' remains one of the most memorable hit singles of the 1980s, a tribute to the creative synergy between Kenny Rogers, Dolly Parton, and The Bee Gees. Albhy summed it up best: 'When Barry was inspired, magic happened'.

'This Woman' (Barry Gibb, Albhy Galuten)

Recorded at Middle Ear, Miami Beach; Lion Share Recording Studios, Los Angeles; Ocean Way Recording, Los Angeles, about May 1983

Barry's enthusiasm for the set's first track, 'This Woman', was evident when he remarked, 'We thought this would make a great opener because it has that immediate punch and grabs your attention right away. It felt like Kenny, but with a slightly new edge'. Released as a single in the US in January 1984, it reached number 23 on the *Billboard* Hot 100, proving its appeal to both country and pop audiences. The song was co-written with Albhy Galuten, who later reflected on the track's success, admitting, 'Despite my disappointment with some aspects of the album, I was thrilled that 'This Woman' garnered us an Academy of Country Music award and a *Billboard* award for a country record. So, personally, I am glad the record was made in some ways'.

'You And I' (Barry Gibb, Robin Gibb, Maurice Gibb)
Recorded at Middle Ear, Miami Beach; Lion Share Recording Studios, Los Angeles; Strings recorded at Ocean Way Recording, Los Angeles, about May 1983
A heartfelt ballad written by Barry, Robin, and Maurice, 'You And I' showcases Kenny's ability to deliver a tender, intimate performance. The track's stripped-back production allows Kenny's vocals to shine, capturing the vulnerability in the lyrics. Barry recalled, 'This was one of those moments where we wanted to bring Kenny's storytelling into a softer, more intimate space. It's not just about love; it's about connection'.

'Buried Treasure' (Barry Gibb, Robin Gibb, Maurice Gibb)
Recorded at Middle Ear, Miami Beach; Lion Share Recording Studios, Los Angeles; Ocean Way Recording, Los Angeles, about May 1983
Featuring stellar backing vocals by the Gatlin Brothers, 'Buried Treasure' adds a much-needed country edge to the album. Barry shared, 'The song is really about Kenny and his wife, Marianne. It's about the idea that material things don't matter when you have each other'. Kenny's delivery lends authenticity to the narrative, and Barry praised his effort, saying, 'He worked hard on his vocals, and it shows in the final product. It's one of my favourites because of that emotional edge'. Released as the B-side to 'This Woman', which was pushed by RCA, 'Buried Treasure' was picked up by country radio stations and became a hit in its own right, peaking at number three on the *Billboard* Hot Country Singles survey.

'Islands In The Stream' (Barry Gibb, Robin Gibb, Maurice Gibb)
Recorded at Middle Ear, Miami Beach; Lion Share Recording Studios, Los Angeles; Strings recorded at Ocean Way Recording, Los Angeles, about May 1983

The crown jewel of the album, 'Islands In The Stream' is a duet with Dolly Parton that became a cultural phenomenon. Barry reminisced about the recording process, saying, 'Dolly is amazing. She and Kenny recorded their parts live, no separate overdubs, which created such a natural chemistry. The song took on a life of its own – it's a moment in time that feels as fresh today as it did then'. The result was an instant classic that topped the charts worldwide. Barry concluded, 'It's overwhelming to see it become the most successful country song in history'.

In addition to spending two weeks atop the *Billboard* Hot 100 in late October/early November, it was the only American single that achieved RIAA Platinum certification for the entire year.

'Islands In The Stream's title was inspired by the 1970 Ernest Hemingway novel of the same name, although the plot of the book, which follows a reclusive American painter as he grapples with personal loss and the ravages of war, is a world away from the passionate heart-note lyrics of the song. It's not the only time the Gibbs would borrow from Hemingway – The Bee Gees' 1993 single 'For Whom The Bell Tolls' mirrors the name of his 1940 landmark work.

The Bee Gees themselves incorporated 'Islands In The Stream' into the acoustic medley of their *One For All* tour in 1989, segueing it with 'Heartbreaker'. A full live performance followed on 14 November 1997 at the MGM Grand in Las Vegas, later released on the *One Night Only* album in 1998. That same year, Pras Michel's hit 'Ghetto Supastar (That Is What You Are)' borrowed its chorus melody, earning the Gibb brothers songwriting credits and reaffirming the song's cross-genre appeal. It became an international smash, topping the singles charts in ten countries. In the US, the track peaked at number 15, and it placed at number two in the UK.

In September 2001, during what became their final recording session, The Bee Gees revisited 'Islands In The Stream' for their greatest hits compilation *The Record*. This unique rendition, created without Barry, features a hip-hop-inspired backing by Maurice and producer John Merchant, with Robin on lead vocals. Robin's playful addition of a line from 'Ghetto Supastar' underscores the song's lasting influence and links the two tracks in a curious full-circle moment.

The song's legacy took another turn in 2009 when Welsh celebrities Ruth Jones and Rob Brydon, in character from the sitcom *Gavin & Stacey*, released a *Comic Relief* version titled '(Barry) Islands In The Stream'. Featuring Sir Tom Jones and Robin as backing vocalists, the song topped the UK singles chart, securing the Gibb brothers the historic achievement of writing and recording number one hits in five consecutive decades.

The 2025 film *You're Cordially Invited* features no less than three versions of 'Islands In The Stream', each woven into key moments of the story. Will Ferrell's character, Jim, first performs the song with his daughter, Jenni (Geraldine Viswanathan), as part of his heartfelt wedding toast – chosen because it was the lullaby he and his wife used to sing to her as a baby. Later, a slower, more intimate rendition by Ferrell plays over a montage, adding emotional depth to the film. Finally, as the credits roll, audiences are treated to a full duet between Ferrell and Reese Witherspoon (who plays Margot).

'Living With You' (Barry Gibb, Robin Gibb, Maurice Gibb)
Recorded at Middle Ear, Miami Beach; Lion Share Recording Studios, Los Angeles; Strings recorded at Ocean Way Recording, Los Angeles, about May 1983
With backing vocals by all three Bee Gees, 'Living With You' exemplifies the fusion of country and pop. Kenny's rich tones and the layered harmonies of the Gibbs make this a memorable mid-album entry. Barry noted the song is 'What we call the duet with us, The Bee Gees. 'Living With You' is essentially just a pop song with a little powerhouse put in there. It's good, I think, that Kenny is doing some harder songs. He wanted to break new ground, and that's what I think we did'.

'Evening Star' (Barry Gibb, Maurice Gibb)
Recorded at Middle Ear, Miami Beach; Lion Share Recording Studios, Los Angeles; Strings recorded at Ocean Way Recording, Los Angeles, about May 1983
'Evening Star' is one of the album's standout cuts. It is the only song on the album that uses different musicians than Gibb-Galuten-Richardson's usual list of session players – Fred Tackett and Mitch Holder on guitars, John Hobbs on piano, and Paul Leim on drums. They were all seasoned country music session players, giving the track a more authentic country feel. Add Larry, Steve, and Rudy Gatlin's distinctive harmonies in the hook-laden chorus, and it becomes a quintessential country track with its singalong charm. Barry said, 'We also always thought of one of the songs the Gatlin Brothers sang on, 'Evening Star', as sort of a duet. The Gatlins, by the way, were tremendous'.

Evening Star' was later covered by Tommie Babie for the 1984 Italian action film *Blastfighter*, but it remained unavailable in audio format until 2023, when it finally received an official release on CD and a red-and-black vinyl LP.

'Hold Me' (Barry Gibb, Robin Gibb, Maurice Gibb)
Recorded at Middle Ear, Miami Beach; Lion Share Recording Studios, Los Angeles; Strings recorded at Ocean Way Recording, Los Angeles, about May 1983

'Hold Me' is a beautiful, lush, string-drenched ballad with arrangements by Jimmie Haskell that leans into Kenny's ability to convey raw emotion. Barry reflected, 'We wrote this knowing Kenny could handle the deep vulnerability the song required. It's a love song in its purest form'.

The track retains Barry's strummed rhythm guitar from the demo blueprint. While Rogers' vocal also follows Barry's prototype very closely, he does an excellent job of pushing the top end of his register to reach the highest notes at the song's climax with grit.

'Midsummer Nights' (Barry Gibb, Albhy Galuten)
Recorded at Middle Ear, Miami Beach; Lion Share Recording Studios, Los Angeles; Strings recorded at Ocean Way Recording, Los Angeles, about May 1983

The second of two songs by Barry and Albhy Galuten, 'Midsummer Nights' lifts the tempo with its blend of country and soft rock and injects a little more energy into the album, yet it transitions smoothly without jarring the listener. While the catchy melody makes it undeniably engaging, its polished, pop-infused style leans heavily toward the Gibb brothers' signature sound, potentially overshadowing Rogers' established country persona. Nonetheless, it remains a standout for its energy and memorable hooks.

'I Will Always Love You' (Barry Gibb, Maurice Gibb)
Recorded at Middle Ear, Miami Beach; Lion Share Recording Studios, Los Angeles; Strings recorded at Ocean Way Recording, Los Angeles, about May 1983

Not to be confused with the Dolly Parton hit of the same name, 'I Will Always Love You' is a pleasant ballad, written by Barry and Maurice. It's the only song on the album not to feature Barry on backing vocals. Instead, backing vocals from Denise DeCaro, Myrna Matthews, and Marti

McCall (the same exact trio of supporting singers who appeared on Barbra Streisand's 'Woman In Love') elevate the song, providing a contrast to Kenny's commanding lead.

'Eyes That See In The Dark' (Barry Gibb, Maurice Gibb)

Recorded at Middle Ear, Miami Beach; Lion Share Recording Studios, Los Angeles; Strings recorded at Ocean Way Recording, Los Angeles, about May 1983

As the album's title track, 'Eyes That See In The Dark' held a special place in the lineup. Barry explained: 'To me, that song is very contemporary, and we weren't sure it would suit Kenny when we first wrote it. But we sent it along with the first three songs we'd written for Kenny. The immediate reaction was that it was a hit single and that, no matter what else we cut, we'd do 'Eyes That See In The Dark'. It ended up as the title of the album. He's done a beautiful performance of a song I'd like to have sung myself'. It was released as the first single in the UK, reaching number 61, and the fourth single in the US, peaking at number 79 on the *Billboard* Hot 100.

Reflecting on the whole album experience, Barry said, 'We were writing for Kenny, which meant understanding his voice, his emotion and his world. Writing songs is a little like acting – you assume the character and the emotions they need to convey'.

In August 1983, reports surfaced that Maurice was composing music for *Two By Forsyth*, a television adaptation of two short stories by renowned thriller writer Frederick Forsyth. The stories were part of *No Comebacks*, a 1982 collection of ten short stories, each featuring unexpected twists and central characters who, despite appearing ordinary or powerless, navigate high-stakes situations with resilience.

Screenwriter Michael Feeney Callan adapted two of these stories for the screen. The first, 'Privilege', starred Irish actor Milo O'Shea as a mild-mannered stamp dealer who becomes the target of a ruthless journalist. Wrongfully defamed in a scandalous article, he faces the daunting reality that legal action is beyond his financial means. With few options available, he must find an unconventional way to fight back and reclaim his reputation.

The second episode, 'A Careful Man', featured Dan O'Herlihy (best known for his Oscar-nominated turn in the title role of 1954's *Robinson Crusoe*) as Timothy Hanson, a self-made millionaire with a terminal illness. Bitter towards his only surviving relative – his sister – and resentful of the inheritance tax, Hanson devises an elaborate plan to ensure neither benefits from his fortune. His final will stipulates his sister and her husband will inherit his entire estate – but only if they personally push his lead coffin off a boat into the depths of the English Channel.

The production was first broadcast on 28 March 1984 in the US, but the music was ultimately composed by Bill Whelan, the celebrated Irish musician best known for his later work on *Riverdance.*

On 9 September, Robin found himself at the centre of a legal storm that threatened to derail his career and personal life. He was sentenced to two weeks in jail for violating a court order that prohibited him from speaking to the press about his former marriage to Molly Gibb. His emotional interview with the *Scottish Daily Express* in May, in which he discussed his wife, children, financial matters, and the breakdown of his marriage, led to the drastic ruling.

As the sentence was handed down in the London Divorce Court, Molly broke into tears, murmuring, 'I didn't want that to happen'. Robin himself was in shock as Judge Phelan made the decision, and he was taken into custody. The courtroom was tense as his legal team immediately sought leave to appeal. Robin, held under the supervision of his solicitor, wept quietly during the agonising two-hour period that followed.

In a rare move, two High Court judges, Lord Justices Ackner and O'Connor, agreed to hear his appeal during their lunch recess. Robin's lawyer, Andrew Kirkwood, argued that the interview had been an 'emotional outburst' that Robin deeply regretted and assured the court there would be no further violations. Kirkwood presented two additional points to Lord Justices Ackner and O'Connor. First, he emphasised Robin's concerns about his status with US immigration authorities, as he resided in the United States. Second, he reiterated that Molly was not pressing for her ex-husband to go to prison. Her lawyer, Gayle Hallon, confirmed that the intent had only been to ensure Robin upheld his agreement to avoid speaking about their marriage publicly, saying, 'If that has been achieved, Mrs. Gibb does not wish for the serving of the sentence to take place'.

Considering these arguments, the judges overturned the jail sentence, instead imposing a fine of £5,000. Upon hearing the decision, Robin wasted no time in securing his release, paying the fine immediately. Additionally, he also faced an estimated £10,000 in extra legal expenses, plus the substantial cost of chartering a private jet to get him to Italy that same evening.

Emerging from court, Robin did not mince words about his experience. 'Disgusting', he declared to the waiting press. 'I've never seen anything like it in my life'.

Robin made it in time to fulfil his evening engagement, an appearance on a RAIUNO television special with his brothers as part of their promotion for the *Staying Alive* movie. In an unusual step, they performed 'Breakout' rather than one of the more well-known songs extracted as singles from the soundtrack album.

Rarities (1983)

Release date: West Germany: October 1983
Side One: 1. 'Barker Of The U.F.O.', 2. 'Sir Geoffrey Saved The World',
3. 'Sinking Ships', 4. 'Jumbo', 5. 'Gena's Theme', 6. 'The Singer Sang His
Song', 7. 'Tomorrow Tomorrow', 8. 'I've Come Back', 9. 'This Time'
Side Two: 1. 'Railroad', 2. 'I'll Kiss Your Memory', 3. 'Country Woman',
4. 'On Time', 5. 'King And Country', 6. 'Elisa'

In 1983, Polydor in West Germany issued a 17-LP box set consisting of 16 previously released Bee Gees albums and one newly compiled LP called *Rarities* that was available only in the box set. The LP is itself now extremely rare, more so than the original records from which it is drawn.

The special gem here is 'Gena's Theme' in its first appearance since the hard-to-find German LP *Eine Runde Polydor* (1968). It is fairly amazing that its only two appearances were on German LPs that are either rare or extremely rare. Only with *The Studio Albums 1967-1968* project released in 2006 was it finally widely available.

The 5 November edition of *Billboard* reported that country star Larry Gatlin was close to signing with MCA Records. MCA's chairman, Irving Azoff, confirmed the news, adding that Gatlin was heading to Florida to write new songs with Barry for the project.

Earlier in the year, Gatlin had discussions with producer Rick Hall at Muscle Shoals, but speculation grew that Barry was also being considered for the role – a possibility further fuelled by Azoff's remarks. Barry and Larry had previously crossed paths when he and his brothers, Steve and Rudy, recorded vocals for Kenny Rogers' *Eyes That See In The Dark* album earlier in the year.

Ultimately, Larry Gatlin & The Gatlin Brothers' 1984 album *Houston To Denver* was produced by Rick Hall and released under Columbia Records, leaving the potential MCA deal and Barry's involvement unrealised.

In December, The Bee Gees lost a pivotal figure in their early success with the passing of their former producer and mentor Ossie Byrne. Oswald Russell Byrne, an Australian record producer born in 1926, made an indelible mark on music history through his pivotal role in the early success of The Bee Gees, despite remaining a largely uncelebrated figure outside of industry circles. Byrne's story intertwines with The Bee Gees' journey in 1966, when the group, then based in Australia, found themselves needing a studio to refine their sound. Byrne, already a fan of their work, had set up a small studio behind a butcher's shop in Hurstville, Sydney. His enthusiasm for The Bee Gees led him to offer them unlimited recording time, free of charge, which proved invaluable for the group. This access allowed The Bee Gees to experiment and evolve their sound, resulting in their breakthrough single, 'Spicks And Specks'.

When The Bee Gees decided to take their career to England in late 1966, Byrne joined them. In early 1967, the group signed a recording contract with industry heavyweight Robert Stigwood, marking the beginning of their international breakthrough. Working from London's IBC Studios, Byrne co-produced their first British single, 'New York Mining Disaster 1941', which became a substantial hit both in the UK and internationally. This success was followed by the production of The Bee Gees' debut UK album, *Bee Gees' 1st*, a record that showcased the group's blossoming artistry and established them as a major force in pop music. Though they had previously released albums in Australia, *Bee Gees' 1st* represented a new level of artistic and commercial achievement, earning critical acclaim that has endured for decades.

Despite this success, *Bee Gees' 1st* would be the final project Byrne produced with the band. As The Bee Gees' technical skills grew, they gradually transitioned to self-producing, leaving Byrne to seek other opportunities. Although he worked with a variety of bands, including the folk-rock group Eclection and the progressive rock band Cressida, he struggled to replicate the success he had achieved with The Bee Gees. Remaining in London, Byrne opened his own studio, Village Way Recorders, in Rayners Lane, Harrow, North London.

Byrne passed away from cancer in December 1983 at the age of 57 in the borough of Brent, north-west London. In his will, he left Village Way

Recorders to Paul Layton of The New Seekers, ensuring that his influence would persist in the music community he had built.

Although his career largely faded after his work with The Bee Gees, Byrne's legacy was poignantly recognised by the band. Following his death, The Bee Gees dedicated their 1987 album *E.S.P.* to Byrne's memory, acknowledging his instrumental role in launching their global success.

On 12 December, *United Press International* reported that Maurice had been working on a musical score for a promotional tourism film called 'Greater Miami – Where Business and Pleasure Meet'. He had volunteered to write a 15-minute classical score, but Dade County officials said the laid-back musical score would have to be rewritten because it lacked energy.

The music was copyrighted under the title 'Miami: A Musical Score', though it actually consists of eight distinct tracks. The titles may initially seem confusing because they lack punctuation in the registration, but the unique themes of each track make it relatively easy to distinguish one from another: 'Miami', 'Aerial City Hotels', 'Disco Football', 'Golf Tennis', 'Greyhound Horses Jai Alai', 'Miami Lovers Boats City Or Night', 'Planes Landing Cruise Ships', and 'Power Boat Everglades Canal'.

'It was nice of him to donate it. I'm very appreciative of the music. But it needs some work, that's all', said Hank Goldberg, an advertising executive who represents the Metro-Dade County Department of Tourism. 'The way the music is structured now, people are going to fall asleep. We're not looking to replace Valium', he said. 'It's all very classical sounding ... it's dull'. But Goldberg said only portions of the score were inappropriate and he did not intend to scrap the entire composition. The film, in production for two years, was intended to highlight South Florida's natural beauty.

On 24 December, British television audiences were treated to a festive special with *Cilla Black's Christmas Eve*, a variety programme produced by London Weekend Television which was broadcast on all regional channels within the ITV network. Set in a festive living room-style studio, Cilla opened the show with a rendition of Lionel Richie's 'All Night Long'. The show also featured performances from international stars, including Julio Iglesias and George Benson, along with British comedian Frankie Howerd, who brought his signature humour to the proceedings. The most memorable moment, however, came from The Bee Gees, who appeared via satellite surrounded by their families: Barry with his wife Linda and sons Stephen, Ashley and Travis; Maurice with his wife Yvonne and his son, Adam, and daughter Samantha; and Robin with his then girlfriend Dwina and baby son Robin John.

The Bee Gees' performance was a simple rendition of 'Silent Night' accompanied by Barry on acoustic guitar. The entire family sang along, as did Cilla, who also encouraged her studio audience to join in. In a time before video calls were commonplace, seeing such an intimate family moment broadcast into homes on Christmas Eve was both innovative and slightly surreal.

1984

At the end of a very busy 1983, The Bee Gees revealed ambitious plans for the year ahead, announcing no fewer than five album projects slated for 1984. The schedule included a new Bee Gees greatest hits collection featuring three brand-new songs, a solo album from Barry Gibb in the spring, a new Robin Gibb album, a full Bee Gees album in the summer and an Andy Gibb album later in the year. Looking even further ahead, the brothers said that albums for Dolly Parton and Diana Ross were already on the horizon for 1985.

The hits retrospective was an especially interesting announcement since there had been such limited output in the roughly four years since the release of the double-disc *Greatest*. The new songs intended for the set were reportedly titled 'It's My Neighborhood', 'Toys' and 'Dimensions'. Curiously, songs with those same titles would surface on separate projects in later years, yet the group has insisted the earlier set were not the same compositions. Robin even clarified in 1985 – when he released his own track called 'Toys', co-written with Barry and Maurice – that the earlier 1983 'Toys' had been nothing more than a working title. While a bit confusing when one looks at the chronology of their work, the Gibbs often came up with song titles that would get tucked away for long periods of time, and they would frequently revisit and revise compositions several times.

Only two of the proposed 1984 releases would come to fruition: a solo album each by Barry and Robin would be on the shelves by autumn. Nothing more was spoken about the remaining Gibb projects or the Dolly Parton album, but the brothers would begin writing songs for Diana Ross later in the year.

The first half of the decade laid bare a culmination of complexities related to the Gibbs' business relationships. While they were now closer to being a fully self-sustaining entity in writing, publishing, and production, they were learning quickly that it came with a cost of having to contend with the problematic arrangements they had made with powerful people earlier in their trajectory.

Bryan Morrison's partnership with Robin began at a critical juncture in the songwriter's career. After his acrimonious departure from The Bee Gees in 1969, Robin's manager, Vic Lewis, approached Morrison for help managing Robin's fledgling solo career. Despite his status as an acclaimed songwriter, major publishers dismissed his potential. 'Robin

Gibb and The Bee Gees are finished' was the blunt response Morrison encountered from publishers. Outraged by their dismissal, he staunchly defended Robin's legacy, arguing, 'You're talking about one of the greatest writers in the world today'. He emphasised Robin's contributions to iconic hits like 'Massachusetts' and 'I Started A Joke' – songs he believed had already attained the timeless quality of 'evergreen' status. When traditional routes failed, Morrison devised an innovative solution: a bespoke publishing company, Robin Gibb Music. He invested £20,000, offering Robin 50% ownership while splitting the remainder with Vic Lewis. 'This idea was jumped upon by Robin', Morrison recalled. The partnership paid off quickly with Robin's first solo single, 'Saved By The Bell', which reached number two on the UK charts in 1969. However, Morrison recognised that the accompanying album reflected 'the songs of a man under pressure', not the unrestrained creativity of his earlier work. Still, the new company provided Robin with stability and a platform to refine his songwriting.

Beyond professional support, Morrison also acted as a stabilising influence in Robin's personal life. Noting that Robin had little to show for his financial success other than a stretch Mercedes-Benz, Morrison persuaded him to invest in a home in Virginia Water, Surrey. This step marked a turning point, as Robin began to rebuild both his career and personal life, even as his next two singles failed to chart. Meanwhile, Barry and Maurice were struggling to keep The Bee Gees' name alive, and by 1970, the group's future seemed bleak.

Robin, buoyed by Morrison's support, assumed the role of 'gentle persuader' in efforts to reunite the band. After a series of meetings, the brothers agreed to work together again, setting the stage for one of music history's most celebrated comebacks. Morrison's unwavering belief in Robin's talent and innovative approach to publishing not only preserved his creative spirit but also played a pivotal role in revitalising The Bee Gees as a musical force.

Bryan Morrison's steadfast belief in Robin's talent helped lay the groundwork for The Bee Gees' remarkable resurgence, but their professional relationship didn't remain harmonious. Though Morrison was instrumental in forming Robin Gibb Music, providing both funding and guidance during a turbulent phase of Robin's career, their partnership later became the subject of legal contention. By the late 1970s, as Robin Gibb Publishing Ltd. continued to operate, tensions between the songwriter and his former ally reached a breaking point.

In January 1984, a London High Court judge ruled that the company had been run in a manner 'unfairly prejudicial' to Robin. Robin's lawyer, Michael Eaton, alleged that Morrison, as chairman of Robin Gibb Publishing Ltd., had excessively benefited from the company, extracting around £70,000 ($100,000) since 1977, while Robin himself received only approximately £10,000 ($15,000) in director's fees during the same period. This marked a stark contrast to the collaborative spirit that had defined their early work together.

The judge, in response, ordered a valuation of the shares of the company with a directive for Morrison to sell his half stake to Robin at a fair market price. He also made an order that Morrison should be removed as chairman of the company. The judge said that Morrison had appointed his own companies, for a 15% commission, to take over the collection of fees and royalties, which was the main purpose for which Robin Gibb Publishing had been set up. While Morrison maintained that an oversight prevented him from mounting a proper defence, the court's findings underscored the complexities of blending artistry with business, even between individuals who once shared a common vision.

On 10 May, the picturesque lakeside town of Montreux in Switzerland became the epicentre of music as it hosted the prestigious Golden Rose Pop Festival. The festival lineup was a who's who of the industry, showcasing a dynamic mix of rock, new wave, and pop, reflecting the diverse musical landscape of the time. Fans were treated to performances by Adam Ant, The Alarm, Nino de Angelo, Bananarama, Roger Daltrey, Thomas Dolby, Duran Duran, Gloria Gaynor, Joan Jett, Elton John, Howard Jones, Kajagoogoo, Cyndi Lauper, Madness, Nena, Pretenders, Queen, Cliff Richard, Peter Schilling, Shakin' Stevens, Slade, Spandau Ballet, Status Quo, Rod Stewart, Bonnie Tyler, UB40, Tracey Ullman, and Ultravox. Among the star-studded lineup was Robin, who performed his current hit, 'Boys (Do Fall In Love)'. The Golden Rose Pop Festival was not just a live spectacle; it was a major television event, reaching audiences across Europe and later in the UK on BBC1 on 28 May.

On 14 May, the Academy of Country Music (ACM) hosted its 19th annual awards ceremony at Knott's Berry Farm in Buena Park, California. The two-hour event, broadcast live on NBC and affectionately known as the 'Hat' Awards, brought together the biggest stars in country music for a night of celebration to recognise the exceptional talent and artistry within the country music industry. A highlight of the evening was the presentation of the Single Record of the Year award. The Academy uniquely honours the contributions of the artist, producer and record label in this category, emphasising the collaborative effort required to create an exceptional single. This year, the accolade went to 'Islands In The Stream' by Kenny Rogers and Dolly Parton. The song, produced by Barry Gibb, Karl Richardson, and Albhy Galuten, and released by RCA, was lauded for its timeless appeal and seamless blend of country and pop. Kenny Rogers and Dolly Parton were also named Top Vocal Duet.

On 19 June, the 32nd annual BMI Awards dinner was held at the Plaza Hotel in New York, celebrating the most performed BMI songs of 1983. The event formally honoured 130 writers and 102 publishers for their contributions to 110 songs. Topping the list was 'Islands In The Stream', earning the distinction of being BMI's most performed song of the year. This award marked the Gibbs' third win in the category, setting a new record (their previous wins were for 'Night Fever' in 1978 and 'Too Much Heaven' in 1979). The Gibbs also celebrated a second win for 'Heartbreaker', performed by Dionne Warwick. During the ceremony, Barry, Robin and Maurice were presented with special engraved glass plaques by BMI President Ed Cramer and Senior Vice President Thea Zavin.

A Breed Apart, directed by Philippe Mora, is an adventure drama set in the breathtaking yet isolated Blue Ridge Mountains in the Eastern US. The film follows reclusive Vietnam veteran Jim Malden, played by Dutch actor and *Blade Runner* alumnus Rutger Hauer, who has dedicated himself to protecting a rare bald eagle species nesting on his private island. The plot revolves around wealthy and obsessive bird egg collector J. P. Whittier, portrayed by Donald Pleasence, who is determined to obtain these eggs for his collection. Whittier enlists mountaineer Mike Walker, played by Powers Boothe, to infiltrate Malden's island by posing as a photographer, while Kathleen Turner rounds out the cast as Stella Clayton, a local shop owner and Malden's subtle love interest.

The film explores themes of obsession, isolation and redemption, underscored by Malden's struggle to connect emotionally with Stella and her son, Adam. Walker's eventual change of heart and the tension between the characters add layers to the story. At the film's end, Malden finds unity with Stella and Adam, while Walker turns against his wealthy employer, exposing Whittier's illegal pursuits to a reporter.

Although the film faced a mixed critical reception, with one review stating it 'lacks reason, dramatic tension or emotional involvement', it holds a special place for Bee Gees fans because Maurice composed the movie's soundtrack. For Maurice, scoring *A Breed Apart* represented a dream come true and an opportunity to explore a solo project distinct from his work with The Bee Gees – and, unlike other previous instrumental work he had recently composed, this one made the final cut. Maurice was thrilled to create a score that could stand on its own musically, as he explained: 'I always wanted to write film scores. I always have since *Saturday Night Fever*. I've been so over the moon about making a certain picture with the music, making a great marriage of music and movie. I'm doing another score called *Ghost Soldiers*'.

Maurice composed the entire soundtrack and recorded it in February 1984 at Los Angeles' famous Gold Star Studio. It was the studio's last recording session before it closed. Gold Star, a landmark of California's music scene, officially shuttered on 2 March, marking the end of an era. Known for its role in crafting the legendary 'Wall of Sound', the studio was famed for its unique echo chambers, which became integral to Phil Spector's signature production style in the 1960s. Founded by Stan Ross and Dave Gold in 1950, the studios quickly became the birthplace of countless hit records from iconic artists like the Beach Boys, Eddie Cochran and Herb Alpert. Following the completion of Maurice's sessions, the Gold Star staff began dismantling equipment for dispersion to various purchasers, and the building was demolished, making way for a new commercial structure. The Santa Monica Boulevard site is now home to a strip mall with a Starbucks and a Yoshinoya Japanese Kitchen restaurant.

The movie's music blends orchestral arrangements by Jimmie Haskell with Maurice's synthesiser work to evoke the film's brooding and atmospheric tone. Maurice's minimalist approach mirrors Malden's isolated life, while moments of intensity underscore Whittier's obsession and Walker's internal conflict. 'The film is about a rare breed of eagle that nests on this man's island', Maurice noted. 'It's basically about a rich man's desire to get this bird's eggs. He's a mad, avid egg collector. I did the eagle sounds. You can make up any kind of sounds if you have the working knowledge of your synthesiser'.

Since Maurice could not read or write traditional sheet music, he collaborated closely with Haskell, who transposed Maurice's synthesiser recordings for a full orchestra. Haskell fondly recalled the experience: 'Maurice is an accomplished composer and plays synthesiser very well.

He created the entire music score on synthesiser and even played the arrangements. My job was to orchestrate his music and conduct the recordings with a real orchestra of symphonic size in Hollywood. I assigned each portion of his notes to the instruments that would best enhance the scene'.

Haskell praised Maurice's skill, particularly his flute-sounding synthesiser parts, which Maurice played with sensitivity. Maurice wasn't aware that these parts made it into the final recording, but Haskell noted that he 'mixed the synthesiser flute into the finished recordings because I liked the sound so much'.

The recordings were mixed at Criteria's Studio A. Recording engineer Samii Taylor remembers, 'It was so intense! It was my second soundtrack engineering session with Maurice, but I took it all so seriously because I didn't want to muck it up. Maurice was amazing to work with and definitely kept the intense moments light. I think that was the first time he dubbed me Cloth Ears'.

A soundtrack album was prepared by Maurice and Jimmie. The titles and running order of the 11 tracks are from the tape box, which lists Maurice as the producer and Dennis Hetzendorfer, who had worked with all four Gibb brothers on a number of projects, as recording engineer. The film's score featured various versions and alternative recordings of the same musical themes.

Side One: 'Hold Her In Your Hand', 'A Breed Apart', 'Jim's Theme', 'Solitude', 'The Intruders'
Side Two: 'On Time', 'Mike And The Mountain', 'Adam's Dream', 'A Touch Apart', 'The Breed Ending', 'Hold Her In Your Hand (Instrumental)'

With the exception of 'Hold Her In Your Hand' and 'On Time', all the other tracks are instrumental. While the title 'On Time' will be familiar to longtime Bee Gees aficionados as the B-side of their 1972 hit single 'My World', this is a re-recording with a more aggressive and punchier sound than the original version. However, the older version is what actually appeared in the movie. Oddly, it doesn't appear in the credits, but 'Crystal Bay' does – which begs the question: did Maurice record it for the film? 'Crystal Bay' is an obscure composition which was written by Maurice and his then brother-in-law, Billy Lawrie, and released as a single by British actor Steve Hodson in early 1973.

'Hold Her In Your Hand' (Maurice Gibb, Barry Gibb)
Recorded at Middle Ear, Miami Beach, in late 1983

'Hold Her In Your Hand' was only Maurice's second career solo single, released 14 years after his first, 'Railroad', in 1970. It would also be his last.

Originally recorded by The Bee Gees during the sessions for *Living Eyes* in 1981, it was not used for the project. Maurice revamped the song and included it in the soundtrack to *A Breed Apart*.

A country ballad, which Maurice recorded with himself on piano, guitar, and bass, became the film's main title and serves as both a theme for Stella's character and a metaphor for the eagle. Jimmie Haskell, who arranged the film's score, later stated that he was not responsible for the arrangement of this song.

Maurice explained how the song fitted *A Breed Apart*'s plot:

What happens is, Rutger Hauer, the man who owns this island in the Carolinas, has been out of touch with love and communicating with ladies and so forth. Kathleen Turner plays the love interest in the film, and she owns the main shop on the mainland where he buys all his groceries and spades and things. She has a little son who's madly in love with him, worships him and he doesn't know how to communicate. ['Hold Her In Your Hand'] is basically the song about how he should go about it. Because it's from a film and the film is set in the Carolinas, I thought this was the most appropriate song that Barry and I wrote quite some time ago. I thought this would be really appropriate for the movie, so I re-cut it, re-polished it and made it lovely.

'Hold Her in Your Hand' was issued as a single in Britain in September on the Audiotrax label. It was housed in a glossy gatefold sleeve, which was unusual for a single, featuring a photo of Maurice taken during the filming of the promotional video. The centrespread was a still from the movie showing Rutger Hauer sitting on a cliff, watching over an eagle's nest. The back cover was effectively the lobby poster for the movie. It was also released in South Africa on the Principal Record Company label and in Australia on RCA Victor. It failed to chart in all territories.

The record label for 'Hold Her In Your Hand' shows the music publishing companies as Gibb Bros. Music and Filmtrax plc, a London-based music publishing company that specialised in film soundtracks.

The company operated as a straightforward music publisher, creating copyrights through the production of film music. Filmtrax provided producers with a complete package, commissioning composers and recording soundtracks while also managing record sales through its associated label, Audiotrax.

In addition to *A Breed Apart*, Maurice also composed music for the 1986 American zombie horror film *The Supernaturals*, according to the British music trade magazine *Music Week*, and a movie called *Republics*. Filmtrax, through Audiotrax, capitalised on these soundtracks, adding them to their growing catalogue of film scores. The company had a strong roster of composers, including John Barry, Nino Rota, Stanley Myers, and Paco de Lucía, whose works were associated with major cinema and television productions.

Filmtrax was led by industry figures – chairman John Hall, managing director Tim Hollier, and production director Simon Heyworth. Their expertise and connections allowed the company to amass an extensive collection of soundtracks. By the mid-1980s, Filmtrax owned or co-owned copyrights in around 40 soundtracks.

Audiotrax, as the label associated with Filmtrax, played a crucial role in bringing these soundtracks to market. It released a variety of scores, including *Howling II* by Steve Parsons, *Return Of The Living Dead* by Denis Haines, *Bill The Minder* by Barrie Guard, *The Miracle* by Sal Paradise, and *The Chain* by Stanley Myers, featuring a theme song by Barbara Dickson. Additionally, the label had success with projects like *Paddington Bear's Golden Record* and albums by Jackie DeShannon and Peter Sarstedt. Sadly, the soundtrack for *A Breed Apart* was not released as an album.

Maurice's involvement with Filmtrax and Audiotrax demonstrated his ability to create compositions suited for cinematic storytelling. His association with them positioned him within a broader network of respected composers in the world of film music.

Although Filmtrax plc eventually faded from prominence, its impact on the film music industry was significant during its time. The company's ability to merge music publishing with film production allowed composers like Maurice to explore new creative avenues.

'Hold Her In Your Hand' was the only song from the soundtrack to be released legitimately, gaining a wider audience when it was included on Maurice's disc of The Bee Gees' *Mythology* box set compilation in 2010.

Maurice's daughter, Samantha, recorded an acoustic version of 'Hold Her In Your Hand' that was independently released on CD in 2013.

'Hold Her In Your Hand (Instrumental)' (Maurice Gibb, Barry Gibb)

Recorded at Middle Ear, Miami Beach, in late 1983

The instrumental version of 'Hold Her In Your Hand' was intended to be the closing track on the soundtrack album. The mix Maurice made for the B-side of the single still includes some of his backing vocals.

While it must have been quite disappointing for Maurice not to have his passion project receive a full album treatment, it wasn't to be his last flirtation with the film world.

A Breed Apart premiered at the Cannes Film Festival in 1984, where it received a lukewarm response. *The Hollywood Reporter* critiqued it as a 'picturesque but illogical, uninvolving tale', and Orion Pictures delayed its US release until March 1986, by which time Maurice's single had largely been forgotten. However, over the years, the soundtrack has gained a cult following, with fans praising its dark, haunting quality and Maurice's willingness to step outside The Bee Gees' usual style.

Reflecting on his experience, Maurice acknowledged that not every project reaches a massive audience, but valued the creative freedom he had: 'Sometimes the things you love the most don't find a big audience right away. That's okay – it was about making something I believed in'. The project allowed Maurice to experiment with a mood-driven, instrumental style that was new territory for him.

Robin, meanwhile, sought to capitalise on the momentum of *How Old Are You?* by following it up almost exactly a year later with this third solo album, *Secret Agent*.

Secret Agent – Robin Gibb (1984)

Personnel:
Robin Gibb: vocals
Maurice Gibb: vocals, keyboards, synthesisers
Rob Kilgore: keyboards, synthesisers, guitars
Chris Barbosa: sequencers
Jim Tunnell: guitar
Backing vocals: Robin Gibb, Maurice Gibb, Jim Tunnell, Evan Rogers, Cindy

Mizelle, Audrey Wheeler, Arlene Gold, Lari White, Lori Ellsworth
Engineers: Dennis Hetzendorfer, Richard Achor, Mike Fuller
Producers: Maurice Gibb, Robin Gibb, Mark Liggett, Chris Barbosa
Recorded at Criteria Studios, Miami, between March and June 1984
Release dates: UK: July 1984, US: June 1984
Chart positions: Switzerland: 20, West Germany: 31, US: 204

Robin understood that forging a solo identity after being part of a hugely successful pop group was no simple task. Yet, as one-third of The Bee Gees, he was willing to take the leap. He signed a new deal with Mirage Records, focusing on the North American market, while Polydor retained the rights to his music in other territories. This partnership signalled a strategic shift toward establishing a stronger foothold in the US, building on his recent success in Europe.

Founded by Jerry and Bob Greenberg in 1980, Mirage Records was initially distributed through Atlantic Records, but by this time, it had transitioned to Atco Records, which had previously released the vast majority of The Bee Gees' 1967-1972 albums and singles in North America. Jerry, a long-time friend of the group, played a pivotal role in securing this collaboration.

Seeking a fresh direction and inspired by the chart success of American singer Shannon's groundbreaking dance-pop hit 'Let The Music Play' the previous year, Robin sought out Mark Liggett and Chris Barbosa, the production team behind the song. Barbosa, who also co-wrote the hit, recalled, 'Robin really wanted a dance hit; he specifically wanted to avoid a Bee Gees soundalike record'. Robin's vision aligned perfectly with the duo's expertise and marked a bold departure from the signature Bee Gees sound, leaning into a techno-pop and urban aesthetic and the innovative freestyle dance music scene that was gaining traction in the mid-1980s.

The studio team also included session musicians Rob Kilgore on keyboards, synthesisers, and guitar, and Jim Tunnell on guitar. Maurice is also credited for keyboards and synthesisers. As Barry and Robin were recording solo projects simultaneously in early 1984, Barry utilised The Bee Gees' Middle Ear studio, while Robin chose the familiar surroundings of Criteria Studios, where The Bee Gees had previously recorded a number of their albums. This setting offered him the benefit of a recognised presence in recording engineer Dennis Hetzendorfer, who was assisted by Richard Achor.

In September 2025, Hetzendorfer offered some insight into the
sessions at Criteria:

It was a long, meticulous project, recorded and mixed entirely in Studio
E. [Liggett and Barbosa] were great – very techno, very electronic – and
we had a good time. It was a creative atmosphere. But they had to
learn how the Gibbs liked to work. The brothers liked to build a song
in steps so that by the time they sang, what they heard in their
headphones was virtually the finished record. The vocals were almost
the last thing to go on, but everything else was already there. Mark and
Chris came from a different school of production. They focused more
on the track itself; the singing wasn't as central. And that was fine, it's
just a different approach. But Robin and Maurice wanted to keep the
focus on the voice and the harmonies. And of course, Robin had one of
the great voices of our lifetime.

Discussing their work on the album, Mark Liggett shared insights into
their typical production approach: 'Once we agree to work with an artist,
a budget is proposed. Costs hover around $6,000 a side. That is a pretty
consistent figure lately, but of course, that's when we control the budget'.
However, Robin's project stood out as an anomaly. 'The Gibb project was
different for us in that way. We're not usually working with mega-
budgets, and it's better that way. All that money comes out of your
pockets anyway', he added.

Secret Agent was another collaborative effort between Robin and
Maurice, with two songs co-written by Barry. Robin and Maurice
entered the studio without demos for the album, instead crafting songs
on the spot. Assistant engineer Richard Achor recalled that the brothers
arrived at the studio with only rough song ideas, with Robin constantly
writing and refining the lyrics and experimenting, while Maurice would
often begin by creating drum and synthesiser parts, and they would
build the songs collaboratively.

The resulting sound of *Secret Agent* leaned heavily on electronic
elements, dominated by thick synthesiser lines and programmed bass
and drum tracks that created a crisp sound. It was hard-edged, but
rather sterile and soulless, accented only occasionally by electric
guitar. Most of the intricate keyboard and synthesiser parts were
handled by Rob Kilgore, whose contributions were central to the
album's polish.

This shift toward a more modern, layered sound reflected Robin's desire to create something fresh and current. 'I don't like songs of the past', he explained. 'I like to get ahead; these songs are very 1984, maybe even more futuristic. You'd never associate them with The Bee Gees'.

Robin emphasised the album's innovative qualities. 'It's a different sound', he said. 'Very Black and urban, with strong storylines. It reflects street music. I'm not singing at all the same as I did on our early records. It's definitely not disco. It's very urban dance-oriented, actually. I'm influenced by the sounds that are coming out of Europe, but also the sounds that are coming out of New York City'.

He also contrasted *Secret Agent* with his previous album. 'I didn't want *How Old Are You?* to come out in North America because the music was different on that – it was more European – more continental than anything'.

The album is relatively short in length, with only nine tracks and a total runtime of just over 36 minutes, yet it somehow feels overly long. Much of the disappointment stems from its radical departure from the signature Bee Gees sound that fans had come to expect. Strangely, though, while the album as a whole falls flat, the individual songs are surprisingly good – a contradiction that's hard to reconcile, leaving listeners pondering its overall impact.

The front cover of *Secret Agent* is a striking representation of its time, combining bold visuals with a clean, colourful design. Robin, wearing a black blouson jacket paired with grey cargo pants, stands as the central figure, confidently posing with his hands raised to adjust his dark sunglasses. His hair is voluminous, with blonde highlights and a somewhat wild and untamed look. He stands against a pale blue, panelled background, providing a subtle industrial texture that underscores the album's modern vibe.

The typography plays a significant role in the overall design. At the top left, the bold red lettering of 'Robin Gibb' grabs attention immediately, its stylish serif font lending an air of classic sophistication. Below it, the title *Secret Agent* is written in a contrasting yellow script. Together, the fonts create a dynamic visual hierarchy that draws the eye.

Bob Defrin and Roland Schmidt's contributions to the artwork, along with Mark Tucker's photography, reflect a stylish and deliberate design choice that perfectly suits the mood of *Secret Agent*, radiating the sleek confidence of the 1980s.

The back cover features the same pale blue panelled background, creating visual continuity. This minimalist backdrop allows the key design elements to stand out prominently.

On the left side, the tracklist is displayed in a bold red font on the European edition of the album, sharply contrasting against the muted blue background. The typography is clean and spacious, giving the design a polished and professional feel. The album's production credits appear below in smaller text, although prominence is given to Maurice and Robin as producers. On the North American editions of the album, the credits were styled differently and appeared in a significantly smaller font size.

On the right side, an artistically blurred image of Robin creates a dynamic focal point, adding movement and energy to the scene. It contrasts sharply with a static background and the tidy, structured typography, giving an abstract quality to the design and introducing an air of mystery and intrigue.

'Boys Do Fall In Love' (Robin Gibb, Maurice Gibb)

Recorded at Criteria Studios, Miami, between March and June 1984
Chart positions: South Africa: 7, Italy: 10, Brazil: 13, Spain: 13, West Germany: 21, Canada: 34, US: 37, Australia: 48, UK: 70, France: 71
Gold certification: Canada, US

'Boys Do Fall In Love' was released in May 1984 as the first single to be extracted from the album, with 'Diamonds' on the B-side. It marked a stylistic shift towards synth-driven dance-pop and was engineered for club play. It was released with extended and dub mixes on a 12" single, clearly aimed at DJs and dance floors rather than traditional pop charts alone.

The single peaked at number 37 on the US *Billboard* Hot 100 and was certified gold in the US and Canada. It reached number seven in South Africa and number ten in Italy, but only managed to inch up to number 107 in the UK. In some countries, it was released under the slightly altered title with the addition of brackets – 'Boys (Do Fall In Love)'.

The song's production leans heavily on the Fairlight CMI, evident in the stuttering 'B-b-b-b-b-boys' vocal effects that feel both playful and futuristic, albeit now charmingly dated. The verses are sung in an unusually deep register, with Robin sounding quite a bit like The Human League's Philip Oakey – certainly the lowest vocal he'd used since 1966's 'Monday's Rain'. The chorus, however, returns him to his instantly recognisable normal vocal range with female backing vocals. There is also more prominent guitar work than on the other tracks, giving the song a grittier edge. Tape editing techniques used in the break were consistent with early remix culture, involving free-form editing and new material insertion, aligning with the emerging format of the dance remix.

Lyrically, the song reflects Robin's cynicism toward romantic themes at the time: "Boys Do Fall In Love' is quite tongue-in-cheek. I'm very cynical about love ballads right now because I went through a dreadful divorce back in 1980. I don't feel like doing love ballads, quite honestly'. There's an ambiguity to the phrase, too – whether it's about romantic desire between a man and a woman or hints at same-sex attraction is left open, reflecting the sexually fluid sensibility of 1980s dance music culture.

The extended and dub mixes take things further into club territory, with the dub version in particular stripping the song of its lyrical narrative to emphasise rhythm, instrumental elements and effects like reverb and delay – perfect for DJs seeking to sustain momentum on the dancefloor and consistent with dance music trends of the time.

The music video for 'Boys Do Fall In Love', directed by Mike Brady, adopts a low-budget sci-fi aesthetic, set in the imagined future of 2184. Featuring silver-painted men performing robotic movements, it reflects the period's fascination with futurism and pop surrealism.

The single was promoted across a steady stream of European television show appearances. There were two dates in West Germany: *Show & Co Mit Carlo* on 3 May and *Na Sowas!* on 9 May, followed by a performance on *Eldorado* in Denmark on 8 May. On 11 May, he appeared at the Montreux Golden Rose Festival, which was broadcast throughout Europe. Further engagements included *Azzurro '84* in Italy on 28 May, *Superstar* in Spain on 8 June (where he also performed 'Juliet'), *Festivalbar* at Arena di Verona in Italy on 8 September and *TopPop* in the Netherlands on 11 November.

Critical reception at the time was positive. *Billboard* described the song as 'a really flawless pop record', while *Cash Box* noted that 'the classic Bee Gees sound and knack for a hook is intact though noticeably updated'.

'In Your Diary' (Robin Gibb, Maurice Gibb, Barry Gibb)
Recorded at Criteria Studios, Miami, between March and June 1984
The theme of a man reading his lover's journal and uncovering painful truths in 'In Your Diary' is not entirely original, as it closely mirrors an earlier 1972 song, 'Diary' by American rock outfit Bread. Both songs

revolve around the same central motif, but while Bread's version is gentle and sorrowful, depicting quiet resignation as the man realises his lover loves someone else, Robin's take is more intense and emotionally charged, expressing anguish and a sense of betrayal. Despite the shared concept, the songs differ significantly in tone and emotional delivery.

Although this was the first song on any solo Bee Gee album credited to all three brothers, 'In Your Diary' opts for a surprisingly simple structure with a straightforward verse-chorus format favoured by Robin and Maurice.

The production is unashamedly of its era, boasting crisp electronic drums, dramatic fills, a solid instrumental break and a dramatic key change near the end – it's all very much by-the-numbers for 1984 pop. The track features a Fairlight CMI introduction, the bell-like tones shimmering with digital clarity that analogue synths of the time could only dream of achieving.

Robin uses his rich, low register in the verses, and later adds some quirky vocal inflections, which help break up the repetition. The upbeat, almost cheerful melody clashes with the lyrical content, creating a strange contrast – the music is catchy, bouncy pop, but the lyrics describe a man feeling erased from someone's life.

Lyrically, it's blunt. The narrator, having dared to read his lover's written reflections, is crushed to find he's not a part of them. The repeated line 'You didn't mention my name' drives the message home. There's also a fair question: why is he looking in the first place? Regardless, once he does, he can't unsee it.

Released as a single in the US only in November 1984, with 'Robot' on the B-side, 'In Your Diary' was positively received overall. *Cash Box* called it 'a pleasing piece which suffers slightly from its formula quality but benefits strongly from the familiar strength of the Gibbs' reliable performance, production and styling'. The review concluded that the track has what it takes to succeed strongly on CHR [Contemporary Hit Radio] stations. Despite this, it failed to make an impact on the charts.

'Robot' (Robin Gibb, Maurice Gibb)

Recorded at Criteria Studios, Miami, between March and June 1984

'Robot' employs a choppy, offbeat chord technique that gives it a mechanical, shuffling feel – an intentional nod to the concept of a robot as imagined in the early 1980s. The rhythm progresses in a methodical, deliberate fashion, mimicking the gait and precision associated with early depictions of humanoid machines.

The track is notable for its blend of reggae and synth-driven production, a hybrid sometimes referred to as 'techno-reggae'. This groove underpins the entire song and is one of its strongest features. The use of a vocoder adds an effective layer of texture, transforming his voice into a synthesised, robotic counterpart. This contrasts well with Maurice's natural vocal interjections, particularly the repeated line 'never no way', creating a dialogue that emphasises the artificial versus the human.

The vocoder was first employed by the group under the guidance of George Martin during the 1978 *Sgt. Pepper's Lonely Hearts Club Band* soundtrack. In 'Robot', it's central to the song's identity and theme. It manipulates the vocals in a way that is both stylistically fitting and thematically aligned, reinforcing the track's mechanical aesthetic. It wasn't an original idea, however, having been used to similar effect by Kraftwerk on 'The Robots' from *The Man-Machine* in 1978.

The song likely developed through the in-studio creative approach typical of Robin and Maurice during this period. Richard Achor recalled that they often began sessions with only rough ideas, building from drum and synthesiser grooves before adding vocals and structure. 'Robot' feels like a direct result of that process, with the vocoder possibly serving as the original conceptual spark.

The instrumental section of 'Robot' includes 'scratching' – sometimes referred to as 'scrubbing' – a DJ technique most commonly associated with hip hop in which a vinyl record is moved back and forth on a turntable to create percussive or rhythmic sounds. Its presence here adds a contemporary, urban texture that contrasts with the track's otherwise synthetic and programmed feel.

'Robot' appeared as the B-side to both 'Secret Agent' and 'In Your Diary' on Mirage's US 7" releases. An Extended Dub Mix, found on the US and Canadian 12" editions of 'Secret Agent' (on Mirage and Polydor, respectively), runs a minute and a half longer than the album version and features a longer introduction and additional drum elements.

Robin performed 'Robot' on *Tocata*, a music programme broadcast on Spain's RTVE channel on Christmas Day, giving the track some additional exposure beyond its B-side status.

'Rebecca' (Robin Gibb, Maurice Gibb)

Recorded at Criteria Studios, Miami, between March and June 1984

'Rebecca' sits uneasily in the middle of side one of the album, where the creeping fatigue of the persistent electronic approach starts to set in. It's a critical point in the record, marking a moment where what initially seems like one of the weaker tracks begins to signal that this unrelenting sonic style isn't just a phase, but the defining character of the entire album.

But beneath the dense layers of synthetic textures and polished electronic sheen, a genuinely compelling song is fighting for air beneath layers of cold, manufactured production. The track opens with a long, somewhat wearying 30-second introduction, but once Robin enters, almost narrating his way through the verse in a mellow vocal tone, he draws you into the narrative. The pitch shift going into the chorus is dramatic, almost jarring, but also memorable – it's a fine art, and one Robin was truly a master of.

The second chorus is slightly extended before leading into an instrumental break and, unusually for a Robin and Maurice co-write, a bridge section before the chorus returns and carries the track through to the fade-out.

Rebecca, the character, remains an enigma. Is she a figment of longing, an idealised fantasy, or perhaps an ex-lover lingering in memory? Or, veering into more provocative territory, the lyric 'so wrong' hints at a moral tension, echoing the kind of ambiguity also found in the track 'How Old Are You?'. Is she meant to be a sex worker, catering to a world of kink or fetish? The lyrics 'satin and lace, she's so fine in leather' and 'you only live for the night' perhaps point to something more performative, or maybe even transactional? The song resists clarity, leaving just enough ambiguity to keep the question open.

It's a shame the song's catchy melody is almost lost beneath the weight of its era-specific production. The verses, static and repetitive, don't help matters when Robin's voice is buried in the mix. 'Rebecca' might not be a standout on first listen, but it rewards those who persevere, letting its hooks and quirks sink in slowly.

'Secret Agent' (Robin Gibb, Maurice Gibb)
Recorded at Criteria Studios, Miami, between March and June 1984
The title track, released as the second single from the album, stands as a compelling, if commercially overlooked, highlight. It was issued in various markets with different B-sides: 'King Of Fools' in Spain, West Germany and Canada, and 'Robot' in the US. It commands attention as the album's longest track, and arguably its most fully realised. The 7" single was shortened by a full minute from the album version, while the 12" featured an extended dub mix, emphasising the song's dancefloor potential.

It's a brisk, up-tempo piece with a strong rhythmic drive and well-defined melodic hooks. It exemplifies Robin's ability to create dance music that feels dramatic without descending into pastiche. He's in strong vocal form, using his high register with greater control than on parts of his previous album. The result is expressive without strain, and in passages such as the chorus – where Maurice provides supporting vocals – there's a clear, steady quality that supports the song's more dramatic moments.

'Secret Agent' occupies the territory of a narrative song, though rather than unfolding a coherent plot, the song presents a series of brief scenarios – shadowy meetings, sudden twists and a mood shaped by Cold War tension – that echo both spy thrillers and the news stories of the early 1980s. Incidents like the Combe-Ivanov affair and the Cyprus Seven Trial were still present in the public mind at the time. The opening sets a stylised, fictional tone, establishing the song more as a piece of imaginative storytelling than a realistic account. The reference to *Casablanca*, a film known more for its romantic and cinematic legacy than for espionage accuracy, reinforces the sense that this is a playful nod to spy fiction rather than a serious reflection on real-world events.

The promotional video, directed by Philip Davey, was filmed on location in Glasgow, which stood in for Vienna in 1951. It interprets the song's fragmented storyline with considerable fidelity. The production makes effective use of several distinctive Glasgow landmarks. The South Portland Street Suspension Bridge, which crosses the River Clyde, is prominently featured as one of the key locations. The glass canopy over Queen Street railway station is used to evoke a sleek, modernist setting, while The Glasgow Necropolis, a Victorian cemetery, is used in the video for its atmospheric setting with its elaborate statuary and the prominent column topped by the statue of John Knox featured in several shots. The café sequence was shot at Nico's on Sauchiehall Street, a well-known gathering place for the city's fashionable youth during the 1980s. These carefully selected locations lend the video both period character and urban texture. Maurice appears briefly as the pilot of the aircraft referenced in the song, dragged from the cockpit in uniform – a moment of levity in an otherwise stylised narrative.

'Secret Agent' received limited promotion. The only televised performance Robin gave at the time the single was released was on the popular West German music programme *Musikladen*, broadcast on 20 September. Later in the year, Robin appeared on the Spanish show

Tocata in a special Christmas episode, which aired on 25 December. While *Billboard* described the track as 'powerfully emphatic dance music' in its 15 September issue, this endorsement did not translate into significant airplay or sales.

'Livin' In Another World' (Robin Gibb, Maurice Gibb, Barry Gibb)
Recorded at Criteria Studios, Miami, between March and June 1984
The second track, written collaboratively by all three brothers, raises expectations from the outset. Seeing all their names on the credits alongside the intriguing title 'Livin' In Another World' sets the stage for something potentially bold or visionary. The a cappella introduction, brief though it is, hints at a level of ambition, capturing a moment of anticipation that, sadly, fizzles rather than flourishes.

Once the full arrangement kicks in, the promise begins to unravel. The lyrics dive headfirst into abstraction – and not in a poetic or resonant way. While some individual lines pop with vivid imagery, the cumulative effect is nonsensical rather than surreal. There's a difference between mysterious and muddled, and unfortunately, the lyrics lean into the latter. Lines like 'Check the Dow Jones index' or 'Cable television' appear seemingly at random, leaving the listener more confused than intrigued.

Musically, this is a weak opener to side two. The track attempts to inject energy with rock motifs and some edgier guitar riffs, but they feel tacked on rather than integral. The instrumental passages, particularly the use of reverse-sounding drums – a nod to 1967's 'Barker Of The U.F.O.' perhaps – come across as more of a technical trick than a creative triumph. It's worth noting that the use of the Fairlight to create this effect makes the execution easier, but also more sterile, robbing it of the charm and challenge of its predecessor.

Ultimately, 'Livin' In Another World' tries to be a statement piece but stumbles under the weight of its own disjointed ambition. The chorus repetition becomes numbing rather than anthemic, and without lyrical coherence or a strong melodic anchor, it ends up sounding like a missed opportunity – a track full of ideas but devoid of cohesion.

'X-Ray Eyes' (Robin Gibb, Maurice Gibb)
Recorded at Criteria Studios, Miami, between March and June 1984
'X-Ray Eyes' is an upbeat, commercial pop song that dives headfirst into retro sci-fi kitsch: a girlfriend with literal X-ray vision, peering through

walls and minds. There's more than just a sense of improvisation in the air, with Robin and Maurice making it up as they went along – having fun with the knobs and buttons rather than chasing emotional depth. It's hard to ignore how juvenile 'X-Ray Eyes' feels coming from two seasoned 34-year-old songwriting veterans – it seems more suited to teenage novelty records than adult pop.

The titles of the songs 'Robot', 'X-Ray Eyes' and 'Secret Agent' appear to garner influence from mid-20th-century cinema – *Forbidden Planet* and *The Day The Earth Stood Still*, with their iconic robots Robby and Gort, and *X: The Man With The X-Ray Eyes*. There's also a nod to the intrigue of old spy thrillers like *The 39 Steps* and *The Ipcress File*. But these references, instead of feeling sophisticated or knowing, feel like they've been filtered through a childlike lens. Perhaps that's the point. This could have been a deliberate retreat into fantasy, a way to escape the weight of expectation and the shadow of earlier musical personas. Trading ballads for sci-fi quirkiness might have been an effort to reset, even if it meant embracing silliness to do so. Whether that's endearing or disposable depends on how much playful absurdity you're willing to embrace.

'King Of Fools' (Robin Gibb, Maurice Gibb)
Recorded at Criteria Studios, Miami, between March and June 1984
'King Of Fools', the penultimate track, provides a much-needed lift to what has otherwise been a rather uninspired second side. It's a song that, while far from perfect, stands out due to some striking vocal choices and a few melodic swells.

It opens with a stark, mechanical drumbeat – cold, consistent, and somewhat detached. This chilly foundation leaves plenty of space for the warmer elements to shine, particularly in the vocals. Robin's voice is the real highlight here. In the verses, he reaches into his upper register to great effect, adding emotional tension to otherwise straightforward lines. There's a pleasing melodic contour to these moments – not flashy, but enough to catch the ear.

Unfortunately, the chorus doesn't quite deliver on that promise. It lacks a big, defining hook – the kind that might have lifted the track to another level. It feels slightly flat and underpowered on its first appearance. However, the second time around, the chorus is prefixed with a couple of extra lines, giving it a sense of development and acting almost like a bridge. It's an improvement, even if it's frustrating that this expanded section is never repeated.

As the track progresses, things begin to fill out sonically. Layered harmonies are introduced, giving the later sections a fuller, richer sound. These harmonies don't overwhelm – instead, they gently build, giving the impression of a song finding its own form as it unfolds. One of the most interesting moments comes during the instrumental section. Here, the analogue synthesiser creates a subtly unstable tone – the kind of 'pitch drift' you get when a low-frequency oscillator modulates the pitch of the main signal. It's a small but effective detail, evoking that warm imperfection of vintage gear, and it adds character to what might have otherwise been a filler moment.

Lyrically, 'King Of Fools' leans into a theme of romantic disillusionment, but it's all wrapped in a playful tone. The repeated 'alright' chant gives the song an almost resigned shrug – like someone laughing at their own misfortune.

In the end, 'King Of Fools' isn't a standout track, but it does help to redeem a flagging album side.

'Diamonds' (Robin Gibb, Maurice Gibb)
Recorded at Criteria Studios, Miami, between March and June 1984

The album's closer is 'Diamonds', which was also the B-side to 'Boys Do Fall In Love'. It's one of the earliest tracks recorded for the project and, in many ways, feels like a sonic blueprint for the rest of the album. There's a sense that the production team had a formula, and they stuck with it; the two-line bridge here works well, but it doesn't push any boundaries. The chorus is undeniably catchy – proof the Gibb twins hadn't lost their commercial instincts – but Robin's high-register verses occasionally become a bit indecipherable, a familiar issue that also cropped up on the *How Old Are You?* album.

The lyrics tell the story of a relentless adventurer, driven since boyhood by a vision to find a legendary diamond in the depths of the Amazon and Peru. Steeped in myth and danger, the song paints a vivid picture of holy temples, sacrificial rites and cryptic warnings – evoking the perilous, exotic energy of *Indiana Jones And The Temple Of Doom*, which was released around the same time the album was recorded. As the quest intensifies, the hero deteriorates – feverish, starving and ultimately falling into an icy tomb with the treasure forever out of reach. The repeated refrain, 'he won't stop, the kid goes on and on', underscores a tragic irony: the unstoppable drive that fuels the journey is also what destroys him.

Side two, having opened weakly, is redeemed by 'Diamonds', a bold and strong closing track.

The legal battle between Ronald H. Selle and The Bee Gees spanned four years, from its initiation in March 1980 to the final appellate ruling on 23 July 1984. What began as an allegation of copyright infringement gradually unfolded into a notable legal examination of musical similarity and access.

After the initial ruling, the case was overturned by Judge George N. Leighton on 22 April 1983, and Selle decided to appeal the decision. The appeal was heard by the United States Court of Appeals for the Seventh Circuit on 13 April 1984. In his appeal, Selle argued the district court had improperly overturned the jury's verdict, asserting there was sufficient evidence to support his claim of copyright infringement. Selle maintained that the similarities between his song 'Let It End' and The Bee Gees' 'How Deep Is Your Love' were not coincidental and that there had been a significant possibility of access to his work by The Bee Gees.

The Seventh Circuit carefully reviewed the case, including the evidence presented during the initial trial and the legal basis for Judge Leighton's decision to grant a motion for 'judgment notwithstanding the verdict'. The appellate court emphasised the standard required to prove copyright infringement, which involves demonstrating both substantial similarity and access. They found that while there were some notable similarities between the songs, Selle had not provided convincing proof that The Bee Gees had actually accessed his work.

On 23 July, the appellate court issued its ruling, affirming the district court's decision to overturn the jury's verdict. The appeals court ruled:

In essence, the plaintiff failed to prove to the requisite degree that the similarities identified by the expert witness – although perhaps 'striking' in a non-legal sense – were of a type which would eliminate any explanation of coincidence, independent creation, or common source, including, in this case, the possibility of common source in earlier compositions created by The Bee Gees themselves or by others. In sum, the evidence of striking similarity is not sufficiently compelling to make the case when the proof of access must otherwise depend largely upon speculation and conjecture.

Selle's loss in the appellate court finally marked the end of his legal challenge. The case remains a significant example of the complexities involved in proving copyright infringement, particularly in the context of popular music, where accidental similarities can and do occur. Selle v. Gibb is even more interesting to contemplate in the 2020s, where digital music and social media have made access and appropriation – both coincidental and intentional – possible for almost anyone.

Now Voyager – Barry Gibb (1984)

Personnel:
Barry Gibb: vocals, guitar
Olivia Newton-John: vocals on 'Face To Face'
George Bitzer: keyboards, synthesiser
George Terry: guitar, bass guitar
Harold Cowart: bass guitar
Ron Ziegler: drums
Dennis Bryon: drums
Joe Lala: percussion
Lenny Castro: percussion
Michael Brecker: saxophone
Randy Brecker: trumpet
Brass section: Bob Findley, Walt Johnson, Lew McCreary, Harold Diner, Terry Harrington, Vince DeRosa, David Duke
Backing vocals on 'Fine Line': Olivia Newton-John, Roger Daltrey, Harry Wayne Casey, Kitty Terry
Backing vocals on 'Shatterproof': Denise DeCaro, Myrna Matthews, Marti McCall
String arrangements: Barry Gibb, Jimmie Haskell
String conductor: Jimmie Haskell
Recording Engineers (Middle Ear): Larry Janus, Steve Klein, Neal Kent
Engineer (Ocean Way Studios): Steve Crimmel
George Marino: mastering engineer
Producers: Barry Gibb, Karl Richardson
Recorded at Middle Ear, Miami Beach, in early to mid-1984. Strings recorded at Oceanway Recording, Los Angeles
Release dates: UK and US: September 1984
Chart position: US: 72, UK: 85
Gold certification: Canada

In August 1983, Barry signed a major recording deal with MCA Records, marking the beginning of his first official solo project, *Now Voyager*. The agreement, brokered by industry heavyweight Irving Azoff, aimed to showcase Barry's individual artistry beyond The Bee Gees. The project was ambitious, involving not only a studio album but also a companion 'visual album', a concept that was ahead of its time. The idea was compelling to Barry, though he admitted, 'It's something I always wanted to do, but I never quite felt comfortable enough to do it. The man who really made me think seriously about it was Irving Azoff, who convinced me that there was possibly a market out there for me'. The project became a turning point in Barry's career, reflecting both ambition and underlying tensions.

Barry approached *Now Voyager* with a desire to push creative boundaries to produce something different from his work with The Bee Gees. Working largely with George Bitzer and Maurice, with contributions from Robin on one track, Barry extrapolated on the signature pop-leaning foundations of his songwriting.

The result was a dense and eclectic mix of musical styles, from techno-pop to ballads, designed to appeal to a wide audience. However, this eclecticism also created challenges, as the album sometimes lacked cohesion and, perhaps even more importantly to the sales-conscious elder Gibb brother, a clear commercial quality that could edge out other contemporary music on the charts in 1984.

Barry described George Bitzer as a pivotal collaborator, saying, 'George ... who is a co-writer on this album, is a very fine pianist and he helped me to broaden some of my scope with my chord progressions'. Maurice and Robin were notably absent from the recording sessions, leaving Barry to work closely with the house band and arranger Jimmie Haskell. The sessions were produced by Barry and Karl Richardson, with their usual third co-conspirator, Albhy Galuten, conspicuously absent from the sessions.

Albhy had grown weary of the painstaking, months-long process the production team had adopted of piecing together albums from perfectly played and engineered components. Barry savoured the control and precision of that approach, but Albhy longed for their pre-*Spirits Having Flown* projects that were energised and inspired by musicians and artists building performances together in the studio.

That widening disparity led to Albhy bowing out of the *Now Voyager* project. Reflecting on the situation, he explained his vision for the album and the frustration that led to his decision to leave:

I would have loved to have worked on it if he had done it in the way I thought he could. I said to Barry: 'Your ability to write songs is great, let's book a Broadway theatre, some nice sounding theatre in New York for a week, or two weeks' worth of shows, and rehearse a band … you love working with The Sweet Inspirations, and Steve Gadd, Richard Tee, Randy Brecker, David Sanborn, Harold [Cowart] the bass player, George Terry the guitar player, Cornell Dupree … '.

Albhy envisaged a dynamic, live-recording approach for the album:

We could have put together the ideal band, even a string section, the whole nine yards; written about 15 songs, more than enough for an album, and record it, like seven shows, and put together a live album of solo Barry Gibb. I said, 'This would be great, it would be so much more stimulating and inspiring than sitting in a room by ourselves for nine months with a click track'. And he just said, 'I can't do it, man'. And I said, 'Well, I just can't stay and do another one of these records'.

This creative disagreement marked the beginning of the end of their collaborative relationship. Albhy admitted: 'I know [Barry] was very hurt by my leaving'. Years later, he contemplated what might have been had they taken a more organic route:

It would have been so unbelievable. His ability to sing is great, and we would have had background singers. And with seven or eight versions of each song, we could have had unbelievable takes. At that point, the technology was such that you could repair anything in a live take you wanted to. We could have had guest appearances by people coming in and singing verses. It would have been an amazing record.

Albhy departed for California to pursue new projects, settling permanently in Los Angeles, although he would return to the fold in 1985 to work with the team one last time on the forthcoming Diana Ross album.

Karl chose to stay behind and continue working with Barry, comfortable in his surroundings and not wishing to uproot himself from his home or the Miami music scene he had been immersed in for most of his career. While Albhy had grown frustrated with the album's direction, Karl was excited by it, as he told the authors in December 2024:

I was really getting off on it – and so was Barry's wife, Linda. She turned to me one day and said, 'Wow, you guys are doing a little more rock 'n' roll. I love it!' She could feel it, that looseness in the room. I'd brought in some L.A. players – real sharpshooters, top-tier studio musicians – and they gave the sessions this edge, this swagger that made the music move in a new way.

George Bitzer was there, too. George is blind, but he's got phenomenal ears and a deep sense for harmony and texture. I leaned on him a lot for the arrangements, and that partnership gave Barry a kind of creative freedom he hadn't had in a while. He could just go out there, follow his instincts, and build whatever world he wanted. The sessions felt open and alive.

Recording took place at Middle Ear in Miami, with additional string sections recorded at Ocean Way in Los Angeles. Barry utilised familiar session players like Harold Cowart and Ron Ziegler, along with arranger Jimmie Haskell.

The album's title, *Now Voyager*, was inspired by Barry's love of the 1942 film starring Bette Davis, although the album bore no thematic connection to the movie. Instead, it presented a dense, experimental collection of songs with extended lyrics and varied musical genres. This ambitious approach, while creative, often felt disjointed as Barry attempted to appeal to multiple markets. The result was an uneven album that lacked the cohesive polish of his Bee Gees hits. Critics noted its mix of calypso, rap, easy listening, and funk as both innovative and problematic. Barry himself acknowledged the challenges of working solo, stating, 'I do miss working with Maurice and Robin. It's mutual, all three of us need some time to work as individuals, but it doesn't mean we don't miss working together'.

The brass at MCA apparently also had issues with the album's trajectory – or at least that's what they presented to the production team, who were baffled by the abrupt change in tone after Irving Azoff and his label brass had so enthusiastically signed Barry and championed his artistry. Karl Richardson recalled to the authors in December 2024 that support from the label began to wane before the album was even finished:

When we sent the rough mixes over to the label, that's when the trouble started. Irving Azoff, who was running the show at the record company, didn't respond the way we hoped. The feedback came back sounding cautious, even dismissive. 'It's a little self-aggrandising', they said. 'It's too much'.

In truth, it had nothing to do with the music. Irving just didn't want to spend the money to promote it. Politics, internal games – it was all that. From our end, we thought we were flying. The band were on fire, Barry was inspired, and everyone in the room was having the time of their lives. But at the label, the enthusiasm just wasn't there. They pulled back, and the project drifted. We were having too much fun, really. It was one of those rare projects where the process itself was so electric that you didn't imagine it could fade away. Yet somehow, it did. Sometimes I still catch myself wondering what happened.

Despite moderate success for the single 'Shine Shine', the album struggled to gain traction. It debuted at number 72 on the *Billboard* Top 200 Albums chart and quickly faded. Many attributed this to the lingering '*Fever* backlash' in the US. While *Now Voyager* had potential, MCA's lack of commitment after its underwhelming reception effectively ended Barry's solo run with the label.

The front cover of *Now Voyager* features a striking composite image: a portrait of Barry is superimposed over a photograph of the Males 1st Class/Gala Pool at Victoria Baths in Manchester. Barry's photo was taken by photographer Alex Henderson, known for his distinctive work on album covers such as Boxer's *Below The Belt*, Neil Ardley's *Harmony Of The Spheres*, Donovan's *Love Is Only A Feeling*, Roger Waters' *The Pros And Cons Of Hitch Hiking*, and Pete Townshend's *White City*.

The background photograph of Victoria Baths, which wraps around onto the back of the sleeve, was captured by Lawrence Lawry, contributing a grand setting to the composition. The same photograph was also used for the 'Fine Line (Extended Dance Version)' 12" single in the US without Barry's image over it.

Additional photography on the inner sleeve was provided by Richard Evans, who served as a stills photographer on location during the filming of the *Now Voyager* film.

The overall album package was designed by ICON, who presented the tracklist over a marbled backdrop – an aesthetic mirrored on the inner lyric sleeve. The UK edition features cerise-coloured text, while the US release opts for a vivid red.

In the lower-right corner of the cover appears a stylised compass rose, forming the album's logo. At its centre are the initials 'BG' for Barry Gibb, with the letters 'N' and 'V' positioned near the upper compass point, referencing *Now Voyager*.

The *Now Voyager* project included a ground-breaking visual album directed by Storm Thorgerson, featuring a surreal narrative about a man navigating a liminal world between life and death. Veteran British actor Sir Michael Hordern played Barry's guide. The concept was innovative but struggled to find its audience. MCA's reluctance to fully fund the project left Barry financing much of it himself, which limited its reach.

Reflecting on the album years later, Barry admitted that the project had been a learning experience. 'I [had] gone out of my way to create something for everybody', he explained. Yet, the broad approach diluted the album's impact. Fans and critics alike noted that the album might have been more successful had it been released earlier in Barry's career, when his star power alone could have carried it.

Although *Now Voyager* didn't achieve the commercial success Barry hoped for, it remains an ambitious effort, highlighting his willingness to take risks and explore new creative avenues, even at the cost of mainstream success. While it didn't achieve the high impact of his Bee Gees work, the album and its accompanying video were enterprising projects that hinted at the possibilities of multimedia storytelling in music.

As Barry himself observed, songwriting and artistry are crafts that evolve with time: 'You've got to really put an emotion into the song – whether it's a good one or a bad one. It isn't a song until it has something in it that actually makes you think, or makes you move – gives you an emotion'. Ultimately, *Now Voyager* demonstrates Barry's drive, and his bold experimentation has earned the album a cult following among fans, despite the results falling short of commercial expectations.

Now Voyager was among the very first ten compact discs released by MCA Records in the US. The LP and cassette versions were released in September, with the CD edition following just a few weeks later on 10 October.

In 2008, it had been reported by *The New York Times* that the master tapes for Barry's MCA solo work had been destroyed by a fire on the Universal Studios Hollywood backlot, among over 170,000 others that belonged to hundreds of Universal Music Group-affiliated (the conglomerate the MCA label was eventually folded into in the mid-1990s) artists. However, as details unfolded, it became less clear how many, and even if, most of the named artists actually experienced losses in the fire. Nobody in the Gibb camp has confirmed any impact on Barry's material since, but it would seem the tracks from *Now Voyager* have been preserved in some form since the full album was available briefly on streaming platforms like Spotify, but has since been removed. A remastered 'Face To Face' resurfaced in 2021 and 2023, attached to two Olivia Newton-John projects.

'I Am Your Driver' (Barry Gibb, George Bitzer, Maurice Gibb)
Recorded at Middle Ear, Miami Beach, in early to mid-1984
'I Am Your Driver' introduces the album with a conceptually driven song that blends themes of cosmic exploration with the metaphor of airline travel. The lyrics position the narrator as a pilot or cosmic guide, navigating listeners through both fantastical interstellar landscapes and the more grounded turbulence of everyday life. Lines such as 'there's been good times, some were bad, some were just appalling' balance reassurance with candid admissions of past missteps.

Barry delivers the vocals with a clipped, staccato phrasing, and his enunciation style, at times bordering on aggressive, renders parts of the lyrics difficult to discern. The verses tend to meander, and the mechanical, almost robotic rhythm track contributes to a rigid structure that diverges from the more fluid arrangements typical of The Bee Gees.

Despite its challenging vocal delivery and unconventional structure, the track is an exciting entry point into the album and the melodic flow of the verses are memorable.

'Fine Line' (Barry Gibb, George Bitzer)
Recorded at Middle Ear, Miami Beach, in early to mid-1984
The second song on the album, 'Fine Line', stands out as a daring and dynamic track with Barry pulling out all the stops and cramming the song with musical ideas. The song transitions through a verse-bridge-chorus structure before launching into a rap section. It should be noted that this was during the era of 'old school rap' (1979-84) and the only rap record by a white artist that had made the mainstream was Blondie's 1981 hit 'Rapture', so this was a very bold move by Barry. The chorus features an all-star ensemble, including The Who's Roger Daltrey, Olivia Newton-John, and Harry Wayne 'KC' Casey of KC & The Sunshine Band.

Barry explained his inspiration for the track during a *Westwood One* interview:

> I wanted to do something that's kind of sensual for a long time. I recently did a guest appearance on a show with Stevie Wonder in Miami, where we sang 'Happy Birthday' – and apart from that, he did something with the audience that I thought was wonderful. He kept on doing things with his voice, and the audience – 5,000 of them – would answer just the same way, you know. And although not many people in the audience could physically sing when everybody's doing it – it works, you know – they do sing, it does find a pitch centre. So, the atmosphere in that situation was amazing. And since that day, I've been thinking, how come he doesn't do that on record? How come we don't hear that? So, I decided to do it – I decided to do a record that had that crowd – like an audience answering me.

'Fine Line' was released in an edited form as the second and final single from the album, but only in select regions: the US, Canada, Australia and Japan. Instead of a widespread European release, it was limited to France and Spain. In North America, where MCA handled the release, 'Stay Alone' was chosen as the B-side, while in other territories under Polydor, 'One Night (For Lovers)' was selected. Although the single didn't make an impact on mainstream charts, the 12" release featuring an extended dance mix by Larry Patterson helped it reach number 50 on the *Billboard* National Disco Action chart.

'Face To Face' (Barry Gibb, George Bitzer, Maurice Gibb)
Recorded at Middle Ear, Miami Beach, in early to mid-1984. Strings recorded at Oceanway Recording, Los Angeles
'Face To Face' was first recorded as a solo demo version in late 1983 and then re-recorded for the album release as a duet with Olivia Newton-John in 1984. The collaboration results in a sweet and soft song that showcases both singers' vocal strengths, particularly Barry's falsetto in the closing moments.

Barry remarked in the *Westwood One* interview: 'I do love doing ballads – I like doing all kinds of different things, but I do love ballads, there's no question about that, and I think over the years, that's probably become painfully obvious to some people. I guess I'm a bit of a romantic – I love romantic songs. I mean, I'm a Perry Como fan, would you believe?'

While the duet showcases beautiful vocal chemistry between Barry and Olivia, who certainly have some tonal similarities in their higher registers, and emotional depth, its placement on *Now Voyager* feels somewhat jarring. It could have shone on an Olivia Newton-John album, but here it contrasts sharply with the experimental nature of the preceding tracks. Despite its charm, the ballad disrupts the album's flow, making it a missed opportunity to thrive elsewhere. Interestingly, the song is not credited as a duet with Newton-John anywhere in print on the album product.

'Face To Face' was considered for release as a single, with promotional copies pressed in West Germany, Spain, Argentina, and the Philippines. However, Olivia Newton-John was hesitant about a full-scale release. In a July 1986 interview with the Dutch fan club *Brothers Gibb Information*, Barry revealed, 'Olivia and her manager pulled out at the very last minute, just before the single was supposed to be released. I tried various ways to find out why, but I never did – so that question remains unanswered to this day'. It could have landed both of the singers a hit, given its radio-friendly sound; Olivia was still having significant chart success at the time.

Additionally, there were complications with the song's planned video for the *Now Voyager* video album. Barry recalled, 'The video was in the hands of a pretty ruthless director. Even when Olivia Newton-John refused to allow the single or video to be released, they actually wanted another girl to lip-sync to Olivia's voice. I said, 'No".

Despite the curious friction with Newton-John and her camp over the song, 'Face To Face' was a surprise inclusion as a bonus track on the 'deluxe' version of the 40th anniversary reissue of her landmark album, *Physical*, in October 2021 – especially since it hadn't even been conceived when the set was originally released in 1981. It appeared again in May 2023 on another Newton-John compilation, *Just The Two Of Us: The Duets Collection (Vol. 1)*. In both cases, the track sounds as if it's been recalibrated to some extent, with a louder and more vibrant mix than on the original album.

'Shatterproof' (Barry Gibb)

Recorded at Middle Ear, Miami Beach, in early to mid-1984

'Shatterproof', a Barry-only composition, continues the experimental tone of the album but doesn't quite match the impact of the opening tracks. While it's an intriguing addition and offers insight into Barry's creative experiments, it lacks the immediacy to sustain the album's momentum. It's more of a transition than a highlight, paving the way for the buoyant closer of side one, 'Shine Shine'.

'Shine Shine' (Barry Gibb, George Bitzer, Maurice Gibb)
Recorded at Middle Ear, Miami Beach, in early to mid-1984
Chart positions: Italy: 23, Netherlands: 32, US: 37, West Germany: 45, Canada: 53, Australia: 87, UK: 95
The first single from the album, 'Shine Shine', was released in August 1984 – the same month as Robin released 'Secret Agent' as a single. With its upbeat tempo, Caribbean-inspired rhythm and catchy melody, it stood out – but it didn't reflect the overall sound of the album.

The song became Barry's highest-charting solo single, significantly outperforming 'I'll Kiss Your Memory' from 1970. On the US Billboard Hot 100, it rose to number 37 (interestingly matching the chart position of Robin's 'Boys Do Fall In Love'). It saw its strongest success on the adult contemporary charts, reaching number eight in the US and number five in Canada, though its performance on the mainstream charts was underwhelming. Unlike Robin's 'Saved By The Bell' (1969) and 'Juliet' (1983), 'Shine Shine' didn't achieve major commercial success, reflecting the general struggle of Barry's solo material to connect with record buyers. Still, it generated enough attention to give the album some chart presence in both the UK and the US.

Lyrically, the song takes an unusual path, with the singer wishing his former love happiness as she marries someone else. In addition to the regular 7" and 12" formats, Polydor in the UK also issued a special silver mirror disc – a playful nod to the song's title.

'Lesson In Love' (Barry Gibb, Maurice Gibb, George Bitzer)
Recorded at Middle Ear, Miami Beach, in early to mid-1984
Side two opens strongly with 'Lesson In Love', a gritty track where Barry channels the growling vocal style of his performance on 1976's 'Boogie Child'. The song's bold energy contrasts sharply with the gentler ballads on the album. Barry continues to explore different vocal approaches, demonstrating his versatility even if the track doesn't entirely land with all listeners.

'One Night (For Lovers)' (Barry Gibb, George Bitzer)
Recorded at Middle Ear, Miami Beach, in early to mid-1984. Strings recorded at Oceanway Recording, Los Angeles

A lush, romantic ballad, 'One Night (For Lovers)' envelops the listener in pure sophistication. George Bitzer's Rhodes electric piano sets a mellow, velvety foundation, while the sultry saxophone weaves through the arrangement, adding warmth and sensuality. The interplay between these two instruments creates a rich, intimate atmosphere, perfect for the song's late-night allure.

Barry's smooth, expressive vocals glide effortlessly over the track, with his delivery made even more captivating by a few lines sung in Spanish. This subtle detail enhances the song's allure, making it a refined highlight of the album's second side.

While undeniably beautiful, 'One Night (For Lovers)' plays it safe, favouring smooth, classic romance over bold innovation. Its polished, understated delivery makes it a graceful addition to the album's second side, even if it doesn't steal the spotlight.

'Stay Alone' (Barry Gibb, George Bitzer)

Recorded at Middle Ear, Miami Beach, in early to mid-1984. Strings recorded at Oceanway Recording, Los Angeles

A beautiful piano-driven ballad, 'Stay Alone' is one of the album's hidden gems. The simplicity of its arrangement highlights the thoughtfully composed lyrics, which Barry himself considered a triumph as he quipped in his *Westwood One* interview:

There are fragments of things, like feelings, that aren't necessarily viable in today's recording market. So, you know, therefore – Barry or Bee Gees – you shouldn't sing ballads because it's not something that will happen. In other words, there's too much of a concentration on what the marketplace is, and not enough concentration on the art form itself. And I think what I tried to prove by writing a song like this is that a deep, thoughtful, moving song can still be written by somebody, somewhere, and I wanted to try that as a challenge just to see if anybody would recognise it – that carefully crafted lyrics still exist. I believe that my lyrics in that song are carefully crafted – and I'm proud of that song – I think it came out better than I ever thought it would.

Its organic sound and sincere delivery make it a standout track, even if its stripped-back style feels out of sync with the album's more ambitious arrangements.

'Temptation' (Barry Gibb, George Bitzer, Maurice Gibb)
Recorded at Middle Ear, Miami Beach, in early to mid-1984
'Temptation' continues the album's exploration of complex emotions and layered arrangements, and contributes to the thematic diversity of *Now Voyager*, although it doesn't quite match the standout moments of the first half.

'She Says' (Barry Gibb)
Recorded at Middle Ear, Miami Beach, in early to mid-1984
'She Says' blends a soft beat with smooth harmonies and offers a moment of calm, which doesn't demand the listener's attention in the same way as some of the album's bolder tracks. That said, the melody has a dark edge and some compelling chord changes.

Attentive listeners may notice a familiar melody. Whether intentional or not, Barry borrows the melody of two lines from a track from The Bee Gees' unreleased album *A Kick In The Head Is Worth Eight In The Pants*. The lines 'I never meant a thing to you/All I did was waste your time' and 'One song was all she sang to me/All her words were soft and low' in 'She Says' share the same melody as 'I tried so hard to reach you/A song I tried to teach you' from 'A Lonely Violin'. Also, the lyric 'we hide the sun' reappeared just a few years later on the chorus of The Bee Gees' hit single, 'One'.

Despite this, 'She Says' carves its own space on the album, offering a moment of quiet reflection with its understated charm.

'The Hunter' (Barry Gibb, Maurice Gibb, George Bitzer, Robin Gibb)
Recorded at Middle Ear, Miami Beach, in early to mid-1984
Closing the album on a high note, 'The Hunter' is a dramatic and dynamic collaborative effort credited to all three Gibb brothers and George Bitzer, and the result is electrifying. The track builds from a relatively quiet opening to a powerful climax, Barry singing with clarity and emotion, delivering the song's sense of urgency and impending doom. His performance gives weight to lines like 'there is danger on the earth tonight', creating a fittingly solemn atmosphere for the album's conclusion. Alan Kendall is afforded a rare chance to shine with a guitar solo, and if there's any critique to be made about this song, it's that the solo is too short. The track ends with a sudden halt. It's a brilliantly executed dramatic effect. 'The Hunter' delivers a sense

of foreboding and uncertainty, enhanced by its enigmatic lyrics and dynamic range. It's a superb finale.

The BMI Awards banquet in Nashville on 9 October honoured songwriters for their work based on broadcast performances from 1 April 1983 to 31 March 1984. Barry, Robin, and Maurice, and their publishing company, Gibb Brothers Music, received two BMI citations for 'Buried Treasure' and 'Islands In The Stream'. They also won the 16th annual Robert J. Burton Award for 'Islands In The Stream', which was the most performed BMI country song of the year. Dolly Parton accepted the award on behalf of the brothers. As guests departed, they were treated to a spectacular fireworks display spelling out the song's title.

In an interview published in the Norwegian daily newspaper *Verdens Gang* (VG) on 9 October 1984, conducted during the filming of the *Now Voyager* video, Barry offered a clear indication of how he saw the immediate future unfolding: 'I will be far from idle in 1984/85. I will write and produce an LP with Julio Iglesias, and there will probably be a new LP with Barbra Streisand. The Bee Gees will be back on the market again. I am also on the committee for a major gala performance for UNICEF next year'. No work with Julio Iglesias ever materialised, of course, and the public would need to wait another three years for a new Bee Gees album. Anyone hoping for a Gibb-Streisand redux would be holding out for another twenty years.

On 25 October, the Swiss fan club, BG News, released The Bee Gees' final ever fan club record. Previously, the Barry Gibb Fan Club released an EP in 1971, followed by Brothers Gibb Information's Maurice Gibb EP in 1975, and 'A Personal Message From The Bee Gees' from the Official Bee Gees Fan Club in 1979. Titled 'Bee Gees – Barry, Robin & Maurice Gibb In Interview 1984', the release came as a 7" 33⅓ RPM EP. It contained interviews with Barry, Robin, and Maurice, all conducted by Andreas Anderegg on 6 February 1984. On Side A, the record featured Barry's interview at Middle Ear and Robin's interview at Criteria Studios. Side B was dedicated to Maurice's interview, also conducted at Criteria. The EP was pressed by the Swiss record label Turicaphon AG, with the catalogue number BGN-1-200, where the '200' indicated the total number of records produced. The black and white cover featured individual photographs of the brothers taken by Anderegg during the interviews, accompanied by typewritten credits.

1 December was a day of double celebration for Barry and his family. At 6:03 am, Barry's wife, Linda, gave birth to their fourth son, Michael David, at Mount Sinai Hospital in Miami. The baby weighed seven pounds, eight ounces. His arrival coincided with another special occasion – the 11th birthday of their eldest son, Stephen.

Just five days later, Barry hosted the inaugural Love and Hope Tennis Festival, a charity event to support the University of Miami's Diabetes Research Institute. Held at the Doral Country Club in Miami, the festival brought together celebrities, socialites and fans for a weekend of tennis, golf, music, and entertainment. Barry was joined by Robin and Maurice, as well as Andy, who not only participated in the tennis matches but also contributed to the evening's entertainment. The celebrity lineup included notable figures such as actor Don Johnson, tennis players Arthur Ashe and Tracy Austin, Miami Dolphins head coach Don Shula, Florida Governor Bob Graham, and martial arts star Héctor Echavarría. The festival's grand finale was a gala dinner and ball, where Barry and Andy performed a short set featuring 'You Should Be Dancing', 'Shadow Dancing', and 'Words' for the assembled guests. The entire weekend's activities were captured in a 50-minute television special directed by Carole Myers, showcasing the star-studded charity event and its purpose of supporting diabetes research, and extending its reach beyond those in attendance.

Also in 1984, a mysterious 12" single was released. 'Rockin' Reggae Jam' by Surfside appeared on the Surf Records label. There were scant other details on the label – no songwriters or producers were credited. As the only record to have been released by Surf Records, it would appear to have been a vanity label. The song appeared on both sides of the 45rpm 12", the A-side timed in at 3:10, with an extended 4:58 version on the flip-side.

In May 1985, 'Rockin' Reggae Jam' reappeared on the Soaring Records label, as both 7" and 12" singles. The label this time revealed far more about the recording. 'Rockin' Reggae Jam' was written by Geoffrey Williams, and produced by Maurice and Dr. Ron Stander, the Bee Gees' physician, and also Soaring Records' owner, for Doc Ron Productions. The label also claims that the A-side is from an LP called *I Step Ahead*, but no evidence of this has ever surfaced. *Billboard* reported the recording was engineered by Dennis Hetzendorfer at Criteria Studios, and that Maurice played steel drums. The 12" single, which played at 33rpm, featured the extended version on both sides, but the B-side version was instrumental. The 7" single version of 'Rockin' Reggae Jam' was another edit of 3:36, but most interestingly, the B-side featured another Geoffrey Williams composition, 'Feel A Need', which was again produced by Maurice and Dr. Ron Stander.

1985

In mid-January, CIC released *Sgt. Pepper's Lonely Hearts Club Band* on VHS in the UK for the first time, bringing the Robert Stigwood-produced 1978 musical fantasy to home audiences. Featuring The Bee Gees and Peter Frampton, the movie reimagined The Beatles' classic music through a unique narrative. Although critically panned on its original release, the video offered fans a chance to revisit the film's soundtrack and story, cementing its status as a cult curiosity of late 1970s pop culture.

In January of 1985, Maurice began scoring a film titled *Ghost Soldiers*. As production evolved, the movie was rebranded *The Supernaturals*. The story follows a modern-day US Army unit on a seemingly routine training exercise. However, the soldiers unknowingly enter a cursed battleground haunted by Confederate soldiers who were brutally killed during the Civil War. As eerie occurrences escalate, the soldiers confront resurrected Confederate soldiers driven by a supernatural thirst for revenge, led by a mysterious child with unearthly powers. The soldiers' mission quickly spirals into a fight for survival as they are hunted by the vengeful undead.

The Supernaturals featured some notable stars, including two actors who gained fame within the *Star Trek* franchise. Nichelle Nichols, celebrated for her role as Lieutenant Uhura in the original *Star Trek* series, played Sergeant Leona Hawkins, bringing her distinctive presence to the horror genre. LeVar Burton, who starred in the iconic 1977 television miniseries *Roots* and would later become known as Geordi La Forge in *Star Trek: The Next Generation*, appeared as Private Michael Osgood. The film also featured Maxwell Caulfield as Private Ray Ellis. Better known for his leading role in *Grease 2* alongside Michelle Pfeiffer, he later went on to co-star in the epic Civil War drama, *Gettysburg*.

Maurice not only contributed musically to the film but also appeared in an uncredited cameo in one of the introductory scenes as a Union, or 'Yankee', Civil War soldier, wearing a blue uniform. This implies that he was most likely hired to compose the score by October 1984, when filming began.

Maurice's score was registered for copyright as a single non-tracked work titled 'The Supernaturals: A Film Score' in July 1985. It was also registered as 'Supernaturals – BG Cues'. 'BG Cues' stands for Background Cues (not Bee Gees, as one might assume at first glance), which are short musical or sound cues used in the background of a scene in film, television, or theatre. These cues are typically subtle pieces of audio or music that help set the mood, reinforce the atmosphere, or fill silence without drawing too much attention to themselves. They're often used to enhance emotions, create tension, or add continuity within scenes. For example, in a suspenseful scene, a BG Cue might include a low, droning sound to build unease, while in a light-hearted moment, it might feature a gentle melody. These cues are important tools in sound design and scoring because they add depth to a scene without overpowering the main dialogue or action.

Despite his significant involvement, his score was ultimately not used in the film's theatrical release, with Robert O. Ragland's composition replacing it. However, a version of the film featuring Maurice's original score was broadcast on Sky Movies, a British satellite channel, in 1992. This unexpected development prompted Maurice to contact his lawyer, Michael Eaton, upon learning that his work had been used without his knowledge or compensation.

In response to the situation, Dick Ashby, The Bee Gees' personal manager, shared insight into the unexpected twist:

It would appear that Maurice has never been paid for this project and was told it never came to anything. As for the two different scores, I presume that was the company being cheap, originally doing a cable/movie/TV deal without the inclusion of home video sales rights. Rather than re-approach Maurice – who, after all, had been told the project was not happening – they got someone to do a second, cheap and nasty score.

Although it may seem harsh, it's not uncommon for movie directors to commission multiple scores from different composers before selecting the one that best complements the film. In this case, Maurice's score, while competent, revealed his limited experience in composing for film soundtracks. In contrast, Robert O. Ragland was a seasoned professional in this field, with a strong background in both classical training and film scoring. Ragland attended Northwestern University, earned degrees at the American Conservatory of Music in Chicago and studied at the University of Music and Performing Arts in Vienna. By the time he worked on *The Supernaturals*, Ragland had already scored over two dozen films and had gained experience across genres, including blaxploitation, horror, monster movies and thrillers. From an objective standpoint, Ragland's score demonstrated a level of skill and nuance that elevated the film in ways that Maurice's score, despite his talents, couldn't fully achieve.

Now Voyager (Visual Album) – **Barry Gibb** (1985)

In the mid-1980s, as the music video medium was rapidly maturing into a defining component of the pop landscape, Barry was quietly working on a bold new experiment – one that would stretch the limits of what a music video could be. The result was *Now Voyager*, an 80-minute visual album born from his solo album of the same name, and a project he envisaged not as mere promotion, but as something more innovative.

'I've always wanted to do a visual album as opposed to just a collection of tracks', Barry told *Billboard*. 'It was while I was recording the LP earlier this year that the idea came to me to do something that covered the whole album rather than a single promotional video'. This vision quickly evolved into an ambitious, multi-million-dollar production – co-financed by Barry himself and PolyGram Music Video to the tune of $1.8 million.

When Barry set out to bring *Now Voyager* to life as a visual album, he knew he needed more than just a director – he needed a creative force with a proven visual imagination and cinematic flair. He found that in Storm Thorgerson, co-founder of the iconic 1970s design studio Hipgnosis, renowned for crafting some of rock's most memorable album covers for the likes of 10cc, Pink Floyd, Led Zeppelin and Genesis.

By the early 1980s, Thorgerson had teamed up with fellow Hipgnosis alum Aubrey 'Po' Powell and visual artist Peter Christopherson to form Green Back Films, a production company specialising in high-concept music videos and commercials. Their reel quickly filled with striking promos for artists like Paul Young ('Wherever I Lay My Hat'), Belouis Some ('Imagination'), and David Gilmour ('Blue Light'). Their sharp eye for narrative visuals and a more cinematic style corresponded with Barry's vision.

For *Now Voyager*, Powell took the reins as producer and Christopherson handled the lighting, helping shape a narrative-driven film that leaned on performance, atmosphere and stylised roles for Barry. In an interview with David English for the *Inside Now Voyager* promotional video, Barry said:

Like any other artist, I watched a number of videos and chose the company that had the best videos, in my opinion, and the people who had this company, Green Back – Storm Thorgerson and Aubrey Powell, very creative people, very, very strong people. And I wanted that. I didn't want to be in control of the situation. I needed other people's input, other creative minds. This is not a thing I do every day, so I need people who know what they're doing – and their videos, like 'Owner Of A Lonely Heart' [by Yes] and 'The Big Log', I think it's called, the Robert Plant video, appeal to me very much.

From the start, Barry was clear-eyed about the project's commercial prospects. 'We're not going out to make a killing', he said candidly to *Billboard*. 'The market isn't big enough yet to really do much more than help us break even'. Yet profit was never the driving force. Instead, Barry saw *Now Voyager* as a chance to innovate. 'It's time somebody made more than a video promo film', he explained. 'I think it's time that an artist, any artist, should start applying themselves to things that are a bit more, for want of a better word, *pioneeristic*'. Indeed, with cinemas beginning to ask for longer visual content – 'not just video promos, but longer programmes' – *Now Voyager* emerged as an answer to the unspoken question: could the music video grow up?

As Barry's cinematic journey began in early 1985, it was billed as the 'first true video album', a title that encapsulated both its novelty and its enterprising approach. Whether or not it would spark a trend remained to be seen, but one thing was certain: Barry had set out not just to promote music, but to tell a story, and in doing so, helped redefine what a solo artist could do with sound and image. The film is as much a metaphysical journey as it is a musical showcase. Barry described the plot during the *Inside Now Voyager* interview:

Now Voyager is about a young man, myself of course, who crashes his car off a bridge and enters the place between life and death, which, for the sake of this story, is a swimming bath in Manchester ... He emerges from the river in this holy place, and the man who rules this place is called the Trickster, played by Sir Michael Hordern, who takes me on a series of adventures which make up the 60 minutes, which make up the whole of the album *Now Voyager*. Each adventure is completely different. And by the adventures themselves, I'm supposed to learn something.

Sir Michael Hordern, a towering presence known for his Shakespearean gravitas, became more than just a co-star. Barry reflected on their time together with deep admiration:

> Here is a person who gave me an education in acting in five days. All of the seasons that one could spend in an acting school could not equal what this man taught me. He is one of my favourite actors of all time, amongst very few that I have, and I did have a great desire to work with him.

Despite being new to acting, Barry took the craft seriously. 'I definitely think acting is extremely hard work', he said. 'I think you have to be a dedicated actor. And I think Jane Fonda said once, 'If you don't feel it in your stomach when you go to sleep, and you don't feel it in your stomach when you wake up, you shouldn't be doing it".

Barry had to play a range of characters – including a Vietnam War veteran, an astronaut, and an American Southern gentleman. It was a tall order for someone just finding his feet in acting. But Powell remembered Hordern's calm assurance: 'Sir Michael was wonderful. He said, 'Part of my responsibility, dear boy, will be to train this man to become an actor'. He was so patient with Barry, who accepted his guidance and wanted to learn from the master'.

The responsibility of guiding Barry through this dramatic shift didn't fall solely on Hordern. David Gale, who co-wrote the script and served as Barry's dialogue coach, recalled the intense behind-the-scenes preparation:

> I'd written the script and was honoured to become Barry Gibb's dialogue coach. He had no acting experience and started to panic. Barry was staying in a hotel in Manchester, and every morning, I would knock on the door, and his minder would answer, and Barry's wife, an ex-Miss Edinburgh, would welcome me in. Then I'd sit there with Barry in his bathrobe and go through the script together.

Visually and narratively, *Now Voyager* was a bold departure from the typical music video formula. The marriage of the music with Hipgnosis visuals creates an interesting, if somewhat surrealistic, sojourn. Barry made it clear that while *Now Voyager* flirted with the structure of a concept album or rock opera, it resisted easy categorisation:

In a sense, it's a rock opera, because when you put the film and the music together, it relates as one whole story in sort of pieces, but it relates, nevertheless. You can sit at home and listen to the album, and I believe with this album that I've gone out of my way to create something with a little bit of something for everybody.

Though the project had no overt message, Barry hoped it would resonate visually and emotionally:

There's no real moral to the special, just entertainment, visually and audio, and there's no great sort of serious message. What I should say is there are other elements that I cannot tell you – there are other surprises that I cannot tell you about. Sir Michael Hordern is not just the Trickster, and everything is not exactly what it seems ...

Aubrey Powell explained, 'The idea was that there was more to life than being a debauched rock star'.

What began as a promising artistic collaboration would soon spiral into a gruelling, surreal three-month ordeal that all involved would come to regret. The project quickly unravelled under the weight of egos, creative differences and a steadily disintegrating working relationship between its two key players. 'I had a nightmare with the guy who was directing it', Barry would later admit, his words tinged with lingering frustration. 'I should have stopped in the beginning and got somebody more friendly to work with, Steven Spielberg, perhaps. But I let it go on, and I shouldn't have done. So, for me, I don't think of what it is now. I think of all the horrible times I had trying to do it'. It was a partnership doomed from the start, and according to those closest to the production, the warning signs were clear. 'I foolishly kept Storm and Barry apart because I felt they wouldn't get on', said Powell. 'The chemistry wasn't right. A $2 million budget was the equivalent of $10 million today, and I couldn't risk that'.

After initial scenes were shot in Manchester, the production relocated to the opulent, pastel-pink Don CeSar Hotel in St. Petersburg, Florida. It was there that tensions truly began to boil. Thorgerson, known for his eccentric personality and confrontational sense of humour, challenged Barry to a game of tennis – a seemingly innocuous invitation that would set the tone for the chaos to come. 'Storm thrashed Barry, which you just don't do', recalled stills photographer Richard Evans. 'If it's the first day before the shoot, you let the client win. Of course, Storm wasn't going to do that. Then the next thing Storm says to him is, 'Right, Barry, you're going to have to shave that beard off!' That, unsurprisingly, didn't go over well. Barry, deeply attached to his image, was unwilling to part with his signature beard and flowing hair. 'Storm quite rightly told Barry, 'If you are an actor and you want to play a part, you can't be Barry Gibb, so the beard has to go', Powell explained. 'But Barry wanted to keep the beard and the flowing locks because that was his image'.

And so began what Evans called a 'Mexican standoff'. Neither individual would budge, and Powell found himself trapped in a no-man's land between an unyielding director and a high-profile artist backed by the powerful Polygram label. 'Time was money, and I now had to defend Storm and the script,' Powell said, 'but Polygram had to defend their artist. So, I was caught in the middle. Storm kept threatening to leave, and Barry was saying the same'.

As the crew basked in the Florida sun and enjoyed the local nightlife, production was halted. 'We're all thinking, 'this is great'', Evans admitted. 'We're in Florida, the sun's shining, someone was sent out to get the Charlie [cocaine], and we were all having fun'. But behind the scenes, the tension had reached a boiling point. The drama reached an almost comical peak when two emergency doctors were called to the hotel: Barry believed he was having a nervous breakdown; Storm thought he was having a heart attack. The bizarre medical episode finally prompted a compromise. Barry would keep his beard for scenes with Sir Michael Horden, which had already been filmed, but would shave it for later parts of the film. 'Absolute hell', Barry later said about the beard ordeal. 'I did it because I thought it was important to do it. I hate myself without my beard, really. I think we all have these idiosyncrasies about ourselves, and I just personally don't like me without my beard'.

The compromise wasn't enough to smooth the creative fissures. Storm, ever headstrong, wanted his production company, Green Back, to pull out entirely. 'But we took a vote between the three of us, and he was outvoted', said Powell. 'We made the video, but it was very trying'. For Thorgerson, the feeling was mutual. In the documentary *Taken By Storm: The Art Of Storm Thorgerson And Hipgnosis*, he described working with Barry as nothing less than 'cosmic punishment'. And for Barry? The scars were lasting. 'If you're actually doing it, and you hated doing it, you can't see the beauty in it', he said, reflecting on the experience. The glitz of the Florida shoot, the glitter of the production budget and even the final product itself were overshadowed by the torment behind the scenes. 'Sadly,' Powell recalled, 'Barry's pearly white smile belied what I now remember as three months of unbearable hell'.

'Theme From Now Voyager'

Although there was no official track titled 'Now Voyager' on the album, Barry composed an instrumental 'Theme From Now Voyager' that bookends the film – hauntingly ethereal and cinematic, it sets the tone for what's to come. The opening scene, which was the last to be filmed, unfolds with striking drama on the remote fenlands near King's Lynn in Norfolk.

Barry is seen driving a 1967 Mercedes 250S along a quiet country road before a tractor pulls out from a side road in front of him. In reality, the car was later taken over by stuntman Ken Shepherd for what became the most spectacular – and nearly fatal – sequence of the production. The bridge, located on a road known as Wretton Fen Drove in Norfolk, spans a stretch of water known as Cut-off Channel. The stunt was intended to be relatively straightforward: the front-loaded car would crash through the railings, nosedive into the water and sink slowly, giving the driver time to unbuckle, don breathing apparatus and escape safely. But what unfolded was far from the plan.

The vehicle unexpectedly flipped mid-descent, plunging upside down into nine feet of water, embedding itself in the muddy riverbed. Shepherd, trapped underwater in the driver's seat, could not escape. In a tense, real-life emergency, divers who were standing-by in case of such an incident sprang into action, broke into the vehicle and pulled the stuntman to safety. As he was stretchered into a waiting ambulance, barely conscious, he gave a feeble thumbs-up. 'Ken is an amazing guy', Barry marvelled. 'When I spoke to him in the ambulance, he wanted to know if the director was happy and if he would need to shoot it again'.

As the camera follows Barry escaping the submerged car, the scene transitions into an entirely different world – he emerges into the waters of a swimming pool where he is greeted by Sir Michael Hordern in the role of the Trickster.

The next sequence was shot over 200 miles away at the historic Victoria Baths in Manchester, located just three miles from the Gibb family's former home on Keppel Road in Chorlton-cum-Hardy. Built between 1903 and 1906, with a construction budget of £59,000 – an extravagant sum for a public facility at the time – the baths were once a shining symbol of civic pride and luxury.

Barry surfaces in the Males 1st Class/Gala Pool, the grandest of the building's three pools. It once catered to Manchester's elite swimmers, complete with elegant poolside cubicles. This is the pool that features on the front cover of the *Now Voyager* album. But despite its stately appearance, the glamour was skin-deep. Beneath the waterline, Barry remembered an entirely different reality: 'We worked virtually on a sea of cockroaches. They were all in my shoes, you know, and they were everywhere we were working, especially in bare feet. I can't be objective about it – it was a nightmare to do'.

'I Am Your Driver'

Barry finds himself cast as the captain of a spaceship called *The Merry Widow*, embarking on a cosmic voyage that channels the spirit of classic British sci-fi – most notably *Doctor Who* – complete with bizarre characters and futuristic visuals. In early takes, Barry's eldest son, Stephen, made a cameo as an alien creature, although he appears to have been cut from the final edit.

Barry's striking futuristic outfit is actually a modified high-altitude pressure suit, originally developed in the 1950s for RAF pilots. Designed to be worn beneath a flying suit, it kept aircrew cool in the stifling heat of a jet cockpit – a perfect fusion of vintage innovation and space-age style. This isn't the suit's first appearance in pop culture, either; David Bowie wore one in the promotional video for 'Ashes To Ashes' (1980), as did Kate Bush in 'The Dreaming' (1982).

As the scene draws to a close, Barry suddenly begins to behave erratically, eventually collapsing to the floor while continuing to sing. In a moment of confusion and shock, the passengers tear open his suit – only to reveal a circuit board. The captain of the spaceship was actually an android.

In the follow-up scene at Victoria Baths, Barry is seen sitting in an Aeratone – a full-body therapeutic bath that delivers a vigorous underwater massage, once used to treat a range of medical conditions. Installed in 1952, this particular Aeratone was the first of its kind to be housed in a public bathhouse in England.

'Temptation'

Barry and his on-screen girlfriend sit in a red 1966 Volvo 1800S sports car, tension thick in the air. Whatever had been brewing between them has reached its boiling point. She throws the door open, steps out with finality and slams it shut, telling him she's done – done with the secrets, the betrayals, the deception that's been unfolding behind her back.

Then suddenly, reality fractures. Barry now finds himself strapped into a motorised chair, gliding through a stark, clinical courtroom of the future. A dystopian tribunal surrounds him, cold and imposing. It isn't just judgment from others he faces – this is a self-confrontation with the parts he's tried to suppress or deny. The air is sterile, humming with an eerie calm, broken only by a voice that begins to read out a list of charges. They're not legal accusations in the traditional sense, but emotional ones – betrayals, lies, absences of conscience.

As the introduction of 'Temptation' begins to play, the room seems to come alive with imagery. Screens flicker on, surrounding him with scenes of his past transgressions. On one, his girlfriend sits with private detectives who slide damning photographs across a table – Barry, arms around someone else, lips pressed where they shouldn't be. She looks at the images, face stony, then rips them in half as if trying to destroy the proof and the pain in one motion.

Another screen flickers. She enters a bedroom. A woman sits on the bed, half-dressed. Barry is there, too, pulling on a shirt, caught in the act. Yet, among these betrayals, there is another image – Barry in a studio, headphones on, singing the very song that now scores his trial. He performs it with intensity, as if the lyrics could somehow redeem him, or at least explain him.

But no lyric is strong enough to overwrite what he's done. As the song fades out, so too does the last hope of reprieve. The chair halts. Silence. Then the verdict: guilty. The floor beneath him opens without warning. He plunges into deep water. When he finally breaks the surface, he finds himself in another swimming pool – this time it's the Females' Pool at Victoria Baths. Waiting for him is the Trickster – the reckoning isn't over; it's only just begun.

'Lesson In Love'

The video for 'Lesson In Love' is set in the 1930s and follows a young man's experience inside a high-class brothel. The narrative begins as he is let into the establishment, where he is seen navigating the emotional and physical complexities of love and lust. Barry's character appears as an observer, dressed in a smart suit with a tie, hat and cane. Though he moves through bedrooms and hallways filled with people in various states of undress, his presence is unnoticed by the other characters. He remains visible only to the audience, creating a quiet separation between him and the unfolding events.

As the video nears its end, the atmosphere begins to shift and the calm is broken as police burst in, rushing through hallways and forcing doors open. Their presence is abrupt and forceful, creating a stark contrast to the subdued elegance of the setting. Although the brothel appears to be in a British residential area, the officers are dressed in American-style uniforms, complete with eight-point caps traditionally worn by some US police forces.

The video was filmed across three separate locations. The young man is first seen entering 46 Duncan Terrace in the London borough of Islington. At the close, he exits from a different address – 1 Canonbury Place, around a mile away, also in Islington. Barry does not appear in either of these scenes.

The interior sequences, which do feature Barry, were filmed at Hosey Rigge, a country house in Westerham. Built in the early years of the 20th century, the house carries a quiet historical resonance, having served as the temporary home of Winston Churchill and his family between 1923 and 1924, while their nearby residence at Chartwell was undergoing renovation.

'Shatterproof'

'Shatterproof' opens with vivid imagery of circus performers and dancers, creating a surreal backdrop. Barry appears in a donkey jacket, beanie hat, and neckerchief – attire historically associated with Britain's working class in the 1950s to 1980s. He walks down a dim corridor beside a scruffy companion, peering into small doors that open onto strange, unsettling scenes.

One door reveals women armed with spears and nets, apparently hunting men. Another reveals a classic circus freak show featuring a tattooed lady, a bearded lady, Siamese twins, a three-headed man, a werewolf and a strongman. The corridor itself becomes increasingly surreal as a latex wall begins to bulge with human forms pushing through, echoing the aesthetic used in Ultravox's 1981 video for 'The Thin Wall'. This stretch membrane effect is well-known in stage and film production for its eerie, otherworldly quality, and is frequently employed in horror and sci-fi.

As they continue forward, masked dancers begin to appear. These dancers wear neutral masks – smooth, expressionless faces common in mime and performance art – creating an uneasy, anonymous atmosphere. The dancers surround Barry and eventually propel him into a hall of mirrors. As Barry stands in the hall of mirrors, the glass begins to shatter. The video then cuts between this and scenes set in an empty pool at the Victoria Baths, where the Trickster is spinning Barry around while the mirrors continue to break.

The video reaches its conclusion with the pair climbing out of the empty pool and sitting on its edge. The Trickster begins telling a story, and the pool slowly fills with water, signalling a transition into the next visual sequence.

'Stay Alone'

The video for 'Stay Alone' is set in the 18th century and was filmed on location in Lyme Regis, a historic town in Dorset, England's south coast. Barry appears as the captain of a ship, the *TS Royalist*, a brig launched in 1971 and operated by the Marine Society & Sea Cadets as a training vessel.

The video features Maryam d'Abo, who is best known as the cello-playing Bond girl Kara Milovy in the 1987 James Bond film *The Living Daylights*. D'Abo is the first cousin of Mike d'Abo, a member of the 1960s pop group Manfred Mann, and of Olivia D'Abo, best known for her turn as Karen Arnold on the American television dramedy series *The Wonder Years*.

One of the most memorable images in the video is Barry and d'Abo together on the upper level of The Cobb, Lyme Regis' curved harbour wall, originally built to protect ships and the town from the sea. The structure has long been a notable feature of the town and has appeared in other films and literary works.

'Shine Shine'

The scene opens in the opulent male first-class entrance hall of the Victoria Baths. Barry turns to the Trickster, his tone wistful, and says, 'I'd just like to go somewhere where there's a bit of fun'. The Trickster, always quick to tease with half-mockery, half-sincerity, arches a brow. 'A sort of jamboree or something, is that what you mean?' – Barry nods, a small, hopeful smile forming. 'A sort of party would be nice'. The Trickster barely misses a beat. 'A wedding. Want to go to a wedding?' There's a flicker of amusement in Barry's eyes as he glances down at his crumpled blue suit. 'I'm not dressed for it', he says, sniggering. The

Trickster waves the concern away – 'It doesn't matter. No one will notice you'. Barry cocks his head, playful but probing – 'Where's the fun in that?' The Trickster, with a knowing glint, answers, 'Well, that's the point'.

They wander over to a fish tank. 'What do you see in there?' asks the Trickster. Barry peers in. 'A bunch of weed'. 'Look a little closer', the Trickster urges. As Barry does, the greenery transforms – the tank becomes a lake, and Barry emerges soaked but composed, wearing a white suit. Before him rises a grand Southern mansion, the Phipps Plantation at Ayavalla, located on the outskirts of Tallahassee, Florida. A wedding reception is underway. The band begin to play 'Shine Shine' as Barry enters. He moves through the crowd, unseen – just as the Trickster had promised, no one notices him. Although he doesn't sing on screen at first, his voice haunts the soundtrack. When the guests suddenly freeze, Barry begins to sing, stepping through the frozen moment toward the bride – an old flame. She doesn't see him, but he sings to her directly.

The party resumes, and the guests move again – Barry fades from their awareness, and his voice once more blends into the background music. During the instrumental break, everyone dances outside – until they freeze again. Barry seizes the moment. He approaches the bride, sings to her, and this time, leads her away, if only briefly. They dance – quietly, privately – before he returns her to her husband just before time resumes.

As the scene ends, the wedding photographer gathers everyone for a group photo. Surprisingly, he calls out to Barry, inviting him to join. Barry steps in as the shutter clicks. The photo – the only evidence he was ever there – appears framed in the next scene, as Barry and the Trickster now stand together once more, poised on the grand staircase of the first-class entrance hall, to continue their discussions.

'One Night (For Lovers)'

The setting is the Don CeSar Hotel in St. Pete Beach, Florida, bathed in the warm light of sunset. A couple stroll along the beach, waves gently lapping at their feet. Inside the hotel, a bell boy receives quiet instructions from an enigmatic man, along with a bundle of roses – each to be delivered with care and precision. The bellhop carries out his task, leaving roses in unexpected places: one on the beach, others on balconies and terraces, even handing one each to a couple in an elevator. Meanwhile, Barry appears alone on his balcony before retreating indoors to prepare for the evening, dressing in a white tuxedo.

Later, the bellhop knocks on the door of Room 601 – Barry's room – and presents a rose. Barry accepts it, his expression marked more by intrigue than understanding. As night falls, the hotel comes to life. Couples gather by the pool, dancing beneath soft lights as music floats through the air. Barry descends the grand staircase and joins them, eventually approaching a woman seated by the pool – they dance.

In the final moments, the bellhop returns to the man who gave him the roses. Only one remains. The man, now revealed as the Trickster, tells him the last rose is for him – a reward, or perhaps the final move in a carefully orchestrated plan.

'Fine Line'

The clip for 'Fine Line' was released commercially in black and white. However, a colour version of the video is included on the promotional video *Inside Now Voyager*, providing a more vivid take on the same footage.

The video was filmed at a venue named Dougie's Dine And Dance in the on-screen credits. In reality, the location was known as Dougie's Night Club, situated at 229 Lower Clapton Road in the Borough of Hackney, London. The club was owned by Irvine Douglas and was a notable local venue during the period.

It served as the backdrop for the performance-style video, which featured Barry miming to the track alongside a band of notable musicians. He appears without his trademark beard and with his hair slicked back – a distinct departure from his usual image. The band included guitarist Mick Ralphs, known for his work with Mott the Hoople and Bad Company, and drummer Simon Kirke, who was in Free and also Bad Company.

They were joined by session musicians Jerome Rimson on bass, Ray Carless on saxophone, and Foster Patterson on keyboards. Also featured is Raphael Ravenscroft, best known for his iconic saxophone solo on Gerry Rafferty's 'Baker Street'.

'The Hunter'

The closing chapter sees Barry in the role of a United States Marine Corps veteran haunted by the ghosts of his past. The video is cinematic and intense, blending flashbacks of tanks and military helicopters with scenes of quiet domesticity. At his desk, he studies a framed photograph of himself, alongside a smaller inset of his wife, Linda. He doesn't perform the song directly, but at one point he mouths the lyric, 'Let me live, let me hide away' – a subtle, poignant touch.

The tension builds when the doorknob to his room begins to turn from the outside. Barry bolts the door, his mind flashing back to the memory of a comrade betrayed and stabbed by an enemy soldier. Back in the present, he is shown poring over a map, showering and handling a California driver's license, before the scene cleverly transitions to a pair of hands closing a file containing photos of Barry in combat gear.

The drama escalates with the arrival of a black Jaguar XJ6. Four men storm up the stairs, forcing their way into Barry's room. In a desperate scramble, he burns papers, stuffs belongings into a suitcase and arms himself with a pistol. A brutal fight follows – Barry holding his own until he is finally overpowered by one of the intruders, played by his long-time friend David English. Dragged downstairs and bundled into the waiting car, Barry sits bloodied and exhausted, flanked by his captors.

The sequence suddenly shifts. Barry is back behind the wheel of his Mercedes, revisiting the film's opening imagery of the bridge. This time, he swerves just in time, narrowly avoiding disaster. On foot, he hears cries for help and dives into the water to rescue a floundering old man – the familiar Trickster who has shadowed him throughout the film. No words are exchanged, but their reconciliation is clear as they walk together to Barry's car and drive away.

Dark, fragmented and symbolic, this final video captures the central themes of *Now Voyager*: struggle, survival, and the blurred lines between nightmare and redemption. It is not simply a music clip but a short film, closing the video album on a note of ambiguity and hard-won hope.

PolyGram released *Now Voyager* on 14 February in the UK. It was originally scheduled for release in November 1984, but was delayed to capitalise on the planned release of a second single from the album, which ultimately did not materialise. In the US, MCA Home Video released *Now Voyager* in the first week of June.

Music Week reporter Chris White commented that 'Gibb is no great shakes as an actor but benefits from the professionalism of Sir Michael Hordern and a wide array of special effects that maintain viewer interest. Gibb takes on a different role with each song, and the album tracks are cleverly interwoven into the storyline, supporting the claim that this is one of the first genuine 'video albums".

In the UK, *Now Voyager* was released on VHS and Betamax by PolyGram Music Video with a still from the 'Temptation' video used on the cover. Later UK reissues by Channel 5 and Hendring featured a still from the video for 'The Hunter' on the cover. In the US, the VHS and Betamax versions released by MCA used the same picture as the LP cover. In Japan, a Laserdisc version was released by PolyGram Music Video on 21 April 1985.

On 30 March, *Now Voyager* entered the UK video charts at number 30. It peaked at number 28 the following week before dropping back to number 30 in its final showing on 13 April.

In 2006, the film was remastered and released on DVD by Universal Music Group with new cover art, featuring enhanced audio and bonus content, including *Inside Now Voyager – The Making Of The Film*.

On 15 July, the budget-priced compilation album *Massachusetts* was released for the third time by the Contour label. Originally released in 1973, it was first reissued in 1978. Each version is easily distinguishable due to its unique artwork. The 1973 edition features a photo from The Bee Gees' March 1972 tour of Japan, with the group's name displayed in bold white letters against a dark background. The 1978 reissue uses a photograph from the medley portion of their rehearsal for the American TV show *The Midnight Special* on 10 October 1975, framed with a blue border and a stylish graphic logo in the top right corner. The latest 1985 reissue showcases a photograph from their 6 April 1973 appearance on *The Midnight Special*, framed with a red border and a bold orange logo. Contour justified this second reissue by citing the strong sales of the previous editions and the desire to keep the album visible in record stores. The album achieved BRIT certified silver status in February 1978 and went on to receive gold status in April 1979.

Robin and Dwina's relationship reached a new milestone on 31 July when they were married in Wheatley, Hampshire, after nearly five years together. The wedding date was carefully selected by Dwina to coincide with the eve of Lughnasad, a Druid festival that symbolises the turning of the year, reflecting her lifelong connection to Druidism.

In September, BMI honoured 75 new inductees into the ranks of its 'Million-Airs'. Among the newly inducted songs were the Gibb brothers' compositions 'Grease', 'Islands In The Stream', and 'Woman In Love'. These songs joined BMI's catalogue of 650 other songs that had each surpassed one million plays. A 'Million-Air' designation signifies that a song has achieved over 50,000 hours of radio airplay.

Swedish singer Carola was soon to join the ranks of artists who benefited from having an album written and produced by the Gibb brothers. While she was a major star in her native Sweden, she was not widely known internationally.

Carola Maria Häggkvist was born on 8 September 1966 in Stockholm and grew up in Norsborg, south of the Swedish capital. She was educated at Adolf Fredrik's Music School. In 1977, she won a talent competition and made her first television appearance. After several additional small screen performances, she was discovered by Mariann Records in 1981. Performing 'Främling' at Melodifestivalen 1983, she was selected to represent Sweden at the Eurovision Song Contest in Munich, where she placed third.

She quickly became Scandinavia's most in-demand singer and scored a number of top ten hits, all of which achieved gold certification. During the summer of 1983, she toured Sweden, drawing a total audience of 220,000 people. In February 1984, she had her own television special that was broadcast across Scandinavia.

In an effort to launch her international career, she travelled to Los Angeles for a photo shoot for a *Pepsi* commercial. She performed at the UNICEF Gala in Canada in 1984 and visited Japan twice, where she was very well received. Her second album featured a mix of Swedish and English songs, and soon after, she released a full English-language album.

Maurice explained, 'I was introduced to her by a guy called Franz Auffray, who represents Polydor International, and they were looking to see if they could introduce her to the rest of the world besides just being a Swedish artist. They wanted to make an international album, and they asked the guys and me to write, and me to produce the album'. The agreement was inked in July, and Maurice set to work writing songs, enlisting the help of his brothers along the way. Carola and her manager, Thomas Nordlund, travelled to Miami Beach on 6 September to meet Maurice and Barry for the first time. They discussed plans for the new album and what they envisioned for her. During this visit, she also recorded demos at Middle Ear.

'It's wonderful to work with the Gibb brothers', Carola enthused. 'It's really incredible! Just to think that Michael Jackson worked in the same studio just one day before I was here the first time!' Despite being a big star in Scandinavia, Carola was starstruck by the Gibb brothers, veterans of the music industry. 'It was really wonderful to meet Barry and Maurice. I was really nervous before I met them – after all, they are superstars. But they were very nice, and they invited us to their homes – we were there for dinner and talked with their families'. She celebrated her 19th birthday during the visit, recalling that Barry and Maurice came in with a beautiful birthday cake and sang "Happy Birthday' to me! I wonder how many people ever celebrated their birthday like that'.

While the social aspect of the trip was enjoyable, Carola understood the importance of the opportunity. She expressed, 'I have to work very hard now. A chance like this, I just must not miss. Our cooperation is perfect. We got a terrific contact right from the start, and I think that they understand what I can do and want to do'.

Maurice and Barry had only good things to say about Carola, and they loved her voice. After meeting her and gaining a better understanding of her style and personality, they felt more confident in crafting songs that suited her. 'This new album will show a new side of me', Carola revealed. 'It will really swing – that I promise. I do not know yet which musicians Maurice has picked out for me, but I'm sure that they are all well-known artists. The Gibb brothers usually get what they want!'

Returning to Sweden on 13 September with some demos and some early lyrics, the brothers would remain in contact over the following months, regularly sending her new song demo backing tracks and lyrics to work with. Carola would next meet with Maurice at a business meeting in London in December.

Several press discussions had hinted at the Gibbs' forthcoming collaboration with Diana Ross. The result was *Eaten Alive*, which arrived in the third quarter of the year.

Eaten Alive – Diana Ross (1985)
Diana Ross: vocals
Barry Gibb: vocals, guitar
Michael Jackson: vocals ('Eaten Alive')
John J. Barnes: keyboards
George Bitzer: keyboards, synthesiser, piano
Albhy Galuten: synthesiser
James Newton Howard: keyboards
Greg Phillinganes: keyboards
Larry Williams: keyboards
Don Felder: guitar

George Terry: guitar
Nathan East: bass
Steve Gadd: drums
Paul Leim: drums
Michael Fisher: percussion
Gary E. Grant: horns
Jerry Hey: horns
Bill Reichenbach: horns
Kim S. Hutchcroft: saxophone
Tim Scott: saxophone
Bruce Albertine: background vocals
Myrna Mathews: backing vocals
Marti McCall: background vocals
Arranged by Barry Gibb, Albhy Galuten
Engineers: Jack Joseph Puig, Karl Richardson
Mixed by Jack Joseph Puig ('More And More', 'Don't Give Up On Each Other', 'I'm Watching You', 'Chain Reaction'), Elliot Scheiner ('Oh Teacher', 'Crime Of Passion', 'Love On The Line'), Karl Richardson ('(I Love) Being In Love With You'), Humberto Gatica ('Eaten Alive', 'Experience')
Assistant Engineers: Dan Garcia, Scott Glasel, Julie Last, Larry Ferguson
Producers: Barry Gibb, Karl Richardson, Albhy Galuten; Michael Jackson ('Eaten Alive')
Recorded at Bill Schnee's Studio, Los Angeles; Middle Ear, Miami Beach, in July 1985
Mixed at Studio 55, Los Angeles; Middle Ear, Miami Beach; Lion Share Recording Studios, Los Angeles
Release dates: UK: October 1985, US: 24 September 1985
Chart positions: Sweden: 3, Netherlands: 8, Norway: 9, Switzerland: 10, Australia: 11, UK: 11, Austria: 14, Italy: 14, West Germany: 14, Japan: 20, Finland: 27, Canada: 43, US: 45

The final project for the Gibb-Galuten-Richardson production team marked the end of a prosperous and innovative era. The trio, who had been responsible for some of the biggest hits of the late 1970s and early 1980s – and, in the rearview mirror, some of the most impactful songs in pop music history – came together one last time to produce an album for Diana Ross. It was an idea that had been floating around for years. Ross, an icon in her own right, was an intriguing collaborator, but by the time the project materialised, the once-unshakable creative chemistry among the production team had begun to fade. The result was an album that, while boasting moments of brilliance, lacked the seamless magic of their earlier work.

Adding to the sense of transition, the team found themselves working with a different engineer for the first time. Albhy, who had relocated back to California, had started collaborating with Jack Joseph Puig. Looking back on the shift, he explained, 'We used him on the Diana Ross stuff along with Karl. Karl is an excellent engineer, but there are some engineers who are brilliant, like Bob Clearmountain, certainly, and Bill Schnee, who are another order of magnitude. Karl did the engineering, but we went to do the mixing with Jack'. It was a telling moment – an indication their established creative process was evolving, or perhaps unravelling.

Throughout her storied career as one of the cornerstones of the Motown stable, Diana Ross had been surrounded by whispers of diva-like behaviour, and those working on the album were well aware of her formidable reputation. However, their personal experience with her was relatively smooth, at least on the surface. Albhy reflected, 'Now, [Diana] was a piece of work. Not particularly troublesome for us because we got along fine, but the stories about her are legion. I know a lot of people who've worked for her, and she is an unbelievable piece of work. Makes everybody call her Miss Ross. But we did fine'. While he was careful not to level direct criticism at the singer, his words carried the weight of an industry insider who had seen and heard enough to recognise a pattern.

Barry, meanwhile, was a little more candid in describing the challenges of working with Ross. 'It's only difficult because she's very much in control of her own destiny, and it's very difficult to work with an artist who is very single-minded like that', he admitted, though he conceded that he himself had a similar personality. 'That's why there's a clash', he added. Barry was no stranger to working with legendary divas – his collaborations with Barbra Streisand had produced major hits – but even he acknowledged that working with Ross presented unique difficulties.

'Barbra was totally focused and studying the songs', he explained. 'The thing is, when you go into the studio, you need to be ready. Diana was doing a million other things. She was hosting the Academy Awards one week, attending rehearsals, going here and there, and when it came time to record, you just wouldn't see her. Being a record producer, when you put the other hat on, it's very frustrating to see that the artist doesn't always learn the songs when they're supposed to be recording them'. He was quick to clarify, however, that this was not a criticism, merely an observation. 'I wouldn't call it unprofessional – I'm not saying that – but I will say, it wasn't comfortable'.

One of the most anticipated tracks of the album was its title song and lead single, 'Eaten Alive', co-written by Barry and Maurice with input from Michael Jackson, who also co-produced the song. With these pop powerhouses collaborating, expectations were sky-high. And yet, it did not become the defining hit of the album, something the production team found disappointing.

Albhy had high hopes for the song. In his view, it was something special. 'The most amazing track we cut', he recalled. The production team had approached it with fresh eyes and technical ambition, using the cutting-edge Synclavier digital synthesiser to create what Albhy believed was a groundbreaking drum track. 'It was the first full Synclavier drum track that had ever been done', he revealed. 'In fact, Michael was so impressed by the stuff that I did on the Synclavier that he went out and bought one. He ended up using it himself'.

Barry wholeheartedly agreed. "Eaten Alive' should have been the big hit off that album, but incidentally just wasn't', he lamented. He also shared a glimpse into Jackson's creative input:

Michael was lovely – he's a very shy person. He came along one day to the house we were renting in L.A., and he heard the songs from the Diana Ross album. He heard part of a song called 'Eaten Alive', which was unfinished, and it was just the verses, you know. And he just said that there should be something else in this song, there should be another place to go to. And I was cheeky enough to say, 'Well, Michael, if you feel like there's something else to put in there … if you have any thoughts, you let me know because we'd be delighted to share the song with you if you want to do that'. So, he said, 'Well, give me a cassette of the song', and he went away, and a few days later, he came back with the chorus area.

Despite their belief in 'Eaten Alive', the final product was altered before its release in a way that Albhy felt would hurt its commercial success. 'We did a mix that I thought was incredible and was a smash that Barry loved', he explained. However, Michael had his own thoughts on how the song should sound and brought in his preferred engineer, Humberto Gattica. 'He used metal cassettes that were louder and knew how it would sound on Michael's ghetto blaster, and it would be louder than the other. We ended up settling for Humberto's mix, which was awful. But the original mix was a great record'.

Surprisingly, it wasn't 'Eaten Alive' but rather the album's second single, 'Chain Reaction', that became the standout hit. The song's success caught even Barry off guard. He recalled the moment it was discovered, saying, 'The one song that really broke out was 'Chain Reaction', and it was a complete surprise. The funny thing is, the song had been there all along. We'd written it, but we hadn't had the nerve to play it for her. Then one day, she said, 'Well, we still need one more song from somewhere'. That's when we brought it up'.

There was initial scepticism about the song's suitability for Ross, given that it bore an undeniable resemblance to some of the bouncy soul hits from her days with The Supremes. 'We said, 'We think it's time you did something which you would have done with The Supremes, not as Diana Ross", recalled Barry. 'It's time to do that. It had been long enough since The Supremes, and she needed to reintroduce that sound. But it wasn't until she heard it all come together that she finally agreed. It turned out to be a credible tribute to her past'.

Albhy described the creation of 'Chain Reaction' as a snap decision that turned into a hit. 'It was done kind of at the last minute', he admitted. 'We threw it together, just put it on the Synclavier to get something done fast, but it had great vibes'. The track had a warmth and an energy that resonated with audiences in a way the team hadn't entirely expected.

'Eaten Alive' (Barry Gibb, Maurice Gibb, Michael Jackson)
Recorded at Bill Schnee's Studio, Los Angeles, around July 1985
Chart positions: Italy: 10, Finland: 14, Sweden: 14, Switzerland: 17, Belgium: 24, Netherlands: 17, New Zealand: 26, West Germany: 38, UK: 71, US: 77, Australia: 81

The original copyright registration for the song 'Eaten Alive', dated 11 March 1985, listed Barry Gibb and Maurice Gibb as the songwriters. However, when Michael Jackson, who had become a friend of the Gibbs, heard the demo, he suggested changes to the chorus. This feedback led to a new version and a writing credit for Jackson, prompting a second copyright registration on 1 June 1985, with a note stating that the words and music in the choruses had been entirely rewritten.

RCA touted the release of both the *Eaten Alive* album and its titular track single as a 'major musical event', generating considerable excitement not just for the collaboration between Diana Ross and Barry Gibb, but also for the added star power of Michael Jackson.

Initial feedback on the single was positive and R&B radio swiftly embraced the song, and within just two weeks, it became a top 20 Dance Club Play hit. However, after a month, 'Eaten Alive' had only reached number 77 on the *Billboard* Hot 100, a disappointing outcome for a single whose creators alone should have ensured top ten status.

While there have been instances where the record-buying public missed the mark on great singles created by the Gibbs, 'Eaten Alive' is not one of them; the song fell short. Diana Ross' voice is drowned in echo on the verses, making it barely discernible. She is overshadowed on the refrain by the shrill falsetto vocals of both Barry and Michael Jackson. The frantic pace and layered sound effects make it difficult to decipher the lyrics, and repeated listens only lead to greater confusion regarding the lyrics and the song's intended message.

At the 13th Annual American Music Awards, held at the Shrine Auditorium in Los Angeles on 27 January 1986, Ross kicked off the event with a live performance of the song. The arrangement featured an extended, mainly percussive instrumental section, allowing the MC to announce all the evening's performers while dancers added a visual dimension to the ongoing performance. After a costume change, Ross returned to the stage, seamlessly continuing her singing while joining the dancers in their choreographed routine.

The music video for 'Eaten Alive' drew inspiration from H. G. Wells' novel *The Island Of Doctor Moreau*, and its 1977 film adaptation, which starred Burt Lancaster and Michael York. Directed by David Hogan, the video features a storyline where a singer, depicted as a cat-like demon, seduces a man portrayed by Joseph Gian, who is best known for his role as Detective Tom Ryan in the TV show *Knots Landing*. The video also includes scenes where chimeras chase the main character, adding to the eerie atmosphere.

'Oh Teacher' (Barry Gibb, Robin Gibb, Maurice Gibb)
Recorded at Bill Schnee's Studio, Los Angeles, around July 1985
'Oh Teacher' was one of the first demos crafted by Barry for the album, a synth-heavy track with a dark, driving vibe that sets the tone for the entire album. It offers a glimpse into Barry's vision for Diana Ross, aiming to create a sexy pop album that played to her image as a glamorous, sensual woman. The song was co-written with Robin and Maurice and had undeniable hit potential. However, the final recording

exemplifies how closely Ross followed Barry's original demo. A comparison between the two versions reveals her mimicking his every breath, resulting in a high, raspy vocal performance that diverges significantly from her signature style. From the outset, Ross's voice is overshadowed by other elements; Barry's own vocals are overly prominent, almost to a fault, while the synthesisers dominate the mix. Consequently, Ross's lead vocal becomes nearly indiscernible, blending into the background rather than standing out.

'Experience' (Barry Gibb, Robin Gibb, Maurice Gibb, Andy Gibb)

Recorded at Bill Schnee's Studio, Los Angeles, around July 1985
Chart positions: Ireland: 14, Netherlands: 45, UK: 47, Australia: 64

Upon the release of *Eaten Alive*, music critics consistently highlighted 'Experience' as a standout track. *Rolling Stone* lauded it as a 'flawless ballad', while *Billboard* dubbed it 'lovely'. What immediately catches attention is its relative simplicity compared to the album's more intricate arrangements, giving it a timeless quality. It is a beautiful composition.

The songwriting credits include Andy as well as the usual trio of Barry, Robin and Maurice. Andy lived in Los Angeles at the time and reportedly stopped by the studio during the recording sessions and offered some form of input on the track, but it's never been discussed what his contribution exactly was.

Diana's vocal delivery, while occasionally powerful, often veers into an uncanny resemblance to Barry's breathy whisper, especially evident in the clipped pronunciation of the second verse. Unlike Dionne Warwick, who maintained her distinctive style on her *Heartbreaker* album, Diana struggles to carve out her own identity within the song's framework, often overshadowed by Barry's multitracked background vocals and the echo-y percussion. At least some of the falsetto harmonies Barry assembled for the demo survived to the final mix.

Nevertheless, 'Experience' enjoyed moderate success when it was released as a single in April 1986. It peaked at number 64 in Australia, number 47 in the UK and number 45 in the Netherlands. Its best placing was number 14 in Ireland.

'Chain Reaction' (Barry Gibb, Robin Gibb, Maurice Gibb)

Recorded at Bill Schnee's Studio, Los Angeles, around July 1985
Chart positions: Australia: 1, Ireland: 1, UK: 1, New Zealand: 3,

South Africa: 4, West Germany: 11, Finland: 15, France: 20, Switzerland: 20, Belgium: 35, Canada: 40, Netherlands: 40, US: 66

Undoubtedly, 'Chain Reaction' stands as the album's crowning achievement, marking Diana's first chart topper hit in the United Kingdom since 'I'm Still Waiting' in 1971. The song was added only after all other tracks had been completed. According to the Gibbs, they proposed the idea to Diana as a nod to her earlier work, aiming to create a quintessential Supremes-style record with her lead vocals. 'The whole album was done, and Diana was still looking for that one song she could call a single', Barry recalled in an interview with Billboard in 2001. 'We asked her, 'How do you feel about doing something that you might have done 25 years ago?'' Maurice further explained, 'We thought, 'Wouldn't it be great to make a great Supremes record? We've got the lead singer''.

Barry, Robin and Maurice succeeded in crafting a compact and captivating pop single, adorned with a lively beat and an irresistibly catchy refrain. While the lyrics venture into more suggestive territory than Holland-Dozier-Holland's compositions for The Supremes, the melody is sharp and instantly memorable, providing Ross ample room to shine. Her vocal performance on this track is unmatched throughout the album; her delivery is clear and commanding, effortlessly rising above the rollicking instrumental. Notably, she displays newfound power, particularly evident when she belts out the title phrase amidst the dynamically changing musical keys.

Moreover, Diana's performance cleverly evokes her early days as a recording artist, as seen in subtle nuances reminiscent of her time with The Supremes. It's worth noting that Barry's demos for the album initially excluded 'Chain Reaction', suggesting that Diana may have had no vocal reference to mimic. It remains a standout track, encapsulating the fun, retro vibe that defines the album.

Despite its undeniable quality, 'Chain Reaction' faced a disappointing reception upon its US release as the second single extracted from the album in November 1985, peaking at a dismal number 95 on the *Billboard* Hot 100 and number 85 on the R&B chart. However, its international release, accompanied by an energetic music video, propelled it to immediate success, jumping to number one in the UK, Australia and West Germany.

Seemingly determined to make the song an American hit, RCA remixed and re-released the song in the United States in early 1986, but it failed to secure a significant foothold. It achieved a slightly improved peak of number 66 on the *Billboard* Hot 100 the week of 24 May. It's regrettable that 'Chain Reaction' didn't grant Diana Ross the pop hit she deserved in her home country, marking her final appearance on the pop singles chart. Nevertheless, its enduring popularity internationally solidifies its status as a timeless classic.

'More And More' (Barry Gibb, Andy Gibb, Albhy Galuten)
Recorded at Bill Schnee's Studio, Los Angeles, around July 1985
If 'Chain Reaction' represents a brilliant homage to the qualities that propelled Diana Ross to superstardom in the 1960s, then the bluesy 'More And More', composed by Barry and Andy Gibb and Albhy Galuten, is a purposeful nod to Diana's Oscar-nominated turn as Billie Holliday in the 1972 film *Lady Sings The Blues*.

Adopting almost the exact vocal tone from Barry's demo and aiming to convey vulnerability by whispering throughout the entire song, Ross sounds so feeble that it appears she's on the verge of losing her voice altogether. It's a shame Barry didn't push her to put more of her own personal stamp on this.

'I'm Watching You' (Barry Gibb, Robin Gibb, Maurice Gibb)
Recorded at Bill Schnee's Studio, Los Angeles, around July 1985
The next four songs on the tracklist are credited to Barry, Robin and Maurice, the first of which is a cool, ethereal ballad, 'I'm Watching You', which stands out as one of the album's most enchanting tracks. The distinctive synthesiser line that introduces and concludes the song is both lovely and memorable, possessing the potential to attract pop airplay on its own. Diana delivers a relatively straightforward performance, albeit with a lingering breathiness that could have been toned down a little.

'Love On The Line' (Barry Gibb, Robin Gibb, Maurice Gibb)
Recorded at Bill Schnee's Studio, Los Angeles, around July 1985
The fiery 'Love On the Line' exudes instrumental swagger, but by now the synth-driven composition carries a dated charm, yet it stands out as one of the few tracks on *Eaten Alive* that instantly captures the potential for hit status. Diana's performance on the verses is surprisingly strong; the song's structure complements her breathy delivery better than several others, and she infuses certain lyrics with a passion that's noticeably absent elsewhere. Unfortunately, when the impeccably crafted

refrain kicks in, Ross seems to fade into the background amidst the sharp, pop-infused, swaying falsetto background vocals, which detract from its potential street-swagger appeal.

'(I Love) Being In Love With You' (Barry Gibb, Robin Gibb, Maurice Gibb)

Recorded at Bill Schnee's Studio, Los Angeles, around July 1985

'(I Love) Being In Love With You' bears a striking resemblance to Barry's singing style rather than Diana Ross's usual delivery. Much like her earlier attempt with 'Oh Teacher', this ballad underscores her efforts to emulate The Bee Gees' sound. Her pronunciation mirrors Barry's demo vocals so closely that it becomes difficult to distinguish between them.

'Crime Of Passion' (Barry Gibb, Robin Gibb, Maurice Gibb)

Recorded at Bill Schnee's Studio, Los Angeles, around July 1985

'Crime Of Passion' is a lively track, which injects much-needed vigour into the album. The mere presence of an electric guitar provides a welcome break from the onslaught of synthesisers that dominate previous tracks (although it must be noted that synthesisers still play a significant role here). The song exudes pure pop-rock, featuring an assertive melody that demands more power and range from Ross, who rises to the occasion. She's accompanied on the chorus by Barry's prominent background vocals, which complement the song's sharp and edgy tone.

'Don't Give Up On Each Other' (Barry Gibb, George Bitzer)

Recorded at Bill Schnee's Studio, Los Angeles, around July 1985

The delightful 'Don't Give Up On Each Other', composed by Barry and George Bitzer, stands out as one of the album's finest compositions, with heartfelt lyrics that beautifully complement the achingly pretty melody. Ross delivers a crisp vocal performance that effectively conveys the song's message. While her performance may feel somewhat restrained, she still manages to infuse the track with emotion. It's a strong, fitting close to the album.

Despite the initial criticism directed at its lead single, 'Eaten Alive', Diana Ross's album garnered some favourable reviews. *Rolling Stone*, in particular, described it as 'deep and intelligently crafted'. However, the lack of widespread support for the single resulted in poor album sales, peaking at only number 45 on the *Billboard* 200 chart the week of 16

November 1985. It fared better in the UK, where it placed at number 11, and had a top ten showing in Norway, Sweden, Switzerland, and the Netherlands.

Barry released *The Eaten Alive Demos* via iTunes in 2006, which includes the album's full tracklist minus 'Chain Reaction', which had no demo due to its very late addition to the project.

In 2014, *Eaten Alive* received an expanded treatment with a two-disc set assembled by Funkytowngrooves Ltd. – an independent label based in Northampton, UK, specialising in R&B, soul, and disco reissues. The label had revisited several of Diana Ross' 1970s and 1980s albums in addition to releases by Dionne Warwick, KC & The Sunshine Band, Martha Reeves, Melba Moore, and Earth, Wind & Fire, among hundreds of other artists. The first disc of the *Eaten Alive* reissue included the album's original tracklist, while disc two contained previously released mixes and instrumental versions of 'Eaten Alive' and 'Experience', and dance and single mixes of 'Chain Reaction'.

The central problem with much of the album appeared to be the lack of soul, a critique emphasised by UK magazine *Blues & Soul* upon its release. Even in a relatively positive review, the magazine pointed out that it was 'a good collection of songs if you immediately disregard the fact that Diana was once an integral part of a soulful trio and a leading soul artist through her early Motown recordings'.

In an article titled 'Year of Surprises on the Charts' at the close of 1985, *Billboard* writer Paul Grein labelled *Eaten Alive* as the number one disappointment of the year. However, this narrative only tells part of the album's story. The success of 'Chain Reaction' provided a significant boost, leading to major international acclaim. The album peaked at number 11 in the UK. It reached the top ten both in Norway, where it peaked at number nine, and in the Netherlands, where it reached number eight. Its best placing, however, was in Sweden at number three.

In the spring of 1985, Larry Gatlin, following a stint in rehabilitation for his drug and alcohol issues, embraced a calmer, more measured approach to life and music, signalling a profound personal transformation. It was in this frame of mind that Gatlin travelled to Miami for a creative collaboration with Barry. The two had first crossed paths in 1983 when the Gatlin Brothers provided backing vocals on two songs for Kenny Rogers' *Eyes That See In The Dark*. The respect between them was mutual, and the opportunity to work together again was one both artists welcomed. This time, they sat down to write a new song: 'Indian Summer'.

The track was recorded for the Gatlin Brothers' album *Smile*, which was released in October 1985. Larry Gatlin took the lead vocal, with his brothers Rudy and Steve Gatlin providing backing vocals. Barry also contributed backing vocals and guitar, while Maurice played keyboards. Pop legend Roy Orbison – long a vocal inspiration for the Gibbs – joined them as well, lending his haunting tenor to the background harmonies.

Although the finished track suggested a seamless collaboration, the circumstances behind the recording were more complicated. Initial accounts claimed the instrumental parts and the Gatlin Brothers' vocals were laid down in Tennessee, with Orbison recording his contribution at an unspecified location, and Barry and Maurice adding their parts at Middle Ear in Miami. Yet video footage, dated 18 June 1985, emerged showing all five singers together in the studio recording the song. If the sessions were indeed conducted separately, the footage might be an artful reconstruction – or perhaps the recording took place more collaboratively than originally reported. Despite the speculation, the chemistry between the artists is undeniable in the audio and video that remain.

Upon its release, the album, *Smile*, reached number 35 on the *Billboard* Top Country Albums chart. 'Indian Summer' also found a second life as a single in Australia and New Zealand, and it later appeared on several Roy Orbison anthologies, including *Rare Orbison* in 1989, and the comprehensive *Legendary Roy Orbison* box set in 1990.

'Indian Summer' wasn't the only product of the Barry Gibb-Larry Gatlin partnership. Another song, 'Didn't We Call It (Falling In Love)', was written around the same time, with copyright registration in March, about a month earlier than 'Indian Summer'. Unlike its sibling, this song was never released, although it's likely that demo recordings of it exist.

At the time of these sessions, Barry was reportedly exploring other major production projects, including potential albums for Neil Diamond and his Miami neighbour, Julio Iglesias.

Walls Have Eyes – Robin Gibb (1985)
Robin Gibb: vocals
Maurice Gibb: vocals, keyboards, bass
Barry Gibb: vocals ('Toys')
Duane Hitchings; keyboards
Mitchell Froom: keyboards

Phil Chen: bass ('Gone With The Wind')
Sandy Gennaro: drums
George Terry: guitar
Steve Farris: guitar
Alto Reed: saxophone
Ed Calle: saxophone
MIDI programming and sampling: Scott Glasel
Engineers: Dennis Hetzendorfer, Leslie Shapiro (Middle Ear and Criteria Studios), Bill Schnee, Glen Holguin (Studio 55), Doug Sax (Mastering Lab)
Produced by Tom Dowd and Maurice Gibb
Recorded at Middle Ear, Miami Beach, and Criteria Studios, Miami, in August/September 1985
Release dates: UK: November 1985, US: November 1985

Produced by Maurice and the renowned Atlantic Records producer Tom Dowd, Robin's third solo album of the 1980s, *Walls Have Eyes*, was released in November 1985. Recorded at Criteria Studios and Middle Ear, the album showcased Robin's unmistakable vocal style paired with a refined and sophisticated production approach. Contributions from all three Gibb brothers hinted at an evolving creative dynamic within the family, edging them closer to a Bee Gees reunion. However, the project was shaped by tight budgetary constraints and creative compromises imposed by Polydor UK, which ultimately limited its potential despite notable artistic strengths. As a result, while the album delivered several musically satisfying moments, it struggled to achieve commercial success.

The songwriting on *Walls Have Eyes* marked a broader collaborative effort, with Barry co-writing eight of the album's ten tracks. Tom Dowd recalled that much of the material was prepared in advance of the sessions, reflecting Robin's preference for straightforward verse-chorus structures. Barry's melodic craftsmanship added an extra dimension to the material, blending with Robin's characteristic simplicity of form. Dowd praised Robin's vocal interpretation, noting, 'Robin has an uncanny way of taking a melody and making it soar above the production. He made the fantasy come alive, and the production became part of the storytelling'.

However, the production process was not without challenges. Dowd described frequent clashes with Polydor UK's A&R team, whose demands often conflicted with the artistic freedom he and Robin desired. 'It was, 'I want this, and something that'll do that, and it's got to fit this", Dowd explained. 'You realise – I'm not here to make the best record this artist is capable of making; I'm here to make a record that fits this guy's concept of what he can sell'. This tension between artistic vision and commercial considerations is a recurring theme in the album's narrative.

Robin and Dowd were also apparently at odds during the sessions. Robin had hoped that Dowd being the protege of the Gibbs' mentor, Arif Mardin, would result in a closer working relationship, but they apparently grew to dislike one another. Dennis Hetzendorfer, the album's engineer, agreed that the working dynamic was somewhat problematic. He praised Dowd as 'a legend in the industry, but it was at a point where Tom was getting older. It just wasn't as much fun as making *Secret Agent*'.

The sessions featured a mix of familiar collaborators and fresh talent. Maurice contributed bass, keyboards, and backing vocals, with this album marking the final time he played bass on a recording. Guitarist George Terry, a regular on past Gibb projects, returned alongside Steve Farris of Mr. Mister, fresh off the success of their massive hits 'Broken Wings' and 'Kyrie'. Keyboards were handled by the young Mitchell Froom – who would later achieve fame for his work with Crowded House, Suzanne Vega, and Elvis Costello – and veteran Duane Hitchings, co-writer of Rod Stewart's hits 'Da Ya Think I'm Sexy?' and 'Young Turks'. Hitchings later recalled that Maurice played most of the keyboard parts, with his own contributions being minimal. The drums were a blend of live performances by Sandy Gennaro and programmed tracks by Scott Glasel, reflecting the era's evolving production techniques. Robin and Maurice were playfully credited for backing vocals as 'The 'G' Twins' on the album's inner sleeve – perhaps inspired by Mick Jagger and Keith Richards' pseudonym, The Glimmer Twins.

Barry contributed lead vocals on 'Toys', but his involvement in the recording of the album was otherwise limited. Dowd speculated that involving all three brothers on 'Toys' was a strategic move by the record company: 'Because things weren't going as planned, it was, 'Hey, maybe if we get the brothers on it, we'll come out smelling better''.

The album's lead single, 'Like A Fool', while well-crafted, lacked the distinctiveness needed to stand out in a competitive market. In contrast, its B-side, 'Possession', allowed Robin to explore a darker and edgier tone. The second single, 'Toys', featured the full participation of the Gibb brothers, but despite these efforts, neither track made a significant impact on the charts. Barry later reflected that 'Robin didn't receive the feedback he wanted'.

The release strategy for *Walls Have Eyes* complicated its legacy. EMI America re-sequenced the tracklist for its US release but failed to issue it on CD, making it the last Gibb album in the US available only on vinyl and cassette. Polydor's international release included a CD version, but poor sales rendered it a rarity.

UK: Polydor
Side One: 1. 'You Don't Say Us Anymore', 2. 'Like A Fool', 3. 'Heartbeat In Exile', 4. 'Remedy', 5. 'Toys'
Side Two: 1. Someone To Believe In', 2. 'Gone With The Wind', 3. 'These Walls Have Eyes', 4. 'Possession', 5. 'Do You Love Her?'

US: EMI America
Side One: 1. 'Someone To Believe In', 2. 'Like A Fool', 3. 'Gone With The Wind', 4. 'Toys', 5. 'These Walls Have Eyes'
Side Two: 1. 'Do You Love Her?', 2. 'Possession', 3. 'Heartbeat In Exile', 4. 'You Don't Say Us Anymore', 5. 'Remedy'

Dennis Hetzendorfer also recalled that the label wasn't happy with how the final product sounded. 'We mixed it at Middle Ear, but they didn't care for the mixes, so we took everything out to California to remix with Bill Schnee – another legendary engineer – at Studio 55, Richard Perry's place in Hollywood'.

The album's artwork by The Cream Group featured reversible cover art with two nearly identical photos of Robin by Tim O'Sullivan – one a headshot and the other showing him standing on a beach at night – while the inner sleeve displayed a curious grainy close-up of Robin's hair. These choices, though intriguing, did little to elevate the album's visibility.

Financial limitations also influenced the recording process. Dowd reflected on the obstacles, saying, 'We were sitting on a tight monetary consideration, and here we were recording in the United States for a record company in England. Once in a while, somebody shows up, and the rest of the time it's like, 'What did you do? You should have told me!"

Walls Have Eyes balanced artistic ambition with external pressures and thriftiness, offering moments of melodic sophistication and vocal brilliance. However, the lack of a standout hit and strained relationships with the label hindered its commercial performance. Despite these setbacks, the album remains a compelling snapshot of Robin's solo artistry and the Gibb brothers' collaborative strengths. As Dowd poignantly noted, 'Sometimes you can pull it off, and sometimes it isn't a very good marriage'.

'You Don't Say Us Anymore' (Robin Gibb, Maurice Gibb)
Recorded at Middle Ear, Miami Beach, and Criteria Studios, Miami, in August/September 1985

'You Don't Say Us Anymore' opens the album in all regions where it was released on Polydor and establishes its tone with the fastest tempo on the record at 134 beats per minute. It stands out not only for its pace but also for being one of only two tracks on the album not co-written with Barry.

Robin delivers the verses using a deeper vocal register, similar to his performance on 'Boys Do Fall In Love', before transitioning to his more familiar voice in the pre-chorus. This shift adds dynamic range and helps lift the track as it builds. Midway through, Robin embarks on a vocal tangent that provides a notable variation in the song's structure and is repeated three times.

The production incorporates electronic drumbeats and a brisk keyboard riff, creating a layered, synth-driven sound. However, in contrast to the more aggressive electronic style of the previous album, *Secret Agent*, the synthesisers here are handled with more restraint. This more refined approach is attributable to producer Tom Dowd, whose experienced hand brings greater subtlety and nuance to the arrangement.

The instrumental section features a synthesiser tone that flirts with dissonance. This slightly off-kilter sound adds a jarring but effective texture that complements the song's emotional tension.

Lyrically, the track captures themes of disconnection, frustration and emotional erosion. The song paints a picture of a relationship unravelling, punctuated by an energetic and sharp-edged musical backdrop.

'Like A Fool' (Robin Gibb, Barry Gibb, Maurice Gibb)
Recorded at Middle Ear, Miami Beach, and Criteria Studios, Miami, in August/September 1985

'Like A Fool' appears as the second track on the album in both the Polydor and EMI America releases – a coincidental consistency for an album issued in varying formats across regions. Released as the first single from the album in November, with 'Possession' as its B-side. It also appeared in an extended 12" mix tailored for dance markets, despite its slower ballad tempo. It failed to chart in all major territories, but it became a modest hit in Brazil.

The track follows a conventional verse-chorus structure and moves at a slow, measured pace reminiscent of Robin's earlier solo single 'Another Lonely Night In New York'. The arrangement features soft, atmospheric production with restrained instrumentation, allowing space for the vocals to carry the song's lyrical weight.

Robin sings in his natural voice throughout, a decision that noticeably improves the clarity of his delivery and adds emotional depth to the lyrics. His vocal performance is understated but expressive, complementing the song's themes of regret and emotional vulnerability.

Dennis Hetzendorfer recalled to the authors in September 2025 that 'we brought in this huge hundred-piece adult Black choir from Bethune-Cookman University to sing on 'Like A Fool'. They came into Middle Ear and did some gospel-style choral singing – that was a lot of fun'. The choir, not credited anywhere in the album's notes, was either dropped from the track or they're so far back in the mix that they simply blend in.

A promotional video was shot over three days in London in July, directed by Jay Dubin, best known for his work on Billy Joel's 'Uptown Girl'. Robin also promoted the single on German television, appearing on *Wetten, Dass..?* on 27 October and *Tele-Illustrierte* the following day, as well as on *Sterrenshow* in the Netherlands on 30 October.

'Heartbeat In Exile' (Robin Gibb, Barry Gibb, Maurice Gibb)
Recorded at Middle Ear, Miami Beach, and Criteria Studios, Miami, in August/September 1985
'Heartbeat In Exile' was one of the last three songs submitted for copyright registration for the album in September 1985, slightly later than the other seven tracks. Along with 'Do You Love Her?' and 'Remedy', it is assumed to have been recorded toward the end of the sessions.

The track opens with a percussion and bass groove that runs for almost 30 seconds before Robin's vocal kicks in. His delivery is rapid, pushing through the verses with urgency. The lyrics deal with loss and regret, but the music doesn't dwell on it. Instead, the upbeat tempo and pop-leaning arrangement give the song more energy than the subject matter might suggest. That contrast works well here and keeps the track from becoming too heavy.

A notable feature is the saxophone solo by Alto Reed, best known as a long-time member of Bob Seger and the Silver Bullet Band. His part adds a smooth, expressive break in the middle of the song without disrupting the pace before the chorus repeats into the outro fade.

'Remedy' (Robin Gibb, Barry Gibb, Maurice Gibb)
Recorded at Middle Ear, Miami Beach, and Criteria Studios, Miami, in August/September 1985
'Remedy' is the second of three songs on the album submitted for copyright registration in September 1985. Driven by a relentless, fast-paced rhythm, the track features a constant backbone of bass drum, snare, and hi-hat, with the unusual inclusion of a persistent cowbell. Notably, the programmed drums remain consistent throughout, with no fills interrupting the momentum.

The chorus is divided into two contrasting sections. The first showcases impressive high register layered harmonies from Robin and Maurice, while the second brings Robin's vocals back to his regular range. Two short synthesiser interludes – each built around a repeated riff – appear after the first and second choruses, adding subtle instrumental interest without detracting from the vocal focus.

With its crisp arrangement and commercial appeal, 'Remedy' is a well-crafted pop song that could have performed strongly as a single. It's a fitting and memorable closing track for the album's US release.

'Toys' (Robin Gibb, Barry Gibb, Maurice Gibb)
Recorded at Middle Ear, Miami Beach, and Criteria Studios, Miami, in August/September 1985
'Toys' closes the first side of the Polydor edition of the album with a theatrical intensity that stands out as a highlight, not least for bringing together all three Bee Gees after a significant hiatus. It was released as the second single in February 1986 in limited territories: Canada, Spain, West Germany, and the US. It charted modestly, reaching number 27 on the Canadian Adult Contemporary chart. Still, its strength lies more in its dramatic arrangement and haunting lyrical content than in its chart performance.

Set in a minor key with a slow, deliberate tempo, 'Toys' unfolds as a brooding piece rich in gothic atmosphere, layered with themes of madness, control, and dark eroticism. Robin delivers a tortured, expressive vocal performance, perfectly suited to lines like 'don't tell me not to stare at you, I see the danger in your eyes'.

The language is psychologically fraught, hinting at obsession and voyeurism, while the imagery of 'your secret hall of pain' and 'bedroom point of view' implies twisted intimacy without crossing into outright vulgarity.

Barry's contribution adds contrast, particularly as he croons the ambiguous 'I want to play with your toys, be one of your special friends', a line which, through his understated delivery, becomes chillingly suggestive. The use of shared lead vocals between Barry and Robin harks back to an earlier era of their work. It certainly made fans hungry to hear The Bee Gees work together again.

Musically, the production is meticulous. Deep drum tones, a keyboard line following the second chorus, and Barry's signature falsetto flourishes in the outro all contribute to a layered and textural listening experience.

On an early demo version, Barry sings the entire second verse and pre-chorus in addition to the choruses as he does on the final version.

A remixed version of 'Toys' later appeared on the *Tales From The Brothers Gibb* box set in 1990, offering a slightly cleaner, more polished version of the original that highlighted the dense instrumentation and vocal layering.

Prior to its release as a single, a promotional video was filmed over two days – 16 and 17 December 1985 – in London, directed by Nigel Dick for NAWGO Productions and produced by Mark Freedman and Ruth Orme. A key television appearance followed on 11 January 1986, when Robin performed the track on *Solid Gold*, giving American audiences a glimpse into the single's theatrical and emotionally fraught world.

Although its suitability as a single may be questioned – most likely chosen more for the nostalgic value of a Bee Gees reunion than for commercial viability – 'Toys' remains a compelling recording.

'Someone To Believe In' (Barry Gibb, Robin Gibb, Maurice Gibb)

Recorded at Middle Ear, Miami Beach, and Criteria Studios, Miami, in August/September 1985

'Someone To Believe In' serves as a strong opening track on the EMI America edition of the album and appears as the first track on side two of the Polydor version. It begins with a syncopated bass and drum pattern, paired with pulsing keyboards, immediately creating a sense of urgency that is sustained throughout. Set in a minor key, the track leans into a darker, more dramatic atmosphere, with Robin's impassioned vocals amplifying the tension.

The lyrics introduce a gothic tone, while the repeated plea for 'someone to believe in' underlines the song's desperate emotional core.

Musically, the song benefits from a more cohesive band feel, with guitar present throughout. While it mostly mirrors the keyboard line, it stands out during the brief but effective power chord sections and a short, harmonised solo that adds real texture without overstaying its welcome.

'Gone With The Wind' (Robin Gibb, Maurice Gibb)

Recorded at Middle Ear, Miami Beach, and Criteria Studios, Miami, in August/September 1985

'Gone With The Wind' stands out as a striking and necessary departure from the dominant electronic aesthetic that defined much of the parent album – as well as *How Old Are You?* and *Secret Agent*.

It is one of only two tracks not co-written with Barry, and while the absence of his input is notable, the song's divergence lies more in its overall approach than in authorship alone. This melodramatic ballad moves away from the prevailing synth-driven production of the album, offering instead a more organic arrangement.

Maurice's contribution on piano, paired with live instrumentation from seasoned session musicians Phil Chen on bass and Sandy Gennaro on drums, gives the track an authentic depth that many of the album's other songs lack. The song follows a simple verse-chorus structure, with a tasteful guitar solo providing further dynamic lift without overshadowing the vocal performance.

Robin delivers one of his most compelling vocals here. His voice on the verses is tender and raw, capturing the emotional weight of the lyrics with remarkable sensitivity. As the song builds, his delivery becomes increasingly impassioned, carrying the listener through the narrative of vulnerability, heartbreak and longing. The lyrics themselves are direct, with recurring themes of emotional fatigue and the desperate pull of needing someone despite the pain they've caused.

'Gone With The Wind' is a reminder of Robin's strength as a balladeer when allowed space to move away from rigid production. Its power lies in its restraint – simple instrumentation, uncluttered structure and a vocal performance that is both nuanced and soaring. It is, without question, one of the album's standout moments.

'These Walls Have Eyes' (Barry Gibb, Robin Gibb, Maurice Gibb)

Recorded at Middle Ear, Miami Beach, and Criteria Studios, Miami, in August/September 1985

'These Walls Have Eyes' closes side one of the EMI America edition of the album and effectively functions as its title track, despite the slight variation in name. The song again has a somewhat gothic tone, both lyrically and musically, with a minor key structure that reinforces its shadowy atmosphere. A relentless walking bassline underpins the track, providing a steady pulse that remains unchanged throughout, lending it a hypnotic, almost claustrophobic feel.

The vocal arrangement in the pre-chorus is one of the track's standout features. Overlapping vocal lines build tension, adding a sense of unease that complements the lyrical themes. A brief a cappella passage near the song's end offers a stark contrast before the rhythm section returns for a fade-out.

The phrase 'walls have eyes' reimagines the familiar idiom 'walls have ears', intensifying its connotation to suggest not just passive overhearing but active surveillance. This idea draws a possible parallel with the 1969 erotic thriller film *The Walls Have Eyes*, in which the manager of the True Vue Motel secretly films couples during illicit encounters using hidden cameras, then blackmails them. Its narrative revolves around voyeurism, control, lust, betrayal, and the violation of privacy – elements that strongly echo through the song's lyrics. Lines such as 'someone making love to you, it shows under the skin' and 'even all that is sacred ... is mine' evoke a sense of unseen observers intruding upon deeply personal experiences.

The constant bassline and minor key heighten the atmosphere of unease, reinforcing the sense that no action or emotion is truly private within the song's dark, watchful setting.

'Possession' (Robin Gibb, Barry Gibb, Maurice Gibb)
Recorded at Middle Ear, Miami Beach, and Criteria Studios, Miami, in August/September 1985

'Possession', the B-side to the single 'Like A Fool', is a slow ballad that leans into dark, gothic territory – making it the third track on the album to do so. Originally titled 'Soul Passion', the song evolved into a more haunting and obsessive meditation on desire. The lyric paints a portrait of obsessive desire, where love blurs into obsession and desperation. Lines like 'You know I would sell you my soul for possession' and 'I'd break every rule in the book' underscore the intensity and unhealthy fixation of the narrator, reinforcing the song's gothic tone.

The track is anchored by a constant tom-heavy drum pattern that maintains a steady, pulsing undercurrent throughout. The verses are carried by a primitive, but pleasing, string synth sound, creating a tense, atmospheric backdrop. In contrast, the choruses shift to a piano-led sound, giving them more emotional weight. From the bridge onward, the string synths and piano combine, helping the song build towards a more dramatic conclusion.

The word 'possession' is emphasised in the choruses with layered harmonies. The bridge, placed between the second and third choruses, is a high point – Robin lifts both his vocal range and volume, giving the moment a heightened sense of urgency and climax before the track returns to its refrain.

'Do You Love Her?' (Robin Gibb, Barry Gibb, Maurice Gibb)
Recorded at Middle Ear, Miami Beach, and Criteria Studios, Miami, in August/September 1985

'Do You Love Her?' serves as the closing track on the Polydor edition of the album, while also opening side two on the EMI America version. Both placements are significant: album closers often act as a parting statement, while a side-two opener can serve to re-engage the listener. Additionally, its appearance as the B-side to the single 'Toys' further underlines its role as more than mere filler.

This is the third and final song submitted for copyright registration in September, making it one of the last songs to be recorded for the album. The track is driven by a fast-paced, straight rock rhythm. The arrangement is structured to build tension; the first chorus features only Robin's solo vocal, while subsequent choruses incorporate harmonies that steadily increase the song's energy. A brief percussion interlude after the bridge adds a sense of suspense before the final choruses fade out.

On 13 and 14 December, Barry hosted his second Love and Hope Tennis Festival at the Doral Country Club in Miami, to benefit the Diabetes Research Institute at the University of Miami. The event began on Friday, 13 December with a gala dinner at the Fontainebleau Hilton Hotel in Miami Beach, attended by 300 guests. A highlight of the evening was a charity auction, where Barry donated two gold record awards – *Saturday Night Fever* and *Guilty* – along with a guitar and his first tennis racket. Attendees also had the chance to win a date with Andy Gibb and one of his T-shirts. Barry and Andy, accompanied by the Peter Graves Orchestra, performed a short concert. Their setlist featured 'To Love Somebody', 'Shadow Dancing', 'Words', the Jackie DeShannon classic 'Put A Little

Love In Your Heart' and a festive rendition of Bing Crosby's 'White Christmas'. The following day, the much-anticipated tennis tournament took place despite unfavourable weather conditions. Barry, partnering with tennis professional Harold Solomon, emerged victorious in a celebrity doubles match against Andy and fellow pro Gardnar Mulloy.

Also in 1985, Barry, Robin, and Maurice were officially inducted as members of the Academy of Motion Picture Arts and Sciences (AMPAS). Being accepted into AMPAS, the governing body of the Academy Awards (Oscars), signified a rare acknowledgment for musicians outside the traditional film composer circles and underscored the evolving role of popular music in cinema.

Despite their immense success, The Bee Gees, like many other legendary artists, faced a perplexing lack of recognition from the Academy Awards. One of the most glaring omissions in Oscar history is the lack of nominations for any of The Bee Gees' tracks from *Saturday Night Fever*. The film's soundtrack featured multiple chart-topping hits, propelling the film to legendary status and solidifying disco's place in popular culture. However, none of them earned a nomination for Best Original Song at the Academy Awards.

The soundtrack itself became a cultural phenomenon, winning the Grammy Award for Album of the Year in 1979 and selling over 40 million copies worldwide, making their exclusion from the Oscar race even more baffling. Instead, the Academy-nominated songs have since faded into obscurity, raising questions about how they overlooked a soundtrack that became a generational landmark.

This was not an isolated case. The Oscars have a long history of snubbing commercially and critically successful songs in favour of more traditional, ballad-driven choices. Over the years, many legendary tracks – whether from The Beatles' 'A Hard Day's Night' or Elvis Presley's 'Can't Help Falling In Love' – have been ignored by the Academy, proving that mainstream appeal and cultural impact do not always translate to industry recognition.

1986

As the year began, the Gibbs remained in the spotlight with various public appearances. Barry played in the Pringles Light Classic Pro-Celebrity Tennis Tournament in Palm Beach on 5 January, partnering with Martina Navratilova in a mixed doubles match against actor Alan Thicke and Chris Evert Lloyd. On 9 January, Maurice appeared on *Good Morning Britain*, and later in the month, on 22 January, Robin travelled to New York to promote his new album, *Walls Have Eyes*. His promotional tour included interviews on VH1 with Bruce Leddy, *Showbiz Today*, *Radio Today*, NBC's *Live At 5*, CBS's *Morning News* and CNN.

On 15 February, Barry, Robin, and Maurice, along with their wives, attended the Love and Hope Ball at the Fontainebleau Hilton Hotel in Miami Beach. As in previous years, the event raised significant funds for the Diabetes Research Institute through an auction, with Barry performing a selection of songs.

In March, The Bee Gees travelled to Los Angeles for a series of meetings that would shape the next phase of their career. With their longtime record deal with RSO having ended in 1983, the brothers began negotiating privately with Warner Bros. Records for a new contract, aiming to secure a fresh start for their music under a new label. Discussions also included a change in management, signalling a strategic shift in how they would navigate the industry moving forward.

As negotiations progressed, plans emerged for The Bee Gees to begin work on a new album in the autumn. Several high-profile producers were considered for the project, including Rupert Hine (who had previously helmed albums for Rush, Howard Jones, and Tina Turner), legendary Beatles producer George Martin, and their former mentor Arif Mardin. Although details were still being finalised, the move to Warner Bros. promised a new chapter for the group, setting the stage for their next era of music.

In early 1986, Barry expressed his intent to record his next solo album live in the studio, aiming for a more direct, performance-based feel. Inspired by a more spontaneous approach (one that was fervently rejected for *Now Voyager* when urged by former co-producer Albhy Galuten), he aimed to move away from the time-intensive process of multi-layered track dubbing. While the musicians would eventually record many instrumental parts live for the project, Barry's lead and backing vocals were still tracked separately afterwards.

The sessions took place at Middle Ear over two primary phases: February to March and April to May, with a brief visit to the UK in between. This album brought together both long-time collaborators and some new faces in Barry's circle. Notably, guitarist Alan Kendall returned to work with Barry after several years away, and George Bitzer, a frequent co-writer and musician involved in many Gibb projects, also contributed. Karl Richardson returned to the control booth one final time to co-produce the set with Barry. The album evolved with the working titles *When Tomorrow Comes* and *My Eternal Love* before finally being called *Moonlight Madness*.

However, MCA's president, Irving Azoff, rejected the album before its release. It must have been baffling news for Barry to receive since Azoff had been the one to convince him to join the label two years earlier because he believed strongly there was a market for Barry's solo work. Azoff had been deeply disenchanted by the commercial performance of *Now Voyager*, which he made public in a 29 January 1985 interview with the *Los Angeles Times* that called Barry's signing to MCA one of the label's 'biggest disappointments in the past year'. 'You can't be right all the time', Azoff commented, although he then followed his statement with an admission that attracting an established artist like Barry was still a boost for the label, who 'had to prove to the industry that we were willing to step up and be competitive'. With that, it would seem Azoff may have had more of an issue with the album artistically, given he didn't even allow Barry an opportunity to prove himself with a follow-up.

Despite the album being shelved, seven of its 12 tracks were released two years later on the *Hawks* film soundtrack album: 'Moonlight Madness', 'My Eternal Love', 'System Of Love', 'Where Tomorrow Is', 'Cover You', 'Not In Love At All', and 'Letting Go'. However, some mixes differed slightly from the original 1986 recordings. The remaining five songs further developed the album's style, blending sharp songwriting with carefully arranged production. *Moonlight Madness'* direction is decidedly less experimental than *Now Voyager*, leaning on clean, crisp production with a rock-forward edge on its up-tempo tracks. The album's ballads soften the aesthetic with a mix of R&B, country and pop.

'The Savage Is Loose' stands out with its bold arrangement, while 'Words Of A Fool' is more reflective. Together, they add to the album's contrast of energy and restraint, hinting at the full picture that was ultimately left unreleased.

'In Search Of Love' was one of the final songs written for the album, co-penned with one of Barry's close associates, Richard Powers, who is not known as a songwriter. With its warm melodies and introspective lyrics, 'In Search Of Love' has a timeless quality, capturing the yearning that often threads through Barry's songwriting and giving the song a personal touch. It adds to the album's mix of introspection and sophistication. It's a beautiful piece that resonates with those who appreciate Barry's softer, more contemplative side.

'The Savage Is Loose' is a bold and gritty track that sees Barry, alongside bassist and future *American Idol* judge Randy Jackson and George Bitzer, taking a brassy, rock-oriented approach with a hint of protest. The song carries a fierce, rebellious energy, channelling raw emotion into biting lyrics and an intense, driving rhythm. Unlike Barry's typical themes of love and contemplation, this track veers into darker territory, expressing frustration and critique.

Lyrically, 'The Savage Is Loose' doesn't shy away from controversy, particularly with the line 'The woman in Dallas with a runny nose', widely interpreted as a jab at actress Victoria Principal, who dated brother Andy. This thinly veiled reference, a comment on the struggles that affected Andy, adds a layer of raw personal anguish to the song, making it one of the album's most emotionally charged moments. Its edgy tone and provocative lyrics most likely contributed to the track remaining unreleased, but 'The Savage Is Loose' stands out as a striking piece in Barry's solo catalogue – gritty, unfiltered, and powerful.

'Words Of A Fool' is a soulful country ballad with a melody that evokes shades of Barry's composition 'Rest Your Love On Me', taking its time to fully unfold with a two-minute build-up before returning to the main theme. It has left its mark well beyond its inception. It was covered by Chubby Tavares (lead singer of R&B group Tavares, who recorded and charted with a version of The Bee Gees' 'More Than A Woman' for the *Saturday Night Fever* soundtrack) in 2012 on his solo album *Jealousy*, and it was revisited by Barry himself in a 2021 duet with American singer-songwriter Jason Isbell on his 2001 solo album, *Greenfields*. The song's appeal, steeped in gentle country roots and Barry's signature melodic complexity, makes it a standout ballad, whether in its original form or later renditions.

'Distant Strangers' showcases a live-band energy that sets it apart from Barry's typical layered studio approach. Co-written with session players Carlos Vega, Steve Farris, and Neil Stubenhaus, the track gives the impression of a dynamic, in-the-moment performance rather than the multi-layered overdubs Barry often relied on. This collaborative writing style infuses the song with a vibrant, authentic feel, as though the musicians are playing off each other in real time. Despite its impromptu sound, 'Distant Strangers' is far from simple. It unfolds with complex rhythms and subtle shifts that reveal a carefully crafted piece, blending Barry's vocals with the nuanced instrumentation of a skilled ensemble.

'Change' is a rhythmic, groove-heavy track written by Barry, George Bitzer, and Alan Kendall. While it's not officially listed in the album's copyright lineup, the songwriting credits suggest its place among the project's dynamic numbers. Driven by an infectious beat, 'Change' balances Barry's smooth vocal style with the rhythmic expertise of Bitzer and Kendall, merging danceable energy with a polished musicality.

The intended running order for the album was:

Side One: 1. 'Moonlight Madness', 2. 'My Eternal Love', 3. 'System Of Love', 4. 'Where Tomorrow Is', 5. 'In Search Of Love', 6. 'Cover You (With Kisses)'
Side Two: 1. 'The Savage Is Loose', 2. 'Not In Love At All', 3. 'Words Of A Fool', 4. 'Distant Strangers', 5. 'Change', 6. 'Letting Go'

Plans were well advanced for the album's release, with a promotional photo shoot having been conducted and a stunning album cover design created by American artist Rick Garcia, painted in oil on canvas.

Garcia studied at the Art Institute of Miami before gaining recognition for his surrealist-inspired work. In the 1980s, his paintings appeared on Miami Vice, including a three-storey mural created for the show. He went on to receive commissions from both Barry and 1960s legend Dion, and after Hurricane Andrew devastated Homestead, Florida, in 1992, he was tapped to create a poster for the Hurricane Relief concert at which The Bee Gees performed. Garcia later served as official artist for the GRAMMY Awards in 1998, 1999 and 2001, designing program covers and related artwork. His other music-related projects include portraits of artists such as Coldplay, Destiny's Child, Ricky Martin, and Santana, along with custom-painted guitars created for Rock & Roll Hall of Fame fundraising events. In the autumn of 1990, as preparations were underway for the spring 1991 release of an Andy Gibb greatest hits album, Garcia was the preferred choice to create the cover artwork.

The intended front cover image for *Moonlight Madness* had a surreal quality, featuring Barry with long, flowing hair and a contemplative expression against a vibrant backdrop. The scene combined natural and abstract elements: on the left, a tilted palm tree and a serene ocean scene with a small sailboat under a moonlit sky evoking a sense of tranquillity, aligning with the 'moonlight' theme. Meanwhile, the right side explodes with intense colours and fragmented shapes, conveying a sense of 'madness' or chaotic energy.

The back cover is a continuation of the front cover, enhancing the surreal atmosphere with a striking, otherworldly landscape. It featured a floating landmass with a waterfall cascading into an expansive blue ocean. The waterfall appears to defy gravity, emerging from an elevated, rocky platform under an intense, sunset-coloured sky. To the right, a line of palm trees bends and twists in unnatural directions, with their reflections rippling in mid-air clouds, giving the impression of a surreal mirage. This visually echoes the dreamlike and chaotic mood of the front cover, balancing tranquillity with a sense of disorientation.

Runaway – Carola (1986)

Personnel:
Carola Häggkvist: vocals
Rhett Lawrence: keyboards, programming
Maurice Gibb: synthesiser, vocals
Robin Gibb: vocals
Efva Nyström: vocals
Ed Calle: horns ('Brand New Heart', 'Everlasting Love')
Engineers: Dennis Hetzendorfer, Scott Glasel
Producer: Maurice Gibb
Recorded at Panther House, Miami Beach, from March to April 1986
Release date: Norway: 12 May 1986, Sweden: 12 May 1986
Chart positions: Sweden: 2, Norway: 9

In the spring of 1986, Swedish pop star Carola Häggkvist took a significant step in her career by recording her first internationally focused album, *Runaway*. The recording took place between March and April entirely at Maurice's home studio, Panther House – not Middle Ear as stated in the album credits.

The album was produced by Maurice himself, with instrumental contributions from Rhett Lawrence, a sought-after session musician who would later work with global stars such as Mariah Carey and Kelly Clarkson, as well as The Bee Gees on 1987's *E.S.P.* album. Carola provided lead and backing vocals, while Maurice, Robin, and Swedish singer Efva Nyström offered additional backing harmonies.

Dennis Hetzendorfer, who engineered the album, remembered some of the nuances of making the album in close quarters in what was essentially Maurice's converted garage:

[Maurice] had a home studio with a soundboard – a very adequate one, but, you know, it was like the Chevrolet of consoles [*laughs*]. Still, we had to make it work because that's what you do. He had a 24-track MCI machine, and he brought in this really good producer, arranger and programmer named Rhett Lawrence. Rhett was great, but soon we realised we needed more equipment. So, we brought in a second board – I think it was a B&H board or something – which we borrowed from Mike Harris [owner of Harris Audio Systems in Miami, who supported several Gibb projects]. We hooked that up because Rhett needed a lot of inputs to handle all the instruments coming out of the synthesisers. We ran two boards, mixed everything down and kept it all on 24-track.

We mixed the whole thing in Maurice's studio. It was fun. We even did the vocals right there. Carola sang right next to us, so we just turned off the monitors, and everyone put on headphones. We set the mic up right in the middle of the room. The place was cramped, maybe the size of a bedroom, with a couple of consoles, the tape machine and the vocal mic all packed in together. But it worked just fine.

Dennis remembers Robin was regularly present during the sessions, but was a far less active collaborator on *Runaway* than Maurice had been on Robin's solo projects:

At that point, Robin wasn't busy; we had just finished *Walls Have Eyes*. Maurice was looking for something new to dive into, so this was really his baby. He handled the daily work, the nuts and bolts. Robin would drop by around four or five o'clock every afternoon, sit and listen, throw in his two cents, stay for a few hours, then head out. But everyone was getting along great, and both of them were in a very relaxed, creative mood.

Carola recalled the sessions in an interview with the International Carola Fan Club:

> Maurice takes the responsibility as the producer of the album, but as always, Robin and Barry will cooperate with him. Barry is the big writer, Robin tried to get the right sound on the tape and Maurice took care of the technical part of the songs.

The recording process was a meticulous one, with every step planned down to the smallest detail. Carola stated at the time:

> We don't know when the album will come out. At this time, you must not rush into something! It can take from Christmas until June until the album is out. We want to go forward being calm without any stress, but with harmony. Everything is planned to the smallest detail! Lawyers have been checking and watching over the contracts, photographers from London have been engaged and special people will create the right image. The basis for all this is, of course, our worldwide contract with Polydor International, a contract arranged by Thomas Nordlund.

The Bee Gees studied Carola's singing style and watched videos of previous performances extensively before selecting and composing the right material for her voice. Carola herself was equally dedicated. During the recording period, she immersed herself in music and sought inspiration from live performances. 'I listened to lots of music, and we went to see Bruce Springsteen in Miami's Super Bowl, which gave me a real kick. I took some singing lessons, too. Everything must be perfect until the last little detail', she said, emphasising her dedication to getting everything just right.

At the time, Carola was seeking to evolve beyond her previous image as a teenage pop star, saying, 'I don't want to be little sweet Carola who only has fans who are 12-13 years old anymore. With the record contract I have been given – and with such professional helpers as The Bee Gees – I do not hide the fact that I have ambitions to be the best in the world'.

In the studio, she worked closely with Maurice and Robin, who played key roles in shaping the album. She recalled, 'Maurice and Robin were in the studio every day. Maurice is very modest, and we do have the same kind of humour. Robin is very concentrated when he's working. He had helped me with the pronunciation, and he does have many musical specialities'.

Franz Auffray, vice president for A&R and marketing for Polydor International, saw the project as more than a regional success. 'The Nordic region is important, but we have not invested between one and a half and two million Norwegian Kroner on the record for it to only be successful in Stockholm and Oslo. The plan includes Europe, the US, Japan and other important sales areas'.

When asked if she secretly dreamed of reaching the top ten on the charts in the UK and the US, Carola was candid in her response:

> Yes, but I am completely clear that it takes time to build up a name on an international basis. One thing is certain – the record has turned out much better than we ever imagined. Maurice thinks there should be ten singles on the LP, and only when he has finished mixing them all will we decide which song will be the first single. But deep down, I hope that the singles will give me a top spot on the charts abroad.

Carola collaborated on the album cover in London with The Cream Group, who had worked on Robin's *Walls Have Eyes* the previous year. The art direction was led by Maximillian S. W. Kirsten, who designed the cover, while the striking photographs were captured by Tim O'Sullivan – the British photographer known for his work on Paul McCartney's *All The Best!*, T'Pau's *Bridge Of Spies* and, most notably, Tears For Fears' *Songs From The Big Chair*.

The album cover features a soft, high-contrast, black-and-white portrait of Carola. She has an intense and dreamy gaze, giving the image a sense of contemplation or wonder. A striking detail is the white dove, resting gently on her hand, which enhances the serene and delicate atmosphere of the cover. Another notable element is her earrings – small ichthus (Christian fish symbol) designs, subtly reinforcing a spiritual or symbolic undertone. The typography at the top spells out Carola in a modern, spaced-out font, and the album title, *Runaway*, is placed in a small, rectangular blue box on the right side. At the bottom, song titles are listed in a clean, sans-serif font. The overall aesthetic is elegant and minimalistic, with a nostalgic 1980s feel. The combination of monochrome photography, bold yet refined styling, the symbolic presence of the ichthus earrings and the dove conveys a sense of purity, strength, and a hint of mysticism.

A press conference with Carola and Maurice took place on 6 May in Stockholm, marking a key moment in the album's rollout. Carola's television appearances – including performances in both Norway and Sweden to promote the single in early April – played a key role in boosting interest in the album. On 17 May, SVT aired the *Carola Special*, featuring specially recorded video clips for five songs: 'Spread Your Wings (For Your Love)', 'Lost In the Crowd', 'Radiate', 'Nature Of The Beast', and the extended version of 'The Runaway'. The video for 'Spread Your Wings (For Your Love)' includes a performance by a four-member male dance group known as the Scenique Dancers. Between the musical segments, interview clips with Carola – conducted by Fredrik Grundel as she drives through Stockholm – offer a behind-the-scenes perspective. One notable moment comes during the 'Nature Of The Beast' segment, in which a man emerges from the bushes and later lifts Carola and carries her off. The man is Dragan 'Jokso' Joksović, a prominent figure in Stockholm's criminal underworld at the time.

Despite his criminal background, Joksović was known for his flashy presence – frequenting upscale clubs, socialising with celebrities, and dressing in designer clothes. He cultivated a 'gentleman gangster' image that intrigued the public and media. His life came to a violent end on 4 February 1998, when he was shot and killed at close range by a hitman inside a restaurant at the Solvalla horse racing track.

Despite Polydor's enthusiasm, *Runaway* struggled internationally. Released in Sweden and Norway on 12 May, it peaked at number two and number nine, respectively, on the album charts. While it was later made available in France, West Germany, Portugal, and Spain, it was never released in the UK, US, or Japan as originally planned. Additionally, when Franz Auffrey, the project's key supporter at Polydor, left the label, the album was quickly withdrawn from circulation. Despite this, it still achieved platinum status in Scandinavia, selling over 200,000 copies.

Of the album's ten tracks, five were written by Maurice and Robin. They collaborated with Rhett Lawrence on one song, while Barry joined them for three others. The final track was a collaboration between Maurice, Robin, Rhett Lawrence, and Carola.

'Radiate' (Robin Gibb, Maurice Gibb)
Recorded at Panther House, Miami Beach, from March to April 1986
'Radiate' launches the album with a rush of energy, laying the groundwork for Carola's shift toward a more dance-driven sound. With

sharp hooks and sleek, modern production, it sets a confident tone for what follows.

The track opens with vocoder-treated vocals and shimmering Fairlight CMI effects, adding a retro-futuristic texture that nods to electronic pop's past while keeping the sound fresh and contemporary.

The verses move through late-night city scenes and emotional highs and lows, delivered with urgency and flair. The chorus repeats like a mantra, building momentum as the song unfolds. Carola's voice cuts through with clarity and force, especially in the chorus, where she rejects shallow affection with a firm, catchy refrain.

Backed by layers of synthesisers and a pulsing groove, 'Radiate' is a stylish, confident opener that captures attention without overcomplicating things, making it a strong introduction to the album's mood and energy.

'The Runaway' (Robin Gibb, Maurice Gibb)
Recorded at Panther House, Miami Beach, from March to April 1986
Chart position: Sweden: 3

As the lead single, 'The Runaway' was chosen for its strong hooks and commercial appeal – it was a clear choice to represent the album. It was an instant success in Sweden, reaching number three shortly after its release on 7 April. Despite its Scandinavian success, the single's international rollout was delayed until September, during which time Carola performed it on the German television show *Die Spielbude*.

The song opens with a steady, reflective verse, where heartbreak and regret are quietly laid out. The shift into the chorus brings a notable lift in energy, as Carola's voice pushes forward with urgency and emotional force. The repeated phrase 'Someone is breaking your heart' becomes a kind of refrain, echoing the theme of emotional fallout and misconnection.

The bridge, while not typical of Robin and Maurice's compositions, serves to steady the flow between two choruses. Rather than shifting dramatically, it maintains the song's atmosphere, offering a moment of stillness before the final chorus resumes.

The 12" featured an extended dub mix of 'The Runaway' mixed and engineered by Maurice and Robin, with Dennis Hetzendorfer and Middle Ear engineer Scott Glasel.

The music video aimed to highlight Carola's stage presence in a natural setting with minimal visual effects. Carola recalled the intense filming process: 'The video took two days. We woke up at three o'clock on Monday morning, and we were out there at five, and we filmed until ten o'clock at night. The next day we woke up at five o'clock and worked until eight in the evening'.

In 2019, Swedish heavy metal band Gathering of Kings covered 'The Runaway', giving it a fresh edge on their debut album, *First Mission*. In its review, *Melodic Net* described the track as 'a killer AOR song' and named it 'one of the highlights' of the album.

'Brand New Heart' (Robin Gibb, Maurice Gibb)
Recorded at Panther House, Miami Beach, from March to April 1986

'Brand New Heart' is a mid-tempo ballad that reflects on the pain of starting over after heartbreak. The recurring line 'breaking in a brand new heart' poignantly captures both the struggle and the quiet strength required to move on. The song features a smooth, layered arrangement with prominent backing vocals from Robin, adding depth and warmth.

An instrumental break, highlighted by a saxophone solo from Venezuelan-American session player Ed Calle, provides a melodic pause, deepening the mood before the chorus returns with renewed intensity. The arrangement remains clean and focused throughout, allowing the song's message to shine without distraction.

Released as the second single in Sweden only, it was performed by Carola on national television, including appearances on *Flyktinggalan* and *Sweden Today,* giving it a strong domestic presence despite its limited release.

'Brand New Heart' was released as a single on the Irish Ritz Records label in 1988 by Luv Bug, a group from Newry in Northern Ireland. They are best known for representing Ireland in the 1986 Eurovision Song Contest with their song 'You Can Count On Me', which placed fourth in the competition.

'Spread Your Wings (For Your Love)' (Barry Gibb, Robin Gibb, Maurice Gibb)
Recorded at Panther House, Miami Beach, from March to April 1986

'Spread Your Wings (For Your Love)' is the first of three songs on the album written by Barry, Robin, and Maurice. Initially titled 'Something For Your Love', the song blends rhythmic pop with notable vocal interplay. Maurice delivers the chorus using the original title phrase, while Carola leads with the soaring line 'spread your wings', which is not found in the lyrics on the inner sleeve of the LP, hinting at an evolving creative direction during production.

The song's complex narrative follows a woman caught in the emotional turmoil of a love triangle or failing relationship. She watches as the man she loves becomes captivated by another woman who 'plays that game that only she can win'. The lyrics capture the tension between power and vulnerability, longing, and resignation, all within a few lines.

The track ends abruptly, cutting off mid-flow, a jarring contrast to typical fade-outs and possibly mirroring the unresolved nature of the lyrics.

'Spread Your Wings (For Your Love)' was the B-side of the 'Brand New Heart' 7" single, which was only released in Sweden. On the 12" release, it was given more visibility, listed as the lead track on the cover, but placed as the second track on the first side of the record itself. The flipside featured an extended dance version. This dance version was also the featured track on a special numbered 12" pink vinyl promo, where it was paired with remixes of 'The Runaway' – previously available on the commercially available 12" single – and 'Radiate', the latter being exclusive to this release.

'Nature Of The Beast' (Robin Gibb, Maurice Gibb)
Recorded at Panther House, Miami Beach, from March to April 1986

A more serious and thought-provoking track, 'Nature Of The Beast' demonstrates Carola's ability to tackle dramatic material. It's a brooding, synth-driven track that delves into the darker corners of human instinct. The introduction sets the scene with subtle jungle sound effects, placing the listener in a shadowy, primal landscape that mirrors the song's themes.

Alternating vocal lines from Maurice and Carola in the chorus give the song a tense, back-and-forth energy, while Carola's lead in the verses brings a dramatic intensity that underscores the song's central theme: the collapse of restraint under pressure.

A brief instrumental break – punctuated again by distant jungle sounds and a marimba-like synthesiser – adds a moment of eerie calm before the final section, where the song fades out in a cycle of repeated choruses, reinforcing its central message of inescapable, animalistic drive.

Overall, 'Nature Of The Beast' is a taut, atmospheric song that reflects on how easily animal instincts can surface when tested.

'When Two Worlds Collide' (Barry Gibb, Robin Gibb, Maurice Gibb)

Recorded at Panther House, Miami Beach, from March to April 1986

'When Two Worlds Collide' is the second track on the album co-written by Barry, Robin, and Maurice, and it showcases a commanding vocal performance by Carola. The song opens with a marimba-style synthesiser before launching into forceful, fast-paced drums that set a brisk, urgent tempo.

The track is structured to highlight Carola's dynamic vocal range, but Robin and Maurice also play a key role in shaping the track's atmosphere, providing wordless backing vocal countermelodies during the pre-chorus. Their presence is especially felt in the chorus, where they reinforce the title phrase, which Carola herself never sings.

The instrumental break, played on the Fairlight CMI, includes digital effects that evoke comparisons to elements of Yes' 'Owner Of A Lonely Heart'. It adds a sharp, contemporary edge to the track's otherwise melodic foundation.

Despite the shared writing credits and strong contributions from Robin and Maurice, it's Carola's powerful delivery that defines the song.

'(We Are) Atomic' (Robin Gibb, Maurice Gibb)

Recorded at Panther House, Miami Beach, from March to April 1986

'(We Are) Atomic' is a power ballad that channels the dramatic flair of 1980s pop-rock, blending a restrained, atmospheric verse with a chorus that bursts into full force. The song plays with contrast, building emotional intensity through an unusually long verse structure before releasing it in the explosive refrain.

Carola delivers a striking lead performance, despite later admitting the vocal range pushed her limits. 'The songs were a bit too high for me, I think. Maurice made me sing so high – especially on the track '(We Are) Atomic", she recalled. Yet there is no audible sign of strain; her voice soars confidently across the song's demanding range, maintaining clarity and power even at its highest points, moving seamlessly between delicate whispered phrases and full-throated declarations.

Backing vocals by Robin enhance the melodic texture, particularly between the first chorus and second verse, and reappear in the instrumental break – this time digitally manipulated for effect. A whispered line from Carola in the breakdown adds to the haunting atmosphere, leading into an extended outro of repeated choruses where the soft phrases overlap with bold vocal ad-libs.

'Lost In The Crowd' (Barry Gibb, Robin Gibb, Maurice Gibb)
Recorded at Panther House, Miami Beach, from March to April 1986
'Lost In The Crowd' is the third and last song on the album with a songwriting contribution from Barry, together with Robin and Maurice. It was originally known as 'Rock #3' during its creation prior to the addition of lyrics. Evidence points to Barry having written the verse melody, which features his signature broken lines. Carola delivers with a breathy vocal in the verses before transitioning into an energetic chorus. There's a subtle elegance in her performance, with certain vocal traits reminiscent of both Diana Ross and Olivia Newton-John, suggesting the song could easily have suited either of them stylistically.

Carola insisted on a slight lyric change to those printed on the inner sleeve. Her religious beliefs made her uncomfortable singing 'the devil in me', so she amended the line to 'the feelings in me' instead.

'So Far So Good' (Robin Gibb, Maurice Gibb, Rhett Lawrence)
Recorded at Panther House, Miami Beach, from March to April 1986
Initially developed under the working title 'Rock #4', 'So Far, So Good' evolved into one of the album's more vibrant tracks. Co-written by Robin and Maurice alongside producer Rhett Lawrence, it was also released as the B-side to the single 'The Runaway'. Its distinctive hook lies in the syncopated phrasing of the title line – 'So far, so [pause] good' – which punctuates the chorus with a memorable rhythmic punch.

Musically, the song is layered with contemporary pop-rock elements but features a rare moment of organic instrumentation: a saxophone solo in the instrumental break. This is notably the only non-digital instrument on the album, providing a moment of warmth and contrast within the track's otherwise synthesised soundscape. It's bright, aggressive tone takes on a raspy quality, giving the solo a piercing, urgent feel.

'Everlasting Love' (Robin Gibb, Maurice Gibb, Rhett Lawrence)
Recorded at Panther House, Miami Beach, from March to April 1986
The album's closing song, 'Everlasting Love', was written by the four key contributors to the project – Robin, Maurice, Rhett Lawrence and Carola herself, who appears to have woven subtle religious overtones into the

lyrics. Reflecting on the songwriting process, Carola explained, 'I was sitting in the hotel and wrote some text to it, then I went to Maurice with these ideas, so we've written the text to that one, in a way, together'. However, she did not receive a printed credit on the album acknowledging this. She also shared her personal connection to the track, saying, 'I like the whole album, but the first song I fell for is 'Everlasting Love' – it has lovely harmonies'. The harmonies she refers to appear most clearly in the striking a cappella introduction and outro, which bookend the song. The lines 'In the power, feed the fire, follow you and you follow me' evoke a mutual devotion that can be interpreted as both romantic and spiritual.

The chorus, with its repeated plea to 'Live in everlasting love', is the emotional centre of the song. Uplifting and melodic, it carries a tone of triumph, envisaging a connection so profound that even heaven might not be enough. By the final bars, the music circles back to the initial refrain, bringing the album to a close on a note of clarity and optimism. The result is a subtly powerful and gently anthemic finale.

Despite its success in Scandinavia, *Runaway* did not receive the international reception originally hoped for. One major setback was Carola's sudden religious conversion, joining the Livets Ord fundamentalist sect, leading to speculation that she had refused to promote the album, although she later denied this:

I wanted to do a lot of promotion. In fact, I was up to it. But the communication between The Bee Gees and me was not up and running. They heard things from other sources, and they probably believed those stories. Anyway, the album died, and I went on to other projects.

Maurice reflected on the experience in a 1993 Swedish TV interview:

I have to say that Carola is probably one of the most talented singers that I've ever worked with. She's a true professional. The album didn't do that well because, during those days, the record company was rebuilding, and they were trying to sort things out, so she didn't get the full support that she needed. But she was a great lady to work with and a great singer, and I hope one day in the future we can work together again. She was great.

Looking back, Carola remains proud of the album: 'I think *Runaway* still today ranks as a very modern and up-to-date album, having been made in the 1980s. It was at the forefront of technology in those days. I still like it a lot'.

While *Runaway* may not have catapulted Carola to global stardom, it remains a fascinating chapter in her career and a reminder of what might have been had circumstances aligned differently. Looking back, she acknowledged this herself: 'In retrospect, I was perhaps not ready for eventual international stardom'.

On Sunday 25 May, during the Memorial Day weekend in the US, Hands Across America, a public fundraising event, took place. An estimated 5.4 million people held hands for 15 minutes in an attempt to form a continuous human chain across the contiguous United States. The attempt to have a complete line of people across the country failed, although the number of participants would have been sufficient to succeed if they had been spread out over the full length of the planned course. While Barry was in Los Angeles earlier in the year, he made a public service announcement on *The Dick Clark Show* to publicise the event. Participants were asked to donate $10 to be part of the chain. An estimated 1,320 people would be required to cover one mile of the route, and celebrities and companies were able to sponsor a mile by donating $13,200. Having always been generous and charitable benefactors, The Bee Gees were quick to contribute. The proceeds were donated to local charities to fight hunger and homelessness and help those in poverty.

The Bee Gees spent part of the summer of 1986 in England, attending high-profile events and making several media appearances. On 29 June, Barry, Robin, and Maurice, along with their wives, attended the Jackie Stewart Celebrity Challenge clay pigeon shoot at the North Wales Shooting School at Sealand near Chester, an exclusive gathering that also included Wham!'s Andy Ridgeley and actor Sean Connery. Barry joined the Rocking Team alongside Ridgeley, while newly engaged and soon-to-be-married Prince Andrew and Sarah Ferguson competed on the Royal Team.

A few weeks later, on 27 July, the brothers and their wives attended the Cartier International Polo match at Smith's Lawn, Guards Polo Club in Windsor – a prestigious event featuring Prince Charles and organised by Major Ronald Ferguson, father of Sarah Ferguson. Among the notable attendees were Eric Clapton and his wife Pattie Boyd, Ringo Starr and his wife Barbara Bach, and actress Jane Seymour. During the match, the England II team, led by the Prince of Wales, faced off against Chile. Princess Diana was also in attendance to support her husband and later presented the prizes at the award ceremony.

During their stay in England, the brothers remained active in media and music. Robin gave an interview for BBC Radio 2, spoke with David Frost in a telephone interview, and appeared on *Good Morning Britain*. Barry also made several television appearances to promote The Bunburys, including segments on *Good Morning Britain*, *Wogan* and special features aired during cricket matches. As part of the Bunbury project, Barry had the opportunity to record a song with Eric Clapton and met England's renowned cricketer, Ian Botham.

The brothers also made the most of their social time. Maurice and Yvonne attended a Rod Stewart concert, while Robin and Dwina were invited to a dinner at a local manor house, where Robin was the guest of honour of Princess Margaret.

In August, Maurice received an anonymous death threat. He was targeted by an unknown individual, prompting authorities to take immediate action to ensure his safety. While Maurice initially dismissed the threat as the work of 'a crackpot', Scotland Yard treated it with the utmost seriousness. The situation was deeply unsettling for Maurice and his family. 'My house in Britain has been raided by the police, and they have done a marvellous job in looking after me', he said. As a precaution, Maurice was placed under armed guard during his visits to the UK. He was even escorted by police at Heathrow Airport as he boarded a flight, a stark reminder of the lingering threat looming over him. Despite the security measures, he admitted the experience had been difficult. 'It's been a horrible time, but I hope the ordeal is coming to an end. We've heard nothing more, and we're none the wiser about who made the threat'. He remained determined to return to Britain for Christmas. 'I hope by then this business will be over. But nothing would keep me away', he stated.

David English, a former president of RSO Records, initiated *The Bunbury Tails* project. A close friend of The Bee Gees, particularly Barry, David had gained recognition in Bee Gees fandom as the author of The Bee Gees' cartoon biography, *The Legend*, illustrated by Alex Brychta. David and his friend Jan Brychta, Alex's father, were inspired to create a team of cricket-playing rabbits while watching a cricket match. He had no hesitation in calling his old friend Barry, who willingly agreed to lend support to the project. Central to the project were animated cartoons aired on Channel 4, featuring music – much of it penned by The Bee Gees – and a series of books authored by David and illustrated by Brychta. These works aimed to promote cricket and good sportsmanship.

On 23 July, Barry spoke to Anneke Koremans and Lies Spruit of the Brothers Gibb Information fan club for *The Spirit* magazine about the upcoming release tied to The Bunburys project, describing the first single as imminent. 'The single comes out in about two weeks in England, and perhaps in Europe, called 'We're The Bunburys', which is me singing, but it says The Bunburys, not me', he said. The concept behind The Bunburys involved more than just music. 'The Bunburys are a team of rabbits that play cricket and also save people and bring families together – it's for children and adults', Barry explained. He added that a full album, featuring 'five songs and a story by David English, will come out within four or five weeks. There will probably also be a cartoon TV series'.

The recording sessions for the project lasted around five days at producer David Mackay's studio, The Factory, in Woldingham. The Bee Gees wrote several songs and recorded backing vocals. Barry shared the tentative lineup of songs and performers at this point: 'We're The Bunburys', sung by Barry; 'Bunbury Afternoon', performed by The Bee Gees; 'Fight', sung by Eric Clapton; 'Revolution', by Errol Brown and Hot Chocolate; and two other tracks recorded by Shakin' Stevens and No Hat Moon.

On 8 September 1986, Robin discussed the project on *Good Morning Britain*, recalling its origins: 'It goes back about a year now. And David English got us all involved'. He described the collaborative nature of the sessions and noted the participation of English cricketer Ian Botham. 'We worked along with Ian Botham in the studio, who is on the next single from the project', he said.

Robin outlined plans for multiple singles to be released under The Bunburys name, stating, 'There's about four or five other singles which are coming out either before the end of the year and afterwards, including a Christmas single, all by The Bunburys, but with artists such as Eric Clapton, The Bee Gees, and Ian Botham'. Commenting on Botham's musical contribution, Robin said that 'he played on the actual record and did some singing. So, he's actually on one of the singles called 'Fight'. I wouldn't call him one of the best singers in the world, but he did a good job. He did well'.

Despite the brothers' enthusiasm and optimism about the imminent release of the Bunburys material, the entire project, from inception to completion, would eventually span six years, running from 1986 to 1992, with some changes made prior to the album's eventual release.

'We're The Bunburys' (Barry Gibb, David English)
Recorded at Middle Ear, Miami Beach, in April or May 1986
Chart position: UK: 80

The first Bunburys record, 'We're The Bunburys', had no reference to The Bee Gees on the sleeve or the record, although, of course, Barry's name appeared as one of the songwriters on the record label. The sound, however, has unmistakable Bee Gees trademarks, although neither Robin nor Maurice appeared on the recording.

The UK edition of the single was released on the Island Records label on 22 August 1986 and had the catalogue number LBW1. Those from countries not familiar with the game of cricket would not understand that 'LBW' stood for 'leg before wicket', one of the ways in which a batsman can be dismissed in the sport.

The single appeared in three formats in the UK; the first and most common included a nine-page story book, written by David English and illustrated by Jan Brychta, within the gatefold sleeve. The second was a standard picture sleeve, but the package included a poster, and finally, a cassette single, which was, at that point, mandatory for a single to be considered for inclusion in the charts.

Other countries to release the single were big players in world cricket: Australia and South Africa. Appearing on the Island label in all territories, it came with the standard company label, opposed to the custom picture label used in the UK. The Australian edition came in a standard picture sleeve bearing the same design as the UK, while the South African edition came in a plain cover but bore the catalogue number BUN 1.

Although the single received some low-key television promotion, including a video by celebrated British animator Bob Godfrey MBE, it fared poorly in terms of chart performance. It entered the UK singles chart at number 80 on 30 August, dropping to 89 in its second and final week.

'We're The Bunburys' was credited to The Bunburys on the single, but to The Bee Gees on *The Bunbury Tails* album, which was eventually released in 1992.

'Chapter One: Record Breakers' (David English)
Recorded at Middle Ear, Miami Beach, in April or May 1986
The B-side of the 'We're The Bunburys' single wasn't a song, but a children's story called 'Record Breakers' that introduced the Bunbury cricket team. It contained a few excerpts from the A-side song, but in the main, it was David English narrating the story and some character voices from both David and Barry.

On 6 September, Barbra Streisand hosted a historic fundraising concert at her Malibu ranch. She cited the inspiration for the event in her autobiography, *My Name Is Barbra*, tracing its origins to the catastrophic Chernobyl nuclear disaster earlier that year. The accident, which spewed radioactive material across Europe, deeply disturbed her. 'The news was apocalyptic', she wrote. 'I kept thinking, how can we allow this kind of threat to our environment? Because we're all connected. We all share this one planet … and suddenly I was reminded how fragile it was'.

The calamity spurred Streisand to take action. Encouraged by her friend and musical collaborator Marilyn Bergman [who had co-written the classic Streisand song 'The Way We Were', among many others], she decided to leverage her voice to support the midterm campaigns of the Democratic Party in the US, which she hoped would challenge current President Ronald Reagan's policies. Initially hesitant to perform live, she was persuaded by Bergman's pragmatic question: 'What's more frightening … singing live, or nuclear annihilation?' Streisand admitted, 'Good point'.

Choosing her Malibu ranch as the venue, Streisand transformed her back garden into a natural amphitheatre. 'After all,' she explained, 'what could be more appropriate than celebrating nature while we were in the midst of nature?' The setting not only minimised costs but also gave the evening a unique intimacy. Invitations were sent as cassette recordings encased in pretty tin boxes filled with potpourri, and the $5,000 per couple tickets quickly sold out. Streisand was thrilled: 'Everyone accepted, and I felt very supported by the Hollywood community because so many turned out, including Quincy Jones (who brought Whitney Houston), Barry Diller, Jack Nicholson and Anjelica Huston, Sydney Pollack, Jane Fonda and Tom Hayden, Goldie Hawn and Kurt Russell, Whoopi Goldberg, Bette Midler, Henry Winkler, Sally Field, Bruce Willis, Chevy Chase, Penny Marshall and Rob Reiner, and Norman Lear. Steven Spielberg was in London, but he sent a cheque for $5000, and so did Bruce Springsteen, even though he couldn't come, either'.

The evening began with drinks and dinner served on her tennis court. Robin Williams then delivered a 'brilliant monologue', easing Streisand's nerves before her performance. Reflecting on her apprehension, she recalled, 'I was scared stiff, as always. I had to keep reminding myself that these were my friends out there, but still, I made sure we wouldn't start until it was dark so I couldn't see them'.

Streisand opened the concert with 'Somewhere', emerging from the shadows to thunderous applause. The concert's centrepiece came when Barry joined Streisand for duets of 'Guilty' and 'What Kind Of Fool'. None of the hits from the massively successful *Guilty* had been performed live to date, and Barry had been absent from the concert stage for nearly seven years at that point. Both artists were in excellent voice, and it was exciting for both Streisand and Bee Gees fans to see them together again years after their landmark partnership.

Streisand described the collaboration as a joyful highlight: 'The audience heard Barry Gibb's voice before they saw him … then he came out of the shadows and joined me for the song. I was surprised by how much fun I was having. You can't help but move to that music. I think I forgot some words or missed a beat, but I did do some dipping and swaying. That's about as much dancing in public as I've ever done! It was a magical night'.

The event's legacy was profound. Five of the six supported candidates won their races, flipping the Senate to Democratic control. Reflecting on the concert's success, Streisand wrote, 'It actually helped change the direction of the country'. Beyond the political victories, the concert marked a turning point in her activism. Proceeds from the performance, as well as subsequent album and video releases, were used to establish the Barbra Streisand Foundation, supporting a broad range of causes, including women's rights and civil rights. The concert was broadcast by HBO under the title *One Voice* in December, followed by an album release of the programme in April 1987.

On 7 September, Robin joined a host of renowned pop artists at the legendary Abbey Road Studios to record 'Live In World', an anti-drug anthem aimed at raising awareness and funds for the Phoenix House Charity. The single was officially released in the UK on 25 October. Among the notable artists involved were The Thompson Twins, Zak Starkey [son of Ringo Starr], Cliff Richard, Bonnie Tyler, John Parr, and Holly Johnson of Frankie Goes to Hollywood. The song's release was widely covered by media outlets such as MTV, *Entertainment Tonight* and *Good Morning Britain*.

'Live In World' was part of a broader initiative, The Anti-Heroin Project, which aimed to harness the power of music for social change. Inspired by the success of Band Aid's 'Do They Know It's Christmas?' and USA For Africa's 'We Are The World', selected members of the all-star cast took turns to sing one line of the verses, while everybody sang the choruses. Robin sang the first line of the second verse, following on from Mel Collins' saxophone solo.

Charley Foskett, the mastermind behind the project, was inspired by personal loss. Having lost friends to heroin addiction, he launched a campaign to raise money for Phoenix House, a rehabilitation centre focused on recovery from substance abuse. As word of the project spread, more and more artists joined in. Foskett pitched his idea to EMI Records, who agreed to produce a single and a double album and offered free use of Abbey Road Studios for recording sessions.

The double album, *It's A Live-In World*, featured a mix of existing songs and new recordings from Ringo Starr, Elvis Costello, Paul McCartney, Chris Rea, Eurythmics, Dire Straits, Wham!, Bucks Fizz, and many others. The album's title track, 'Live In World', was the centrepiece of the project. Its recording brought together a diverse array of musicians, including Fish from Marillion, Nik Kershaw, Cliff Richard, and Bonnie Tyler. The accompanying video, filmed at the recording session, featured appearances from Robin, Elkie Brooks, Kim Wilde, Poly Styrene, Suggs, Steve Harley, Genesis P-Orridge, The Three Degrees' Sheila Ferguson, The Alarm's Mike Peters, Hayley Mills, Roy Harper, Sinitta, Chas & Dave, and more.

Despite a star-studded lineup, both the single and album struggled to gain mainstream traction, and, unlike previous anti-drug campaigns, such as the UK government's *Heroin Screws You Up* or the Grange Hill cast's hit single 'Just Say No', failed to make an impact on the charts. Foskett later alleged that political interference contributed to their failure. According to him, government officials had approached him to take part in a national anti-drug initiative. When he declined – instead proposing a collaboration with The Anti-Heroin Project – he claimed that the Home Office pressured EMI to suppress their release. However, EMI executives firmly denied these allegations, insisting that no such directive was given. The truth behind the commercial failure of the records remains a matter of speculation.

On 8 September, the day after the recording session, Robin appeared on *Good Morning Britain* to discuss the recording of 'Live In World' and

The Anti-Heroin Project. In his interview, he highlighted the impact of drug addiction and the need for rehabilitation support, and the importance of using music to drive social change. When asked by host Ann Diamond about his stance on drugs, Robin stated firmly, 'I think today, children, teenagers, people are very vulnerable to the wrath of drugs. And I think it's time for everybody, not just the kids themselves, the parents, to be very, very much on guard'. Reflecting on the music industry's reputation for drug use, Robin noted:

It's the image entirely. It doesn't mean that everybody in it is taking drugs because there's a lot of great people, great sensible people in this business – and then there are those that are not sensible, and those who are irresponsible. There are a lot of them, and there are a lot that are very conscientious about the kind of music and the kind of image that they reflect. But the image of the rock industry goes on, and it's very hard to fight this kind of image when it's perennial; it goes on. It's because of what the actual rock industry represents.

Diamond pressed Robin, suggesting, 'You must have gone to the sort of rock, crazy rock parties and all those wacky times when you must have been offered drugs, surely?' Robin acknowledged:

Yes, absolutely. But that didn't mean that we took them, and I'm not saying that we didn't try things – we did. But because a lot of groups that have gone on that have been around a long time, like The Rolling Stones and The Beatles – of course, they tried everything, but they learnt from their experiences, and they don't take them anymore.

Robin expressed hope that his experience could positively influence others. 'There are younger, newer groups and artists that know already that it's wrong,' he said, 'but young people tend to want to experiment when the opportunity is there, and they make a lot of money very quickly'.

On 30 October, The Bee Gees finally signed a long-term, worldwide exclusive contract with Warner Bros. Records. The deal was formally announced by Warner Bros. Records Chairman Michael 'Mo' Ostin and Ken Kragen of Kragen & Co., The Bee Gees' new management team, during a luncheon reception hosted by Ostin at New York's Water Club. Ostin, celebrating the signing, expressed the significance of the group's impact:

There is no way to overstate the impact of Barry, Maurice, and Robin Gibb on contemporary music. Their influence isn't just traced in hit singles and number one albums, as impressive as that track record may be, but in music itself. The Bee Gees have changed the state of the musical art across an extraordinary two decades. They are true artists and innovators, and I join with all of Warner Bros. Records staff in proudly welcoming them to the company.

Ken Kragen shared his elation: 'It is an exciting opportunity to work with such talent; whether recording, writing, or producing for themselves or for other major artists, they continue to excite, astound, and make history'.

Warner Bros. Records' official press release celebrated the band's achievements: 'In over 20 years of their recording career, they have had songs on the charts for an astounding 443 weeks – over eight-and-a-half years of Bee Gees music over the airwaves! The global sales records for their 18 albums and nearly 30 hit singles put them among the best-selling artists of all time'.

Discussing the decision to join Warner Bros., Barry explained:

We came to the conclusion that we would go after what we considered to be the best record company. Our opinion at that point – and it still is – was that Warner Bros. is the best. Rich Fitzgerald [Warner Bros. vice president of promotion] went through all the *Saturday Night Fever* stuff with us at RSO, so it seemed natural to go with them if they would have us.

The Bee Gees' choice of Kragen & Co. for management followed a similar mindset. 'We decided we should go with what we considered the best management team, and, right now, Kragen's is the best', Barry added.

Barry's third Love and Hope Tennis Festival took place on 15 and 16 November at The Turnberry Isle Yacht and Country Club in Aventura, Florida. Robin and Maurice were unable to attend due to commitments in New York, where they were working on the new Bee Gees album. The event began with a grand gala dinner, an auction and a concert. The auction proved to be the highlight of the evening, featuring an array of exclusive items. Among the most sought-after were a gold record of *Saturday Night Fever,* which sold for $11,000, a T-shirt signed by all three Bee Gees, a *Sgt. Pepper's Lonely Hearts Club Band* photograph and a lap around the Miami Grand Prix circuit. Other unique offerings included a dinner for two with Channel 7's Jill Beach and Steve Dawson, an Andy Gibb tour jacket, and a cocker spaniel puppy. Barry himself successfully bid on an Akita puppy.

The festival attracted several notable celebrities, including David Soul, Sonny Bono, Alan Thicke, and Jermaine and Tito Jackson. The world of professional tennis was also well represented, with players such as Harold Solomon, Eddie Dibbs, and Gardnar Mulloy joining the event.

To conclude the evening, Barry and Andy performed a short concert, delighting the audience with a setlist that included 'To Love Somebody', 'Words', 'Shadow Dancing', 'I Don't Wanna Be Alone' – a duet between Barry and family friend Noeleen Batley Stewart, for whom he had written songs during their 1960s stint in Australia – and 'What'd I Say'.

The following day was entirely dedicated to tennis. Barry and his guests spent the day on the courts, culminating in a thrilling doubles match. Barry teamed up with Florida Governor Bob Graham, while Andy partnered with Alan Thicke. The match ended in victory for Barry and the Governor, providing an exciting close to the tournament. The festival raised over $100,000 for the Diabetes Research Institute.

Also in 1986, Barry was invited to write and perform the title song for the movie *The Morning After*, a psychological thriller starring Jane Fonda, Jeff Bridges, and Raúl Juliá. The plot follows a washed-up, alcoholic actress who wakes up on Thanksgiving morning next to the dead body of a photographer in his loft, with no memory of the previous night. Desperate to uncover the truth, she teams up with a former police officer she meets while on the run. The film received generally positive reviews, and Fonda earned an Academy Award nomination for Best Actress for her performance. Barry, however, declined the offer to become involved with the music.

1987

In February, it was revealed that Maurice had partnered with producer
Sydney Rose to launch a new creative production and development
company for film and television. Sydney Rose, a British-born
entrepreneur and producer with a remarkable career spanning over 25
years, brought extensive experience to the collaboration. His diverse
background included roles as a producer, writer, personal manager, and
agent, with expertise in movies, television, stage productions, large-scale
arena events and sports.

The Gibb Rose Organisation Ltd. (GRO) was officially established in
July 1986 and was based at Pinewood Studios. At the time of the
announcement, the company had already secured several international
film and television deals. In April, Maurice and Sydney announced their
first major project: a mini-series chronicling the lives of the influential
Rothschild banking dynasty. Additionally, they revealed plans for four
television productions in various stages of development. Among them
was a celebration of British music since 1920, complemented by a book
and record release, and another show focusing on British composers,
envisaged as a live broadcast. Despite these ambitious announcements,
no further progress on these projects was ever reported. Rose continued
to work in the film industry until his death in 2007.

On 12 April, The Bee Gees were celebrated at the Royal Palm Polo Club
in Boca Raton, Florida, where they received the prestigious Decade
Achiever's Award. Barry and his wife, Linda, along with Andy Gibb, made
a grand entrance in a century-old horse-drawn carriage to accept the
honour. Presented by neuroscientist and technology entrepreneur Tom
Oxley, the award featured a stunning bronze sculpture crafted by visual
artist Thomas Holland. The Decade Achiever's Award recognised
individuals and groups who have made significant contributions in their
fields, with past recipients including the likes of like Bob Hope and Burt
Reynolds. Beyond their impact on music and entertainment, The Bee Gees
were also acknowledged for their dedication to the Diabetes Research
Institute (DRI). As part of the event, a donation was made to DRI by the
Royal Palm Polo Club. Following the ceremony, guests enjoyed a polo
match before Barry and Andy took to the tennis court for a doubles match,
partnering with professional players Juan Nunez and Mario Martinez.

Barbra Streisand's *One Voice* album, which featured live performances
of 'Guilty' and 'What Kind Of Fool' with Barry, was released on 20 April,

capturing her first full-length concert in 20 years. Sales of the album and its video releases went to the Barbra Streisand Foundation, which supports causes such as anti-nuclear initiatives, environmental preservation, civil liberties and human rights. Commercially, *One Voice* was a success around the world. It reached number two in the Netherlands, number seven in New Zealand, and number nine in the US, while also charting strongly in Australia, Spain, the United Kingdom, Canada, Finland, West Germany, Sweden, and Japan. The album went on to achieve silver certification in the UK, gold in Australia and Canada, and platinum in the Netherlands, New Zealand, and the US.

An interesting footnote in the album's history comes from American singer-songwriter Richard Marx, who at the time was still working as a session vocalist, having not yet broken out with his eponymous debut album. He recalled:

I was doing some background vocals for Kenny Rogers when Barbra Streisand walked in. She asked, 'Is there somebody named Richard here?' Then she said, 'They tell me you can imitate people. Can you sound like Barry Gibb? You've got to sing on 'Guilty". During the concert, Barry had missed the first line, 'It ought to be illegal', and she needed it for the album mix. So, I put on headphones and sang the line. She said, 'Perfect! Thank you so much because I'm not paying you'. She did give me a credit, though, and years later, when I reminded her of it, she said, 'That was you!?'

American actor Bruce Willis took on a surprising alter ego in the comedic 'mockumentary' *The Return Of Bruno*, where he starred as Bruno Radolini, a fictional 1960s rock legend whose influence shaped the course of popular music. As described by *Billboard*: 'Bruce Willis is the incomparable, incredible, unbelievable, uncontrollable Bruno Radolini. Bruno wrote the book on rock 'n' roll – then he burned it'.

The film, which originally aired on 7 February as a one-hour HBO special in the US, and on 31 August on BBC2 in the UK. It was commercially released on VHS in June 1987. It featured Willis's satirical portrayal of Bruno as a blues icon who supposedly inspired some of the most famous musicians of the era. Narrated by Dick Clark, the film included appearances from a star-studded cast of musicians and industry figures, including Ringo Starr, Brian Wilson, Joan Baez, Phil Collins, Elton John, Grace Slick, Jon Bon Jovi, Freddie Garrity, Graham Nash,

Stephen Stills, Melvin Franklin and Paul Stanley, alongside cultural icons like Bill Graham, Wolfman Jack, Michael J. Fox, Clive Davis, Henry Diltz and Don Cornelius. The film was nominated for a 1988 ACE Award (Award for Cable Excellence), now known as the CableACE Awards.

The Bee Gees delivered a playful tribute in the film. In a scene featuring all three brothers huddled around a piano, Robin humorously credited Bruno's influence on their most famous works: 'I don't think we could have actually created the songs that we've done in our careers had it not been for Bruno's assistance. He was there when we wrote 'How Deep Is Your Love' – he came up with 'How Deep', and when we were writing *Saturday Night Fever*, he came up with 'Saturday''.

This tongue-in-cheek acknowledgment was part of the film's overall comedic tone, blending satire with affectionate nods to the music industry. The Bee Gees' appearance underscored their willingness to engage in humour and self-parody, demonstrating a lighter side of their character while adding to the mockumentary's charm. By blending fictional narratives with real-life musical legends, the film offered a unique, comedic perspective on the mythos of rock 'n' roll.

In 1986, as The Bee Gees prepared for a comeback, they signed with the Los Angeles-based management firm led by Ken Kragen. At the time, Gary Borman and Harriet Sternberg were working at Kragen & Co. and began closely overseeing the group's affairs. A year later, in June 1987, Borman and Sternberg made the decision to leave Kragen's company to start their own venture, Borman/Sternberg Entertainment. 'Harriet and I had been very involved with The Bee Gees on a day-by-day basis', Borman recalled. 'When we decided to leave and do our own thing, Ken called The Bee Gees and told them. I guess they gave it a lot of thought, and then they asked to join us. Harriet and I left not knowing what The Bee Gees were going to do. We planned to go either way, but the fact that they asked us to represent them was very exciting'.

Despite obvious enthusiasm for The Bee Gees' relaunch, Borman said management and the group were both trying to avoid a hype overkill: 'What we didn't want to do was set up a backlash to *Saturday Night Fever* and that whole disco thing. Going out there with a mega-event and super-hype would only encourage that. The way to discourage it is just to come up with a product you believe in and really let the music speak for itself. Over the last year, especially at Kragen & Co., we went from trying to create the mega-event around the release of The Bee Gees' record all the way down to where we're at now. We decided in the long run that all that matters is the music, so that's our approach. And I think perhaps one of the reasons The Bee Gees ended up coming with Harriet and me was probably that they felt our approach was more suited to their temperaments and personalities'.

Boogie Box High was a short-lived but intriguing British pop project that made a splash in the late 1980s. Spearheaded by music producer Andros Georgiou, the group is best remembered for its cover of The Bee Gees' classic, 'Jive Talkin''. Released on 20 June 1987, Boogie Box High's version of 'Jive Talkin'' modernised the original with a sleek, synth-driven production style typical of the era. A key factor in the single's appeal was the uncredited involvement of George Michael, Georgiou's cousin and one of the biggest pop stars of the time. Michael's unmistakable vocals and behind-the-scenes influence added star quality, even though his name didn't appear on the release. The single enjoyed a strong run on the UK Singles Chart, peaking at number seven on 1 August 1987 during an 11-week chart stay.

Andy Gibb returned to the recording studio in June after years of personal struggle and a long hiatus from professional music work. For several years, Barry made it clear he would only collaborate with Andy again if he was able to overcome his drug and alcohol problems. By the spring of 1987, Andy appeared to have achieved sobriety, prompting Barry to begin working with him. Barry and Andy began writing together for the first time in years, and they were joined by Maurice, who had rarely written with Andy in the past.

Although their musical engagements had been limited, Maurice had played a significant role in Andy's earliest foray into studio recording. In August 1973, when Andy was just 15, Maurice booked time at Nova Sound Studio in London, where he played on and produced Andy's very first sessions. Two songs were recorded: 'My Father's A Rebel', written by Maurice, and 'Windows Of My World', most likely a co-write with Andy. Although the recordings remain unreleased, the sessions marked an important milestone in Andy's formal introduction to studio work.

In June, Maurice told staff engineer Scott Glasel that Andy would be coming to Middle Ear to record demos. Although some sources indicate that the sessions took place at Maurice's studio, Panther House, Glasel – who was directly involved as a programmer and recording engineer – confirmed the demos were created at Middle Ear. Andy, Barry, Maurice, and Scott spent the next four or five days recording four songs: 'Man On Fire', 'Hell Or High Water', 'The Price Of Fame' and 'Arrow Through The

Heart'. Although they exist only as demos and were never considered finished recordings, they sound incredibly polished. Jeff Maul, a friend of Glasel's who had performed with him in a band called Veil of Tears, contributed guitar on all four songs. Glasel also recalled that 'Alan Kendall may have played on one or two of those songs'. Glasel praised Andy's vocal abilities during the sessions: 'You didn't have to fix his vocals – he was a great singer, I mean, really, really talented – the guy could sing'. The team believed that Andy was poised for a successful return to music upon securing a new recording contract.

'Man On Fire' is a slow-paced ballad that Glasel considered to be one of the stronger tracks recorded during the sessions, and, as such, it was also the working title for a proposed parent album. The song is a departure from much of the R&B-pop fusion of Andy's previous hits, but hearing Barry's breathy background vocals bubbling under the verses does evoke some shades of *After Dark*. Barry, Maurice, and Andy singing in bright harmonies at the track's climax and on the outro offer a few more truly satisfying moments.

'Man On Fire' became the first song from the sessions to receive an official release, appearing on the posthumous *Andy Gibb* hits compilation issued by Polydor in November 1991. It would also surface on The Bee Gees' *Mythology* retrospective in 2010 (on one of four CDs that contained a specially curated batch of songs featuring each brother), and on *The Very Best Of Andy Gibb* in 2018. 'Man On Fire' was also partially resurrected on Robin's son Spencer Gibb's studio album, *Let's Start Over*, in 2018. A few phrases from the song are incorporated into a track entitled 'Man Burning', on which Barry, Maurice, and Andy are credited as co-writers.

'Price Of Fame' remains one of Andy Gibb's most intriguing unreleased tracks. Glasel called it a 'great song', adding that 'Barry didn't want to release it for some reason'. But with lyrics that feel quite haunting, given Andy's tragic trajectory, it's possible they simply hit too close to home. 'Price Of Fame' stands as a poignant reminder of the burden Andy carried with his success.

'Hell Or High Water' is the longest song of the bunch, and it's also the fastest paced. With its lively arrangement and a guitar solo from Maul, it emerges as the strongest and most commercial-sounding of the four tracks. The energy of Andy's performance shines through, and its upbeat tempo and memorable chorus give it a polished, radio-ready feel. Barry and Maurice's background vocals add urgency to the choruses.

'Arrow Through The Heart' is one of Andy's most poignant recordings, not least because it became the final song he ever completed before his death. It's a minor-key ballad with lyrics reflecting a man's futile search for happiness, with lines like 'I'm too young to die' carrying an ominous sense of prophecy. Robin, who felt the song was a potential hit, later added backing vocals to the track, making it only the second song (after 'Desire') to ever feature all four Gibb brothers singing together. Although a portion of the song surfaced on the VH1 *Behind The Music* programme that featured Andy's story in 1997, the full version remained unreleased until it was included on The Bee Gees' *Mythology* anthology in 2010. With its sombre tone, heartfelt vocal from Andy, and the historic presence of all the brothers, 'Arrow Through The Heart' resonates as both a moving farewell and a reminder of Andy's unfulfilled promise.

Andy's dreams of a comeback were, however, put on hold until the resolution of his long-term financial troubles that had been accumulating since the late 1970s, fuelled by his substance abuse, excessive spending, and infrequent income after his record deal with RSO had been terminated in 1981. They culminated in a bankruptcy case prepared by his attorney, John W. Kozyak of Kozyak Tropin & Throckmorton, a commercial litigation and bankruptcy law firm based in Miami. The case was officially filed on 9 September, marking a low point in Andy's tumultuous career.

Just days later, on 12 September, *United Press International* reporter William C. Trott detailed the filing:

Lawyers, cars and taxes have driven singer Andy Gibb to bankruptcy. Gibb, 29, younger brother of Bee Gees Barry, Maurice, and Robin Gibb, filed a personal bankruptcy petition in Miami, saying he has less than $50,000 and more than $1 million in debts, which his attorney says are mostly business-related.

The biggest creditors are the Los Angeles law firm of Loeb & Loeb, to whom Gibb owes $30,909.94, and Business Jet Airlines, which wants $23,353.59. Gibb, the one-time host of 'Solid Gold', also owes the Internal Revenue Service, a New York accounting firm, Budget Rent-A-Car, a Los Angeles limousine service, a Los Angeles public relations firm, an instrument rental company in Hollywood, RSO Records, the Sun City resort in South Africa, four hospitals, two medical doctors, and a dentist. Once a plan of repayment is worked out, Gibb will be allowed to keep only $1,000 in personal property and any primary residence that he may own. He currently lives in a penthouse apartment overlooking Biscayne Bay.

The media quickly seized on the story, spotlighting every detail of Andy's financial downfall. In late October, a second filing was made, showing a significant revision of the original figures. The downward shift was largely due to the intervention of Robert Stigwood, Andy's former manager, to whom he owed approximately $1 million. Upon learning of the bankruptcy, Stigwood chose to forgive the debt, leading to a dramatic reduction in Andy's liabilities.

Miami News was the first to break the revised story. According to newly filed bankruptcy papers, Andy's debts now stood at $187,041, a far cry from the over $1 million originally reported. His assets were listed at just $1,432. His income had also plummeted – from $24,727 in 1985 to only $7,755 in 1986.

In addition to his personal filing, Andy submitted a bankruptcy petition for his entertainment management company, Andy Gibb Organization Inc., reporting corporate debts of $46,289 and assets totalling just $236. Details emerged that much of the property in his Biscayne Bay apartment – furniture, video equipment, guitars – had been loaned to him by his brothers, their wives and Middle Ear Inc., The Bee Gees' own company. Even his stage clothing and a velvet jacket were said to be borrowed from Barry.

Eventually, the two bankruptcy cases – personal and corporate – were consolidated. Still, the headlines didn't let up, with every number and possession splashed across newspapers, illustrating the steep and very public decline of a once-bright pop star.

In September, as Andy was dealing with his bankruptcy, Barry reportedly made an attempt to bring his younger brother into The Bee Gees – a plan he had first floated as far back as 1979. Barry had long maintained that if Andy could overcome his substance abuse issues, he would be welcomed into the group. Now that Andy was clean and sober, Barry believed the time had come. However, Maurice and Robin remained opposed to the idea, and Andy's recovery did little to change their position.

Scott Glasel had no memory of any serious discussions about Andy becoming a full member of the band while he was working closely with the brothers. 'The Bee Gees were the three of them', he said. 'Andy's dream was to be a Bee Gee, but I think because of the age difference, he was never actually going to be a Bee Gee – that was never going to happen'.

Despite this, both Barry and Maurice would later state that Andy was indeed set to join The Bee Gees for the *One* album and the *One For All* tour. These conversations and internal deliberations were kept entirely out of the public eye at the time. Yet, in the 2020 documentary *The Bee Gees: How Can You Mend A Broken Heart*, a title card appears, starkly stating: 'In 1988, The Bee Gees announced Andy Gibb would join the group as an official member'. The film offers no citation for this claim, but it seems clear that the statement could only have come from Barry.

Still, this declaration does not align neatly with the reality of Andy's life in 1988. Far from preparing to become a Bee Gee, he was focused on relaunching his solo career. The timing of such an announcement, had it been made publicly, would have clashed with Andy's own efforts to reclaim his place as an independent artist rather than becoming a permanent extension of his brothers' legacy.

E.S.P. (1987)

Personnel:

Barry Gibb: vocals; guitar ('You Win Again', 'The Longest Night', 'Angela', 'Overnight', 'Giving Up The Ghost'); drum programming ('Angela', 'Live Or Die')

Robin Gibb: vocals

Maurice Gibb: vocals, keyboards ('You Win Again', 'The Longest Night', 'Live Or Die', 'Crazy For Your Love', 'Giving Up The Ghost'); guitar ('Angela', 'Overnight'); drum programming ('You Win Again', 'Live Or Die'); sequenced guitar ('This Is Your Life')

Robbie Kondor: keyboards ('You Win Again', 'E.S.P.', 'The Longest Night', 'Angela', 'Backtafunk', 'Overnight', 'Giving Up The Ghost'); guitar ('Live Or Die')

Rhett Lawrence: drum programming ('You Win Again', 'E.S.P.', 'The Longest Night', 'Overnight'); keyboards ('Angela'); synthesiser ('E.S.P.', 'The Longest Night')

Greg Phillinganes: piano ('Angela'); keyboards ('Crazy For Your Love', 'This Is Your Life'); drum programming ('Crazy For Your Love'); synthesiser ('Giving Up The Ghost')

Marcus Miller: bass ('E.S.P.', 'The Longest Night', 'Backtafunk')

Brian Tench: programming ('Angela', 'This Is Your Life', 'Giving Up The Ghost')

Nick Moroch: guitar ('Angela', 'The Longest Night', 'Backtafunk', 'Overnight')
Reb Beach: guitar ('E.S.P.', 'Overnight')
Reggie Griffin: guitar ('Backtafunk', 'Giving Up The Ghost'); drum programming ('Giving Up The Ghost')
Tony Beard: drums ('Backtafunk', 'Giving Up The Ghost')
Joe Mardin: programming ('Crazy For Your Love', 'This Is Your Life')
Will Lee: bass ('Angela')
Sammy Figueroa: percussion ('Backtafunk')
Arif Mardin: synthesiser bass ('Backtafunk'); sequenced guitar ('This Is Your Life')
Bob Gay: sax ('Backtafunk')
Basic tracks arranged by Barry Gibb, Maurice Gibb
Orchestral arrangements by Arif Mardin, Robbie Kondor, Reg Griffin
Engineers: Brian Tench, Scott Glasel
Producers: Arif Mardin, Barry Gibb, Robin Gibb, Maurice Gibb, Brian Tench
Recorded at Middle Ear, Miami Beach, between January and March 1987
Release dates: UK: 21 September 1987, US: 12 October 1987
Chart positions: Switzerland: 1, West Germany: 1, Austria: 2, Norway: 2, UK: 5, Netherlands: 9, Italy: 13, Australia: 25, Sweden: 25, Japan: 26, Spain: 32, New Zealand: 44, Canada: 87, US: 96
Gold certification: Hong Kong, Norway, Spain, West Germany (x3)
Platinum certification: Switzerland (x2), United Kingdom

When Barry, Robin, and Maurice walked into the studio to begin writing and recording for their next album in September 1986, they were ready to relaunch The Bee Gees as a successful and, more importantly, cohesive recording group.

One of the main catalysts for The Bee Gees' return to the studio was the work they did collaboratively for Robin's 1985 solo album, *Walls Have Eyes*. All three brothers had written eight of the record's ten tracks, and they all contributed vocals to the song 'Toys', which was released as the set's second single in February 1986. While they had continually written songs together the entire time during the group's self-imposed hibernation, the time they spent together working on *Walls Have Eyes* had re-ignited their passion for creating music as a trio.

The Gibbs had each pursued solo projects during the first half of the 1980s, hoping they'd be able to achieve success with their respective talents outside the confines of The Bee Gees' name and image. While those generated varied amounts of chart impact in different markets, they all seemed to leave the brothers and their audiences wanting something more.

While the brothers were eager to get back to work as a functioning entity, the prospect must have felt at least a bit nerve-wracking. *Living Eyes* was the last Bee Gees studio album on which the brothers had truly all worked together, but the process was turbulent and, in the end, not particularly satisfying commercially or artistically.

And then there was the small matter of their reputation in the eyes of the public and media, which had essentially left them silenced from the airwaves since 1980 – particularly in the US. The Gibbs rightfully found the resistance to their craft frustrating and confusing. A new Bee Gees album, however compelled and enthusiastic they were to make it, was a risky venture.

But maybe there was a silver lining to all of it. Their time out of the spotlight forced them to take a back seat as performers, and they were able to get their personal lives in order, spend more time with their growing families, enjoy their past achievements and, most critically from a creative and artistic aspect, refresh. Considering the three brothers had been performing together since they were children, in retrospect, the enforced time-out must have provided some respite.

But never ones to sit on their laurels, the Gibbs used the time industriously to develop and improve as writers and producers. There was an element of comedy that illustrated how frivolous the ire was against The Bee Gees in name, because most of those commercially lucrative projects fronted by other artists were imprinted so unmistakably with their sound.

The brothers hoped a new record label, new management, and a contemporary revamp of their sound would finally get things back on track. Released in September 1987, *E.S.P.* was the group's first album under their freshly inked contract with Warner Bros. Records.

It was also the first time in 12 years they had worked with Arif Mardin, the legendary producer who had guided them back to success in 1975 with their album *Main Course*. Initially, the Gibbs had announced that long-time Beatles producer George Martin was going to be involved, but that never materialised. The sum of what had happened to The Bee Gees post-1979, especially after parting ways with Robert Stigwood, left them looking for mentorship. Turning to Mardin for direction and support seemed a natural choice given that he'd helped to steer them out of obscurity a decade earlier.

Arif's son, Joe, who had evolved into an accomplished musician in his own right, told the authors in April 2026 that his father was elated to get back to work with the Gibbs to recapture some of the creative magic they had concocted for *Main Course*. 'I remember when the Bee Gees landed at Warner Brothers and expressed interest in working with [my dad] again, and it was a very exciting moment for him. We were very pleased for him – it was definitely a happy happening, so to speak'.

Joe said his father 'felt that they were really doing something cutting edge for the time, and there was a lot of creativity. He always loved Robin's voice – and he especially loved the way Robin and Barry's voices blended together. They would do certain background parts where they would double things in unison. He loved that'.

Mardin, in turn, introduced Brian Tench as co-producer, a partnership that would help define the album's polished sound. Tench had begun his career at Mayfair Studios in 1971 and had since built an impressive résumé across the shifting tides of British pop. He worked with chart acts such as Hello and the Bay City Rollers before moving into the new wave and synth-driven scene of the early 1980s, collaborating with Visage, Landscape, and Orchestral Manoeuvres in the Dark. His first full production credit came with Bow Wow Wow's hit single 'Go Wild In The Country' (1982), while his engineering and mixing work on Kate Bush's *Hounds Of Love* (1985) further showcased his technical finesse. That same year, while engineering former Dollar member Thereza Bazar's ill-fated solo album *The Big Kiss*, Tench first encountered Arif Mardin, who produced the project. Their professional bond formed in those sessions, ultimately drawing him into The Bee Gees' orbit. For the Gibbs, Tench's objective perspective and grounding in contemporary pop acted as a vital counterbalance to Mardin's seasoned leadership, giving *E.S.P.* both a modern edge and a sense of continuity with their past.

Another key figure behind the sound of *E.S.P.* was Scott Glasel, credited as the album's 'synthesiser programmer'. Whereas Tench focused on production oversight and the broader sonic architecture, Glasel worked at the micro level, shaping the very building blocks of the record's sound. He was responsible for creating the extensive custom sound library that underpinned much of the album's distinctive character. Unlike the common practice of purchasing pre-set sounds and tweaking them slightly, Glasel worked closely with the brothers to design textures that were entirely their own. 'Most people buy the sounds and modify them a little bit,' he later recalled, 'but Mo, Barry, and Robin wanted sounds that no one else had'. His work gave The Bee Gees a palette of unique tones that set *E.S.P.* apart from other pop albums and reinforced the group's determination to reassert themselves with a sound that felt both modern and unmistakably their own.

The album was rife with cream-of-the-crop session players that Mardin had likely selected. Rhett Lawrence, Greg Phillinganes, Leland Sklar, Will Lee, and Robbie Kondor were industry juggernauts who had supported dozens of prominent artists of the period.

On the shoulders of the album's first single, 'You Win Again', which had stormed to the top of the charts in the UK, Ireland, Switzerland, West Germany, Austria, and Norway, the album sold very well in Europe, reaching the coveted top slot in West Germany and Switzerland, and achieving top ten status in many others.

Radio response to the single 'You Win Again' had been 'absolutely exceptional', manager Gary Borman told *Billboard*. 'As people are listening to this record, everyone is declaring it a hit'. He admitted that some programmers may have initially approached the track with caution: 'These guys were all of a sudden hit with a Bee Gees record after six years of silence, and they weren't quite sure what to expect. When they didn't hear the disco thing – the heavy falsettos and all that – they were sort of taken aback. But the element of surprise was what we wanted and what we planned on'. For Borman, the album boasted 'a very contemporary sound. It embodies The Bee Gees' writing ability and carries their stamp, but in a definite contemporary way. The group has maintained its pulse, kept its foot in the door and has never lost touch with where the industry is at'.

The only real disappointment was that *E.S.P.* failed to chart higher than number 96 on the *Billboard* Top 200 in the US, where the 'You Win Again' single had also floundered, once again receiving the cold shoulder from radio programmers. For the remainder of their recording career, the once Bee Gees-enamoured US marketplace, with a few exceptions, would be a tougher sell than its global counterparts.

One known outtake of the *E.S.P.* sessions was the track 'Young Love', which has made the rounds in demo form for some years. It sounds quite similar to the rough track made for the album's title song, so perhaps that led to a decision to shelve it and not develop it further.

E.S.P., along with 1989's *One* and 1991's *High Civilization*, would be reissued in 2014 as part of Reprise's *The Warner Bros. Years* box set, which included the original tracks plus some variants and remixes of 'E.S.P.', 'You Win Again' and 'Angela'. Like many of The Bee Gees' later-career albums, it could stand a proper reissue with some competent remastering.

The album overall has remained somewhat frozen in time with the pervasive use of echo in the mix and noisy percussion effects abound, but in 2026, those arrangements now seem to be coming into the forefront of pop music once again.

No known plans were drawn up to support the album with a tour – likely, it felt too soon to take a road trip as they were getting re-established. They did, however, travel extensively to make television and other promotional appearances to reach audiences.

Initial plans for the album's artwork called for a painted or illustrated cover rather than a group photograph. Over time, however, the idea shifted, with Terry O'Neill emerging as the preferred choice for photography. There was also discussion about making slight changes to the now-famous logo designed by Ernie Cefalu, which had been in use since 1975. In the end, none of these concepts were carried through. Instead, London-based photographer Andy Earl was commissioned to create the visuals for the *E.S.P.* album cover and the 'You Win Again' single. Earl's work, known for blending dramatic natural backdrops with striking architectural elements to achieve a surrealistic atmosphere, shaped the final imagery and gave the project its distinctive look. The gothic-styled Bee Gees logo that permeated their 1975-1983 releases was eschewed in favour of the band's name being displayed on the cover, rather unspectacularly, next to the album's title – both in a simple, common serif font.

The photo sessions took place over two days on 13 and 14 July at the Castlerigg Stone Circle near Keswick in Cumbria, one of Britain's most visually impressive prehistoric monuments, dating back to around 3,000 B.C.

Both the front and back covers of the album are matte black with a horizontal spot laminate band across the centre portions. The front cover photograph was a nicely lit photograph of the brothers with the stone circle at dusk, while the back cover photo was taken later in the evening, further back and from a different angle, with floodlighting evident in the foreground.

The inner sleeve included lyrics and credits, and one photograph of the stones on each side, although they did not depict the brothers.

'E.S.P.' (Barry Gibb, Robin Gibb, Maurice Gibb)
Recorded at Middle Ear, Miami Beach, in February/March 1987
Chart positions: Switzerland: 8, Belgium: 12, West Germany: 13, Austria: 21,
Netherlands: 26, Denmark: 32, UK: 51, Australia: 89

A stunning album opener with its haunting a cappella vocal introduction, 'E.S.P.' was an immediate indicator to the listener that The Bee Gees were well and truly back. The song was originally titled 'XTC' or 'Ecstasy' before the brothers recognised it could be considered a drug reference. Released as the follow-up to the smash hit 'You Win Again', the single version had the a cappella introduction edited out. However, 'You Win Again' proved a hard act to follow, and 'E.S.P.' was a comparative failure – peaking at only number 51 in the UK and failing to chart at all in the US.

In truth, the song was worthy of a far better showing as it demonstrated the Gibb brothers' growth as songwriters and performers since their late-1970s chart dominance. Once again, their co-producer and mentor, Arif Mardin, helped reimagine their talents for a late 1980s landscape. Barry takes most of the vocal lead, but Robin also shines in key moments. High-reaching harmonies from all three brothers add power, while sparkling synths and a driving drumbeat complete the production. Guitarist Reb Beach supplies what might be one of the more dynamic electric solos on a Bee Gees record to date.

In the UK, buoyed by the remarkable success of 'You Win Again' and hoping for an equally successful follow-up, Warner Bros. promoted 'E.S.P.' heavily with extensive press advertising and multiple formats: the standard 7" picture sleeve, a 7" poster sleeve, a 7" Christmas card sleeve, a standard 12" single and a special 12" single with Arthur Baker remixes. Yet the eagerness to release it so quickly backfired, as the mid-December release date meant it lost out on valuable airplay during the festive season and failed to receive the attention it deserved.

In Europe and the US, the Arthur Baker remixes were issued as additional formats to help boost sales and secure higher chart positions. No fewer than six different versions were released:

- E.S.P. (Remix – No Guitars) (4:10)
- E.S.P. (Extended Version) (6:15)
- E.S.P. 'Extra Sensory House' (Vocal) (6:31)
- E.S.P. 'Extra Energy' (Dub) (6:42)
- E.S.P. 'E.S.P.N.R.G.' (Vocal) (7:05)
- E.S.P. 'E.S.Piano' (Dub) (8:20)

The Bee Gees would later speak out about their dislike of the industry's tendency to create endless remixes from their original works, and they had a point, as most of the ones released on their behalf over the years added very little value to their prototypes.

The video for 'E.S.P.' was filmed in Los Angeles at the end of October 1987, produced by Tim Clawson for Limelight Productions and directed by Steve Barron. Among the many music videos Barron directed are 'Billie Jean' by Michael Jackson, 'Money For Nothing' by Dire Straits, 'Electric Avenue' by Eddy Grant, 'Africa' by Toto and A-ha's iconic 'Take On Me'. The storyline of the 'E.S.P.' video centres on a boy who has no shadow – until, suddenly, his shadow appears and stays with him, although always moving more slowly than the boy himself.

'You Win Again' (Barry Gibb, Robin Gibb, Maurice Gibb)
Recorded at Middle Ear, Miami Beach, in February/March 1987
Chart positions: Austria: 1, Ireland; 1, Norway: 1, Switzerland: 1, UK: 1, West Germany: 1, Belgium: 2, South Africa: 2, Italy: 4, Netherlands: 5, Sweden: 8, Australia: 10, Finland: 14, France: 14, New Zealand: 18, US: 75
Silver certification: France
Gold certification: UK
Platinum certification: West Germany
Released in September, 'You Win Again' was the first Bee Gees single since 'Someone Belonging To Someone' from 1983's *Staying Alive* soundtrack four years earlier. It is, quite simply, one of The Bee Gees' best-ever tracks, and served as a strong, impressive comeback single to launch them back on the market. It showed them to be completely in tune with contemporary music trends, and it paid off, rewarding them with a number one hit in many parts of Europe. With little interest from US radio, it peaked at a disappointing number 75 on the *Billboard* Hot 100. Its quality and infectiousness should have almost guaranteed them a smash, but even if the American public were willing to buy the single, they had few opportunities to hear the song. Even with a number of high-profile appearances to perform their new song on primetime television and the late-night circuit, including a prominent spot on the 14th American Music Awards broadcast, 'You Win Again' stalled. In Canada, the song fared slightly better by cracking the top ten of the RPM adult contemporary chart, but the song wasn't played regularly on top 40 stations.

As a bit of interesting trivia, The Bee Gees' first UK number one single, 'Massachusetts', topped the UK charts for four weeks beginning on 17

October 1967. Exactly 20 years later to the day, 'You Win Again' matched that achievement, also holding the number one spot for four weeks.

As further recognition of the song's triumph, the Gibb brothers received the 1987 British Academy's *Ivor Novello Award* for Best Song Musically and Lyrically. The Bee Gees also received a British Phonographic Industry Brit Award nomination the following year for Best British Group as a result of the record's success. In a 2011 UK television special, *The Nation's Favourite Bee Gees Song*, it was voted second behind 'How Deep Is Your Love'.

Barry has spoken of how the melody of the song came to him whilst asleep and stumbling around the house in the middle of the night looking for a tape recorder so he wouldn't forget it in the morning. Maurice told *Mojo* magazine:

I loved 'You Win Again' as a title, but we had no idea how it might turn out as a song. It ended up as a big demo in my garage, and I recorded stomps and things. There was just one drum on there. The rest was just sounds. Then, everybody tried to talk us out of the stomps at the start. They didn't want it. 'Take it off. Too loud! Can we have them not on the intro, just when the music starts!?', all this stuff, but as soon as you hear that 'jabba-doomba, jabba-doomba' on the radio, you know it's us!

While Maurice's blueprints for the drums in the demo were used in the released version, session player Rhett Lawrence and Barry fine-tuned the rhythm track.

Robin recalled: 'We absolutely thought that 'You Win Again' was going to be a big hit. It took us a month to cut it and get the right mix'. Although CD singles were not common at the time, a one-track digipak was produced for promotional use in the US and was given to radio stations and reviewers. A two-track 3" CD single was commercially released in Japan. Despite the failure of the single in the US, Warner Bros. would continue to push the song, including it as a bonus track on the American CD and cassette versions of the *One* album two years later in 1989. In the UK, it was also issued as a 12" picture disc and a remixed version was issued as the B-side to the 'Crazy For Your Love' single.

The promotional video, directed by Leslie Libman, continued the theme of the stone circle on the album cover, and indeed the single cover, with clips of the brothers intercut with more rocks. However, these were not filmed at Castlerigg, but the famous strange rock formations at Brimham Rocks near Harrogate, about 100 miles away.

The video showed Maurice playing an unusual instrument – the futuristic Stepp DGX MIDI guitar controller. Stepp produced two very similar-looking instruments – the DG1, which contained an onboard synthesiser, and the DGX, a dedicated MIDI controller. Maurice also brought the DGX to several television appearances, including *Wogan*, *Top Of The Pops*, the Dutch pop show *Countdown* and *Fantastico* in Italy. Other prominent Stepp users included Kate Bush's band (on *Wogan* for 'Experiment IV'), Yes guitarist Steve Howe, who worked directly with the Stepp team and demoed the DG1 around 1987, Pete Townshend of The Who, experimental guitarist David Torn and producers Terry Britten and Steve Levine. The instrument even made a cameo in the 1988 film *Vice Versa*. Despite its innovative, guitar-friendly design – far easier to play than the rival SynthAxe – the Stepp remained a niche product, with only around 250 units ever sold worldwide.

Michael Jackson sampled the infamous intro of 'You Win Again' for use in his 1996 short film, *Ghosts*. While the excerpt didn't appear in one of the official songs included in the film, it's audible during a memorable scene about mid-way through the feature when an army of Jackson's dancing apparitions march in time to the track's unmistakable stomps up the walls of a haunted house.

'Live Or Die (Hold Me Like A Child)' (Barry Gibb, Robin Gibb, Maurice Gibb)

Recorded at Middle Ear, Miami Beach, in February/March 1987

A true 1980s power ballad featuring a robust lead vocal from Barry in his natural voice before relenting to the impassioned chorus, where all three brothers stretch their natural voices into a powerful burst of harmony. Barry also swings into a full-on falsetto for the second pre-chorus and on ad-libs for the remainder of the track. It suits the song and shows the strength of Barry's unique vocal instrument. One of the earliest songs written for the album, it's a standout track.

Strangely, it was only issued as a single in South Africa, with 'Giving Up The Ghost' on the flip-side. It perhaps should have been considered in other territories, as it was a particularly good track. It also appeared as a bonus track on the German 3" CD and 12" singles of 'Angela'.

'Giving Up The Ghost' (Barry Gibb, Robin Gibb, Maurice Gibb)
Recorded at Middle Ear, Miami Beach, in February/March 1987
'Giving Up The Ghost' was one of Robin's favourite songs from the album, and it's one of only two instances on *E.S.P.* where he takes a full lead vocal role. The general absence of Robin as a primary vocalist on this set is surprising, given that he was featured quite prominently on *Living Eyes*. But, as they did during their late 1970s output, the brothers may have decided Barry's voice was the best suited to handle the more cluttered, ambitious arrangements.

It had a bizarre working title of 'Babysitter', which doesn't relate to the finished product in the remotest way. Bee Gees historian Joe Brennan states the song 'sounds like one of the Robin and Maurice collaborations from one of Robin's solo albums'. The demo of the song is very Euro-pop-ish; a bit faster and, frankly, a little more dynamic. It's entirely possible it was born during their collaborations earlier in the decade as another idea and evolved into this one.

No doubt recognising its worth as an up-tempo track that could translate well to the stage, The Bee Gees included it on the *One For All* tour setlist two years later.

'The Longest Night' (Barry Gibb, Robin Gibb, Maurice Gibb)
Recorded at Middle Ear, Miami Beach, in February/March 1987
On the CD edition of *E.S.P.*, 'The Longest Night' is the lengthiest song on the album at 5:46; however, on the vinyl LP, it was edited down to 5:02. It is a sweet, soulful ballad with an excellent lead vocal by Robin. Barry's background vocals are quite prominent, and his falsetto voice is also used sparingly but to good effect.

Although writing credits are given to all three brothers, the drift of the lyric, the diversity of the melody and the song's general arrangement invoke the creative style of Barry, in particular. Unusual for a Bee Gees song, it has no exact repeating chorus.

The song was reportedly considered for release as the album's fourth single.

'This Is Your Life' (Barry Gibb, Robin Gibb, Maurice Gibb)
Recorded at Middle Ear, Miami Beach, in February/March 1987
This song starts up quite well with some funky drums and percussion courtesy of Joe Mardin and Brian Tench and leads the listener to think it's going to be a standard R&B song from the brothers. However,

halfway through, the song shifts into a Barry-led rap section which riffs on the titles of 11 past Bee Gees songs: 'Lonely Days', 'Love So Right', 'Tragedy', 'Stayin' Alive', 'Jive Talkin'', 'Too Much Heaven', 'How Deep is Your Love', 'My World', 'Run To Me', 'How Can You Mend A Broken Heart', and 'Nights On Broadway'. A gimmick or just a bit of fun? Both, probably, but it doesn't really lift the song enough to elevate it beyond being rather ordinary. That being said, the vocals remain excellent.

While the idea of The Bee Gees trying to rap might seem unusual, Barry had attempted it with more success on the song 'Fine Line' on *Now Voyager*.

The title is most likely inspired by the well-known television show *This Is Your Life*, on which, some four years later, The Bee Gees would be the featured guests.

'Angela' (Barry Gibb, Robin Gibb, Maurice Gibb)

Recorded at Middle Ear, Miami Beach, in February/March 1987
Chart position: West Germany: 52

A comparatively uninspiring ballad with an equally unengaging chorus, 'Angela' does feature a reasonably good melody sung by Barry, who is in excellent voice across the entire album.

The inspiration for the song's titular protagonist is unknown, but the Gibbs had occasionally used both fictional and real women's names in their compositions (Louise, Elisa, Fanny, Rebecca, Kathy, to name a few).

On the demo, with the acoustic guitars to the fore, it's a far more persuasive and emotional song, and Barry's voice is allowed to soar with greater emotion. In the repeating refrain, his vocal is clearly double-tracked with Robin's. The final release seems overproduced to its detriment with loud, busy percussion, and until the very end of the song, Barry's lead feels a bit too far back in the mix.

An edited version of the song was released as the third single from the album in West Germany, Spain, Australia, and New Zealand, but it only charted at number 52 in West Germany.

An arty promotional video, very much in vogue in the late 1980s, was produced to support the single.

'Overnight' (Barry Gibb, Robin Gibb, Maurice Gibb)

Recorded at Middle Ear, Miami Beach, in February/March 1987
What was planned as the obligatory Maurice lead vocal on the album was tucked away on its second side. 'Overnight' is, in execution, one of *E.S.P.*'s strongest songs.

Never a particularly confident lead vocalist, Maurice seemed far more comfortable singing harmonies, which he did superbly. But here, his steady tenor vocal, almost with a Gerry Rafferty-esque quality, is a perfect fit for the track. However, when joined by his two brothers for the verse build-up and ensuing chorus, the effect is powerful. Barry's falsetto can also be heard on the edge of the chorus, and Robin sings a few lines solo toward the conclusion.

A wailing guitar solo by accomplished session player Reb Beach drives home its urgency. Beach humorously recalled his session with the Gibbs in a 2019 *MusicRadar* interview:

The Bee Gees flew me out and put me up in Doral, Miami. There were bags of weed *everywhere*. Those guys just smoked and smoked, and that's all they did! But there was a track I played on that didn't have a vocal yet, so they all got around in a circle around me and sang the vocal. It was the most incredible thing because they all had perfect pitch. They just sang for me acapella ... All these voices that I've heard on the radio for all these years, standing around me, in stereo, and singing perfectly. It was a wonderful, wonderful experience.

On the song's original demo, Barry sang the lead vocal but with his falsetto voice, and there are extra lyrics attached to verses that seemed to be edited out to make the journey to the song's big choruses more efficient. The rough version is equally as good, and the choice to use either Barry or Maurice's voice may not have been easy – but ultimately the correct decision was made.

'Overnight' was used as the B-side to the 'E.S.P.' single.

'Crazy For Your Love' (Barry Gibb, Robin Gibb, Maurice Gibb)

Recorded at Middle Ear, Miami Beach, in February/March 1987
Chart position: UK: 79

Dismissed by some critics as 'vapid pop', 'Crazy For Your Love' is one of the most spontaneous songs on the album and it's a lot of fun. If it has a fault to a cynical ear, perhaps it's too commercial – comparisons were made at the time to the Diana Ross hit 'Chain Reaction', with critics not realising, while essentially accusing them of appropriation at the time, that it was also written and produced by them.

Joe Mardin shared a few notes about his contributions to this track and 'This Is Your Life' with the authors in April 2026:

My father asked me to come down and do some programming for the album. I had some of my equipment flown down [to Miami] – my Emulator SP-12 drum machine and my sequencer. I worked on those tracks mainly in a room upstairs at Middle Ear, where I had my stuff set up and a couple of speakers. My dad would come in and make suggestions, and we would work on things together. When it was deemed to be ready, we would go downstairs and start laying down the tracks from the sequences onto a 32-track Mitsubishi digital, if I remember correctly.

Mixing both Barry's natural voice and his falsetto, this fast-paced track with a prominent drum beat was custom-made for the dance floors. It was released as the album's third single in the UK in February 1988, but there was no supporting promotional video made. They did, however, perform it on British television on Terry Wogan's BBC1 prime-time chat show *Wogan*, but despite this, it failed to chart higher than number 79.

'Backtafunk' (Barry Gibb, Robin Gibb, Maurice Gibb)

Recorded at Middle Ear, Miami Beach, in February/March 1987

'Backtafunk' is another playfully abstract track with weightless lyrics that, while catchy, pales when compared to the balance of an excellent album. It certainly confirmed that The Bee Gees could play funky music as efficiently as any other band when they wanted to, and Barry's good vocal makes up for its lack of substance.

Session player Bob Gay furnishes the raspy sax solo near the end of the track, adding to his credentials that included albums by David Bowie, Culture Club, Chaka Khan, and Howard Jones. His work was perhaps most widely heard on American singer Tommy Page's 1990 *Billboard* number one hit, 'I'll Be Your Everything'.

The song saw a wider release as the B-side of the 'You Win Again' single.

'E.S.P. (Vocal Reprise)' (Barry Gibb, Robin Gibb, Maurice Gibb)

Recorded at Middle Ear, Miami Beach, in February/March 1987

This is a 34-second replay of the final two lines of the a cappella vocal portion of 'E.S.P.'s introduction, which opens and fades with a hazy echo effect.

Related Recording
'E.S.P.' (Demo Version) (Barry Gibb, Robin Gibb, Maurice Gibb)

Recorded at Panther House, Miami Beach, between September and December 1986

The original 'E.S.P.' demo was recorded at Maurice's home studio, Panther House, in late 1986 and was included on the 1990 *Tales From The Brothers Gibb – A History In Song 1967-1990* box set. The track features more restrained vocals and fewer harmonies than the final product, but the lift before the chorus – 'and love will take you higher and higher and higher' – is in place at this early stage. It would seem the same drum programming on the demo was preserved for the album version with some enhancements.

It was unusual for the Gibbs to officially release a demo, preferring to present listeners only with songs that were produced and mixed to perfection, but it's always interesting to hear the contrast between their blueprints and the finished product.

In early September, The Bee Gees briefly stopped in New York for press interviews on their way to Miami, where they attended the WEA National Sales Meet in Hollywood, Florida. *Billboard* later published a photo of Barry and Maurice in conversation with WEA president Henry Droz and Warner Bros. Records chairman Mo Ostin, underscoring the scale of their international campaign.

They then launched their European promotional tour on 16 September, beginning with key press interviews. Just two days later, on 18 September, they appeared on BBC1's primetime chat show, *Wogan*, performing 'You Win Again' and sitting down for an interview. By 20 September, the brothers were in Hamburg for a round of press interviews and photo shoots, followed by an appearance on the Dutch pop show *Countdown* in Amsterdam on 21 September.

From 22 to 24 September, they were in Paris for a heavy schedule of press commitments and an appearance on the *Patrick Sabatier Show*. The group then flew to Nurnberg on 25 September, where the following day they appeared on Germany's hugely popular *Wetten, Dass..?* presented by Thomas Gottschalk. Their journey continued into Italy, where they carried out further interviews and performed on *Telemike*, *Pentatlon*, *DeeJay Television* on the youth-oriented channel Italia Uno, and *RAIUNO News*.

Back in Britain, 1 October saw the Bee Gees on *Top Of The Pops*, hosted by Gary Davies and Mike Smith, where they performed 'You Win Again'. It was their first studio performance on the show since 6 July 1973, when they performed 'Wouldn't I Be Someone'. The song's promotional cycle continued on *Top Of The Pops* with a mix of repeats of the appearance and the promotional video as the song steadily ascended the chart.

'You Win Again' reached number one on the UK chart on 17 October and made The Bee Gees the only group to score a number one hit in the 1960s, 1970s and 1980s.

Meanwhile, on 4 October, the British group This Way Up released a cover of 'If I Can't Have You' as a single. The group comprised future Nightcrawlers singer John Robinson Reid and Culture Club guitarist Roy Hay, who also produced the record. It was the duo's second single and spent four weeks on the UK singles charts, peaking at number 76.

Barry reaffirmed his confidence in Andy's recovery when he agreed that summer to finance a lifelong dream of Andy's: learning to fly and obtaining a Private Pilot License (PPL). Andy had taken a few lessons at the Santa Monica Airport during his first short stay in California ten years earlier, but his demanding schedule and eventual substance abuse problems had derailed his ambitions.

In the summer of 1987, Andy went to the CAV-AIR Flight School at Fort Lauderdale Executive Airport and began training with instructor Ken Winters. 'After meeting him on his first trip to the school, we developed a good rapport – we hit it off very well, and he was comfortable with me', recalled Ken. Andy learned to fly a Cessna 152 and earned his private pilot's licence on 7 October after logging 75 solo hours. 'When Andy started, he had doubts, but when he got it accomplished, he was very pleased with himself. He always used good judgment – never missed a lesson', said Ken. Training highlights included a grass-strip landing at Chalet Suzanne near Lake Wales, and even a practice flight with the US Navy's Blue Angels. 'Andy said singing and flying were his first and second loves', remembered Ken, adding, 'He loved flying – his presence always seemed to lighten the moods of those around him'.

In November, The Bee Gees embarked on a brief promotional trip along the US East Coast. On 17 November, they visited *Billboard*'s New York offices, where they met with Michael Ellis, the magazine's assistant director of charts and manager of their Hot 100 survey, along with talent editor Steve Gett, and Valarie Goodman from Warner Bros' local promotion team in New York.

To mark the release of their first album in six years, the South Florida radio station Y-100 hosted a party for The Bee Gees at Club NU in Miami Beach. Before the celebrations began, the group appeared live on the station's airwaves. Around the same time, they also featured on several major American television programmes, including *Good Morning America* and *Entertainment Tonight*, and appeared on Miami's local CBS News affiliate station. Their international reach was further extended when they joined a Japanese television show via satellite link. Meanwhile, their appearance on the British chart show *Top Of The Pops*, then being broadcast in the US, added an extra layer of visibility.

The promotional push was supported by prominent advertisements in *Billboard* magazine, including a double-page spread for *E.S.P.* and 'You Win Again' on 26 September, followed by a full-page ad for *E.S.P.* on 21 November.

On the weekend of 21-22 November, Barry hosted his fourth annual Love and Hope Tennis Festival at the Turnberry Isle Yacht and Country Club in Aventura, Florida. Now in its fourth consecutive year, the event proved to be the best attended and most heavily promoted to date. It was televised in the form of a telethon across Broward and Dade counties and broadcast more widely throughout Florida.

During the evening, Hank Callner presented Barry with an elaborate engraved silver plate on behalf of the Diabetes Research Institute, in recognition of his ongoing support. Musical performances highlighted the celebratory spirit of the festival: Andy sang 'Shadow Dancing'; Barry was joined by Larry Gatlin for 'Words' with Maurice accompanying on piano; Noeleen Batley Stewart performed 'Help Me Make It Through The Night'; and the night closed with a rousing version of 'What'd I Say', delivered by Barry, Larry Gatlin, and Andy together.

The Bee Gees' sister Lesley's eldest daughter, Beri, had long been interested in music. By early 1987, she was actively pursuing her own career, performing and recording with her Los Angeles–based band, Social Fact. Alongside Beri on lead vocals, the band included Chris Wilkening on lead guitar and backing vocals, David Dunn on keyboards and bass, and John Wilma on drums. They performed live around Los Angeles, recorded demos and even produced a video for their song 'Girl Gang', which was written by Barry, Robin, Maurice, and Andy in 1984. It's not known if it was composed specifically for the band, or if it was intended for the tentatively planned but unrealised Andy Gibb album scheduled around the same time.

In late 1987, Beri collaborated with her famous uncles on two demo recordings – 'Naked Feelings' and 'I'm Not Wearing Make-Up'. The recordings were produced by Barry and Maurice at Panther House. Barry and Maurice also contributed instrumentally and vocally, with Andy lending additional vocals, and Scott Glasel assisting with programming and engineering. 'Naked Feelings' remains unreleased, while 'I'm Not Wearing Make-Up' surfaced in 1994 on the Eggbert Records Bee Gees tribute album, *Melody Fair*, featuring Beri's lead vocal with Barry on backup rather than Andy. Notably, the copyrights for these songs, dated 12 and 30 November, respectively, specify that Andy wrote only the lyrics, while his brothers wrote both words and music. These compositions were the very last songs Andy would ever write.

In December, Warner Bros. issued *Yulesville*, a festive promotional album exclusively distributed to radio stations and media outlets. This compilation featured a mix of holiday music and spoken greetings from a variety of artists under the Warner Bros. and Reprise labels, including celebrated names like George Harrison, Fleetwood Mac, Madonna, Prince, and The Bee Gees. Issued on red vinyl and housed in a die-cut sleeve, the album included full-length holiday tracks by artists such as Prince, The Pretenders and Los Lobos, along with short, spoken greetings. The title track, 'Yulesville', originally recorded in 1959 by Edd 'Kookie' Byrnes, added a nostalgic touch. Adding to its quirky charm, the lead-out groove on Side A of the album featured a playful engraving of 'Ho Ho Ho' etched into the runout groove. The Bee Gees' contribution to *Yulesville* was an 11-second Christmas message. They sang a snippet of their 1967 classic 'Holiday', with the lines: 'Ooh, you're a holiday, every day's such a holiday'. Maurice then addressed the audience with a vital reminder for the festive season: 'Hi, we're The Bee Gees. Make it a holiday to remember this year – don't drink and drive!'

As Christmas approached, the wider Gibb family – Barry, Robin, Maurice, their wives and children, their parents Hugh and Barbara, and Andy and Beri – gathered to spend the festive period together in England. Taking advantage of their renewed popularity, the brothers maintained a strong media presence throughout December. On 11 December, Robin appeared on LWT's *Night Network* for a television interview. A few days later, on 15 December, they were featured on the UK pop show *No Limits*, which was hosting its annual awards programme. The Bee Gees came second in the category for best video of 1987. Barry was unable to attend, but Robin and Maurice ensured the group were well represented.

On 23 December, Maurice travelled to Kent to present a Christmas gift to Frances, a young girl suffering from leukaemia. Dressed in a Santa Claus outfit – although without the big white beard – he brightened her day in a moment that was broadcast live on BBC1 with Simon Bates, part of a campaign to raise funds for research into the disease.

On Christmas Day, BBC1 broadcast the *Top Of The Pops Christmas Party*, hosted by Mike Smith and Gary Davies. Andy appeared with a festive greeting before introducing The Bee Gees performing 'You Win Again'.

During this time, Barry was essentially acting as Andy's unofficial manager and decided the best opportunity to find a record deal for him would be in London. Shortly after Christmas, Barry took Andy to the London headquarters of Island Records. Barry had existing ties to the label through The Bunburys project, whose debut single, 'We're The Bunburys', had been released on the imprint in 1986. At the meeting, they played Andy's recently recorded demos for Clive Banks, the label's managing director. Although Banks did not commit to signing Andy on the spot, a tentative agreement was reached, and Andy reportedly left the meeting encouraged by the response.

1988

Encouraged by *E.S.P.*'s solid performance in Europe, The Bee Gees went back into the studio in early 1988 to record its follow-up.

The 15th Annual American Music Awards were held on 25 January at the Shrine Auditorium in Los Angeles. Unusually, however, The Bee Gees were not there to receive an award. Instead, they were co-hosts of the event alongside Whitney Houston, Barbara Mandrell, Smokey Robinson, and Mick Fleetwood. The three-hour ABC TV broadcast included many performances, including The Bee Gees' 'You Win Again'.

After a brief trip to the United States, Andy returned to the UK on 27 January. This time, it was Robin who accompanied him to the London headquarters of Island Records for a meeting with the label's founder and president, Chris Blackwell, where Andy signed a global recording contract. Robin assured Blackwell that The Bee Gees would feature Andy as the opening act on their forthcoming world tour, a commitment that helped secure the agreement.

Janet Kleinbaum, director of national publicity for Island Records in New York, later confirmed that Andy had signed with the label and noted he 'seemed to be very excited about resuming his music career'. While Blackwell and his team had specific plans for Andy's artistic direction – plans Andy did not entirely embrace – he agreed to move forward with them, nonetheless.

Island assigned two of their selected songwriters to collaborate with Andy on new material, although their names are not publicly known. These six songs would complete the ten-track album, alongside the four songs co-written by Barry, Maurice, and Andy that had originally appeared on the demo tape that had secured the contract. Island's initial release schedule included a spring single in Europe, followed by another in the summer, and a full album rollout worldwide in the autumn. Scott Glasel later shared that the album was slated to be recorded at Middle Ear. Andy had asked him to co-produce the project, and Glasel expressed excitement about the opportunity. The album was never started.

Returning to the UK to promote the next single from *E.S.P.*, 'Crazy For Your Love', The Bee Gees appeared on the popular BBC1 chat show *Wogan* on 5 February. The single was released on Monday 8 February.

Wogan was immediately followed in the evening's television schedule by *Comic Relief*, a marathon eight-hour charity fundraiser. Over 150 celebrities and comedians took part, including Kim Wilde, Elton John, Paul and Linda McCartney, and The Bee Gees. The event raised £15 million and attracted a television audience of 30 million viewers for the BBC.

The eighth annual Brit Awards ceremony, organised by the British Phonographic Industry, took place on 8 February 1988 at the Royal Albert Hall in London, and was broadcast live on BBC1 television and simulcast in stereo on BBC Radio 1. The Bee Gees were nominated in the Best British Group category together with Def Leppard, Level 42 and Whitesnake, but the award was ultimately handed to the Pet Shop Boys. The Bee Gees performed 'You Win Again' and also presented an award to Andrew Lloyd-Webber for the best soundtrack of 1987 for his hit musical *The Phantom Of The Opera*.

BMI in the US paid tribute to 112 songs that became 'Million-Airs' by achieving one million or more performances. The Gibbs came away with two certificates for a pair of 11-year-old tracks: 'Come On Over' and 'Nights On Broadway' from *Main Course*.

The Bee Gees resumed work in the studio when unimaginable tragedy struck. Andy Gibb died at the age of 30 on the morning of 10 March 1988 from myocarditis, a viral inflammation of the heart. He had first been rushed by ambulance to John Radcliffe Hospital in Oxford, about 15 miles from where he was staying, on 7 March, complaining of severe stomach and chest pains, but was released. He was admitted twice more – the last time on the night before he died.

Andy had battled drug and alcohol addiction for at least a decade, tumbling in and out of sobriety multiple times. He had reportedly been clean for about a year when he slid downhill again. He had taken up residence in a cottage on Robin's estate in Oxfordshire, charged with writing songs on his own to help fulfil the contract Barry had initiated with Island Records. However, Andy's behaviour, which jeopardised the plans that had been laid out for him to return to form, frustrated his brothers. Many conversations between them turned into arguments.

While his brothers' attempts to help him revive his music career were well-intentioned, the pressure proved to be too much for Andy, and he fell into a deep depression and began drinking heavily in the weeks leading up to his death. The Gibbs' mother, Barbara, had become alarmed by conversations she had with Robin about Andy isolating himself in his cottage and not responding to phone calls or visitors. She flew to the UK and was with him until he died.

Andy's brothers had hoped that making music with him would give him a new lease on life. Robin told *The Washington Post* in 1989:

> We wanted to revitalise him, get his confidence back, refocus him. He was really young when he died. There was a hell of a lot he could have done. Maybe he never should have pursued a solo career. Maybe he should have gotten confidence without having success first; maybe it would have been better for his first four or five records to have died.

Andy's struggle with addiction, interspersed with details about his romantic relationships and financial problems, had been fodder for the media for several years. His death sparked a flurry of global coverage. Several outlets hastily speculated he had died of a drug overdose. While the viral infection was the official cause of his death, Andy's heart had sustained damage after years of drug and alcohol abuse. Many of the headlines were unkind, and some were grievously inaccurate. A cover story in Canadian newspaper, *The Winnipeg Free Press* even wrongfully printed a photo of Robin along with the curt headline 'Gibb Dies Young'. The error was acknowledged in a list of retractions at a later date.

Andy's death shocked his fans, friends, and professional associates. He appeared to be conquering his addiction and getting back in focus. It was later revealed that he had apparently known of issues with his heart for several years before they finally caught up with him.

Shattered, The Bee Gees took most of the year off to contend with the aftermath of Andy's death, not resuming work in the studio for their new album until November. Barry claimed:

> [It] spiritualised the whole family. They say it causes soul growth when you lose somebody. Before, you don't look at the metaphysical side of life much at all. After, you start to look at everything like that: How long have I got ... we're not immortal ... I must get back to making something happen for myself, to working hard, to being fruitful and not taking my family for granted.

Andy was interred on 21 March at Forest Lawn Memorial Park in the Hollywood Hills of Los Angeles. The Gibb family elected to make the well-known cemetery Andy's final resting place as he had lived in the area frequently, and Barbara, Hugh, and Beri Gibb were based in nearby Woodland Hills at the time. Andy's wake took place in their home.

The plaque on his crypt bears the epitaph 'An Everlasting Love'. A memorial stone for Andy was also placed in the cemetery of St. Mary's Church in Thame, Oxfordshire, located just across from Robin's estate, The Prebendal. The stone's inscription, quoting a famous line from William Shakespeare's *Hamlet*, reads: 'Goodnight, sweet prince, and flights of angels sing thee to thy rest'.

On 7 April, the Ivor Novello Awards, presented by the British Academy of Songwriters, Composers and Authors, and sponsored by the Performing Rights Society, were held at the Grosvenor House Hotel in Mayfair, London. Barry, Robin, and Maurice won the best contemporary song trophy with 'You Win Again' and were honoured for their outstanding contribution to British music. Cliff Richard accepted the statuettes on behalf of the Gibbs, who were still mourning the recent death of their brother.

For Barry, Andy's passing was a sobering turning point for The Bee Gees, prompting them to return to live performance after a long absence. 'Andy's death kicked us in the pants and got us going again. It got us motivated to go back on the road. Andy's death stopped us in our tracks and woke us up'.

He further explained how the tragedy fuelled their decision:

The trauma of losing Andy, the idea that we were wasting what we were doing, everything, compounded to make us start performing again. We were a live group before we ever made a record. We're out to show that that's the kind of energy we're prepared to put into our work. We don't want to hide behind our records, which we've done for the last ten years.

While they weren't quite ready to embark on a full tour, the surviving Gibb brothers took the stage at three high-profile events in quick succession. The first of these was the Atlantic Records' 40th Anniversary: It's Only Rock 'N' Roll, a ten-hour spectacular at Madison Square Garden featuring performances by a roster of label superstars on 14 May.

The historic special, presented by the Entertainment Company of America and Atlantic, featured artists from each of the label's four decades, some of whom had either officially split up or not performed together for many years and reformed especially for the occasion. These included The Rascals, Iron Butterfly, and the former members of Led Zeppelin. Other notable performers included Crosby, Stills & Nash, Mick

Jagger and Keith Richards of The Rolling Stones, Pete Townshend and Roger Daltrey of The Who, Phil Collins, Genesis, Yes, Foreigner, Dr. John, Herbie Mann, Vanilla Fudge, and others.

Tickets for the concert were available at prices ranging from $50 to $1000, with all proceeds going toward the establishment of the Atlantic Records Foundation – a newly formed umbrella organisation created to distribute funds to assorted charities.

The Bee Gees' set comprised three songs: 'To Love Somebody', 'Lonely Days', and 'Jive Talkin'', accompanied by Paul Shaffer & The World's Most Dangerous Band, perhaps most well-known as the music director and house band, respectively, for the NBC talk show *Late Night With David Letterman*.

A few weeks later, on 6 June, The Bee Gees gave their first live performance in the UK since 1974 at The Prince's Trust Rock Gala at the Royal Albert Hall. The annual British charity show, now in its sixth year, reportedly raised more than £1.6 million ($3 million) for the Prince's Trust, an organisation founded by the Prince of Wales in 1976 to benefit those between the ages of 14 and 25 who are socially, economically, or environmentally disadvantaged, or physically disabled.

During the first segment of the three-hour concert, Diana, Princess of Wales, seemed relatively subdued as she and her husband, Prince Charles, sat through performances by T'Pau, Leonard Cohen, and Wet Wet Wet. However, enthusiasm in the royal box stepped up when Phil Collins came on stage to kick off the second half of the show. After performing one solo song, the Genesis frontman introduced an all-star band that included singer-songwriter Howard Jones, Queen guitarist Brian May, Big Country drummer Mark Brzezicki, ex-Japan bassist Mick Karn, the Phantom Horns, two backup vocalists, and Midge Ure, the musical director of the event. Following a lively rendition of Jones' 'What Is Love' and two songs by Ure, including the Ultravox hit 'Dancing With Tears In My Eyes', the ensemble provided backup for a variety of acts. Rick Astley won over the crowd with a rousing version of his chart smash 'Never Gonna Give You Up', after which singer Black performed 'It's A Wonderful Life'. Collins then had everyone don sunglasses for his version of 'You Can't Hurry Love' before Joe Cocker emerged for a rendition of 'The Letter'. The Bee Gees scored with their hits 'You Win Again' (reportedly one of Princess Diana's all-time favourite tracks, who could be seen clapping and dancing to the performance on the filmed footage of the event) and 'Jive Talkin'', while Peter Gabriel closed the segment with 'Sledgehammer'.

The concert climaxed with all of the performers uniting for 'With A Little Help From My Friends', led by Joe Cocker, who had a UK number one hit with it in 1969, and Marty Pellow of Wet Wet Wet, who also topped the charts in 1988 with their version of The Beatles' tune. After the event, the Prince and Princess of Wales joined the stars for a post-concert party at the nearby Kensington Hilton hotel.

Just days later, on 11 June, The Bee Gees took part in the Nelson Mandela 70th Birthday Tribute Concert at Wembley Stadium in London in front of an audience of 75,000 people. This was a massive, star-studded event organised to celebrate Mandela's birthday and advocate for his release from prison. The concert aimed to raise global awareness about apartheid and rally support for Mandela's freedom. Broadcast to a television audience of over 600 million in 67 countries, it became a pivotal moment in the anti-apartheid movement, boosting international pressure on South Africa to end apartheid and release Mandela.

The Bee Gees appeared as part of the Midge Ure and Phil Collins All Stars, supported by the house band, which was made up of a number of well-known musicians. They performed one song each with Tony Hadley (Spandau Ballet), 'Harvest For The World'; Joan Armatrading, 'Love And Affection'; Midge Ure (Ultravox), 'Dear God'; Paul Carrack (Ace, Squeeze, Mike & The Mechanics), 'How Long'; Fish (Marillion), 'Kayleigh'; Paul Young, 'Don't Dream It's Over'; Curt Smith (Tears For Fears), 'Everybody Wants To Rule The World'; Bryan Adams, 'Somebody'. The Bee Gees closed the segment with two of their UK number ones: 'You Win Again' and 'I've Gotta Get A Message To You'. During the latter, Barry noticeably broke a guitar string mid-song but played on unfazed.

On 17 June, Barry appeared at the Royal Albert Hall again, where he joined other celebrities in a pro-celebrity tennis tournament. The lineup included Richard Branson, Georgie Fame, Dave Stewart, Bruce Forsyth, John Lloyd and Paul McNamee. The evening raised over £90,000 in aid of the Muscular Dystrophy Group.

In the summer of 1988, Barry, Maurice, and Robin were actively engaged in various high-profile events across the UK. On 26 June, Barry and his family visited Scotland, where he took part in Jackie Stewart's annual celebrity shoot – an event that attracted stars such as Harrison Ford, Sean Connery and Steven Spielberg. Members of the British Royal Family were also in attendance, including Prince Edward and Captain Mark Phillips. At the formal dinner that followed, Barry had the honour of being seated next to Princess Anne.

Around the same time, Maurice attended the Silver Clef Luncheon in London, a fundraising event for the Nordoff-Robbins Music Therapy Centre, alongside Phil Collins and Paul and Linda McCartney. Later that summer, he and his family enjoyed a Prince concert at Wembley Arena during the *Lovesexy* tour. He also attended the annual Cartier polo function with his wife, Yvonne, before joining Robin and Dwina at a party hosted by David Frost.

Meanwhile, Barry and his family were among the audience at one of Michael Jackson's *Bad* tour concerts at Wembley Stadium. The night was made even more special when Barry's son, Ashley, and Maurice's daughter, Samantha, had the chance to dance on stage with Jackson during his performance of 'Bad'.

The Bee Gees also appeared on a few radio shows together and performed 'Massachusetts' live on BBC1 on 2 August.

In a groundbreaking joint venture, Arista Records and NBC Sports partnered to promote and share profits from *The 1988 Summer Olympics Album: One Moment In Time*. The collaboration marked a first in US television history, with a network commissioning original songs from major artists specifically for a prime-time event. The album featured stars like The Four Tops, Eric Carmen, Jennifer Holliday, Taylor Dayne, Odds & Ends, The Christians, Kashif, The Bee Gees, and Eric Clapton. Whitney Houston provided the title track, while renowned composer John Williams provided the spectacular 'Olympic Spirit'.

The project was spearheaded by artist manager Gary Borman of Borman/Sternberg Entertainment, which also served as The Bee Gees' management company. 'Back in 1986, we were approached by NBC Sports, which was seeking ideas for how to incorporate contemporary music into the 1988 Summer Games', Borman explained to *Billboard*. With the Summer Olympics historically under ABC's purview, NBC was determined to do something 'very different, very distinctive this time out', he said.

Borman recognised early on that to succeed, the album needed to feature entirely original compositions by top-tier artists and producers. 'There had been another album for an earlier Olympics that did not do very well', he recalled. 'For this idea to work, I realised the songs had to all be original compositions with the finest artists and producers, and they had to work not only for TV but for contemporary radio as well'.

NBC used the songs from the album extensively throughout its 180 hours of Olympic coverage from 15 September to 3 October, exposing an estimated 80 to 90 million US viewers daily to the music. According to Borman, 'NBC has both vocal and instrumental versions of all the music, so that recurring themes will be played throughout, even when the actual songs themselves are not being played'.

The album artwork featured an Olympic torch in the hand of its carrier and a stylised flame in the form of a treble clef. The album title varied in different territories, some opting to call it *1988 Summer Olympics Album: One Moment In Time*, while others simply ran with *One Moment In Time*.

'Fight (No Matter How Long)' (Barry Gibb, Robin Gibb, Maurice Gibb, David English)

Recorded at The Factory, Woldingham, in August 1986
Chart positions: UK: 88

The Gibbs' first contribution to the album was a collaboration between The Bee Gees and Eric Clapton, two long-standing giants of the industry, using The Bunburys moniker. The song was co-written by The Bunburys' creator, David English, with Barry, Robin, and Maurice. It was produced by Barry, Maurice, Brian Tench, and Australian producer David Mackay at his studio in Surrey in August 1986. While this album was the first time he would work directly with The Bee Gees, Mackay had produced many artists during his early career in Australia who had covered the Gibb brothers' compositions.

'Fight (No Matter How Long)' is a solid rock track and features a great, gruff lead vocal by Clapton and, of course, his lead guitar, with The Bee Gees providing the vocals on the chorus, on which they're joined by legendary English cricketer Ian Botham.

The Gibb brothers and Clapton had known each other since 1967, when they were all under Robert Stigwood's management enterprise, both at NEMS and then at RSO. The three brothers, with the resourceful David English, approached Clapton about recording the song. English, always a great raconteur, told the story:

We trapped him at the polo at Windsor. [It was] a very sociable day, and we said: 'We've written this demo for you, we'd love you to hear it', and he asked, 'Where is it?' We got it out of our pockets, so, as he was eating, he was listening to it on the Walkman. So, he said, 'Okay, I'll do that'. So, we went down to Dave Mackay's studios and recorded it. Ian Botham was on the 'Fight' track doing back-up vocals – it was really getting all your mates together, but singing is a gift and, with The Bee Gees writing, it does help when you've got some songs of that kind of quality.

Eric Clapton and The Bee Gees' involvement was never broadly leveraged, although the Australian and US 7" picture sleeves, along with a sticker on US 12" promotional copies, seemed to favour Clapton and omit The Bee Gees altogether, teasing potential purchasers with this tagline:

In the tradition of famous pseudonyms like Dr. Winston O'Boogie, George Harrysong, Klark Kent, The Glimmer Twins, Suzy and The Red Stripes, Lord Choc Ice, and The Barbusters comes The Bunburys. The lead vocalist and guitarist on this track is a core artist on rock radio, who is currently at the crossroads of his career. One listen, and the mystery will be solved.

The B-side in the US was an instrumental version of 'Fight', which ran to 5:09. In West Germany, a 4:20 edit was used on the 7" and the longer version on the 12" edition.

In the UK, the single was released in early 1989 and bore no relationship to the *One Moment In Time* album and the Olympics, although it did retain a sporting theme.

Japan was the final territory to issue the single. The 7" is very rare, but the 3" CD single edition is now virtually impossible to find.

When *The Bunbury Tails* album was finally released in 1992, the track was credited to Eric Clapton only.

During Barry's *Mythology* solo tour in 2013, much to the delight of the hardcore fans in the audience, his eldest son, Stephen, a fine guitarist in his own right, performed the song with his father beside him, providing vocals on the chorus.

'Shape Of Things To Come' (Barry Gibb, Robin Gibb, Maurice Gibb)

Recorded at Panther House Studio, Mayfair Studios, London, in April/May 1988

The Bee Gees' contribution to *One Moment In Time* under their own name was 'Shape Of Things To Come', which was recorded initially alongside another similar track, 'Wing And A Prayer', earlier in the year. It's unknown if both were slated for inclusion on the album at some point or if they were written with a similar aesthetic, so there was more than one available option.

'Shape Of Things To Come' was entirely played and produced by the Gibbs, with some additional input by Scott Glasel. As a performance, it's a good composition with an incredible hook that should have received more attention than it did. It especially highlighted the staying power of Barry's falsetto, which seemed as strong as ever at that point. The saxophone and electric guitar solo on the track are synthesised sounds; the latter has been rumoured for many years to be played by Barry, which would have been unusual. The track was touched up at Mayfair Studios while The Bee Gees were working on tracks for their new album.

The inclusion of the track on the *One Moment In Time* album became controversial; the Gibbs had reportedly been promised top billing for their participation, with Arista reportedly poised to issue the song as a single. However, the later onboarding of Whitney Houston, a resident Arista artist with surefire hit potential, to the project apparently upended the plan. Instead, Houston's 'One Moment In Time' was released and became a US top-five single.

Until *The Warner Bros. Years* compilation was issued in 2014, which contained a slightly rougher mix than what was on *One Moment In Time*, certainly due to licensing issues with Arista, it remained a relatively obscure Bee Gees track – and became so once again when The Bee Gees moved their catalogue from Reprise to Capitol Records in 2016 and the project completely disappeared from retail and streaming services.

Gary Borman confirmed at the time that an instrumental version also exists.

Hawks – Barry Gibb (1988)

Personnel:
Barry Gibb: vocals, guitar
Maurice Gibb: keyboards ('Celebration De La Vie')
George Bitzer: synthesiser, piano
Larry Williams: keyboards, saxophone
Alan Kendall: guitar
Steve Farris: guitar
George Terry: guitar
Scott Shapiro: guitar ('Celebration De La Vie')
Neil Stubenhaus: bass

Carlos Vega: drums
Engineers: Karl Richardson and Scott Glasel, Brian Tench ('Celebration De La Vie')
Producers: Barry Gibb, Karl Richardson and Maurice Gibb, Brian Tench ('Celebration De La Vie' and 'Childhood Days')
Recorded at Middle Ear, Miami Beach, between February and March 1986, April and May 1986, and in February 1988 ('Celebration De La Vie' and 'Childhood Days')
Release date: UK: September 1988

After his 1986 solo album *Moonlight Madness* was rejected by MCA, Barry sought a new outlet for the work he had completed for the project. That opportunity came with the film *Hawks*. The resulting soundtrack was credited as *Barry Gibb/Music From The Original Soundtrack*.

As early as 1981, Barry and David English had started brainstorming ideas for a film. 'We often chew over silly ideas,' Barry recalled, 'but nothing had ever come to fruition'. However, one scenario resonated sufficiently with both of them to set them on the right course. 'There was news on the radio of a hurricane in Miami, and David and I were driving a car at that moment, imagining what it would be like if it really was bad news, and there was no time left, and you would find out! What would you do? Would you do something you always wanted to do, have a great time somewhere, or would you party all the way out? And that, when we put more notes on it, became the basis of the film'.

That film would eventually be titled *Hawks*. Barry and David had originally copyrighted a preliminary screenplay treatment in April 1982 (then called *A Dutch Treat*, as a portion of the storyline takes place in the Netherlands). The filming started on 28 September 1987 at London's Pinewood Studios, with other footage captured on location at Charing Cross Hospital in Hammersmith. The following week, the entire film crew moved to the Netherlands to film scenes in the Alblasserwaard region.

David elaborated, saying 'We started writing it about two lads in a hospital. It took seven years to make, from actually writing the idea, getting Roy Clarke to do the screenplay, Steve Lanning to produce it and to actually raise the money'.

Barry was passionate about supporting the British film industry and was determined to make the film in the UK. 'The British make the best films in the world, as far as I'm concerned', he said. 'And as long as I can

– in my own small way – I'm going to try and support the industry'.

The film's plot, about two terminally ill young men, wasn't a typical basis for a comedy, but Roy Clarke managed to transform Barry and David's concept into a script filled with humour, emotion, and resilience, focusing on perseverance even in the face of death. Timothy Dalton, the film's star, explained, '*Hawks* is about living and the value of life. It teaches that you can approach the problems of life and death with courage and humour'.

The film also featured Anthony Edwards, known at the time for his role in *Top Gun* alongside Tom Cruise, but who would later achieve greater fame as Dr. Mark Greene on US television series *ER*. Edwards played Deckermensky (shortened to Decker) – an American football player who falls ill while on tour in Britain and ends up sharing a hospital ward with Dalton's character, the cynical lawyer Bancroft. Together, the two men decide to make their last days more enjoyable by stealing an ambulance and heading for the brothels of Amsterdam. Along the way, they meet Hazel and Maureen, portrayed by Janet McTeer and Camille Coduri, and their plans take unexpected turns.

At the time, Dalton and Edwards already had solid acting credits, while *Hawks* came relatively early in the careers of McTeer and Coduri. It was only the third film for both actresses, and each would go on to greater success. McTeer later earned an Academy Award nomination in 1999 for her role as Mary Jo Walker in *Tumbleweed*, and Coduri made a notable appearance in *Nuns On The Run* alongside Robbie Coltrane and Eric Idle.

Timothy Dalton was enthusiastic about taking on the role of Bancroft, seeing it as a welcome departure from his suave portrayal of British secret agent 007, James Bond. 'I jumped at the chance of playing in *Hawks* because scripts of the calibre Roy Clarke has written come along once in a blue moon', he explained. 'I enjoy playing Bond and those movies are great of their type, but I'm an actor who craves variety'.

He noted that while playing James Bond hadn't significantly changed his life, the fame and financial rewards gave him more freedom in choosing roles. 'I know that having me in the movie helped to get it financed because I'm considered bankable as Bond', he acknowledged. 'I don't say that in any egotistical way, but if that leverage means small budget films I want to do can get made, then that's useful'.

Discussing his character in *Hawks*, Dalton said, 'He's a man faced with a huge problem, and he faces it with great pugnacity, verve and humour. *Hawks* is really more about life than death. The lives of Decker and

Bancroft have been brought into very sharp focus through their illness. The film is about the course of action that they take and how they deal with it. It's a film of resilience and courage, good humour and toughness. It's a terrific story, a worthwhile story'.

Seven of the soundtrack album's ten tracks came from the shelved *Moonlight Madness* sessions. The other three included Diana Ross's 1985 hit 'Chain Reaction' and two new recordings: 'Childhood Days' and the instrumental 'Celebration De La Vie'. Three songs – 'Where Tomorrow Is', 'Not In Love At All', and 'Letting Go' – were included on the album as bonus tracks but did not appear in the film.

The soundtrack was released in limited territories: the UK, West Germany, Argentina, Brazil, and Australia. It was not released in North America, limiting its exposure. The film's score was composed by Barry in collaboration with John Cameron.

The movie's star-studded gala world premiere took place on 4 August at the Odeon in London's Leicester Square, followed by a big party at the Empire Ballroom nightclub, conveniently located just a short walk across the square. *Hawks* was released on 14 November 1989 in the US and was screened in select theatres. Barry seemed very pleased with the film, saying: 'Seeing something on the screen for the first time, what you envisaged, is quite a shock, and for me, it was a very pleasant shock'.

Prior to the *Hawks* premiere, there was a press day at Pinewood Studios, which was attended by Barry, Maurice, David English, and Timothy Dalton. Barry also participated in several radio, television and press interviews, including BBC1's *Wogan* on 20 July and an Australian breakfast television show via satellite.

'System Of Love' (Barry Gibb, Alan Kendall)
Recorded at Middle Ear, Miami Beach, in April/May 1986

'System Of Love' kicks off with a gritty guitar riff from Alan Kendall, setting the stage for a rhythm-driven track that showcases Barry's versatility. Co-written with Kendall, this song blends rock and dance elements, building off a compelling riff that later inspired The Bee Gees' track 'My Destiny'. It's a bold, energetic opening track, adding a dose of edge and intensity to Barry's solo repertoire.

He explores a mix of vocal textures here – whispery and understated in the verses, rising into falsetto in the chorus, creating a dynamic contrast. Layered with vocal overdubs, 'System Of Love' feels full and immersive, with each section pulling listeners deeper into its groove. The song's blend of rock energy and danceable rhythm makes it a standout, emphasising Barry's dynamic range as a vocalist. The track is certainly one of the album's defining moments.

'Childhood Days' (Barry Gibb, Maurice Gibb)
Recorded at Middle Ear, Miami Beach, in February 1988
Chart position: West Germany: 60

'Childhood Days', the nostalgic single co-written by Barry and Maurice, is a standout with its bright, folk-pop melody and ringing guitar lines that feel refreshingly pure compared to Barry's 1986 solo tracks. This warmly sung reflection on Barry's youth captures a wistful innocence, offering a heartfelt glimpse into his personal memories. Though it remains largely undiscovered by American audiences, 'Childhood Days' has become a hidden treasure for those who have become familiar with Barry's solo work.

Released as a single in August with 'Moonlight Madness' on the flip side, it was accompanied by a charming promotional video set in a cinema with clips of the *Hawks* movie on the screen showing Maurice playing a keyboard. The single failed to chart in the UK and only managed a paltry peak of number 60 in West Germany.

'My Eternal Love' (Barry Gibb, Richard Powers)
Recorded at Middle Ear, Miami Beach, in February/March 1986

'My Eternal Love' is a heartfelt, carefully crafted ballad that sees Barry returning to his signature falsetto, co-written with close friend Richard Powers (who also contributed to the unreleased *Moonlight Madness* track 'In Search Of Love'). Unlike *Now Voyager*, where he distanced himself from The Bee Gees' trademark falsetto to establish a distinct solo sound, he re-embraces it here, adding an air of vulnerability and intimacy. The song feels personal, with Barry layering his own harmonies, giving it a lush yet solitary quality that adds to its emotional weight.

Slower in tempo and rich in melody, 'My Eternal Love' showcases Barry's skill for powerful balladry, combining delicate falsetto with complex harmonies that he sings solo. The track was strong enough to be a contender for the album's title, and although never released in the US, it's a hidden gem for dedicated fans. Its enduring appeal lies in its mix of nostalgia and romantic melancholy, making it one of Barry's standout, though lesser-known, solo works.

'My Eternal Love' was covered by Annie Haslam, best known as the lead singer of the progressive rock group Renaissance, on her 2007 album, *Woman Transcending*.

'Moonlight Madness' (Barry Gibb, George Bitzer, Alan Kendall)

Recorded at Middle Ear, Miami Beach, in February/March 1986

'Moonlight Madness' is a bold, ambitious song, co-written with George Bitzer and Alan Kendall. Starting out as the title track of Barry's unreleased album from 1986, it immediately sets a cinematic tone with a moody synthesiser intro. Barry's delivery alternates between a breathy, whispery vocal style and his full voice, creating a captivating contrast that draws listeners into the track's dreamlike atmosphere.

Taking its time to unfold, 'Moonlight Madness' spends a full two minutes on its verse and chorus before moving forward, allowing the synth-heavy arrangement to immerse listeners in its surreal mood. The song balances Barry's trademark warmth with an experimental edge, blending lush synth layers and softly haunting vocals to evoke a sense of mystery and nocturnal allure. It's a track that pulls you into its world, blending sophistication with a touch of the unexpected.

Although the song features in the *Hawks* movie, it appears there stripped of its vocal track and is entirely instrumental.

'Where Tomorrow Is' (Barry Gibb, Robin Gibb, Maurice Gibb)

Recorded at Middle Ear, Miami Beach, in February/March 1986

'Where Tomorrow Is' was co-written with Robin and Maurice, adding a touch of Bee Gees spirit to the mix. This rhythmic, groove-driven song straddles the line between dance and rock, showcasing Barry's shift toward a more upbeat sound. Starting off slowly, the track gradually builds into a steady, infectious groove reminiscent of brother Andy's 'After Dark', with a vibe that's both sultry and nostalgic.

While it wasn't included in the *Hawks* film, 'Where Tomorrow Is' holds its own as the final track on side one of the album, bringing a unique energy that hints at the brothers' signature style while leaning into Barry's solo direction.

'Celebration De La Vie' (Barry Gibb, Robin Gibb, Maurice Gibb)

Recorded at Middle Ear, Miami Beach, in February 1988

Opening side two, 'Celebration De La Vie' is an instrumental track composed by all three brothers. This original recording, from which John

Cameron adapted the film version, wasn't directly included in the *Hawks* soundtrack but remains a highlight on the album. The track showcases stunning guitar work by Steve Shapiro, whose skilful playing adds depth and vibrance to the piece, enhancing its celebratory yet introspective tone.

'Chain Reaction' (Barry Gibb, Robin Gibb, Maurice Gibb)
Recorded at Bill Schnee's Studio, Los Angeles, around July 1985
It's unknown exactly why 'Chain Reaction' was included on the soundtrack, but given its two ill-fated releases as a single in North America from Diana Ross' *Eaten Alive*, Barry may have seen it as an opportunity to reacquaint the film's audiences with a worthy performance by Ross, and clever writing and production by the brothers.

'Cover You' (Barry Gibb, Karl Richardson)
Recorded at Middle Ear, Miami Beach, in February/March 1986
'Cover You', originally titled 'Cover You (With Kisses)', is a high-energy dance track that pairs Barry's breathless vocals with an insistent, rapid-fire percussion beat. Co-written with Karl Richardson, the song leans heavily into its driving bassline and rhythmic intensity, delivering a track that's more about vibe and groove than melody.

With its pulsing sequencer and minimalistic approach, 'Cover You' feels like a pure dance track, designed to keep listeners moving. Barry's vocal delivery is quick and passionate, enhancing the track's hypnotic feel and adding a layer of urgency. It's a bit of a departure from his usual melodic ballads, offering a more raw, rhythmic side to his solo work, and its infectious energy makes it stand out among the album's more reflective songs.

'Cover You' is another song that appeared in instrumental form in the *Hawks* movie.

'Not In Love At All' (Barry Gibb, Maurice Gibb, George Bitzer)
Recorded at Middle Ear, Miami Beach, in February/March 1986
'Not In Love At All' is a tender, intricately arranged ballad that sees Barry returning to his signature falsetto lead, co-written with Maurice and George Bitzer. Alongside 'My Eternal Love', this track brings Barry's expressive high register back to the forefront – a notable shift from *Now Voyager*, where he had repressed it. Here, however, he leans fully in, layering his voice with rich overdubs that create a lush, haunting effect.

Somewhat reminiscent of The Bee Gees' 1979 track 'Reaching Out', the song meanders with a gentle, reflective melody, capturing a sense of longing and melancholy. Barry's falsetto lends vulnerability to the lyrics, heightening the emotional resonance, while the multi-layered vocals give the track depth and warmth. 'Not In Love At All' feels like a moment of introspection, balancing complexity with the delicate simplicity of a ballad. Its careful arrangement and emotive delivery make it one of the more poignant pieces on the album, offering fans a glimpse of Barry's introspective side.

The song did not feature in the movie and is noted as a bonus track on the album.

'Letting Go' (Barry Gibb, George Bitzer)
Recorded at Middle Ear, Miami Beach, in April/May 1986

'Letting Go', a standout piano ballad by Barry and George Bitzer, showcases their talent for creating deeply emotional and dramatic music. Initially intended for Barbra Streisand (likely the project Barry had hinted was in the works for 1985), the song found its first release on the *Hawks* album as a bonus track, as it is not featured in the film. Although it was almost overlooked there, Barry himself highlighted it in the *Tales From The Brothers Gibb* box set liner notes. In 2005, he returned to this haunting piece with Streisand, its muse, for the finale of their *Guilty Pleasures* album.

The song opens with Barry's understated, whispery vocals, gradually building into a more natural tone that brings out the track's emotional depth. With its non-repetitive structure, 'Letting Go' feels like a journey – Barry sings the bridge and chorus without revisiting the opening melody, creating a unique flow. The song's ending is particularly striking; as Barry sings the final word, 'go', he stops the music abruptly, letting the word resonate before closing with a synth flourish. Though his falsetto lines add an expressive touch, some might feel they break slightly from the song's otherwise grounded tone. Nevertheless, 'Letting Go' remains a memorable piece with a timeless appeal, demonstrating Barry's versatility and emotional range as both a vocalist and songwriter.

Fresh from his experience working on *Hawks*, Barry seemed increasingly enamoured with the world of cinema. Eager to develop further ties to the film industry, he decided to invest in another screen venture – this time, a nostalgic drama about the rebellious waves of offshore pirate radio.

Rumours of a film based around Radio 270 – one of the prominent pirate radio stations anchored off the Yorkshire coast during the 1960s – had circulated for months. The idea had come from broadcaster Paul Burnett, a former Radio 270 disc jockey, who wanted to capture the spirit of life aboard the station and the golden era of pirate radio.

By May 1988, plans had solidified, and *Anoraks UK* – a long-running radio monitoring and news service dedicated to pirate radio, offshore radio stations and broadcasting developments – reported that filming was scheduled to begin in the first week of August, with the Isle of Man, the birthplace of Barry, Robin, and Maurice, chosen as the primary location. Barry, by now confident enough in his cinematic instincts to back ambitious projects, provided a substantial portion of the film's funding. The working title was *Rock: The Boat,* and its tone was intended to be similar to *American Graffiti*, with music, youth culture, and personal stories woven into a loosely chronological narrative.

A number of former offshore radio DJs and musical acts were expected to appear, lending authenticity to the project. The producer was to be Beryl Vertue, a key figure at one of Robert Stigwood's 1960s companies, Associated London Scripts, and later deputy chairman of RSO. The director attached was Ian Sharp, known for *Who Dares Wins* (1982) and later for staging the action sequences in the James Bond film *GoldenEye* (1995). The script came from Roy Clarke, beloved for sitcoms such as *Last Of The Summer Wine* and *Keeping Up Appearances*. Clarke was already familiar to Barry, having written the screenplay for *Hawks*.

Though much of the filming would take place on land, a ship was essential. Early discussions considered using the *Communicator*, but those plans were abandoned, and the production was still searching for a suitable vessel. Whatever ship was eventually chosen was to have been anchored off Douglas on the Isle of Man to convincingly depict a 1960s-style radio ship.

Speaking at the time, Paul Burnett summarised the intention behind the film: 'The movie is set in that era – the golden age of pirate radio, as well as the age of pop, payola and hype'. *Rock: The Boat* never made it beyond pre-production, but it stands as another example of Barry's brief flirtation with the film industry.

On the weekend of 19-20 November, Barry hosted his fifth annual Love and Hope Tennis Festival at Turnberry Isle Country Club in Aventura, Florida, dedicating the event to the memory of his late brother Andy.

The highlight of the weekend was the charity dinner on 19 November, where Barry was presented with a $5,000 donation from the Andy Gibb Memorial Foundation to support the Diabetes Research Institute. The evening culminated in a special performance by Barry, Robin, and Maurice – the first time the three brothers had performed together at the festival since its inception in 1984. Their setlist included 'Lonely Days', 'First Of May', 'To Love Somebody', and 'Jive Talkin'', along with a duet of 'Islands In The Stream' featuring longtime friend Noeleen Batley Stewart, who also performed 'You Don't Know Me' as a solo.

The tennis tournament attracted several celebrities, including Billy Hufsey (*Fame*), Ted Lange (*Love Boat*) and Robert Hayes (*Airplane*), as well as tennis pros Evonne Goolagong and Mary Jo Fernandez. Unfortunately, Barry was unable to compete due to knee and ankle injuries, but he stayed for the entire event, presenting awards to the participants.

On 21 November, a private screening of *Hawks* was held at the Fontainebleau Hilton Hotel in Miami Beach. Over 100 attendees, including Barbara and Linda Gibb, as well as Linda's mother, May Gray, gathered to support the cause. The event raised over $6,000 for the Andy Gibb Memorial Foundation. Barry and David English made a surprise appearance, engaging in a question-and-answer session with the audience to cap off the evening.

Also in November, Polydor Records began planning a comprehensive Bee Gees anthology, slated for release in late 1989. The collection was envisaged as a multi-record set showcasing the group's legacy. The highlight of the project was to be a newly re-recorded version of their classic hit 'I've Gotta Get A Message To You'. The box set was delayed numerous times but eventually saw release two years later in November 1990 – but the new recording never materialised.

While The Bee Gees' new album was in the final mixing stages, the Gibbs welcomed their future long-time studio engineer, John Merchant, into their camp. While studying music engineering at the University of Miami, Merchant had been researching the AudioFrame Waveframe, a new digital audio workstation with sampler, hard disk recorder, and digital mixer, for a class project. After contacting the manufacturer about finding a local example to study, he discovered that Middle Ear Studios owned one.

John recalled his first visit to the studio in a July 1998 interview with the *Barry Gibb Record* fanzine:

l called and asked if it would be a terrible inconvenience for me to come by and check [the Waveframe] out, and they were very polite and said 'absolutely'. So, I came and took a bunch of notes, checked this thing out, and had a look around. l thought the studio looked kind of cool, so l asked if they had ever employed interns before. They said they hadn't, but they were willing to give it a shot. They mentioned that they needed a piece of computer software written, and if l can do that, the boys will consider that the start of my internship. A couple of days later, l came back with a basic model, not the final program, and I've been working with them ever since.

After a short period, John graduated from intern to studio engineer at Middle Ear, a role he summarised as 'doing all the recording and other mundane things that need to be done day-to-day to keep the studio up and running'.

John said another job responsibility he had been tasked with was to 'try to keep an eye out for new technologies and whether these would make the best sense for us. Running a studio is an expensive proposition, and an awful lot of technology comes down the pike; some of it is the new cool thing, and some of it is garbage. You have to try as best you can to find out what will work best for the way we work'.

1989

1989 would offer The Bee Gees some much-needed solace after a tumultuous nine months. The long post-*Fever* shadow that had followed them for a decade, stymying nearly every attempt they had made to reclaim commercial ground as a group in North America, would also begin to dissipate by the end of the year.

The brothers returned from their usual Christmas break to work on the remainder of their new album. Recording would be finished by March. Shortly after, they began rehearsals for an expansive world tour that would follow.

The 21 January edition of *Billboard* reported that PolyGram had finalised a comprehensive Bee Gees box set, which had been announced by the label late the previous year. The collection planned to chronicle the group's illustrious career, starting from their very first international hit, 'Spicks And Specks', through to the present day. The set would be available in multiple formats, stretched across six LPs, four cassette tapes, or four CDs.

The Bunburys song 'Fight (No Matter How Long)' was released as a single in the UK in February, following its initial inclusion on the *One Moment In Time* project the previous summer. It generated a number of interesting collectibles, appearing in a booklet sleeve as had the first Bunburys single, a regular picture sleeve and a cassette single, which came in a blister pack with the storybook used for the 7" version. The B-side used for these was the previously released track 'We're The Bunburys'.

The single's mid-February drop was timed to coincide with the hype surrounding the upcoming World Boxing Association's championship title fight between Mike Tyson from the US and Britain's Frank Bruno, which took place on 25 February at the Las Vegas Hilton. Bruno was characterised on the single sleeve and the story in the booklet as 'Frank Buno'. The promotional video to accompany the single was once again created by British animator Bob Godfrey MBE.

Despite the superstar collaboration, the song failed to make much of an impact on the charts, peaking at a modest number 88 amidst a very short three-week chart run beginning on 18 February.

On 10 March, commemorating the first anniversary of Andy Gibb's passing, a ceremony attended by the Gibb family and close friends was held to reveal Andy Gibb Drive, the result of a decision by the Miami

Beach City Commission to name the road winding through South Pointe Park at the southern tip of the city. The Gibb family expressed deep gratitude for the tribute. Barry wrote in a letter:

> We promised ourselves when Andy died that something would be done in his memory. We want to thank the Mayor, the City Commission and the people of Miami Beach for helping us fulfil that dream. We found Miami Beach a beautiful, warm and sane alternative to Los Angeles and New York City. It's been our home ever since.

Mayor Alex Daoud and Commissioner Bruce Singer championed the proposal. Mayor Daoud said, 'They and I feel The Bee Gees are a great asset to the community'. Singer noted the Gibb brothers' significant contributions since moving to Miami Beach, including opening their recording studio and supporting numerous local charities like the University of Miami's Diabetes Research Institute, the Police Athletic League and the American Cancer Society. Andy, in particular, had been active in local charity work during the two years he lived in Miami before his death.

Despite the support, not all commissioners agreed with the decision. William Shockett and Stanley Arkin voted against renaming the street. Shockett explained, 'I don't appreciate being in a position to go against motherhood, but this is establishing a precedent. Naming a street, a public thoroughfare, is something we've debated before. You need to be a contributor of major impact. A more appropriate way to honour Andy Gibb would be by installing him in the city's proposed Hall of Fame'.

The 34th Ivor Novello Awards took place on 4 April at the Grosvenor House Hotel in London. Organised by the British Association of Songwriters, Composers and Authors (BASCA) and sponsored by the Performing Rights Society (PRS), the event celebrated outstanding achievements in music. The Bee Gees, who had won the award for Outstanding Services to British Music the previous year, returned to present the same honour to Mark Knopfler and John Illsley of Dire Straits.

Among the nominees for Best Film Theme or Song was 'Childhood Days' from *Hawks*, written by Barry and Maurice. Although it did not win, it stood alongside Phil Collins' 'Two Hearts' from the film *Buster*, written by Collins and legendary Motown composer Lamont Dozier, which took the award, and the theme from *A Fish Called Wanda*, written by British musician and conductor John Du Prez.

In April, The Bee Gees embarked on a series of engagements designed not only to promote their upcoming new album but also to build momentum for their forthcoming tour. This whirlwind of activity saw them visiting major European cities and receiving significant recognition for their work. In Hamburg, they were honoured with gold and platinum record presentations in a ceremony held before an exclusive audience of media and retail professionals. In Zurich, their critically acclaimed album *E.S.P.* earned them additional gold and platinum discs.

Upon their return to Britain, The Bee Gees appeared on the *World Video Awards* with a live via satellite performance of their new single 'Ordinary Lives' from the Hippodrome in London. Their charm and charisma were on full display during appearances on the popular UK television shows *Wogan*, *Rapido* and *Daytime Live*. They also participated in Capital Radio's live radio show *Rockline*, engaging with fans and offering personal insights into their music. Robin and Maurice made an appearance on ITV's breakfast television show *Good Morning Britain*, while Barry was featured on BBC Radio 1's *Singled Out*.

Underscoring their philanthropic activity, The Bee Gees attended a luncheon with Diana, Princess of Wales. The event supported Capital Radio's *Help A London Child* charity and highlighted the brothers' dedication to supporting children in need.

In mid-April, The Bee Gees' 18th studio album, *One,* arrived in the UK.

One (1989)

Personnel:
Barry Gibb: vocals, guitar
Robin Gibb: vocals
Maurice Gibb: vocals, keyboards, guitars
Peter-John Vettese: keyboards, synthesiser
Tim Cansfield: guitar
Alan Kendall: guitar ('It's My Neighborhood', 'Tokyo Nights', 'House Of Shame')
Nathan East: bass
Steve Ferrone: drums
Engineers: Brian Tench, Noel Rafferty, George Marino, Scott Glasel
Producers: Barry Gibb, Robin Gibb, Maurice Gibb, Brian Tench
Recorded at Middle Ear, Miami Beach, between March and April 1988, and Mayfair Studios, London, between April and May 1988, November and December 1988, and February and March 1989

Release dates: UK: 17 April 1989, US: July 1989
Chart positions: West Germany: 4, Switzerland: 6, France: 16, Norway: 19,
Netherlands: 22, Austria: 23, Australia: 29, UK: 29, Italy: 39, Sweden: 42,
Canada: 46, Japan: 63, US: 68
Gold Certification: Australia, France, Netherlands, Switzerland, West
Germany

The majority of *One* was recorded in England, something the Gibbs
hadn't done since 1974 with *Mr. Natural*. The Bee Gees discontinued
working with Arif Mardin for the time being (they would reunite in the
mid 1990s), instead making the record themselves along with their *E.S.P.*
co-producer Brian Tench. After the busy, echoey, programmed
arrangements that adorned the last album, there was a desire to simplify
things and employ a more consistently organic, live sound.

A slate of seasoned session players had been recruited to achieve this,
including drummer Steve Ferrone (a former member of the Scottish
funk/R&B outfit Average White Band), renowned American session
bassist Nathan East, keyboardist and Jethro Tull alumnus Peter-John
Vettese, and guitarist Tim Cansfield. Former Bee Gees band lead guitarist
Alan Kendall, who had been relieved of his duties in 1981 during the
initial recording of *Living Eyes*, was rehired. He remained with The Bee
Gees as part of their studio and touring band until the group's end.

All that being said, synthesisers still do a lot of the heavy lifting on all
the tracks, mostly conceived and played by Maurice. Scott Glasel also
contributed to the arrangements. At this point in the 1980s, many artists
were leaning on the ever-expanding capabilities of keyboards to
replicate real instruments. In some places, like the fluttery flourishes at
the start of 'Bodyguard', and the dark, percussive layers they built into
'Flesh And Blood', the synths add interesting texture that likely could not
have been achieved the same way with real orchestration. But the synth
horns on 'It's My Neighborhood' and 'Will You Ever Let Me', and the faux
saxophone solo on 'Tears', tend to leave one craving the actual brass and
woodwinds The Bee Gees employed just a few years earlier.

Early 'demos' from *One* have floated around the internet for years,
but the Gibbs at this point were making complex blueprints that
essentially sounded like finished recordings. Gone were the days of
Barry making prototypes with an acoustic guitar and a primitive drum
machine. The hired players added nuance and polish, but much of the
scaffolding was already there.

In the aftermath of Andy's death, the making of *One* was an arduously emotional journey for the brothers, but the tensions and competing egos that had complicated the recording of the previous Bee Gees albums were seemingly checked at the door. Spencer Gibb told *Albumism* in 2019:

That wasn't always the case with the Bee Gees' records; everyone was kind of allowed to breathe, and it shows. It's very cohesive, and there are reasons why it is. I heard all the demos, and I was in the studio with them a lot when that record was being made. It was a very formative record for me because it happened at the time when I had chosen to leave home and leave school early to become a professional musician myself. Of course, we were all reeling. Emotions were high, but unity was high, as well. I think *One* is a great example of how tragedy can bring people together artistically.

Barry said in 1989: 'Andy's death made us realise that something can happen at any time, that instead of just making records, it was time to become the group we know we are on stage and in front of a live audience'.

While it's far from being a concept album, *One*'s common thread is, unsurprisingly, the idea of contending with great loss. Barry: 'Losing a member of the family who was that close changes you spiritually. A lot of the album results from this new insight'. The protagonists in the Gibbs' songs are frequently heartbroken and searching for a sense of meaning, but the songs on *One* explore those themes in a much deeper and personal way. 'Wish You Were Here' is the only track the Gibbs claim to have written specifically for Andy, but the album is flush with lyrics that seem to at least imply they had him in mind. The brothers' grief is palpable. Even a ballad like 'Bodyguard', which is rife with romantic innuendo on the surface, still feels reflective and wistful.

Andy's untimely passing shocked and saddened millions of people. It also set the media afire, particularly in North America, where he had been most commercially successful. Sadly, most of the stories surrounding his death didn't focus seriously on his musical contributions or the abundant kindnesses he had extended to his fans, friends and family. Instead, his past struggles with drugs and alcohol, his finances and his relationships were dredged up in headlines for months afterwards.

There did seem to be, however, resounding sympathy for the remaining Gibb brothers and their loss in the public arena, which may have helped to melt the icy reception they'd received for almost a decade and give *One* just enough breathing room to break through.

Billboard writer Jim Bessman penned an article for the 16 September issue, titled 'Bee Gees Success; Sans Disco Beat', that dug into the Gibbs' resurgence in the US and the mechanics of generating media and public support for the new album and single. In a campaign led by their managers, Gary Borman and Harriet Sternberg, the goal seemed to be to make the now oft-ignored Bee Gees virtually inescapable for the North American media.

Warner Bros. executives were invited for an informal conversation with the Gibbs at Middle Ear while production of the album was still in progress, followed by weekly meetings between management and the label to discuss strategy. Once the album was finished, a video press kit, complete with a preview of the 'One' promotional video, a mini-documentary, and interview footage, was delivered widely to media outlets, and advance copies of the single were shipped to radio stations. Ads announcing the upcoming *One For All* tour were also floated in markets that had been mapped out as stops. The push worked. By mid-summer, The Bee Gees were on track to make a triumphant American comeback.

The Bee Gees appeared twice in interviews on Casey Kasem's syndicated television show *America's Top 10* (a companion to his long-standing weekly radio countdown program, *America's Top 40*) on 29 September, alongside singers Gloria Estefan and Siedah Garrett, and on 13 October with Janet Jackson and Roxette.

While the album did not match the commercial heft of their late 1970s output in America (it peaked at number 68 on the *Billboard* album chart the week of 30 September 1989), it did more to renew interest in their contemporary work than anything that had been released post-*Spirits Having Flown*. In the UK and Europe, the album was a moderate hit but still fell somewhat short of *E.S.P.*'s success.

One was later included in its entirety as part of 2014's *The Warner Bros. Years* box set, along with 'Shape Of Things To Come' and three variant mixes of the 'One' single. It was reportedly remastered for the project, but reviews among fans have been mixed in terms of it making more than a trivial difference in sound quality. The proper album has not been reissued in any form since its initial run. For years, the digital version in North America on streaming platforms like Spotify curiously omitted 'Ordinary Lives' (perhaps due to an obscure licensing issue with Warner Bros.), although that has since been remedied.

Martyn Atkins of T&CP Associates' Los Angeles office was credited with *One*'s album design and art direction. Atkins had provided his services to Depeche Mode's *Music For The Masses* and Roy Orbison's *Mystery Girl*, among other high-profile records of the period. Long gone were the days of the ornate handcrafted artwork and logos by the likes of Ernie Cefalu, Drew Struzan, and Tom Nikosey. The Bee Gees' glorious gothic-lettered logo had now been replaced by a simple sans-serif typeface placed in a colour block against a minimalist background; unremarkable, but in vogue for the time. The main focus of the front cover, however, is Larry Williams' three striking black-and-white images of each of the brothers superimposed and faded into one another to create a unified montage of their faces.

Peter Corvin-Brittin took additional photos for the album's inner sleeve, but these never appeared. Instead, the paper liner featured only song lyrics and credits on both sides.

The CD versions of *One* issued outside of North America featured 'Wing And A Prayer' as a bonus track. Later versions of the North American issues of *One* swapped the running order of the tracklist to put the hit single first. They also tacked on 'You Win Again' as an end-of-side-two bonus, supporting a campaign to re-launch it as a single in the US and Canada, hoping the renewed momentum they achieved on the charts with 'One' would urge radio programmers to give it a second look. It worked to some extent, but not enough to return it to the charts.

'Ordinary Lives' (Barry Gibb, Robin Gibb, Maurice Gibb)

Recorded at Mayfair Studios, London, in April/May 1988

Chart positions: West Germany: 8, Switzerland: 9, Austria: 19, Belgium: 22, Netherlands: 23, France: 49, UK: 54

The opening track of *One* – and the first single released outside North America – was 'Ordinary Lives', issued in the UK and Europe on 20 March. The song features an infectious verse-chorus interplay and a double-tracked lead vocal from both Barry and Robin.

Originally titled 'Cruel World', the Gibbs have offered varied meanings behind the song's lyrics over the years; in the classic Gibb tradition, they are contrasting, if not contradictory. Although they're interesting fodder for discussion, pinpointing accurate details is a challenge when discussing their catalogue. As an example, Barry said of the song in 1989:

It's a reflection about ourselves before we became famous – our way of saying we're just ordinary people. The lines 'say goodbye cruel world, no pity no pain tonight, whatever the cost, all is lost' is also a reflection on Andy ... that's what he did.

But a year later, Robin quipped:

This is what I'd describe as a mixture of British type folk, soul and rock. Many things can be read into the lyrics, but autobiographical it ain't! It is, in fact, the story of two lovers who come from different backgrounds, and because of peer pressure, have to escape. It's all a lot of fun, really, nothing heavy.

'Ordinary Lives' became the most significant hit from the album outside of North America, but even at that, its chart success was minor, save for West Germany, where it reached the top ten.

An accompanying video was filmed in Miami Beach, directed by *One*'s cover photographer, Larry Williams, and his spouse, Leslie Libman, who would eventually gain notoriety behind the camera for several successful television series like *Homicide: Life On The Street*, *The 4400*, *NCIS*, *The Wire*, *Oz* and *The Shield*. During the clip, The Bee Gees are backed by Alan Kendall and Nathan East, but Steve Ferrone is missing – instead, drummer Alex Acuña (formerly of American jazz-fusion outfit Weather Report) is behind the kit.

'One' (Barry Gibb, Robin Gibb, Maurice Gibb)

Recorded at Mayfair Studios, London, in November/December 1988
Chart positions: Argentina: 7, US: 7, Brazil: 8, Canada: 11, West Germany: 37, Belgium: 38, Netherlands: 46, UK: 71

Press surrounding the release of *One* was, in many cases, backhandedly complimentary; much of it waffled on whether the Gibbs might ever achieve their hope of staging a comeback in the US.

With perfect timing, The Bee Gees clapped back by releasing the title track and scoring their biggest hit in ten years. It was the album's inaugural single in the US and Canada, released on 13 July. Less than two weeks later, the single debuted at number 73 on the *Billboard* Hot 100, on its way to a peak of number seven the week of 30 September 1989 – their first top ten showing since 'Love You Inside Out' had charted ten years earlier. It fared even better on the *Billboard* Adult

Contemporary singles chart, where it spent two weeks at number one starting on 16 September, ending a six-week run at the top for Richard Marx's massive hit 'Right Here Waiting'.

It was well promoted in North America by Warner Bros., and the Gibbs made acclaimed appearances on *Late Night With David Letterman* and *The Arsenio Hall Show* to support it. Most importantly, radio stations that hadn't played a Bee Gees record since the late 1970s readily added 'One' to their playlists. There really wasn't much room for programmers to argue its omission – it was a well-crafted track that was innocuously catchy, and save for a little momentary background sweetening on the bridge, it was devoid of the falsetto vocals that media types had frequently bemoaned.

'One''s rhythmic similarity to 'Jive Talkin'' also didn't go unnoticed, with some speculating The Bee Gees were slyly replicating the feel of the single that had pulled them out of their last major Stateside commercial dry spell. All that is speculative, but both songs are interestingly in the same key and have the same basic chords in common.

It was reportedly written as the last song for the album in an office in London's Primrose Hill. 'We needed an extra song', Barry told the late Timothy White of *Billboard*, 'So, I took a guitar, and we all sat upstairs in this little room to write one more song and really make it count'.

The concert footage for the single's promotional video was filmed at Shepperton Studios in Surrey on 28 April. The Bee Gees had been using the facility as their rehearsal space for their forthcoming tour. As a promotional gimmick, those purchasing the album at the HMV record store in London's Oxford Street were given a pair of tickets for a special concert at a 'secret' location, along with round-trip transportation. The guests were treated to an abridged concert set in exchange for being used in audience shots for the video filmed during two run-throughs of 'One'. Footage was also included from when the brothers later mingled with the crowd.

A second version of the video also exists in which the same live footage of The Bee Gees performing was retained, but the audience clips were scrubbed in favour of cinematic vignettes using unnamed actors. The result was a choppy video that seemed disconnected from the song's narrative. It has rarely been seen since 1990, when it was occasionally shown on VH1 in the US.

In the UK, a 7" version of the single was released in a limited-edition gatefold pack that featured a set of interlocked hand-drawn (and rather unattractively gnarled) cardboard fingers that opened to reveal a German pressing of the record. Even the extra promotion couldn't usher the single past number 71 on the singles chart.

'Bodyguard' (Barry Gibb, Robin Gibb, Maurice Gibb)

Recorded at Mayfair Studios, London, in November/December 1988
Chart position: Canada: 48

The Bee Gees released 'Bodyguard' as the second single from *One* in the US.

It was sold in record stores only as a cassette single. Radio stations, however, received a two-track promotional CD featuring a shorter, radio-friendly edit and the full-length album version – somewhat confusingly labelled the 'LP version', a term that traditionally refers to vinyl releases. The only other territory to release the single was Australia, where it appeared on 7" vinyl. On both commercial formats, the B-side was 'Will You Ever Let Me'.

Robin said of it in 1989: 'It's a soul ballad, with the same style and spirit of 'Two Occasions' by The Deele, which is itself after ours. We often hear our own music in other groups like this'.

The single caused a stir when its accompanying video, directed by frequent *Playboy* franchise contributor David Kellogg (who would also helm the widely panned feature film debut for American rapper Vanilla Ice, *Cool As Ice*, two years later), was deemed too risqué for 1989 to air on MTV and VH1. It was certainly sensual, but watching the video in 2026, one wonders what all the fuss was about.

The clip may have stifled its prospects as a mainstream radio hit, although it still generated enough airplay and sales to spend 16 weeks on *Billboard*'s Adult Contemporary chart, peaking at number nine the week of 7 April 1990. In Canada, it landed at number 48.

Regardless, Robin's crystalline lead vocal is stunning, and the brothers' layered harmonies are smooth as silk. Considering what was on the pop charts at the time, 'Bodyguard' should have been the album's blockbuster hit.

In a 2019 interview with *Albumism*, Spencer Gibb noted:

'Bodyguard' is one of the best R&B tracks of that period when you compare it to other artists who were making those kinds of records at the time. And also, the duelling vocals between Barry and my dad almost took you back to the *Children Of The World* days a bit, where all of a sudden you had these guys doing double-duty on leads, and it actually worked. Like 'Love Me', where it's all my dad and then Barry comes in with this crazy bridge out of nowhere. 'Bodyguard' is the same.

'It's My Neighborhood' (Barry Gibb, Robin Gibb, Maurice Gibb)

Recorded at Mayfair Studios, London, in February/March 1989

'It's My Neighborhood' (note the American English spelling) is an interesting sonic detour from the rest of *One* – and it may be because it was intended for another project altogether. Instead of the lush pop and R&B of its sibling tracks on the album, it delivers a decidedly tougher guitar-driven punch.

Spencer Gibb confirmed to *Albumism*:

It was originally written for Michael Jackson's *Bad*. They were looking for songs, and then Michael took a turn where he essentially wanted to write more of his own songs. On *Thriller*, he hadn't written the majority of the material. But on *Bad*, almost every one of the songs ended up being written by him because he wanted the songwriting money. But, early on, when he and Quincy Jones were soliciting songs, he'd come to the brothers because they'd just worked on Diana Ross' *Eaten Alive* together. The relationship was there, and Michael said, 'Give me songs for my next record' and 'It's My Neighborhood' was what they submitted. Which makes sense, if you think about it – you can listen to that song and imagine Michael Jackson singing it.

In the end, Jackson ended up not using the song, possibly because it was too thematically similar to the album's title track, which he had written himself in 1986.

'It's My Neighborhood' has a rather long, interesting history. It existed at least as a title when The Bee Gees announced they were releasing a new greatest hits compilation in late 1983, specifically naming 'It's My Neighborhood' as one of three new tracks on the album. A version was also reportedly recorded in 1986 by Andy Gibb. Neither of those ever surfaced.

The track covers similar urban survivalist territory as 'Stayin' Alive' and 'Wind Of Change', although it lacks some of the grit and gusto of those efforts as the brothers sing phrases like, 'You're in trouble if you disagree with me'. The Gibbs have said the track was inspired by incidents of gang violence in Los Angeles during the 1980s.

'Tears' (Barry Gibb, Robin Gibb, Maurice Gibb)

Recorded at Mayfair Studios, London, in February/March 1989

The jazz-pop infused ballad 'Tears' shimmers with synths that seem to mimic falling rain – a fitting backdrop for the wistful lyrics that are focused on loss and loneliness: 'Heaven only knows how much I'm missing you, knowing I had heaven in my hands'. The brothers' harmonies waft like clouds in between the instrumentation. It's a gorgeous piece of music. Barry called it 'Our Beatles reflection – a three-part harmony lament'. Maurice further explained it was The Bee Gees' attempt to capture the feeling of their 1964 classic 'If I Fell'.

The Gibbs' vocal work, their perpetual ace, on this track and throughout *One* is stellar. Their near-perfected blend was especially evident as they embarked on the *One For All* tour – their voices had matured and found a way to coexist to the point where it is often *very* difficult to discern between their individual tones during this period.

'Tokyo Nights' (Barry Gibb, Robin Gibb, Maurice Gibb)

Recorded at Mayfair Studios, London, in February/March 1989

'Tokyo Nights' was reportedly the first song recorded for the album, with writing credits attributed only to Robin and Maurice in a copyright filing dated 19 January 1988. An early version captured at Maurice's home studio in Miami Beach, which perhaps differs the most from its finished product among other demos the Gibbs made for *One*, has a slower tempo and variant lyrics. It was re-recorded in March 1989 with Barry as an added writer.

The song was written as an affectionate tribute to The Bee Gees' enthusiastic Japanese fan base. The Gibbs' music has performed rather well commercially in Japan over the years, despite it being a difficult market for non-domestic acts to break into. Earlier tracks from their catalogue, such as 'Morning Of My Life' and 'Melody Fair', that weren't hits anywhere else managed to find an eager audience there.

According to Barry, the creation of the song was 'all Robin and Maurice', and no doubt its effervescent synths and singable melodic structure are an evolution of the work they did together on Robin's solo albums earlier in the decade. However, the arrangement is brilliantly rich and satisfying. Listening and trying not to be taken in by the infectious 'ooh wee ah … take me to Tokyo' refrain is a near impossibility. Robin said in 1989 that the song 'started off originally as a Beach Boys-influenced track, then switched toward more of an English orientation as opposed to American'.

The single, released in mainland Europe, Australia and Japan, didn't make a significant dent in any chart, but it did become a highlight of their *One For All* tour set when it was added during the last few dates of the European leg and beyond.

'Flesh And Blood' (Barry Gibb, Robin Gibb, Maurice Gibb)

Recorded at Mayfair Studios, London, in November/December 1988

Things take a darker turn with 'Flesh And Blood' and its ominously existential lyrics, which is an outstanding showcase for Maurice's versatility on synthesisers and programming. Like 'It's My Neighborhood', it gives Alan Kendall and Tim Cansfield's guitars a chance to wail a little. Sonically, it's one of the album's most interesting tracks, with dark synth flourishes, stuttered percussion and haunting harmonies by the brothers. Robin's vocal work is outstanding, and it displays his full range from a whisper to a full-throated tenor. Robin called it 'a Steve Winwood reflection with rock, R&B. A hard-edged record with a great uplifting, rousing chorus'.

'Wish You Were Here' (Barry Gibb, Robin Gibb, Maurice Gibb)

Recorded at Mayfair Studios, London, in April/May 1988

Barry: 'A song written for Andy, unconsciously, a week after he died'.

The heart of *One* is undoubtedly 'Wish You Were Here'. It's an absolutely beautiful composition, channelling sadness and nostalgia into a dreamy epic. Maurice said they were inspired to add the calliope melody that plays during the song's introduction because of Andy's youthful, fun-loving personality. 'It's something that everybody can identify with', he explained further in 1989. 'We came up with the title at a hotel, sort of like a belated postcard 'wishing you were here'. We realised we were writing about Andy without having thought about it'. For many fans, especially those who were actively engaged at the time of Andy's death, it's still emotional to hear it all these years later.

The original working version of the song, according to Spencer Gibb, was overwhelmingly difficult for them to sing and was even more emotionally charged than the finished product:

My dad came home, and they'd cut the demo, with his big portable DAT machine, and played it for me. It was just absolutely fucking heartbreaking. I burst into tears, and he choked up. They'd written it that afternoon, and they cut this little demo. Nothing will *ever* touch that demo. When they recorded it, everything became very, very clean. And, of course, it's still beautiful. But on the demo, Barry's doing these falsetto ad libs at the end of the song, and his voice is breaking up like he can't hold it together. I wish they'd kept some of those tracks. I really wish the demo had just stayed intact and they had remixed it and maybe added a few things, because it was so fucking fragile and so beautiful.

The brothers performed it live just one time on the first night of their 1991 European tour to support the *High Civilization* album, and then never did so again because it was too emotional for them.

Although it was never released as a single, 'Wish You Were Here' appeared as the second track on side A of a Brazilian radio promo 12" single, alongside Madonna's 'Oh Father', Eric Clapton's 'Pretending', and Transvision Vamp's Baby I Don't Care'.

'Wish You Were Here' was also gifted by The Bee Gees to *Diana, Princess Of Wales: Tribute*, a 1997 compilation album released in observance of her death on 31 August. A great number of well-known artists also participated, including Queen, George Michael, Aretha Franklin, Seal, Luciano Pavarotti, and Bruce Springsteen. The profits from sales of the album went towards the Diana, Princess of Wales Memorial Fund charity.

Robin recorded a new version of the song for his 2003 solo album, *Magnet*, altering some of the lyrics and giving it a decidedly mid-tempo R&B aesthetic. This was apparently not well received by Barry, who considered the song to be proprietary to Andy's memory, and it reportedly remained a perpetual bone of contention between them.

'House Of Shame' (Barry Gibb, Robin Gibb, Maurice Gibb)
Recorded at Mayfair Studios, London, in February/March 1989
Maurice's instrumental and melodic input helped to define The Bee Gees' sound from the late 1980s onward. While his voice may not have been as dramatically singular as Barry and Robin's, its restraint and subtlety when it was out front added a more contemporary brushstroke to the canvas of their later material, which is audible on 'House Of Shame'. The chorus, which employs all three brothers, is another inescapable earworm.

According to Maurice, the track is about 'love, sex and lies'. He seemed unafraid to tackle more erotically charged material. Unlike later songs like 'Dimensions' and 'Closer Than Close', there is more innuendo here than blatant lust.

The song was Maurice's obligatory solo on the *One For All* tour.

'Will You Ever Let Me' (Barry Gibb, Robin Gibb, Maurice Gibb)

Recorded at Mayfair Studios, London, in February/March 1989

The set closes with 'Will You Ever Let Me', an up-tempo track that's reminiscent of 'One', but with a slightly funkier feel. Robin called it 'a great dance/club record with a very R&B base and a great emphasis on story and lyrics'.

It's far and away the longest track on the album, clocking in at almost six minutes. The meandering verses, one of Barry's songwriting signatures, contain all the melodic interest, while the choruses are a simple repetition of the words in the title. It winds down into a jam session-like outro with Barry repeating the chorus line in a call-and-answer pattern on top of competing keys, drums and synth bass. It likely could have been a few minutes shorter and had more impact.

In the US and Australia, the song was used as the B-side to 'Bodyguard'. In Europe, it was used as the flip side of 'Tokyo Nights' – and, somewhat oddly, it was used again on the Australian release.

'Wing And A Prayer' (Barry Gibb, Robin Gibb, Maurice Gibb)

Recorded at Mayfair Studios, London, in April/May 1988

'Wing And A Prayer' served as the B-side of the 'One' single, and as a bonus track on some versions of the album released outside of North America.

The title is another example of the Gibbs' penchant for writing songs around popular monikers and phrases from historic film and literature. In this case, 'on a wing and a prayer' was thought to originate from the 1942 John Wayne wartime film *Flying Tigers*, and popularised in the song 'Comin' In On A Wing And A Prayer' by British singer Anne Shelton (later recorded by American crooners Bing Crosby and Gene Autry).

The Gibbs produced and played the entire track themselves, with some assistance on sequencers from engineer Scott Glasel, laying it down early on in the process of recording *One*. It's a very close cousin of 'Shape Of Things To Come' lyrically and rhythmically. Barry confirmed it was one of the potential tracks written for the *One Moment In Time* project, but they liked it enough to attach it to the new album.

The Warner Bros. Years Bonus Tracks
'One' (Edit) (Barry Gibb, Robin Gibb, Maurice Gibb)
A flurry of remixes of 'One' were assembled for a 12' single release. The 'edit' here is not of the original song clipped for radio play (which did exist on cassette and 7" formats), but a shortened version of the very lengthy 12" Club Mix that was also part of the tracklist. It's not a really interesting mix, but it does notch up the tempo with added drum programming and synth bass.

'One' (12" Dance Version) (Barry Gibb, Robin Gibb, Maurice Gibb)
It's not known if the Gibbs actually had a hand in remixing these tracks, although it seems feasible that Maurice and Peter-John Vettese might have been in the fold. 'One' isn't a very danceable track to begin with, so it's interesting that the 'Dance Version' really doesn't make it any more so – it's essentially the original track stretched out with some additional synthesised percussion.

'One' (12" Club Mix) (Barry Gibb, Robin Gibb, Maurice Gibb)
Clocking in at over nine minutes, the 12" Club Mix does a better job of translating 'One' for the after-hours crowd than the aforementioned 'Dance Version', but it's still questionable if it's a good derivative of its prototype.

Less than a month after the European release of *One*, The Bee Gees embarked on their first road trip since the *Spirits Having Flown* tour – and their first bona fide worldwide excursion since 1974. In a clever nod to *The Three Musketeers*, the Gibbs' *One For All* tour was their most expansive global trek to date. It would also be their last true world tour. Barry reflected on the significance of this milestone at the time, stating that 'every entertainer needs to perform his music in front of an audience – it's time for The Bee Gees to do it again'.

The decision to tour was partially inspired by their widely acclaimed live sets during the Atlantic Records 40th Anniversary, the Prince's Trust Rock Gala and the Nelson Mandela 70th Birthday Tribute Concert the previous year. A fact acknowledged by Robin:

After those performances, we decided to take the opportunity that came with the release of our new album to go on tour again. We hadn't been playing live for nearly ten years. And when it suddenly started to be fun again, we decided to go on tour. It is extremely exciting.

Maurice added, 'We're also pleased with the new arrangements and ideas for some of our older tunes that we think audiences will enjoy'. Robin additionally acknowledged the challenges of a rigorous schedule but emphasised the importance of giving each performance his all:

I've looked forward to this tour for a long time, even though I know it's going to be a lot of hard work. You've got to make every night your first night. That's important to the audience because, for them, it is your first night, and they want everything you've got.

Barry, too, spoke about the deep gratitude and excitement driving the tour:

We've got a lot of thanking to do. There are a lot of people who've been really good to us over so many years, and I think it would be nice to see them sitting in front of us and be able to please them the same way. The band is in our blood. I just can't wait for the energy you get when it's ten seconds before you go on stage.

The Bee Gees launched the European leg of the tour on 3 May at the Westfalenhalle in Dortmund, West Germany. They also visited the Netherlands, Denmark, Switzerland, Austria, France, and Belgium, and concluded with an open-air concert with an audience of over 50,000 on 1 July at the Niedersachsenstadion, home to the Hannover 96 football club. Norwegian and Swedish fans were disappointed when concerts in Oslo and Stockholm were cancelled shortly before the tour began, as were Italian fans when Milan, Turin and Rome were dropped from the itinerary.

The touring band put in place for the tour included Alan Kendall and Tim Cansfield on guitars, and frequent guest bassist George 'Chocolate' Perry. Keyboard duties were shared by accomplished session musicians Vic Martin, who had played previously with Eurythmics and Boy George, among others, and Gary Moberley, a former member of British glam rock band The Sweet. Chester Thompson would back The Bee Gees on drums, renowned for his work with Frank Zappa, Weather Report, Santana and Genesis. Echoing the setup from their 1979 tour when The Sweet Inspirations were on board, the band featured three backing vocalists: Tampa Lann (credited as Tampa Murphy in associated printed materials), Linda Harmon, and Phyllis St. James.

The opening night setlist was: 'You Win Again', 'Ordinary Lives', 'Giving Up The Ghost', 'I've Gotta Get A Message To You', 'To Love Somebody', 'The Longest Night', 'One', 'Words', 'Juliet', 'Lonely Days', a medley of 'New York Mining Disaster 1941'/'Holiday'/'Too Much Heaven'/'Heartbreaker'/'Islands In The Stream'/'Saved By The Bell'/'Don't Forget To Remember'/'Run To Me'/'World', 'How Can You A Mend A Broken Heart', 'Stayin' Alive', 'How Deep Is Your Love', 'It's My Neighborhood', 'Massachusetts', 'House Of Shame', 'I Started A Joke', 'Nights On Broadway', 'Jive Talkin'', and 'You Should Be Dancing'.

Adjustments were made as the tour progressed. 'The Longest Night' was dropped after the first two shows in Dortmund and Rotterdam, while 'Don't Forget To Remember' and 'Run To Me' were later removed from the medley, although the latter made a brief return during the Munich show. 'You Win Again' was moved from the opening number to the encore, replaced by 'Ordinary Lives'. This nudge made 'Jive Talkin'' the final song of the main set.

The tour was met with overwhelming enthusiasm, particularly in West Germany, where all indoor concerts sold out weeks in advance. According to Ossy Hoppe of Shooter Promotions, 'We sold out all the indoor concerts weeks in advance and had to add four open-air dates to cope with really fantastic public demand'. The Bee Gees travelled with an entourage of five massive trucks to transport their equipment, underscoring the scale of the production. A 10 June article in *Billboard* highlighted the success of the German leg, praising the tour's ability to draw massive audiences; this was celebrated in the 5 August issue with a full-page ad touting the tour's extraordinary reception and solidifying its place as a highlight in The Bee Gees' career.

The Bee Gees returned to the US for a 13 July appearance on *Late Night With David Letterman*, where they performed their hit single 'One'. On 15 and 16 July, VH-1 dedicated a special *Bee Gees Weekend* to the group, celebrating their music and career with several video clips and biographical segments.

On 29 July, The Bee Gees kicked off the 17-stop North American leg of the *One For All* tour with an outdoor concert at Riverfest on Harriet Island in St. Paul, Minnesota, where an enthusiastic crowd welcomed their return. The setlist remained consistent with the one used on their European tour, offering a mix of classic hits and songs from their latest album. Drummer Chester Thompson, unable to join this leg due to other commitments, was replaced by Michael Murphy, the husband of backing vocalist Tampa Lann.

The Bee Gees made two stops in Canada on 15 and 16 August, playing shows at Toronto's Canadian National Exhibition (CNE) Center and Montréal's historic Forum, respectively.

The North American leg concluded on 2 September at the Shoreline Amphitheatre in San Francisco. To mark the end of this successful run, the band hosted a celebration at Fisherman's Wharf for their crew and musicians. The event also doubled as a celebration of Barry's 43rd birthday and his 19th wedding anniversary with Linda. The evening included dinner followed by a show at a comedy club. The Bee Gees remained Stateside afterward for media engagements, appearing on *CNN Showbiz Today* and *After Hours*.

On 1 November, en route to Australia for the next leg of the tour, The Bee Gees made a stop in Los Angeles to appear on *The Arsenio Hall Show*, during which they performed 'One' and 'You Win Again'. Promoted by David Trew and Garry Van Egmond, the trip across the Pacific marked The Bee Gees' first Australian visit in 15 years. David Trew had a long-standing association with the band, having promoted three Australian tours in the early 1970s. His efforts to bring the group to Australia during the quieter period of their international career consistently resulted in a sell-out.

Opening on 7 November in Australia's capital, Canberra, the 11-stop leg visited Adelaide, Perth, Melbourne, and Brisbane, concluding in Sydney on 24 November. The setlist closely mirrored their European tour but featured the addition of 'Spicks And Specks' in the medley as a nod to where their international career took flight. In preparation for the next leg of the tour in Japan, 'Tokyo Nights' was introduced.

As with their previous visits to Australia, the Melbourne concerts were filmed for a television special, which was broadcast shortly after the band's departure. In 1990, the footage was released commercially under the title *One For All*. The video enjoyed enduring popularity, with multiple reissues on VHS, DVD, and Blu-Ray over the years.

The tour also featured some memorable moments. On 17 November, after the first Melbourne concert, The Bee Gees celebrated their mother Barbara's 69th birthday with a small backstage party. Actor Tom Selleck, who attended the show, joined the festivities and met the band. Before one of the Sydney concerts, the group reunited with former bandmates

Vince Melouney and Colin Petersen, both of whom now lived in Sydney. The meeting was initially tentative but soon became warm and friendly, rekindling memories of their earlier days together.

From Australia, the tour continued on to Japan, where The Bee Gees performed six shows. The tour opened on 28 November in Yokohama and concluded on 7 December in Matsuyama. The set list remained consistent with what they had performed in Europe, the USA and Australia, with one notable addition: 'Melody Fair', which was a significant hit in Japan in 1971 due to the popularity of the movie *Melody*, was slotted into the medley. The now geographically fitting 'Tokyo Nights' was retained. At the final show in Matsuyama, the band reappeared for the encore dressed as Samurai warriors, complete with bald wigs and kimonos, bringing a playful end to the tour.

In the 2 September issue of *Billboard*, it was reported that PolyGram had decided to delay the release of The Bee Gees box set originally planned for autumn. The move aimed to avoid overshadowing the group's current Warner Bros. album, *One*. The anthology was now expected to debut in the spring of 1990, with a possible release in April.

In October, ballots were distributed to select new members for the Songwriters Hall of Fame, an American society aimed at 'honouring those whose work represents and maintains the heritage and legacy of a spectrum of the most beloved English language songs from the world's popular music songbook'. The formal induction ceremony was scheduled for the following spring.

The Bee Gees were among the international nominees, which also included Mick Jagger & Keith Richards, Paul Anka, Antônio Carlos Jobim and Michel LeGrand. Brian Wilson, Smokey Robinson, Carly Simon, Otis Blackwell, and the songwriting teams of Ellie Greenwich and Jeff Barry, and Doc Pomus and Mort Shuman were some of the prominent US-based names on the list. Marvin Gaye, Howard Greenfield, Linda Creed, and Sy Oliver rounded out the roster of posthumous nominations.

The individuals ultimately inducted that year were Lee Adams (best known for co-writing the 1960 musical *Bye Bye Birdie* with his partner Charles Strouse), Leslie Bricusse (writer of 'Goldfinger' and 'You Only Live Once' for the James Bond film franchise, among others), Eddie DeLange (an American lyricist who penned several classic tracks for Frank Sinatra, Ella Fitzgerald, Louis Armstrong and Nat King Cole), Anthony Newley (who had scored *Willy Wonka And The Chocolate*

Factory alongside Bricusse) and Roy Orbison. Barry, Robin and Maurice were eventually inducted in 1994.

The One For All Concert 1989 (2014)

Barry Gibb: vocals, guitar
Robin Gibb: vocals
Maurice Gibb: vocals, keyboard, guitar
Alan Kendall: lead guitar
Tim Cansfield: guitar
Vic Martin: keyboards
Gary Moberley: keyboards
George Perry: bass
Mike Murphy: drums
Backing vocals and percussion: Tampa Lann, Linda Harmon, Phyllis St. James
Release date: 18 April 2014
Disc 1: 'Intro', 'Ordinary Lives', 'Giving Up The Ghost', 'To Love Somebody', 'I've Gotta Get A Message To You', 'One', 'Tokyo Nights', 'Words', 'Juliet', 'Lonely Days', 'Medley: New York Mining Disaster 1941', 'Holiday', 'Too Much Heaven', 'Heartbreaker', 'Islands In The Stream', 'Run To Me', 'World', 'Spicks And Specks'
Disc 2: 'How Deep Is Your Love', 'It's My Neighborhood', 'House Of Shame', 'I Started A Joke', 'Massachusetts', 'Stayin' Alive', 'Nights On Broadway', 'Jive Talkin'', 'You Win Again', 'You Should Be Dancing'

It should be pointed out that the *One For All Concert 1989* is not a bona fide live album like *Here At Last … Bee Gees … Live* or *One Night Only*, but it appeared pervasively in so many different configurations and formats between 1989 and 2014 that it is worthy of dissection and discussion on its own.

The Australian leg of the *One For All* tour was The Bee Gees' fourth road trip there since they had ended their eight-year residence to return to England in January 1967 – and it was their first since 1974. Their former adopted homeland had always been a strong market for the group, and this tour, like previous ones, was a sell-out. One show in Melbourne on each of their preceding three tours of Australia was filmed for television, which they repeated this time around. While the group's previous Melbourne concerts were held at the Festival Hall, the 1989 concerts were staged at the newly built Melbourne Tennis Centre (now named Rod Laver Arena) with a capacity of 15,000 people.

Rather than beginning the concert with a known hit, The Bee Gees make an interesting choice to open with 'Ordinary Lives', a track from the new *One* album that was released as its first single, but had only achieved relatively minor chart success in the UK and Europe. It's a strong, singable track, but its atmospheric introduction leads into a tune most of the audience was probably not aware of. The second song, 'Giving Up The Ghost', a deeper cut from the *E.S.P.* album of two years earlier, was likely equally unknown to much of the crowd.

Two familiar songs follow: 'To Love Somebody' and 'I've Gotta Get A Message To You'. The latter's well-known two-chord introduction has a new arrangement somewhat to its detriment, but it is nonetheless an excellent showcase for the Gibbs' vocal work.

The next two songs, 'One' and 'Tokyo Nights', return the set's focus to the new album. The title track had been released as a single locally, but despite the tour, it failed to chart in Australia. Other than making a strong showing in some parts of South America, 'One' was essentially a tailor-made hit for the North American market.

The final three songs of the segment before the medley section include the classics 'Words' and 'Lonely Days'. The former is Barry's now-infamous solo spot in the show, and there is some nice comedic interplay with the audience, and he tries to sing the last line of the song a cappella.

Surprisingly, The Bee Gees add a group rendition of Robin's 1983 solo hit, 'Juliet', to the mix, which seems like an odd choice given that it barely registered on the Australian charts. It was most certainly designed to charm fans on the European leg of the tour, where it had been a significant hit, and was the most successful of the brothers' 1980s solo singles. But Robin's excellent performance and its infectious melody made it a good holdover for the Australian shows. The key and tempo are modified just enough to make it sound a bit more organic.

The medley was traditionally a major highlight of a Bee Gees concert, and this hadn't changed; hearing Barry play an acoustic guitar with Robin and Maurice beside him in front of just one microphone, just the way it started all those years ago, never grew tiresome. As it did on 1977's *Here At Last*, the medley opens with 'New York Mining Disaster 1941', and includes 'Holiday', 'Run To Me' and 'World'. During the performance of 'Holiday', there is some audience laughter as Maurice takes over one of the crew's cameras and films Barry and Robin singing, although those who listen to the audio-only version won't understand the reason for the background hilarity without the context captured on video. The brothers' performance of 'Too Much Heaven' is beautiful and performed in their natural voices just as it was on the *Spirits Having Flown* tour.

Barry introduces the next two tracks, 'Heartbreaker' and 'Islands In The Stream', as 'songs we wrote for other people that we didn't record ourselves'. Both sound fabulous in their stripped-down form, but one can't help but wish for full renditions of both.

The medley finishes to great audience applause whilst Maurice moves to the piano, lifts a single finger (to more laughter from the crowd) and begins to play the unmistakable opening to 'Spicks And Specks', followed by a loud, enthusiastic cheer from the audience. A big hit in Australia in 1966 and New Zealand in 1967, the song had been a regular and popular inclusion in The Bee Gees' concert setlists in those two countries on all previous tours.

Disc 2 opens with 'How Deep Is Your Love', which they dedicated to their late brother Andy. Two more songs, 'It's My Neighborhood' and 'House Of Shame', from the *One* album, are next. 'It's My Neighborhood' had a bit more grit as an album track, but here it's too clean and falls a bit flat. 'House Of Shame' is Maurice's solo for the night, and it's a great performance of a good song.

Following this is 'I Started A Joke', Robin's solo spot, and it is, as usual, beautifully performed, and the crowd's applause for this perennial Bee Gees favourite is particularly loud. It's followed by 'Massachusetts', 'Stayin' Alive', 'Nights On Broadway', and 'Jive Talkin'', which closes the show.

'You Win Again' and 'You Should Be Dancing' serve as the show's encore. 'You Win Again' had been a top ten hit in Australia, but live performances of this fine song never seem to feel as dazzlingly full-bodied as the record. However, it's difficult to emulate the weaving layers of vocals and instrumentation on stage without using backing tracks – a tactic they didn't seem interested in at this point. 'You Should Be Dancing' is great, but perhaps not as powerful as the 1976 live performance on *Here At Last* ... The live horns that coloured the album version and the extended performances on the *Children Of The World* and *Spirits Having Flown* tours were now gone, and the sharp-sounding synths in their place make it sound more like a rock song than an R&B classic. Barry's falsetto vocal on this version is outstanding.

Overall, the *One For All* shows were a very good presentation of The Bee Gees' greatest hits – or at least most of them – and a strong showcase for the *One* album. All three Gibbs are in excellent voice. If there is a fault, it's perhaps a bit too clinical compared to their previous live outings. It's also a shame there weren't more deep cuts among the tracklist, but trying to please everyone now that their catalogue was 25 plus years deep was difficult.

In 1991, the television special of the concert was issued as a video cassette for commercial release under the title *One For All*. For a band that had been internationally successful since 1967 with hundreds of live performances under their belt, it was a rather belated launch for The Bee Gees into the live video market. In 1997, it was re-released in DVD format as *The Very Best Of The Bee Gees Live!*, and in 2018, Eagle Rock Entertainment re-packaged the concert on Blu-Ray and DVD in its original aspect ratio under the title *One For All Tour: Live In Australia 1989*. The audio was presented in a newly mixed and mastered surround sound.

A few individual tracks from the concert were made available as audio releases, including 'How Can You Mend A Broken Heart' (gifted by the Gibbs to the 1990 charity album *Nobody's Child: Romanian Angel Appeal*), 'Juliet', 'To Love Somebody', 'Spicks And Specks', and the medley comprised part of the 'fourth chapter' of Polydor's 1990 retrospective box *Tales From The Brothers Gibb: A History In Song 1967-1990*. 'Massachusetts' and 'You Win Again' had also appeared as B-sides of the 'When He's Gone' and 'The Only Love' singles, respectively, from the *High Civilization* album in 1991. 'Spicks And Specks' also resurfaced in 2009 for the *Ultimate Bee Gees* compilation.

It wasn't until 2014 that the full audio program of the Melbourne show was made available, offered as a double CD as part of *The Warner Bros. Years, 1987-1991* box set issued by Reprise after Warner Music had acquired The Bee Gees' catalogue. For the new CD release, the concert was remixed, and in the process, small bits of between-song talk evident on the DVD format were removed.

Epilogue

By the close of the 1980s, The Bee Gees had achieved a well-deserved return to the global spotlight and rediscovered a renewed sense of unity as a group. The arduous battle to overcome the cruel and unnecessary backlash that followed their *Saturday Night Fever* ubiquity – and to reclaim their rightful place in popular culture – had been both protracted and hard-won. Yet the years the Gibbs spent focusing on outside projects and exploring their individual musical identities as solo performers afforded them a depth of experience and perspective that would serve them well as they entered the next decade.

The Bee Gees had not only rebutted their detractors by surviving the cultural sea change that swept through the end of the 1970s, but had done so by pivoting seamlessly to new roles as high-impact writers and producers – helming some of the most successful records of the era. Barbra Streisand, Dionne Warwick, Kenny Rogers and Diana Ross all received career-defining treatments under the brothers' creative direction, each bearing the unmistakable imprint of their melodic craftsmanship and emotional acuity.

E.S.P. and *One* not only re-established The Bee Gees' prowess as hitmakers; they stood as statements of renewal and skilful adaptation, demonstrating once again the group's ability to transcend professional obstacles and ever-changing industry trends to create music that bridged multiple generations of listeners. The enthusiastic, cross-continental response to the *One For All* tour further cemented their status as industry veterans with one of the richest and most recognisable catalogues in the world.

The tragic and premature passing of Andy Gibb, after years of struggling with substance abuse and personal turmoil, reframed the brothers' perspective on The Bee Gees' place in the music business – and, more profoundly, on their relationship to one another as partners and as family. Losing their youngest sibling seemed to reignite their desire to create and innovate together, grounding their artistry in a renewed sense of purpose and emotional clarity.

As their first world tour in a decade came to a close at the end of 1989, The Bee Gees turned the page on yet another chapter by doing what they knew best: writing a new batch of songs for what would become their 19th international studio album. The music scene was once again shifting beneath their feet, as contemporary pop sensibilities were being increasingly shaped by a growing undercurrent of urban R&B and hip-hop.

The Bee Gees' 1990s output fused their characteristically exquisite melodies and harmonies with a fascination for studio technology – driven largely by Maurice's rising influence and expertise as the group's de facto musical director. The results reflected a creative approach that spanned genres and production styles yet remained grounded in an unwavering commitment to quality over quantity. True to form, the Gibbs continued to navigate an ever-changing musical landscape with diligence and adaptability, carving a path toward the critical and popular recognition that would, by the decade's end, reaffirm their place among the most enduring and accomplished artists in history.

Bibliography

Books

Bilyeu, M., Cook, H., Hughes, A.M., Brennan, J., Crohan, M., *Tales Of The Brothers Gibb: The Ultimate Biography Of The Bee Gees* (Omnibus Press, 2000, 2001, 2003 & 2012)
Bryon, D., *My Life With The Bee Gees* (ECW Press, 2015)
Courtney, D., *Giving It All Away* (Chronos Publishing)
Morrison, B., *Have A Cigar!* (Quiller, 2019)
Arnold, P. P., *Soul Survivor* (Bonnier Books, 2022)
Hild, M., *Arrow Through The Heart: The Biography Of Andy Gibb* (BearManor Media, 2022)
Blake, M., *Us And Them: The Authorised Story Of Hipgnosis* (Nine Eight Books, 2023)
Streisand, B., *My Name Is Barbra* (Century, 2023)

Newspapers & Magazines
UK
Music Week
Record Mirror

US
Billboard

Fan Club Magazines
Brothers Gibb Information: Lamplight (1980-85)
Brothers Gibb Information: The Spirit (1986-89)

Websites
Joseph Brennan's Gibb Songs: www.columbia.edu/~brennan/beegees/
45cat.com
BMI.com
Discogs.com
OfficialCharts.com
TVPopDiaries.co.uk

Sleeve Notes
Tales From The Brothers Gibb box set liner notes (Polydor, 1990)

The Bee Gees in the 1960s
Decades

Andrew Môn Hughes, Grant Walters & Mark Crohan
Foreword by Spencer Gibb & Vince Melouney
Paperback
256 pages
57 photographs
978-1-78952-148-1
£25.00 / $30.00

The first decade in the successful story of The Brothers Gibb is examined in detail.

In April 1967, the Bee Gees launched themselves onto the international music scene with the release of 'New Yok Mining Disaster 1941'. Whilst that haunting classic would be the first of many hits, the Bee Gees - consisting of brothers Barry, Robin and Maurice Gibb - had been releasing records since 1963. As extraordinary as it sounds, with more than ten years of performing and four years of recording behind them, the Gibb twins, Robin and Maurice, were just 17 while elder brother Barry was only 20.

In an incredible career the Bee Gees would go on to sell over 200 million records, making them among the best-selling music artists of all time. They would be inducted into The Rock And Roll Hall Of Fame, The Australian Recording Industry's Hall Of Fame, and The Songwriters Hall Of Fame, and receive lifetime achievement awards from the British Phonographic Industry, the American Music Awards, World Music Awards and the Grammys. According to *Billboard* magazine the Bee Gees are one of top three most successful bands in their charts' history.

Few musical groups have provided the soundtrack to our lives like the Bee Gees, and it all started in the fascinating decade that was the 1960s.

Based in Wales, the United States, and Australia, respectively, Andrew Môn Hughes, Grant Walters & Mark Crohan have over fourteen decades of combined expertise and history tied to the Bee Gees' legacy between them, amassing a lengthy list of credits for their contributions to CDs, DVDs, books, tour programmes, articles, television documentaries, and official websites. In 2000, Andrew and Mark co-authored the expansive biography, *Tales Of The Brothers Gibb*. Andrew's expert contributions can be seen and heard in a myriad of Bee Gees-related productions for the BBC, ITV, A&E, and VH1 networks. Mark, the foremost expert on the Bee Gees' Australian era gifted his collection to the Queensland Library in 2016. He contributed liner notes to the 1998 compilation *Assault The Vaults*. Grant is an award-winning freelance arts writer for *Columbus Underground* and *Albumism*, for which he has penned nearly 300 features since 2015. He is a prolific music interviewer, conversing with a diverse roster of artists including Dionne Warwick, Midge Ure, Melissa Etheridge, Edie Brickell and Bryan Adams.

DECADES
The Bee Gees
in the 1970s
Billboard
Andrew Môn Hughes, Grant Walters & Mark Crohan
Foreword by Spencer Gibb

The Bee Gees in the 1970s
Decades

Andrew Môn Hughes, Grant Walters & Mark Crohan
Foreword by Spencer Gibb
Paperback
320 pages
53 photographs
978-1-78952-148-1
£25.00 / $27.95

The Bee Gees in their Saturday Night Fever pomp – and beyond!.

The Bee Gees' music and image have long been synonymous with the 1970s, and the career trajectory of brothers Barry, Robin, and Maurice Gibb in those ten years meanders between dizzying highs and devastating lows. In 1970, the band was bitterly split after succumbing to the pressures and excesses of their first wave of international fame in the latter part of the 1960s, but by 1979 they were one of the most successful music acts on the planet. In between, the brothers crafted timeless works that defied genre, transcended societal boundaries, and permeated generations of listeners.

The Bee Gees would go on to sell over 200 million records, making them among the best-selling music artists of all time; they would be inducted into the Rock And Roll Hall Of Fame, the Australian Recording Industry's Hall Of Fame, and The Songwriters Hall Of Fame, and receive lifetime achievement awards from The British Phonographic Industry, the American Music Awards, World Music Awards and the Grammys. According to *Billboard* magazine, the Bee Gees are one of the top three most successful bands in their charts' history.

In the 1970s, The Bee Gees established themselves as innovative and versatile artists, and their songs scored a turbulent decade of global cultural change and discovery.

Based in Wales, the United States, and Australia, respectively, Andrew Môn Hughes, Grant Walters & Mark Crohan have over fourteen decades of combined expertise and history tied to the Bee Gees' legacy between them, amassing a lengthy list of credits for their contributions to CDs, DVDs, books, tour programmes, articles, television documentaries, and official websites. In 2000, Andrew and Mark co-authored the expansive biography, *Tales Of The Brothers Gibb*. Andrew's expert contributions can be seen and heard in a myriad of Bee Gees-related productions for the BBC, ITV, A&E, and VH1 networks. Mark, the foremost expert on the Bee Gees' Australian era gifted his collection to the Queensland Library in 2016. He contributed liner notes to the 1998 compilation *Assault The Vaults*. Grant is an award-winning freelance arts writer for *Columbus Underground* and *Albumism*, for which he has penned nearly 300 features since 2015. He is a prolific music interviewer, conversing with a diverse roster of artists including Dionne Warwick, Midge Ure, Melissa Etheridge, Edie Brickell and Bryan Adams.

The Doobie Brothers – Andrew Wild 978-1-78952-462-8
The Doors – Tony Thompson 978-1-78952-137-5
Dream Theater – Jordan Blum 978-1-78952-050-7
Duran Duran – Karen Windle 978-1-78952-368-3
Ian Dury – Opher Goodwin 978-1-78952-374-4
Bob Dylan 1962-1970 – Opher Goodwin 978-1-78952-275-2
Eagles – John Van der Kiste 978-1-78952-260-0
Earth, Wind and Fire – Bud Wilkins 978-1-78952-272-3
Electric Light Orchestra – Barry Delve 978-1-78952-152-8
Emerson Lake and Palmer – Mike Goode 978-1-78952-000-2
Fairport Convention – Kevan Furbank 978-1-78952-051-4
Focus 1969 to 1985 – Stephen Lambe 978-1-78952-463-5
Peter Gabriel – Graeme Scarfe 978-1-78952-138-2
Genesis – Stuart MacFarlane 978-1-78952-005-7
Gentle Giant – Gary Steel 978-1-78952-058-3
Gong (new edition)– Kevan Furbank 978-1-78952-340-9
Green Day – William E. Spevack 978-1-78952-261-7
Dave Grohl and Foo Fighters – Ben L. Connor 978-1-78952-363-8
Steve Hackett – Geoffrey Feakes 978-1-78952-098-9
Hall and Oates – Ian Abrahams 978-1-78952-167-2
Peter Hammill – Richard Rees Jones 978-1-78952-163-4
Roy Harper – Opher Goodwin 978-1-78952-130-6
Hawkwind (new edition) – Duncan Harris 978-1-78952-290-7
Jimi Hendrix – Emma Stott 978-1-78952-175-7
The Hollies – Andrew Darlington 978-1-78952-159-7
Horslips – Richard James 978-1-78952-263-1
The Human League and The Sheffield Scene – Andrew Darlington 978-1-78952-186-3
Humble Pie –Robert Day-Webb 978-1-78952-2761
Ian Hunter – G. Mick Smith 978-1-78952-304-1
Iggy and the Stooges – Robert Day-Webb 978-1-78952-360-7
Iggy Pop 1977 to 1999 – Hans Meertens 978-1-78952-446-8
The Incredible String Band – Tim Moon 978-1-78952-107-8
INXS – Manny Grillo 978-1-78952-302-7
Iron Maiden (new ed) – Steve Pilkington 978-1-78952-380-5
Joe Jackson – Richard James 978-1-78952-189-4
The Jam – Stan Jeffries 978-1-78952-299-0
Jefferson Airplane – Richard Butterworth 978-1-78952-143-6
Jethro Tull – Jordan Blum 978-1-78952-016-3
J. Geils Band – James Romag 978-1-78952-332-4
Elton John in the 1970s – Peter Kearns 978-1-78952-034-7
Billy Joel – Lisa Torem 978-1-78952-183-2
Journey – Doug Thornton 978-1-78952-337-9
Judas Priest – John Tucker 978-1-78952-018-7
Killing Joke – Nic Ransome 978-1-78952-273-0
The Kinks – Martin Hutchinson 978-1-78952-172-6

The Smashing Pumpkins – Matt Karpe 978-1-7952-291-4
The Smiths and Morrissey – Tommy Gunnarsson 978-1-78952-140-5
Soft Machine – Scott Meze 978-1078952-271-6
Sparks 1969-1979 – Chris Sutton 978-1-78952-279-2
Spirit – Rev. Keith A. Gordon 978-1-78952- 248-8
Bruce Springsteen - David Starkey 978-1-78952-471-0
Stackridge – Alan Draper 978-1-78952-232-7
Status Quo the Frantic Four Years – Richard James 978-1-78952-160-3
Steeleye Span 1970-1989 – Darren Johnson 989-1-78952-369-0
Steely Dan – Jez Rowden 978-1-78952-043-9
The Stranglers – Martin Hutchinson 978-1-78952-323-2
Talk Talk – Gary Steel 978-1-78952-284-6
Talking Heads – David Starkey 978-178952-353-9
Tears For Fears – Paul Clark 978-178952-238-9
The Temptations 1960 to 1978 – George Haffenden 978-178952-373-7
The The –Brian J. Robb 978-178952-370-6
Thin Lizzy – Graeme Stroud 978-1-78952-064-4
Tool – Matt Karpe 978-1-78952-234-1
Toto – Jacob Holm-Lupo 978-1-78952-019-4
U2 – Eoghan Lyng 978-1-78952-078-1
UFO – Richard James 978-1-78952-073-6
Ultravox – Brian J. Robb 978-1-78952-330-0
Van Der Graaf Generator – Dan Coffey 978-1-78952-031-6
Van Halen – Morgan Brown 9781-78952-256-3
Suzanne Vega – Lisa Torem 978-1-78952-281-5
Jack White And The White Stripes – Ben L. Connor 978-1-78952-303-4
The Who – Geoffrey Feakes 978-1-78952-076-7
Steven Wilson – Insurgentes-To The Bone – Nick Holmes 978-1-78952-317-1
Wishbone Ash 1970 to 1982 978-1-78952-413-0
Roy Wood and the Move – James R Turner 978-1-78952-008-8
The Yardbirds – Andrew Darlington 978-1-78952-362-1
Yes (new edition) – Stephen Lambe 978-1-78952-282-2
Neil Young 1963 to 1970 – Oper Goodwin 978-1-78952-298-3
Frank Zappa 1966 to 1979 – Eric Benac 978-1-78952-033-0
Warren Zevon – Peter Gallagher 978-1-78952-170-2
The Zombies – Emma Stott 978-1-78952-297-6
10CC – Peter Kearns 978-1-78952-054-5

Decades Series

The Bee Gees in the 1960s – Andrew Mon Hughes et al 978-1-78952-148-1
The Bee Gees in the 1970s – Andrew Mon Hughes et al 978-1-78952-179-5
The Bee Gees in the 1980s – Andrew Mon Hughes et al 978-1-78952-497-0
Black Sabbath in the 1970s – Chris Sutton 978-1-78952-171-9
Britpop – Peter Richard Adams and Matt Pooler 978-1-78952-169-6
Phil Collins in the 1980s – Andrew Wild 978-1-78952-185-6

Also available from Sonicbond

Alice Cooper in the 1970s – Chris Sutton 978-1-78952-104-7
Alice Cooper in the 1980s – Chris Sutton 978-1-78952-259-4
Curved Air in the 1970s – Laura Shenton 978-1-78952-069-9
Donovan in the 1960s – Jeff Fitzgerald 978-1-78952-233-4
Bob Dylan in the 1980s – Don Klees 978-1-78952-157-3
Brian Eno in the 1970s – Gary Parsons 978-1-78952-239-6
Faith No More in the 1990s – Matt Karpe 978-1-78952-250-1
Fleetwood Mac in the 1970s – Andrew Wild 978-1-78952-105-4
Fleetwood Mac in the 1980s – Don Klees 978-178952-254-9
Focus in the 1970s – Stephen Lambe 978-1-78952-079-8
Free and Bad Company in the 1970s – John Van der Kiste 978-1-78952-178-8
Genesis in the 1970s – Bill Thomas 978178952-146-7
George Harrison in the 1970s – Eoghan Lyng 978-1-78952-174-0
Kiss in the 1970s – Peter Gallagher 978-1-78952-246-4
Manfred Mann's Earth Band in the 1970s – John Van der Kiste 978178952-243-3
Marillion in the 1980s – Nathaniel Webb 978-1-78952-065-1
Van Morrison in the 1970s – Peter Childs 978-1-78952-241-9
Mott the Hoople & Ian Hunter in the 1970s – John Van der Kiste 978-1-78-952-162-7
Pink Floyd In The 1970s – Georg Purvis 978-1-78952-072-9
Suzi Quatro in the 1970s – Darren Johnson 978-1-78952-236-5
Queen in the 1970s – James Griffiths 978-1-78952-265-5
Roxy Music in the 1970s – Dave Thompson 978-1-78952-180-1
Slade in the 1970s – Darren Johnson 978-1-78952-268-6
Status Quo in the 1980s – Greg Harper 978-1-78952-244-0
The Sweet in the 1970s – Darren Johnson 978-1-78952-139-9
Uriah Heep in the 1970s – Steve Pilkington 978-1-78952-103-0
Van der Graaf Generator in the 1970s – Steve Pilkington 978-1-78952-245-7
Rick Wakeman in the 1970s – Geoffrey Feakes 978-1-78952-264-8
Yes in the 1980s – Stephen Lambe with David Watkinson 978-1-78952-125-2

Rock Classics Series

90125 by Yes – Stephen Lambe 978-1-78952-329-4
Bat Out Of Hell by Meatloaf – Geoffrey Feakes 978-1-78952-320-1
Bringing It All Back Home by Bob Dylan – Opher Goodwin 978-1-78952-314-0
Californication by Red Hot Chili Peppers - Matt Karpe 978-1-78952-348-5
Crime Of The Century by Supertramp – Steve Pilkington 978-1-78952-327-0
The Dreaming by Kate Bush – Peter Kearns 978-1-78952-341-6
Let It Bleed by The Rolling Stones – John Van der Kiste 978-1-78952-309-6
Purple Rain by Prince – Matt Karpe 978-1-78952-322-5
The White Album by The Beatles – Opher Goodwin 978-1-78952-333-1

On Screen Series

Carry On... – Stephen Lambe 978-1-78952-004-0
David Cronenberg – Patrick Chapman 978-1-78952-071-2

Doctor Who: The David Tennant Years – Jamie Hailstone 978-1-78952-066-8
James Bond – Andrew Wild 978-1-78952-010-1
Monty Python – Steve Pilkington 978-1-78952-047-7
Seinfeld Seasons 1 to 5 – Stephen Lambe 978-1-78952-012-5

Other Books

1967: A Year In Psychedelic Rock – Kevan Furbank 978-1-78952-155-9
1970: A Year In Rock – John Van der Kiste 978-1-78952-147-4
1972: The Year Progressive Rock Ruled The World – Kevan Furbank 978-1-78952-288-4
1973: The Golden Year of Progressive Rock – Geoffrey Feakes - 978-1-78952-165-8
1974: The Year Progressive Rock Came Of Age – Kevan Furbank 978-1-78952-473-4
1977: How Progressive Rock Defied Punk – Kevan Furbank - 978-1-78952-367-6
Apple Of My Eye: The Story Of Apple Records – Andrew Wild 978-1-78952-379-9
Eric Clapton Sessions – Andrew Wild 978-1-78952-177-1
Constellation Heroes – Hans Meertens 978-1-78952-498-7
Dark Horse Records – Aaron Badgley 978-1-78952-287-7
Derek Taylor: For Your Radioactive Children – Andrew Darlington 978-1-78952-038-5
Ghosts – Journeys To Post-Pop – Matthew Restall 978-1-78952-334-8
The Golden Age of Easy Listening – Derek Taylor 978-1-78952-285-3
The Golden Road: The Recording History of The Grateful Dead –
John Kilbride 978-1-78952-156-6
Hoggin' The Page – Groudhogs The Classic Years – Martyn Hanson 978-1-78952-343-0
Iggy and The Stooges On Stage 1967-1974 – Per Nilsen 978-1-78952-101-6
Jon Anderson and the Warriors – the Road to Yes – David Watkinson 978-1-78952-059-0
Magic: The David Paton Story – David Paton 978-1-78952-266-2
Misty: The Music of Johnny Mathis – Jakob Baekgaard 978-1-78952-247-1
Music in the 1980s – Peter Woolliscoft 978-1-78952-347-8
Nu Metal: A Definitive Guide – Matt Karpe 978-1-78952-063-7
Phish- Baker's Dozen – Brent Waltz 978-1-78952-361-4
Philip Lynott – Renegade – Alan Byrne 978-1-78952-339-3
Remembering Live Aid – Andrew Wild 978-1-78952-328-7
Thank You For The Days - Fans Of The Kinks Share 60 Years of Stories –
Ed. Chris Kocher 978-1-78952-342-3
The Making Of Abba – Joe Matera -978-178952-378-2
The Sonicbond On Track Sampler 978-1-78952-190-0
The Sonicbond Progressive Rock Sampler (Ebook only) 978-1-78952-056-9
Tommy Bolin: In and Out of Deep Purple – Laura Shenton 978-1-78952-070-5
Maximum Darkness – Deke Leonard 978-1-78952-048-4
The Twang Dynasty – Deke Leonard 978-1-78952-049-1
Van der Graaf Generator – Pawn Hearts – Paolo Carnelli 978-1-78952-357-7

*... **and many more to come!***

Would you like to write for Sonicbond Publishing?

We are mainly a music publisher, but we also occasionally publish in other genres including film and television. At Sonicbond Publishing we are always on the look-out for authors, particularly for our two main series, On Track and Decades.

Mixing fact with in depth analysis, the On Track series examines the entire recorded work of a particular musical artist or group. All genres are considered from easy listening and jazz to 60s soul to 90s pop, via rock and metal.

The Decades series singles out a particular decade in an artist or group's history and focuses on that decade in more detail than may be allowed in the On Track series.

While professional writing experience would, of course, be an advantage, the most important qualification is to have real enthusiasm and knowledge of your subject. First-time authors are welcomed, but the ability to write well in English is essential.

Sonicbond Publishing has distribution throughout Europe and North America, and all our books are also published in E-book form. Authors will be paid a royalty based on sales of their book. Further details about our books are available from www.sonicbondpublishing.com. To contact us, complete the contact form there or email info@sonicbondpublishing.co.uk